AF358826

Mathematical Modeling with Differential Equations in Biology, Chemistry, Economics, Finance and Physics, Volume 2

Mathematical Modeling with Differential Equations in Biology, Chemistry, Economics, Finance and Physics, Volume 2

Editor

Arsen Palestini

Basel • Beijing • Wuhan • Barcelona • Belgrade • Novi Sad • Cluj • Manchester

Editor
Arsen Palestini
MEMOTEF, Sapienza
University of Rome
Rome
Italy

Editorial Office
MDPI
St. Alban-Anlage 66
4052 Basel, Switzerland

This is a reprint of articles from the Special Issue published online in the open access journal *Mathematics* (ISSN 2227-7390) (available at: https://www.mdpi.com/journal/mathematics/special_issues/Math_Model_Differ_Equ_Vol2).

For citation purposes, cite each article independently as indicated on the article page online and as indicated below:

Lastname, A.A.; Lastname, B.B. Article Title. *Journal Name* **Year**, *Volume Number*, Page Range.

ISBN 978-3-7258-0739-0 (Hbk)
ISBN 978-3-7258-0740-6 (PDF)
doi.org/10.3390/books978-3-7258-0740-6

Contents

About the Editor

Arsen Palestini

Arsen Palestini was born in 1973. He is currently an associate professor at the MEMOTEF department in the Faculty of Economics in the Sapienza University of Rome, Italy. He obtained his Ph.D. in Mathematics at the University of Florence in 2005. He published more than 40 papers in several international peer-reviewed journals, especially on the game theory, differential games, microeconomic modelling, differential equations and graph theory.

 **mathematics**

Article

An Extended Theory of Rational Addiction

Federico Perali [1] and Luca Piccoli [2,3,*]

[1] Department of Economics, University of Verona, 37129 Verona, Italy; federico.perali@univr.it
[2] Department of Sociology and Social Research, University of Trento, 38122 Trento, Italy
[3] IZA Institute of Labor Economics, 53113 Bonn, Germany
* Correspondence: luca.piccoli@unitn.it; Tel.: +39-0461-281307

Abstract: This study extends the rational addiction theory by introducing an endogenous discounting of future utilities. The discount rate depends on habits accumulating over time because of the repeated consumption of an addictive good. The endogeneity of the discount rate affects consumption decisions via a habit-dependent rate of time preference and discloses a patience-dependence trade-off. The existence of a steady state in which habits do not grow and its optimality are proven. The local stability properties of the steady state reveal that the equilibrium can be a saddle node, implying smooth convergence to the steady state, but also a stable or unstable focus, potentially predicting real-world behaviors such as binge drinking or extreme addiction states that may drive to death. The stability of the steady state mostly depends on the habit formation process, suggesting that heterogeneity in habit formation may be a key component to explain heterogeneity in time preferences.

Keywords: addiction; habit formation; endogenous discounting; time consistency

MSC: 34A30; 34A45; 34D20

Citation: Perali, F.; Piccoli, L. An Extended Theory of Rational Addiction. *Mathematics* **2022**, *10*, 2652. https://doi.org/10.3390/math10152652

Academic Editor: Arsen Palestini

Received: 20 June 2022
Accepted: 25 July 2022
Published: 28 July 2022

Publisher's Note: MDPI stays neutral with regard to jurisdictional claims in published maps and institutional affiliations.

1. Introduction

In economics, consumption decisions are the result of an optimizing choice. The consumer chooses the consumption bundle that maximizes their felicity, represented by an utility function, given a budget constraint. Since Ramsey [1], the dynamics of consumption are analyzed considering a representative consumer which maximizes the weighted sum of all their future lifetime utilities, wherein weights decrease with time. In this context, the consumer is seen as a perfectly rational individual, who can exactly predict future earnings and prices and will never change their preferences over time.

However, considering some specific goods, such as alcohol, tobacco or drugs, the phenomenon of addiction may arise and the Ramsey model could be inappropriate for a correct analysis. The state of addiction can lead the consumer to give more importance to the immediate consumption of the addictive good regardless of anything else. In general, addiction creates physical abstinence or withdrawal symptoms when the use of the substance is discontinued, and generates tolerance, which is a physiological phenomenon requiring the individual to use more and more of the substance [2,3]. However, addiction does not arise from one day to another: it is the result of a habitual consumption perpetuated over time. The consumption of possibly addictive goods implies a habit formation process, in which the habit is built day by day through consumption itself. Hence, a habit is formed when past and current consumption are linked by a positive relation. The higher previous consumption was, the larger the habit, and the higher the current consumption level needs to be to deliver the same utility. Pioneer studies on habit formation are due to Gorman [4], Pollak [5], Lluch [6] and Boyer [7], but the reference model for applied studies of rational addiction (RA) is proposed by Becker and Murphy [8].

This model is characterized by a constant discount rate for future utilities that implies a constant rate of time preference. The rate of time preference is a subjective indicator of impatience representing the desire of an agent to anticipate and enjoy the benefits stemming from higher current consumption. A high rate of time preference lowers the propensity towards future utility in determining current consumption choices. This property is known as the time consistency of consumers, as once they have chosen an optimal consumption path in, e.g., time t, they will stick to it even if allowed to reconsider its consumption path in, e.g., $t + x$.

Such a preference structure cannot properly describe situations such as addiction to alcohol (but also in drug use or cigarette smoking), or the existence of goods as holidays and works of art whose benefits continue over the consumption act. For these reasons, several works, starting with Strotz [9], Blanchard and Fisher [10], Deaton [11] and Romer [12], have criticized the assumption of a constant rate of time preference, as suggested more by convenience than economic rationales. Critics have also been made by empirical works, such as Bishai [13] and Laibson et al. [14], who rejected the hypothesis of constant discounting.

One parsimonious attempt at modeling time inconsistency is by introducing the quasi-hyperbolic discounting of future utilities that enable capturing present-biased time preferences. In the formulation proposed by [15], the degree of present bias is modeled through an additional discount parameter $\beta \in (0,1)$, which reduces the weight of all future utilities accordingly. As a consequence, the optimal future consumption path will never be realized because the intertemporal trade-off changes over time as each future period becomes present and the present bias kicks in.

Present-biased preferences modeled through quasi-hyperbolic discounting have been applied to a variety of choices and situations. For instance, refs. [15–19] studied consumption and saving behavior; ref. [20] studied retirement decisions; ref. [21] applied it to economic growth; ref. [22] analyzed caloric intake; ref. [23] applied it to welfare program participation and labor supply; ref. [24] applied it to job search; and ref. [25] applied it to gym attendance). More closely related to our study, ref. [26] introduced quasi-hyperbolic discounting in an RA setting and applied it smoking behavior (also see [27,28] for similar, more recent applications.

Present-biased preferences, however, are not the only way in which time inconsistency may arise, and such a formulation may not be sufficient to capture more complex forms of time inconsistency. For instance, Piccoli and Tiezzi [29], who developed an empirical test for quasi-hyperbolic discounting within the rational addiction framework developed by [26], found no evidence of time inconsistency of this type for Russian smokers.

Given the conspicuous critics of the constant rate of time preference of the RA model and the possibly insufficient complexity of the quasi-hyperbolic discounting extension, this paper contributes to the literature by proposing an extended theory of rational addiction (ERA) that extends the RA model proposed by Becker and Murphy [8]. The relevance of properly introducing time-inconsistent consumers within the RA framework has also recently been highlighted by [30]. In our model, future utilities are discounted by an endogenous discount rate that depends on the stock of habits accumulated over time and is thus capable of describing the behavior of more complex time inconsistent consumers, but remains encompassing to the RA model itself as a special case. In the present paper, we solve the ERA model, study the existence and uniqueness of a steady state in consumption and habits, and analyze its local stability properties. We then open the way for a possible explanation in the observed heterogeneity of the rate of time preference, which is through the heterogeneity of the habit-formation process: individuals that more rapidly accumulate habits will increase their discount rate faster over time and may behave very differently from other individuals. We study these heterogeneity properties of the rate of time preference by a comparative dynamics exercise.

This approach, first introduced by Epstein and Shi [31], generates a non-constant rate of time preference which depends on habits—an index of past consumption. The consumption decision is influenced by the time at which the decision is taken, as different time periods imply different stocks of habits (which evolve over time) and therefore different discount rates. Thus, a consumer that is allowed to reconsider their consumption plan in a future period may choose to change plans, because the accumulated habits have increased their discount rate, and hence the weights given to future utilities. In contrast to Epstein and Shi [31], we keep the general utility structure of the RA model since it allows to model the negative effects that habits can have on consumers, for example, through health problems (see [32–36]). A similar approach has recently been applied by [37,38] to the study of health behavior and its consequences for aging and longevity.

The paper is structured as follows. Section 2 introduces the extended rational addiction model, where the consumer maximizes a lifetime utility function with an endogenous discount rate depending on habits. Euler equations resulting from the ERA model are derived and analyzed. Section 3 proposes a definition of the steady state and derives its properties. Section 4 assesses the stability properties of the steady state. Section 5 discusses heterogeneity in the habit formation process. Section 6 presents the comparative dynamics of the rate of time preferences and Section 7 concludes.

2. The Extended Theory Rational Addiction (ERA)

The reference model in the field of addiction is the rational addiction model proposed by Becker and Murphy [8]. This model endows some characteristics that make it an appealing tool for applied works (see, for example, [32,39,40]), being characterized by a linear Euler equation with a simple test for the presence of addiction. This comes at a cost: a constant discount rate equal to the rate of return to savings is assumed. This assumption has never been supported by theoretical reasoning or empirical evidence and has been widely criticized by the literature. We propose to relax this assumption in favor of an endogenous specification of the discount rate determined by the habits accumulated by the individuals.

The underlying assumption is that habits are likely to influence the discount rate and the rate of time preference inducing increased impatience and, eventually, addiction. In doing so, we follow the work of Epstein and Shi [31], in which the discount rate is a function of the stock of habits, an index of past consumption (Becker and Murphy [8] refers to this concept as the "consumption capital," in a framework in which "past consumption of c affects current utility through a process of learning by doing...." We prefer to use the definition proposed by Ryder and Heal [41], which explicitly talks about habits in determining this index of past consumption.) denoted as z. To enlighten notation, we omit the time indication for time varying variables, except when integrating over time. For instance, $z(t)$ would generally be noted as simply z. An individual's degree of habit is represented by the stock variable z, which accumulates according to a dynamic process. Generally, this process depends on the personal characteristics of the individual and on the consumption level of the addictive good c. The endogeneity of the discount rate implies that the rate of time preference is also endogenous, making the analysis more interesting in terms of optimizing behavior.

In this framework, consumers maximize their felicity, which depends on the consumption of two goods and the stock of habits. The first good, g, is a composite good, which does not cause addiction. The second good, c, is a potentially addictive good (by which we mean a good which generates addiction when consumed under certain conditions, for example, in high quantity) which generates habits in consumption. Alcoholic beverages, for example, are potentially addictive goods. A moderate consumption of alcohol does not lead to addiction, but excessive consumption does. We assume that felicity also depends on the strength of habits, synthesized by the stock of habits z. In line with Becker and Murphy [8], we assume that this effect is negative. Being a potentially addictive good, c generates habits over time, which in turn causes felicity to decrease, so that a larger amount of c needs to be consumed to maintain the same level of felicity.

To keep things simple, we assume that g does not directly interact with c and z in generating felicity, so that the utility function is additively separable and defined by $v(g) + w(c, z)$. In line with Cawley and Ruhm [42], addiction is characterized by enforcement—the marginal utility of current consumption increases with the stock of habits

$(w_{cz} > 0)$. We denote the derivative of a generic function $f(x)$ with respect to some variable x ($\partial f(x)/\partial x$) as f_x. The second derivative ($\partial^2 f(x)/\partial x^2$) is denoted as f_{xx}.—tolerance–and the stock of habits lowers utility ($w_z < 0$)—and withdrawal—as the current consumption of the addictive good increases utility ($w_c > 0$). Other usual regularity conditions impose $v_g > 0$, $v_{gg} \le 0$, $w_{cc} \le 0$, and $w_{zz} \ge 0$.

The endogenous specification of the discount rate closely follows Epstein and Shi [31]. In each instant in time, the discount rate is defined by a discount function $\theta(z)$ which depends on the stock of habits. The discount function $\theta(z)$ is a twice continuously differentiable function assumed to be strictly positive ($\theta(z) > 0$), strictly increasing ($\theta_z > 0$) and concave ($\theta_{zz} \le 0$).

Regarding the habit formation process, the literature proposes two approaches, which we call the partial adjustment approach and adaptive approach. We propose these names to remind, respectively, the partial adjustment model and the adaptive expectation model, which have evident similarities with the habits specifications under discussion. The partial adjustment approach consists of considering the habit formation as an investment process. The stock of habits z accumulates as if it was capital. Investment is represented by current consumption and the stock of habits depreciates at rate σ. As in Becker and Murphy [8], "the rate of habits depreciation σ measures the exogenous rate of disappearance of the physical and mental effects of past consumption of c."The dynamic equation which describes this process is

$$\dot{z} = c - \sigma z. \tag{1}$$

In the adaptive approach, the habits accumulation process is due to the difference between the current consumption of the potentially addictive good c and the current stock of habits z, through the rate of habits adjustment λ. If current consumption c exceeds the current stock of habits z, there will be a formation of further habits, at a rate λ; otherwise, the stock of habits decreases. The dynamic equation which describes this approach is

$$\dot{z} = \lambda(c - z).$$

In this work, we follow the partial adjustment approach, for consistency with the RA model. However, using the adaptive approach, as in [31], would not substantially alter the results.

In the economic literature there is an open discussion if the endogenous discount rate should be considered as increasing or decreasing with respect to consumption c. Koopmans [43] suggests a decreasing rate of impatience, while Lucas and Stokey [44] observe that an increasing rate of impatience is necessary to obtain a single, stable, non-degenerate equilibrium point into wealth distribution in a deterministic horizon with a finite number of agents. According to Blanchard and Fisher [10], the assumption of an increasing rate of impatience is difficult to defend ex ante. On the other side, Epstein [45,46] argues that the more a person consumes, the more she discounts in the future. In line with Epstein, we assume that the endogenous discount rate, $\theta(z)$, is strictly increasing with respect to the stock of habits, and hence consumption. This assumption does not imply an always increasing discount rate. The discount rate may also decrease if, for instance, the consumer quits consuming the addictive good. In this case, the stock of habits z smoothly depreciates at rate σ, and consequently also lowers the discount rate.

This condition is necessary to ensure the stability of the long-run optimal consumption plan, because it guarantees that consumption levels in different dates are substitutes. In this case, as wealth and consumption rise, the marginal private return to further savings, which depends on the marginal utility of future consumption, falls. A discount rate decreasing in consumption would cause consumption in different dates to be complements, so that an increase in present consumption rises the marginal utility of future consumption.

The implication of a discount rate strictly increasing with respect to consumption is that a higher consumption level at time t increases the discount rate applied to utilities after t. An increase in current consumption in t induces an increase in the rate of time preference: the consumer's desire to anticipate the effects of future consumption is picked up by a larger consumption in $t + 1$. An increase in current consumption in $t + 1$ rises the stock of habits in $t + 2$, inducing a further increase in the discount rate: the larger the previous consumption is, the larger the habit and the larger the current consumption must be to deliver the same utility. Moreover, an increase in the discount rate rises the degree of adjacent complementarity and hence strengthens the commitment to all habits.

Defining a cumulative subjective discount rate Θ as (We use this formulation because it allows for some mathematical simplifications. This specification is equivalent to using the integral, from period 0 to t, of the discount function. In fact, $e^{-\Theta}e^{-rt} = e^{-\int_0^t (\theta(z(s))-r)ds}e^{-rt} = e^{rt - \int_0^t \theta(z(s))ds}e^{-rt} = e^{-\int_0^t \theta(z(s))ds}$)

$$\Theta = \int_0^t \theta(z(\tau)) - r \, d\tau, \tag{2}$$

the consumer problem can be written as

$$\max_{g(t),c(t)} \int_0^\infty (v(g(t)) + w(c(t), z(t)))e^{-\Theta(t)}e^{-rt}dt \tag{3}$$

$$\begin{aligned} s.t. \quad &\dot{a} = ra - g - pc, &&a(0) \geq 0 \quad \text{given} \\ &\dot{z} = c - \sigma z, &&z(0) \geq 0 \quad \text{given,} \\ &\dot{\Theta} = \theta(z) - r &&\Theta(0) = 0 \end{aligned}$$

where

$v(g)$ and $w(c,z)$	are the instantaneous utility functions;
g	is current consumption of the non-addictive good;
c	is current consumption of the addictive good;
z	is the stock of habits;
Θ	is the cumulative discount rate;
a	is real wealth;
p	is the relative price of the addictive good (price of $g(t)$ is normalized to 1);
r	is the rate of return to savings;
σ	is the rate of habits depreciation;

and the rate of habit depreciation σ is assumed to be bounded between 0 and 1.

In (3), consumption goods g and c are control variables, while real wealth a, the stock of habits z and the cumulative subjective discount rate Θ are state variables.

This specification nests several models of habit formation and addiction (for a sketch of the proof, see Appendix A), such as:

- The Ramsey model [1,43,47], characterized by a constant rate of time preference;
- The rational addiction model of Becker and Murphy [8], characterized by a constant discount rate and additive utility function with habits;
- The multiplicative habits model proposed by Carroll [48], characterized by a constant discount rate and a multiplicative utility function with habits;
- The Uzawa [49] or Obstfeld [50] models, that assume an endogenous discount rate depending on current consumption, with no explicit modeling of habit formation;
- The Epstein and Shi [31] model, characterized by an endogenous discount rate depending on habits.

The optimization problem is solved according to the maximum principle of Pontriagin (optimal control theory), and the present value Hamiltonian function (note that the relation between the current value and present value Hamiltonian is $H_d = e^{rt}H$, where H_d is the current value Hamiltonian, H is the present value Hamiltonian and r is the rate of return to savings) is

$$H_d = e^{-\Theta}(v(g) + w(c,z)) + \tilde{q}(ra - g - pc) - \tilde{\varphi}(\theta(z) - r) + \tilde{\Psi}(c - \sigma z),$$

where $\tilde{q} = e^{rt}\hat{q}$, $\tilde{\varphi} = e^{rt}\hat{\varphi}$ and $\breve{\Psi} = e^{rt}\hat{\Psi}$ are the discounted costate variables.

The first-order necessary conditions for an interior solution are (to save notation, partial derivatives are denoted with a subscript. Thus, for example, $\partial w(c,z)/\partial c = w_c$)

$$\frac{\partial H_d}{\partial c} = 0 \longrightarrow \tilde{q}p = w_c e^{-\Theta} + \breve{\Psi}$$

$$\frac{\partial H_d}{\partial g} = 0 \longrightarrow \tilde{q} = v_g e^{-\Theta}$$

and

$$\frac{\partial H_d}{\partial a} = r\tilde{q} - \dot{\tilde{q}} \quad \longrightarrow \quad \dot{\tilde{q}} = r\tilde{q} - r\tilde{q} = 0$$

$$\frac{\partial H_d}{\partial \Theta} = r\tilde{\varphi} - \dot{\tilde{\varphi}} \quad \longrightarrow \quad \dot{\tilde{\varphi}} = r\tilde{\varphi} - (v(g) + w(c,z))e^{-\Theta}$$

$$\frac{\partial H_d}{\partial z} = r\breve{\Psi} - \dot{\breve{\Psi}} \quad \longrightarrow \quad \dot{\breve{\Psi}} = (r+\sigma)\breve{\Psi} + \tilde{\varphi}\theta_z - w_z e^{-\Theta}.$$

It is convenient to re-scale the co-state variables in order to eliminate Θ. Letting $q = \tilde{q}e^{\Theta}$, $\varphi = \tilde{\varphi}e^{\Theta}$ and $\Psi = \breve{\Psi}e^{\Theta}$, the first-order necessary conditions become

$$q = \frac{1}{p}[w_c + \Psi] \tag{4}$$

$$q = v_g, \tag{5}$$

and, given that $q = \tilde{q}e^{\Theta}$, and

$$\dot{q} = \dot{\tilde{q}}e^{\Theta} + \tilde{q}e^{\Theta}\dot{\Theta} = 0 + q\dot{\Theta},$$

the remaining conditions are

$$\dot{q} = q(\theta(z) - r) \tag{6}$$

$$\dot{\varphi} = r\varphi - (v(g) + w(c,z)) \tag{7}$$

$$\dot{\Psi} = (r+\sigma)\Psi + \varphi\theta_z - w_z. \tag{8}$$

Differentiating Equations (4) and (5) with respect to time, we obtain

$$\dot{q} = \frac{1}{p}\left(w_{cc}\dot{c} + w_{cz}\dot{z} + \dot{\Psi}\right) \tag{9}$$

$$\dot{q} = v_{gg}\dot{g}, \tag{10}$$

and using Equation (10) with (6), we obtain the following Euler equation for $\dot{g}$

$$\frac{\dot{g}}{g} = \frac{v_g}{v_{gg}g}(\theta(z) - r) \tag{11}$$

Note that, by equating Equations (4) and (5), it is possible to obtain a simple analytical expression for Ψ, which is

$$\Psi = pv_g - w_c. \tag{12}$$

The differential Equation (7) gives a continuous time specification of the recursive structure of consumer preferences for every feasible consumption path. If we solve the differential Equation (7) (recall that the solution for a differential equation with no constant coefficients as $\dot{y} + Py = Q$ is $y = e^{-\int P(t)dt}\int Q(t)e^{\int P(t)dt}dt + Ce^{-\int P(t)dt}$. The value that the solution approaches is referred to as the steady state so the limit for $t \to \infty$ of the solution is $y = \int Q(t)e^{\int P(t)dt}dt$.), we obtain

$$\varphi = \int_t^\infty \left(v(g(\tau)) + w(c(\tau), z(\tau))\right)e^{-\int_t^\tau \theta(z(s))ds}d\tau, \tag{13}$$

which is the present value of future utilities at time t which corresponds to the shadow price of the accumulated impatience rate Θ.

By equating the two equations for $\dot{q}$, (6) and (9), we can solve for $\dot{c}$ and find the Euler equation

$$\frac{\dot{c}}{c} = \eta^c(g, c, z)(\rho^c(g, c, z, \varphi) - r),$$

where, by means of Equations (1), (8), (5) and (12), the rate of time preference for good c is

$$\rho^c(\cdot) = \theta(z) - \frac{w_{cz}(c - \sigma z) + (r + \sigma)(pv_g - w_c) + \theta_z \varphi - w_z}{pv_g} \tag{14}$$

and the elasticity of intertemporal substitution is

$$\eta^c(\cdot) = \frac{pv_g}{w_{cc}c}.$$

In summary, the resulting Euler equations for g and c are

$$\frac{\dot{g}}{g} = \frac{v_g}{v_{gg}g}(\theta(z) - r) \tag{15}$$

$$\frac{\dot{c}}{c} = \frac{pv_g}{w_{cc}c}\left(\theta(z) - \frac{w_{cz}(c - \sigma z) + (r + \sigma)(pv_g - w_c) + \theta_z \varphi - w_z}{pv_g} - r\right). \tag{16}$$

In light of Equation (13), the shadow price of the cumulative discount rate Θ may be seen as an index of impatience. In fact, since φ is the weighted sum of all future utilities from time t, the higher future utilities are, the higher the patience is, since the agent is willing to wait for the realization of their desires of consumption. For this reason, from now on, we will refer to φ as the *rate of impatience*.

This formulation, which involves the non-separability of preferences, is suggested by Ryder and Heal [41], who introduced the notion of adjacent complementarity. Adjacent complementarity occurs when the past consumption of a good raises the marginal utility of present consumption. An increase or decrease in consumption at $t - 1$ can induce a variation of the marginal rate of substitution of current and future consumption at $t + 1$. Complementarity is represented by a utility function that depends on both current consumption c and the stock of habits z, which is a weighted average of past consumption levels. Weights decline exponentially in the past at the exogenous depreciation rate σ, which can be interpreted as a measure of permanence of physical and mental effects of past consumption on present consumption c. As σ becomes larger, less weight is given to past consumption in determining z.

The two Euler equations in (15) and (16) implicitly define the rates of time preference and the elasticities of inter-temporal substitution for the two goods. The rate of time preference for g is simply equal to the discount function $\theta(z)$, as for any standard inter-temporal model of consumption. However, the discount rate is not constant and depends on the stock of habits z, implying that the rate of time preference for g depends on the past consumption of c. The inter-temporal elasticity of substitution for g is completely defined by the preference structure, and in particular, by the shape of $v(g)$. The rate of time preference for c, shown in Equation (14), embeds:

1. Memory of past events through the stock of habits z and the rate of habits depreciation σ;
2. Perception of present events by the current consumption levels of c and g;
3. The anticipation of future events by the present-value of future utilities φ.

Consumer behavior is non-separable over time, revealing complementarity and time inconsistency. The present consumption of the potentially addictive good c and future consumption (represented by φ) depends on the past consumption of the addictive good through the rate of habits depreciation σ, and does not need to be valued equally along a locally constant consumption path. The rate of time preference expresses the propensity that a person reveals towards future utility in determining current choices. This depends on the ability to anticipate the benefits of future consumption and the related physical and mental consequences of present and past consumption effects.

The Euler equation for c is different from canonical expressions mainly because it endows the complementarity between past consumption z, current consumption c and g, and future consumption by the rate of impatience φ through the endogenous rate of time preference and the elasticity of inter-temporal substitution.

3. The Steady State

Given the Euler Equations (15) and (16), the system of differential equations which describes the dynamic behavior of the ERA model is

$$\dot{z} = c - \sigma z \tag{17}$$

$$\dot{\varphi} = r\varphi - (v(g) + w(c,z)) \tag{18}$$

$$\dot{c} = \frac{pv_g}{w_{cc}} \left(\theta(z) - \frac{w_{cz}(c - \sigma z) + (r + \sigma)(pv_g - w_c) + \theta_z \varphi - w_z}{pv_g} - r \right) \tag{19}$$

$$\dot{g} = \frac{v_g}{v_{gg}}(\theta(z) - r) \tag{20}$$

$$\dot{a} = ra - g - pc. \tag{21}$$

Defining the steady state as an optimal solution to program (3) in which the stock of habits z and wealth a do not change over time, ($\dot{z} = 0$, $\dot{a} = 0$), a steady state for system (17)–(21) exists and lies on the optimal consumption path. This definition comes from the consideration that it is physically implausible that a substance continues to generate habits to the infinite, otherwise, to keep a certain level of utility, the consumer should continuously increase the consumption of the addictive good. This, in a world of finite resources, is rather unlikely, although not impossible. If an equilibrium exists where $\dot{z} = 0$, it brings a number of consequences. First, if the stock of habits does not grow, then the consumption of the addictive good c also does not grow at the steady state. In fact, from Equation (17), we find that $c^* = \sigma z^*$ (with the superscript $*$, we denote the variables at their steady state value). Second, if z is constant, Θ is also constant because of Equation (26), and thus $\theta(z)$ is constant and equal to r, as implied by the cumulative discount rate motion equation and $\dot{\Theta} = 0$.

These considerations lead to a first important consequence. At the steady state, the stock of habits z^* is uniquely determined by the discount function $\theta(z)$ and the interest rate r. Hence, the steady state consumption level c^*, which is determined by the stock of habits z^* and the rate of habits adjustment σ, also depends on the shape of the discount factor and the interest rate, but not on the structure of preferences.

The fact that c^* and z^* are constant implies that utility $w(c^*, z^*)$ is constant at the steady state, and so must be the index of impatience φ, which is the discounted value of the future streams of utilities. From Equation (18), considering that $\dot{\varphi} = 0$, we obtain

$$\varphi^* = \frac{v(g^*) + w(c^*, z^*)}{r}. \tag{22}$$

The fact that, at the steady state, $\theta(z) = r$ has another important consequence: g does not grow at the steady state. A condition for this to happen is that marginal utility v_g is constant, whereby Equation (5) implies that q is also constant, i.e., $\dot{q} = 0$. From condition (4), we find that

$$q^* = \frac{1}{p}(w_c + \Psi^*),\qquad(23)$$

which in turn, by condition (5), defines the steady state value of g^*.

Finally, assuming that, at the steady state, real wealth a does not grow, from Equation (21), we obtain the steady state value of wealth

$$a^* = \frac{g^* + pc^*}{r}.$$

To date, we determined the steady state levels of the variable involved in the dynamic system of the ERA model. To verify the existence of the steady state and that the steady state is an optimum solution to the maximization program, we can use Equation (19). We know that in the steady state, $\dot{c}$ must be zero. For this to be verified, the term in square brackets must also be zero, and since $\theta(z^*) - r = 0$, we can concentrate on the term

$$w_{cz}^*(c^* - \sigma z^*) + (r + \sigma)\left(pv_g^* - w_c^*\right) + \theta_z^* \varphi^* - w_z^*.$$

Considering that, from (17), $(c^* - \sigma z^*)$ is 0 and substituting Equation (12), we obtain

$$(r + \sigma)\Psi^* + \theta_z^* \varphi^* - w_z^*,$$

and using Equation (12), Equation (8) can be set to 0, and

$$\Psi^* = \frac{w_z^* - \theta_z^* \varphi^*}{r + \sigma},$$

which implies that

$$(r + \sigma)\frac{w_z^* - \theta_z^* \varphi^*}{r + \sigma} + \theta_z^* \varphi^* - w_z^* = 0.$$

Then, the steady state lies on the optimal solution to the ERA model. The steady state defined as $(\dot{z} = 0, \dot{a} = 0)$ is unique. To verify the uniqueness of the steady state, we consider the case in which $\dot{z}$ is still 0, but assume that this hypothetical steady state level of $z^{\#}$ is such that $\theta\left(z^{\#}\right) - r \neq 0$, i.e., $z^{\#}$ can be any value different from z^*. This implies that at the steady state, the cumulative discount rate Θ constantly changes because $\dot{\Theta}$ is constant. By Equation (20), g also constantly changes at the steady state.

Since z is constant, by Equation (17), the consumption of addictive good c must also be constant. The fact that g grows indefinitely at the steady state while c does not suggests that this hypothetical steady state may not satisfy all optimality conditions, so we need to verify that $\dot{c} = 0$ even when $\theta\left(z^{\#}\right) - r \neq 0$. The steady state levels of φ and Ψ are not constant and will change at a constant rate proportional to $\dot{g}$. From (19), the necessary condition for $\dot{c} = 0$ is

$$\theta\left(z^{\#}\right) - r - \frac{w_{cz}^{\#}\left(c^{\#} - \sigma z^{\#}\right) + (r + \sigma)\left(pv_g - w_c^{\#}\right) + \theta_z^{\#}\varphi - w_z^{\#}}{pv_g} = 0,$$

but since $\left(pv_g - w_c\right) = \Psi$ and $\dot{\Psi} \neq 0$, using Equation (11), the expression can be written as

$$\frac{pv_{gg}\dot{g} - (r + \sigma)\Psi - \theta_z^{\#}\varphi + w_z^{\#}}{pv_g},$$

which, by Equation (20), is 0 if and only if

$$(r+\sigma)\Psi + \theta_z^{\#}\varphi = w_z^{\#} + \theta\left(z^{\#}\right) - r. \tag{24}$$

Note that the right-hand side of Equation (24) is constant, which would either imply that both Ψ and φ were constant and take some specific values, which is not the case, or that

$$\Psi = \frac{w_z^{\#} + \theta\left(z^{\#}\right) - r - \theta_z\varphi}{r+\sigma},$$

which, again, is not the case. This implies that this alternative steady state is infeasible. It follows that, if we define the steady state as an optimal solution to the optimization problem (3) in which the stock of habits is stationary ($\dot{z} = 0$), the unique feasible solution implies that the discount rate $\theta(z^*)$ has to be equal to the interest rate r. Other steady states may exist when the definition of the steady state is different. However, at least we proved the existence and uniqueness of at least one steady state. This, in turns, defines the steady state value of the stock of habits z^* and the consumption of the addictive good c^* purely as a function of the habit-generating process (through σ) and the discount function shape. This sounds intuitively reasonable, since a steady level of the stock of habits could be reached only if the process that generate habits stabilizes and does not affect preferences for the addictive good.

4. Local Stability Properties

The system described by (17)–(21) generates a five-dimensional hyperplane which is divided into a number of regions ($2^5 = 32$, to be precise), each of which is characterized by a force leading the system toward the steady state or away from it.

We can reduce the dimension of the system, noting that a is only present in the wealth accumulation equation. Since a does not influence other dynamic equations, we can consider the accumulation equation of wealth (21) as exogenous to the system and drop it from the stability analysis. Because a is recursively determined for each value of c and g by Equation (21), when considered in the system, it would imply an eigenvalue equal to r, which would not influence the stability properties of the system. The new system generates a four-dimensional hyperplane, which allows for an easier mathematical analysis.

Rewriting Equation (19) as

$$\dot{c} = c\varepsilon^c(\cdot)(\rho(\cdot) - r)$$

where

$$\rho(\cdot) = \rho(g, c, z, \varphi)$$
$$\theta(z) - \frac{w_{cz}(c - \sigma z) + (r + \sigma)(pv_g - w_c) + \theta_z\varphi - w_z}{pv_g}$$
$$\varepsilon^c(\cdot) = \frac{pv_g}{w_{cc}c};$$

Equation (20) as

$$\dot{g} = g\varepsilon^g(\cdot)(\theta(z) - r)$$

where

$$\varepsilon^g = \frac{v_g}{v_{gg}g};$$

and making each dynamic equation equal to 0 at the steady state (and since every function is intended to be evaluated at the steady state), the system can be written as

$$
\begin{aligned}
(z) \quad & 0 = c^* - \sigma z^* \\
(\varphi) \quad & 0 = r\varphi^* - w(c,z) - v(g) \\
(c) \quad & 0 = c^* \varepsilon^c(\cdot)(\rho(\cdot) - r) \\
(g) \quad & 0 = g^* \varepsilon^g(\theta(z) - r). \\
(a) \quad & 0 = ra^* - g^* - pc^*.
\end{aligned}
$$

To analyze local stability, we first drop the (a) equation, since the corresponding eigenvalue is trivial and equal to r, and then we linearize the system by a first-order Taylor expansion, obtaining

$$
\begin{aligned}
\dot{z} &\cong c^* - \sigma z^* \\
\dot{\varphi} &\cong r(\varphi - \varphi^*) - w_c(c - c^*) - w_z(z - z^*) - v_g(g - g^*) \\
\dot{c} &\cong A(c - c^*) + B(g - g^*) + C(z - z^*) + D(\varphi - \varphi^*) \\
\dot{g} &\cong E(g - g^*) + \theta_z(z - z^*)
\end{aligned}
\tag{25}
$$

where $A = (\varepsilon^c(\cdot) + c^* \varepsilon^c_c(\cdot))(\rho(\cdot) - r) + c^* \varepsilon^c(\cdot)\rho_c(\cdot)$, $B = c^* \varepsilon^c(\cdot)\rho_g(\cdot)$, $C = c^* \varepsilon^c(\cdot)\rho_z(\cdot)$, $D = c^* \varepsilon^c(\cdot)\rho_\varphi(\cdot)$ and $E = \varepsilon^g(\theta(z) - r) + g\varepsilon^g_g(\theta(z) - r)$. The resulting Jacobian matrix J is

	z	φ	c	g
z	$-\sigma$	0	1	0
φ	$-w_z$	r	$-w_c$	$-v_g$
c	C	D	A	B
g	θ_z	0	0	E

The stability properties of system (25) are determined by the eigenvalues of matrix J, through its characteristic polynomial

$$
\alpha_0 + \alpha_1 \lambda + \alpha_2 \lambda^2 + \alpha_3 \lambda^3 + \lambda^4,
$$

where

$$
\begin{aligned}
\alpha_0 &= r\theta_z B + v_g \theta_z D - E(rC + r\sigma A + \sigma w_c D + w_z D) \\
\alpha_1 &= C(r + E) - AE(r - \sigma) + r\sigma(A + E) + D(\sigma w_c + w_z - w_c E) - \theta_z B \\
\alpha_2 &= (r - \sigma)(A + E) + AE - r\sigma + w_c D - C \\
\alpha_3 &= \sigma - r - A - E.
\end{aligned}
$$

The stability of the system is determined by the number of stable and unstable eigenvalues for matrix J, and in particular, if all eigenvalues are real and positive, the steady state is an unstable point; if they are all real and negative, the steady state is a stable point; if they are all real but some are positive and some negative, the steady state is an saddle node; if some of them are complex, the steady state is a saddle focus. The saddle node is the multidimensional equivalent of the saddle point. The system will converge towards the steady state only if the starting point lies on the stable eigenspace. In the saddle, focus convergence (if the real part of the eigenvalue is negative) or divergence (if the real part of the eigenvalue is positive) will be cyclical.

The roots of the characteristic polynomial correspond to the eigenvalues of matrix J. We know that an analytical solution exists for the roots of polynomials of the fourth degree, and that it is given by the Ferrari method. However, the analytical solution and the relative stability analysis are by far too complex to be meaningful, even if we decided to use the Routh–Hurwitz stability criterion.

It is clear that the existence and stability of the steady state depends on the parameters values. For example, if the discount function $\theta(z)$ is always greater than r, a steady state is not possible because of the increasing property of $\theta(z)$. For this reason, to characterize the stability properties of the steady state, we conduct a numerical simulation. The strategy of the simulation is as follows: first, we choose a functional form for the utility functions and the discount function; second, we select plausible numerical values for the parameters of the system and compute the steady state; third, we let the parameters vary and calculate the numerical value of the eigenvalues of matrix J.

In the choice of the functional form of the utility function, we depart from Becker and Murphy [8]. In fact, a quadratic utility function is characterized by a point of maximum and the non-satiation property, commonly assumed in consumption studies, would not hold. The model could still reach the steady state, if lower than the global maximum of utility, but this would imply an additional set of restrictions on the parameters which we prefer to avoid. Instead, we use logarithmic utility functions, and, for simplicity, a linear specification for the discount function:

$$\theta(z) = \theta_1 + \theta_2 z \tag{26}$$
$$w(c,z) = \beta \ln c - \gamma \ln z$$
$$v(g) = \alpha \ln g.$$

The discount function parameters θ_1 and θ_2 are both chosen to be 0.02. Utility parameters α and β are set to 0.8, while γ is 0.2. The relative price of the addictive good p is fixed to 1.2, the rate of returns to savings r is equal to 0.05 and the rate of habits depreciation σ is 0.2. To evaluate the stability of the steady state, we allow each parameter to vary.

The results of the simulations (The table with all eigenvalues is available upon request, together with the program that generates the results.) indicate that the system is a saddle node in the neighbor of the parameters values. The eigenvalues are all real—three are positive and one is negative. This means that the system monotonically approaches the steady state, provided that the starting point lies on the stable eigenfold. This situation is depicted in Figure 1. This phaseplot for the variable current consumption of the addictive good c_t and the current value of future utilities ϕ_t represents in red the stable eigenfold and black arrows represent the forces driving the system away from the steady state if out of the stable eigenfold.

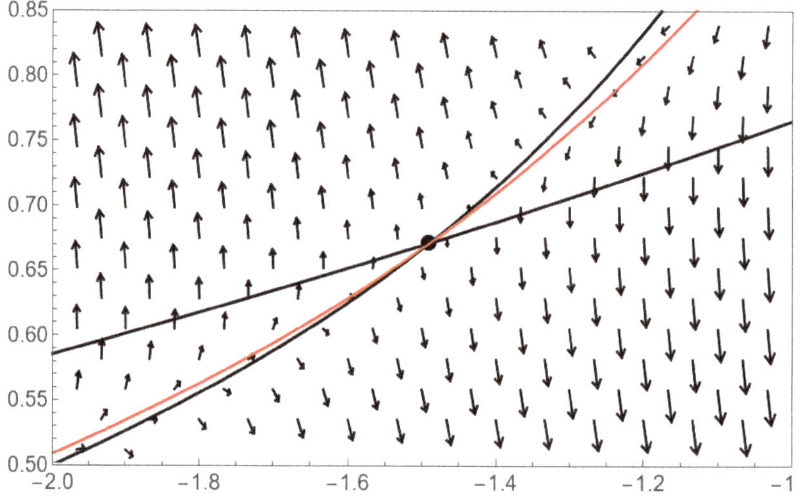

Figure 1. Phaseplot of the steady state.

The stability of the system with respect to the variations of the parameters is less trivial. For example, the steady state keeps being a saddle node for values of σ in the range $(0.1, 0.25)$. For values smaller than 0.1 or greater than 0.25 and smaller than 0.47, the equilibrium is an unstable focus, with a cyclical behavior that diverges from equilibrium. Then, it becomes a stable focus and for values greater than 0.55, again a saddle node. Aside from the numerical values, that depend on the actual choices for the parameters and the consequent steady state's values, this means that the rate of habit depreciation is a key parameter for the behavioral interpretation of the model, and a fundamental ingredient to analyze heterogeneity in habit formation. Normal people with reasonable rates of habit depreciation can find an equilibrium in the consumption of the addictive substance and enjoy a moderate consumption. People with a small σ may be more likely to develop an addiction and for them, a stable equilibrium might not be possible. The cyclical fluctuations of the equilibrium for values in between 0.25 and 0.55 could be interpreted as binge drinking, while a very large rate of habits depreciation may not result in problematic behaviors.

Other parameters that could possibly be of interest from the behavioral point of view are the discount function parameters. In particular, θ_2 determines the degree of dependence of the discount rate on the stock habits z. The discount rate corresponds to the rate of time preference of g and is one of the main determinants of that of c. We observe that for very small values of the parameter, the system becomes an unstable focus. This seems reasonable since one of the equations that must be verified at the steady state is $\theta(z) - r = 0$. If $\theta(z)$ does not grow sufficiently quickly with z, then the equilibrium could be unstable. On the other side, for any value larger than the chosen one, the system behaves as a saddle node.

Furthermore, the disutility caused by the stock of habits, through the utility parameter γ, plays an important role. We observe that the equilibrium becomes an unstable focus with a cyclical path if the disutility of habits is small (below 0.1). This may indicate that people with an insufficient perception of the health issues related to the consumption of alcohol, for example, may fall into binge drinking. For larger values, the equilibrium is always a saddle node. Other parameters' variations do not show unexpected results, and in general, result in a saddle node equilibrium for wide intervals.

A similar result was observed using isoelastic utility functions, while, as mentioned above, the case of a quadratic utility function is slightly more complicated. Our simulations suggest that the model behaves as in the previous cases in several situations, however, depending on the parameters of the utility function, the steady state may be infeasible, since it can lie above the global maximum of the utility functions.

5. Heterogeneity in the Habits Formation Process

Heterogeneity is a necessary feature for almost any work on consumer demand. In fact, it is a common opinion that each individual has their own preference structure and that a correct demand analysis should take this into account. When considering a dynamic context, heterogeneous preferences can be captured through the rate of time preference, as suggested by Fuchs [51] and Lawrance [52]. Following this path, in this section, we concentrate on introducing heterogeneity through the rate of time preference for c.

The definition of an endogenous rate of time preference permits separating the effects of heterogeneity from a generic habit effect. This is achieved through the definition of a rate of habits depreciation σ as a function of personal characteristics d. This implies that each individual develops habits and eventually addiction with a different consumption–habits path and achieve a different steady state. In particular, in Section 3, we have seen how the steady state level of the stock of habit z^* only depends on the discount function $\theta(z)$ and on the interest rate r. As a consequence, the steady state level of consumption of the addictive good c^*, which is equal to $\sigma(d)z^*$, depends on the individual characteristics of the consumer d. Moreover, these characteristics may not be constant over time, as for age, which, as suggested by Bishai [13], may influence the rate of time preference.

An example can help one understand our hypotheses. Define two categories of agents which constitute society, e.g., myopic (m) and forward-looking (f) (any resemblance between the symbols used to indicate the two kind of agents and those used to indicate males and females is purely coincidental). An agent is myopic if they are characterized by strong a preference towards actual consumption, with a large degree of impatience. The impatience is caused by a large discount rate $\theta(z)$, which in turn is caused by a large stock of habits z. A large stock of habits may be caused by a rapid growth of z induced by a small rate of habits depreciation $\sigma(d)$.

An agent is forward-looking if they are characterized by a preference towards future consumption, with a small degree of impatience. The discount rate $\theta(z)$ is small, due to a small stock of habits z, which remains small thanks to a relatively large rate of habits depreciation $\sigma(d)$.

The likelihood that they reveal addiction is picked up by the rate of habit depreciation $\sigma^f(d)$ and their preferences towards alcohol consumption and habits. The larger is $\sigma(d)$, and less weight is given to past habits in determining current habits z. Therefore, even if preferences towards alcohol are strong, the large value of $\sigma^f(d)$ and the strong adversity against health injuries caused by habits, can prevent falling into addiction. Two simulations with a plausible value of $\sigma(d)$ to ensure a saddle node steady state are depicted in Figure 2. Here, the forward-looking agent is characterized by a larger σ, which ensures a lower level of consumption of the addictive good and achieves the steady state later in life.

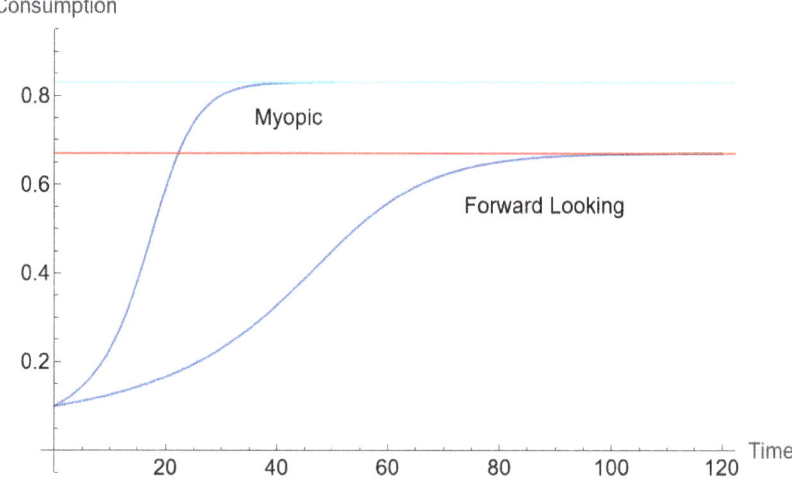

Figure 2. Heterogeneity analysis: paths to the steady states for a myopic (small σ) and a forward-looking (large σ) individuals.

Regarding the shape of the rate of habit depreciation $\sigma(d)$, to ensure the needed regularity properties of the maximization problem, it is necessary to bound it between 0 and 1. In fact, allowing for a negative rate of habit depreciation would rule out the existence of a steady state since habits would arise and continuously accumulate over time even if the consumption of the addictive good happened just once. On the other hand, for values of $\sigma(d)$ greater than 1, the stock of habits z would respond more than proportionally to a change in consumption c, allowing for a negative stock of habits z which would have no sense from a behavioral point of view. The limiting case of $\sigma(d) = 1$ implies that the stock of habits fully depreciates each period, thus excluding the possibility that habits accumulate and addiction ensues.

Other characteristics of $\sigma(d)$, which are not relevant for obtaining an interior solution to the optimization problem, such as slope and concavity, may have important implications for the behavioral analysis.

For example, one appealing feature could be an inverse-U-shape with respect to age, which would imply that an individual is more likely to develop addiction when young or elder, rather than when they are middle-aged. Another example is provided by recent medical evidence that suggests that men and women have different a predisposition to addiction. For example, a research conducted by Mancinelli et al. [53] links the stronger effects produced by alcohol abuse, with a scarce presence of alcohol dehydrogenase (ADH), which is an enzyme involved in the metabolization of alcohol. It is observed that, in general, women have smaller quantities of ADH than men. This may lead to a physiological differences in the process that generates addiction, in which women may be more exposed to the risk of become addicted. However, even if women need less alcohol than men to become addicted to alcohol, they may have different preferences with respect to both alcohol, which may be less valued, and to habits, regarded as the negative health effects that habits may bring, which could be greater valued (in negative). The result may be that there is a smaller probability that women become addicted, since, even if women are more likely to become addicted for a given amount of consumed alcohol, they may be much less inclined to consume than men.

6. Comparative Dynamics

The comparative dynamic analysis investigates how a variation of a variable or parameter of interest, such as c, z, φ and σ, affects the endogenous rate of time preference $\rho(g, c, z, \varphi)$ in the neighborhood of the steady state.

The rate of time preference $\rho(g, c, z, \varphi)$ is strictly decreasing with respect to current consumption c. In the neighborhood of the steady state $c - \sigma z \approx 0$, the partial derivative of the rate of time preference with respect to current consumption is thus

$$\frac{\partial}{\partial c}\rho(\bar{g}, c, \bar{z}, \bar{\varphi}) = -\frac{1}{pv_g}(w_{cz} - (r + \sigma)w_{cc} - w_{zc}) = \frac{(r + \sigma)w_{cc}}{pv_g} < 0.$$

The rate of time preference is decreasing with respect to an increase in the current consumption of the possibly addictive good $c(t)$. This implies that the consumer is more concerned with immediate consumption rather than future consumption. In such cases, the need to "*save against a rainy day*" becomes less urgent and there is higher willingness to consume today. In other words, a rise in current consumption causes an increase in the level of impatience. The rate of time preference $\rho(g, c, z, \varphi)$ strictly decreases with respect to the stock of habits z. In the neighborhood of the steady state $c - \sigma z \approx 0$, the partial derivative of the rate of time preference with respect to the stock of habits is impatience

$$\frac{\partial}{\partial z}\rho(\bar{g}, \bar{c}, z, \bar{\varphi}) = \theta_z - \frac{1}{pv_g}(-w_{cz}(r + 2\sigma) + \theta_{zz}\varphi - w_{zz}) > 0.$$

The rate of time preference $\rho(g, c, z, \varphi)$ is strictly decreasing with respect to the rate of impatience φ. The partial derivative of the rate of time preference with respect to the rate of impatience is

$$\frac{\partial}{\partial \varphi}\rho(\bar{g}, \bar{c}, \bar{z}, \varphi) = -\frac{\theta_z}{pv_g} < 0.$$

An increase in the rate of impatience φ indicates that the consumer is less impatient, giving more weight to future consumption. Hence, the rate of time preference is reduced and the consumption of the addictive good grows at a smaller rate. The rate of time preference $\rho(g, c, z, \varphi)$ is strictly decreasing with respect to the rate of the habit depreciation

σ if $w_c < pv_g$. In the neighborhood of the steady state $c - \sigma z \approx 0$, the partial derivative of the rate of time preference with respect to the rate of habits depreciation is thus

$$\frac{\partial}{\partial \sigma} \rho(\bar{g}, \bar{c}, \bar{z}, \bar{\varphi}) = -\frac{1}{pv_g}\left(pv_g - w_c\right) < 0 \quad iff \quad w_c < pv_g.$$

An increase in the rate of habits depreciation implies that the rate of time preference declines, i.e., a decrease in the habit effects of the possibly addictive good tends to reduce the growth of consumption of c. This is true provided that the marginal utility of the possibly addictive good w_c is smaller than the marginal utility of the non-addictive good, pv_g. Hence, unless preferences are biased towards the addictive good, an increase in the rate of habit depreciation lowers the rate of time preference, reducing the growth path of c.

The analysis of the variation of the rate of time preference with respect to a variation of the stock of habits is more complex, with no meaningful results.

The analytical and behavioral properties of the rate of time preference allow us to describe the dynamic evolution of an agent from a condition of potential habit to a state of addiction.

Reconsider the case of the myopic and forward-looking agent introduced above. The degree of impatience of the myopic agent is generally higher (lower φ) than the degree of the forward-looking and so will be the degree of habits ($\sigma^m < \sigma^f$). The propensity to exchange current for future consumption becomes less and less considerable. The myopic agent reveals an increasing impatience since their stock of habits is larger.

The subjective rate of time preference of the myopic agent encloses reinforcement and tolerance, two behavioral factors that are closely related to the concept of adjacent complementarity. Reinforcement means that, to obtain the same level of utility, the consumption of the addictive good has to increase when current consumption increases, while tolerance means that given levels of consumption are less satisfying when past consumption has been greater.

The analysis reveals a patience-dependence trade-off. A patient person tends to have a lower stock of habits than an impatient person, since the desire to anticipate future consumption is lower. It is not surprising that addiction is more likely for people who discount the future heavily since they pay less attention to the adverse consequences. Becker et al. [40] suggested that poorer and younger persons discount the future more heavily while Chaloupka [32] found that less educated persons may have higher rates of time preference. The ability of anticipating the consequences of present and past consumption depends on income, education, rank and degree of awareness of dangers.

In line with Becker and Mulligan [54], we find that "*... the analysis of endogenous discount rates implies that even fully rational utility-maximizing individuals who become addicted to drugs and other harmful substances or behavior are induced to place less weight on the future, even if the addiction itself does not affect the discount rate.*"

7. Conclusions

Traditionally, the economic literature represents the structure of preferences in a dynamic context through utility functions discounted by a constant rate. This choice, often adopted for the sake of mathematical tractability, does not allow explaining situations where the discount rate changes over time for the same individual (see, for example [10–14]).

Starting from the rational addiction model proposed by Becker and Murphy [8], this paper develops an extension which allows for time-inconsistent consumers. Assuming an endogenous discount rate depending on past consumption as adopted in Epstein and Shi [31], this study develops a formulation of intertemporal preferences that generalizes several rational models of habit formation and addiction. The proposed rate of time preference supports a subjective structure of preferences that comprehends the memory of past events, the perception of present events and the anticipation of future events, revealing adjacent complementarity. The behavioral contents delivered by the ERA model are consistent with the results of the theory of rational addiction proposed by Becker and Murphy [8] but introduce a further dimension in the analysis—an endogenous discount rate—that allows the consumer to be time inconsistent in a more complex way with respect to the quasi-hyperbolic discounting used by [26].

The proposed model presents a steady state in which the stock of habits, consumption of the possibly addictive and non-addictive goods, the shadow price of habits and the index of impatience do not grow. This steady state shows the interesting property that the consumption level of the addictive good and the stock of habits are not determined by the corresponding preferences, but only by the discount function parameters, the interest rate and the rate of habit depreciation.

Numerical simulations show that the steady state tends to be a saddle node, but some parameters variations, in particular the rate of habits depreciation, can introduce instability in the equilibrium by being cyclical. This introduces a strong motivation for analyzing heterogeneity in the consumption of addictive goods, with the possibility of finding the conditions under which habits generate addiction or even binge drinking behavior. A further feature of our specification is that it allows us to analyze how heterogeneity in time preferences may in part arise by how easily individuals accumulate habits over time.

The main limitation of the current study is that the presented model is not suitable—as it currently is—to be used in empirical applications. To overcome this limitation, our future research agenda foresees an econometric implementation of our extended rational addiction model in the form of a discrete time/finite time model which will produce an estimable Euler equation allowing us to test the hypotheses derived in the comparative dynamics analysis of the model and to estimate the subjective individual specific rate of time preferences. This parameter would then be used to calibrate our ERA model and run dynamic simulations reproducing the competitive evolution leading to the prevalence of the patient and forward-looking sub-population over the impatient and myopic sub-population that are more exposed to the risk of addiction. From a policy perspective, this evolutive exercise would show the importance for society to invest in the "production" of young people with a greater endowment of non-cognitive skills such as patience, which may increase the share of forward-looking individuals in the population, much in the spirit of the so-called Heckman equation line of research [55].

Author Contributions: Conceptualization, F.P. and L.P.; methodology, F.P. and L.P.; formal analysis, F.P. and L.P.; writing—original draft preparation, F.P. and L.P.; writing—review and editing, F.P. and L.P. All authors have read and agreed to the published version of the manuscript.

Funding: This research received no external funding.

Institutional Review Board Statement: Not applicable.

Informed Consent Statement: Not applicable.

Data Availability Statement: Not applicable.

Conflicts of Interest: The authors declare no conflict of interest.

Abbreviations

The following abbreviations are used in this manuscript:
RA   Rational addiction
ERA   Extended rational addiction

Appendix A

Here, we present a sketch of the proof that the ERA model is encompassing with respect to the models listed in the introduction. We show how imposing restrictions on the parameters or on the utility function of the proposed model is reduced to each of those models.

We start specifying the representative consumer optimization problem for the ERA model, i.e.,

$$\max \int_0^\infty u(g(t), c(t), z(t)) e^{-\int_0^t \theta(z(\tau))d\tau} dt$$

$$s.t. \quad \dot{a} = ra - g - pc,$$
$$\dot{z} = c - \sigma z.$$

This specification is different from (3) in two ways: the utility function that here is not divided into the non-addictive and addictive parts, and the discount rate, which, as shown in footnote 14, is perfectly equivalent to the alternative specification.

Epstein and Shi. The ERA model reduces to the endogenous discounting model with habits proposed by Epstein and Shi [31] by setting $u(g, c, z) = u(c)$ and assuming an adaptive habits accumulation process. Under these restrictions, the consumer maximization problem is

$$\max \int_0^\infty u(c(t)) e^{-\int_0^t \theta(z(\tau))d\tau} dt$$

$$s.t. \quad \dot{a} = ra - c,$$
$$\dot{z} = \lambda(c - z),$$

which corresponds to Epstein and Shi [31] (page 63 Equation (2.1)).

Uzawa and Obstfeld. The model proposed by Uzawa [49] and Obstfeld [50] is obtained by assuming that the utility function only depends on the consumption of a non-addictive good, i.e., $u(g, c, z) = u(g)$, and that the endogenous discount rate depends on the current consumption of the non-addictive good. This would be equivalent to set $\theta(z(t)) = \theta(g(t))$. The maximization program, taking into account that the habits accumulation equation must not be considered, becomes

$$\max \int_0^\infty u(g(t)) e^{-\int_0^t \theta(g(\tau))d\tau} dt$$

$$s.t. \quad \dot{a} = ra - c,$$

which correspond to Obstfeld [50] (page 14, Equations (20) and (21)).

Carroll. The multiplicative habits model by Carroll [48] is characterized by a constant discount rate, such that $\theta(z) = \theta$, by a utility function which depends on the ratio between the consumption of the addictive good c and the stock of habits z, so $u(g, c, z) = u(c, z)$, and by an adaptive habits formation process. Even though the author explicitly sets up a CES-like utility function from the beginning and uses a capital investment equation rather than a wealth equation, the following program

$$\max \int_0^\infty u(c(t), z(t)) e^{-\theta t} dt$$

$$s.t. \quad \dot{a} = ra - c,$$
$$\dot{z} = \lambda(c - z),$$

can be considered equivalent to Carroll [48] (page 7, Equations (4) and(5)).

Rational addiction. The rational addiction model proposed by Becker and Murphy [8] is characterized by a constant discount rate and by an utility function which depends on the current consumption of an undifferentiated good g, a possibly addictive good c and the stock of habits z. Hence, the RA model can be easily obtained by setting $\theta(z) = \theta$ and taking into account the fact that the authors prefer to use a lifetime budget constraint rather than a motion equation for wealth. It is worth noting that the authors initially consider an additional term, the expenditure on endogenous depreciation D, which is not present in the ERA model. Since the authors soon assume $D = 0$, we consider the program

$$\max \int_0^\infty u(g(t), c(t), z(t))e^{-\theta t}dt$$
$$s.t. \quad \dot{a} = ra - g - pc,$$
$$\dot{z} = c - \sigma z$$

to be equivalent to Becker and Murphy [8] (page 677, Equations (2)–(4)).

Ramsey. The Ramsey model, often referred to as the basic consumption model, is characterized by a constant discount rate and a utility function depending on an undifferentiated good. Hence, we can recover it by assuming $u(g, c, z) = u(g)$ and $\theta(z) = \theta$. The resulting maximization problem is

$$\max \int_0^\infty u(g(t))e^{-\theta t}dt$$
$$s.t. \quad \dot{a} = ra - g,$$

which is one of the possible representations of the Ramsey model.

References

1. Ramsey, F.P. A Mathematical Theory of Saving. *Econ. J.* **1928**, *38*, 543–559. [CrossRef]
2. Kennedy, J.G. *The Flowers of Paradise. The Istitutionalized Use of the Drug Qat in North Yemen*; Reidel Publishing Company: Dordrecht, The Netherlands, 1987.
3. Stein, J.; Bentler, M.; Newcome, M. Structure of Drug Use Behaviour and Consequences Among Young Adults: Multitrait-Multimethod Assesment of Frequency, Quantity, Work Site, and Problem Substance Use. *J. Appl. Psychol.* **1988**, *73*, 595–605. [CrossRef] [PubMed]
4. Gorman, W.M. Tastes, Habits and Choices. *Int. Econ. Rev.* **1967**, *8*, 218–222. [CrossRef]
5. Pollak, R.A. Habit Formation and Dynamic Demand Functions. *J. Political Econ.* **1970**, *78*, 745–763. [CrossRef]
6. Lluch, C. Expenditure, Savings and Habit Formation. *Int. Econ. Rev.* **1974**, *15*, 786–797. [CrossRef]
7. Boyer, M. A Habit Forming Optimal Growth Model. *Int. Econ. Rev.* **1978**, *19*, 585–609. [CrossRef]
8. Becker, G.S.; Murphy, K. A Theory of Rational Addiction. *J. Political Econ.* **1988**, *96*, 675–700. [CrossRef]
9. Strotz, R.H. Myopia and Inconsistency in Dynamic Utility Maximization. *Rev. Econ. Stud.* **1956**, *23*, 165–180. [CrossRef]
10. Blanchard, O.; Fisher, S. *Lectures on Macroeconomics*; Harvard University Press: Cambridge, MA, USA, 1989.
11. Deaton, A.S. *Understanding Consumption*; Oxford University Press: Oxford, UK, 1992.
12. Romer, P. Cake Eating, Chattering and Jumps: Existence Results for Vaiational Problems. *Econometrica* **1986**, *54*, 897–908. [CrossRef]
13. Bishai, M.D. Does Time Preference Change with Age? *J. Popul. Econ.* **2004**, *17*, 583–602. [CrossRef]
14. Laibson, D.; Repetto, A.; Tobacman, J. *Estimating Discount Functions with Consumption Choices over the Lifecycle*; NBER Working Paper Series; Working Paper 13314; National Bureau of Economic Research (NBER): Cambridge, MA, USA, 2007.
15. Laibson, D. Golden Eggs and Hyperbolic Discounting. *Q. J. Econ.* **1997**, *62*, 443–478. [CrossRef]
16. O'Donoghue, T.; Rabin, M. Doing it Now or Later. *Am. Econ. Rev.* **1999**, *89*, 103–124. [CrossRef]
17. O'Donoghue, T.; Rabin, M. Addiction and self-control. In *Addiction: Entries and Exits*; Elster, J., Ed.; Russell Sage: New York, NY, USA, 1999.
18. O'Donoghue, T.; Rabin, M. *Addiction and Present Biased Preferences*; Working Paper Department of Economics, University of California at Berkeley: Berkeley, CA, USA, 2002; p. E02-312.
19. Angeletos, G.; Laibson, D.; Repetto, A.; Tobacman, J.; Weinberg, S. The Hyperbolic Consumption Model: Calibration, Simulation and Empirical Evaluation. *J. Econ. Perspect.* **2001**, *15*, 47–68. [CrossRef]
20. Diamond, P.; Köszegi, B. Quasi-Hyperbolic Discounting and Retirement. *J. Public Econ.* **2003**, *87*, 1839–1872. [CrossRef]
21. Barro, R. Ramsey meets Laibson in the neoclassical growth model. *Q. J. Econ.* **1999**, *114*, 1125–1152. [CrossRef]
22. Shapiro, J. Is There a Daily Discount Rate? Evidence from the Food Stamp Nutrition Cycle. *J. Public Econ.* **2005**, *89*, 303–325. [CrossRef]
23. Fang, H.; Silverman, D. Time-Inconsistency and Welfare Program Participation. Evidence from the NLSY. *Int. Econ. Rev.* **2009**, *50*, 1043–1076. [CrossRef]
24. Della Vigna, S.; Paserman, D. Job Search and Impatience. *J. Labour Econ.* **2005**, *23*, 527–588. [CrossRef]
25. Acland, D.; Levy, M. Habit Formation, Naiveté, and Projection Bias in Gym Attendance. *Manag. Sci.* **2015**, *61*, 146–160. [CrossRef]
26. Gruber, J.; Köszegi, B. Is Addiction "rational"? Theory and Evidence. *Q. J. Econ.* **2001**, *116*, 1261–1303. [CrossRef]
27. Levy, M. An Empirical Analysis of Biases in Cigarette Addiction. *MIMEO*, unpublished.

28. Chaloupka, F.; Levy, M.; White, J. *Estimating Biases in Smoking Cessation: Evidence from a Field Experiment*; NBER Working Paper Series; National Bureau of Economic Research (NBER): Cambridge, MA, USA, 2019; p. 26522. [CrossRef]
29. Piccoli, L.; Tiezzi, S. Rational Addiction and Time Consistency: An Empirical Test. *J. Health Econ.* **2021**, *80*, 102546. [CrossRef] [PubMed]
30. Grossman, M. The demand for health turns 50: Reflections. *Health Econ.* 2022, *in press*. [CrossRef]
31. Epstein, L.; Shi, S. Habits and Time Preference. *Int. Econ. Rev.* **1993**, *34*, 61–84.
32. Chaloupka, F.J. Rational Addictiove Behaviour and Cigarette Smoking. *J. Political Econ.* **1991**, *99*, 722–742. [CrossRef]
33. Dragone, D. A rational eating model of binges, diets and obesity. *J. Health Econ.* **2009**, *28*, 799–804. [CrossRef]
34. Dragone, D.; Savorelli, L. Thinness and obesity: A model of food consumption, health concerns, and social pressure. *J. Health Econ.* **2012**, *31*, 243–256. [CrossRef] [PubMed]
35. Chavas, J.P. On the microeconomics of food and malnutrition under endogenous discounting. *Eur. Econ. Rev.* **2013**, *59*, 80–96. [CrossRef]
36. Strulik, H. Smoking kills: An economic theory of addiction, health deficit accumulation, and longevity. *J. Health Econ.* **2018**, *62*, 1–12. [CrossRef]
37. Strulik, H. Intertemporal choice with health-dependent discounting. *Math. Soc. Sci.* **2021**, *111*, 19–25. [CrossRef]
38. Strulik, H.; Werner, K. Time-inconsistent health behavior and its impact on aging and longevity. *J. Health Econ.* **2021**, *76*, 102440. [CrossRef] [PubMed]
39. Becker, G.S.; Grossman, M.; Murphy, K. Rational Addiction and the Effect of Price on Consumption. *Am. Econ. Rev.* **1991**, *81*, 237–241.
40. Becker, G.S.; Grossman, M.; Murphy, K. An Empirical Analysis of Cigarette Addiction. *Am. Econ. Rev.* **1994**, *84*, 396–418.
41. Ryder, H.E.; Heal, G.M. Optimum Growth with Intertemporally Dependent Preferences. *Rev. Econ. Stud.* **1973**, *40*, 1–33. [CrossRef]
42. Cawley, J.; Ruhm, C.J. The Economics of Risky Health Behaviors. *Handb. Health Econ.* **2011**, *2*, 95–119.
43. Koopmans, T. Stationary Ordinal Utility Impatience. *Econometrica* **1960**, *28*, 287–309. [CrossRef]
44. Lucas, R.E.; Stokey, N.L. Optimal Growth with Many Consumers. *J. Econ. Theory* **1984**, *32*, 139–171. [CrossRef]
45. Epstein, L. The Global Stability of Efficient Intertemporal Allocation. *Econometrica* **1987**, *55*, 329–355. [CrossRef]
46. Epstein, L. A Simple Dynamic General Equilibrium Model. *J. Econ. Theory* **1987**, *41*, 68–95. [CrossRef]
47. Cass, D. Optimum Growth in an Aggregate Model of Capital Accumulation. *Rev. Econ. Stud.* **1965**, *32*, 233–240. [CrossRef]
48. Carroll, C. Saving and Growth with Habit Formation. *Am. Econ. Rev.* **2000**, *90*, 341–355. [CrossRef]
49. Uzawa, H. Time Preference, the Consumption Function, and Optimal Asset Holdings. In *Value, Capital and Growth: Papers in Honour of Sir John Hicks*; Wolfe, J.N., Ed.; Edimburg University Press: Edinburgh, UK, 1968; pp. 485–504.
50. Obstfeld, M. Intertemporal Dependence, Impatience and Dynamics. *J. Monet. Econ.* **1990**, *26*, 45–75. [CrossRef]
51. Fuchs, V.R. Time preference and health: An exploratory study. In *Economic Aspects of Health*; Fuchs, V.R., Ed.; University of Chicago Press: Chicago, IL, USA, 1982; pp. 93–120.
52. Lawrance, E.C. Poverty and the Rate of Time Preference: Evidence from Panel Data. *J. Political Econ.* **1991**, *99*, 54–77. [CrossRef]
53. Mancinelli, R.; Vitali, M.; Ceccanti, M. Women, alcohol and the environment: an update and perspectives in neuroscience. *Funct. Neurol.* **2008**, *24*, 77–81.
54. Becker, G.S.; Mulligan, C.B. The Endogenous Determination of Time Preferences. *Q. J. Econ.* **1997**, *112*, 729–58. [CrossRef]
55. Cunha, F.; Heckman, J.J.; Schennach, S.M. Estimating the technology of cognitive and noncognitive skill formation. *Econometrica* **2010**, *78*, 883–931.

Article

Higher-Order Asymptotic Numerical Solutions for Singularly Perturbed Problems with Variable Coefficients

Chein-Shan Liu [1], Essam R. El-Zahar [2,3] and Chih-Wen Chang [4,*

[1]   Center of Excellence for Ocean Engineering, National Taiwan Ocean University, Keelung 20224, Taiwan
[2]   Department of Mathematics, College of Sciences and Humanities in Al-Kharj,
      Prince Sattam bin Abdulaziz University, Alkharj 11942, Saudi Arabia
[3]   Department of Basic Engineering Science, Faculty of Engineering, Menofia University,
      Shebin El-Kom 32511, Egypt
[4]   Department of Mechanical Engineering, National United University, Miaoli 36063, Taiwan
[*]   Correspondence: cwchang@nuu.edu.tw

Abstract: For the purpose of solving a second-order singularly perturbed problem (SPP) with variable coefficients, a mth-order asymptotic-numerical method was developed, which decomposes the solutions into two independent sub-problems: a reduced first-order linear problem with a left-end boundary condition; and a linear second-order problem with the boundary conditions given at two ends. These are coupled through a left-end boundary condition. Traditionally, the asymptotic solution within the boundary layer is carried out in the stretched coordinates by either analytic or numerical method. The present paper executes the mth-order asymptotic series solution in terms of the original coordinates. After introducing $2(m+1)$ new variables, the outer and inner problems are transformed together to a set of $3(m+1)$ first-order initial value problems with the given zero initial conditions; then, the Runge–Kutta method is applied to integrate the differential equations to determine the $2(m+1)$ unknown terminal values of the new variables until they are convergent. The asymptotic-numerical solution exactly satisfies the boundary conditions, which are different from the conventional asymptotic solution. Several examples demonstrated that the newly proposed method can achieve a better asymptotic solution. For all values of the perturbing parameter, the method not only preserves the inherent asymptotic property within the boundary layer but also improves the accuracy of the solution in the entire domain. We derive the sufficient conditions, which terminate the series of asymptotic solutions for inner and outer problems of the SPP without having the spring term. For a specific case, we can derive a closed-form asymptotic solution, which is also the exact solution of the considered SPP.

Keywords: linear singularly perturbed problem; higher-order asymptotic-numerical method; initial value problem method; iterative method; modified asymptotic solution

MSC: 65L11

Citation: Liu, C.-S.; El-Zahar, E.R.; Chang, C.-W. Higher-Order Asymptotic Numerical Solutions for Singularly Perturbed Problems with Variable Coefficients. *Mathematics* **2022**, *10*, 2791. https://doi.org/10.3390/math10152791

Academic Editor: Arsen Palestini

Received: 16 July 2022
Accepted: 3 August 2022
Published: 5 August 2022

Publisher's Note: MDPI stays neutral with regard to jurisdictional claims in published maps and institutional affiliations.

1. Introduction

Inside the singularly perturbed problem (SPP) is a second-order derivative term multiplied by a small parameter, whose perturbation operates over a thin region across which the solution varies rapidly. This phenomenon happens for the boundary layer in fluid mechanics, the edge layer in solid mechanics, and the skin layer in electronics. To properly simulate this sort of thin-layer behavior, some special numerical methods have been developed in [1–12] by taking the singularity for the SPP into account.

The most common asymptotic approximation to the SPP is the matched asymptotic expansion method, which includes the solutions to outer and inner problems and their matching technique [13,14]. However, the asymptotic solution only satisfies a one-side boundary condition within the boundary layer, and it does not exactly match the boundary condition on another side. A modified asymptotic approximation can improve the conventional asymptotic solution. Some researchers have solved the SPP by dividing the domain of the problem into non-overlapping outer and inner regions with a terminal point near the boundary layer [15–18]. Within each region, a different type of governing equation is given with two boundary conditions being attached.

Instead of the process of determining the outer and inner expansions, matching them and then performing a composite expansion, many authors directly decomposed the asymptotic solution as the superposition of an outer solution in terms of the original variable and an inner solution in terms of stretched variable. The decomposition methods [19–22] have been broadly used to find an asymptotic expansion of the SPP due to its advantages toward the asymptotic analysis by resolving two sub-problems, which modified the original problem into a reduced problem and a boundary layer correction problem. There exists no discrepancy about the reduced problem to find the outer solution; however, there are different techniques to construct the boundary layer correction problems for the inner solutions. Padmaja and Reddy [23], according to the idea of [19], developed a numerical patching method with the Padé approximation to solve the linear SPP.

In the text books [24,25], there are many different methods, such as the WKB, a method to eliminate the first derivative term and then use the exponential phase function to approximate the singular solution, and the reproducing kernel method to reconstruct the solution in the Hilbert space. Recently, Xu et al. [26] have applied the reproducing kernel method to solve some BVPs with the optimal convergence rate.

There are different initial value methods appearing in the literature [27–32]. Some methods are replacing the original SPP by an asymptotically equivalent first-order differential equations system and solving them as the initial value problem. Reddy and Chakravarthy [30] have factorized the original problem into three first-order initial value problems. These are different from our approaches outlined above. In [33], the method of the reduction of order was proposed for solving SPP, which is replaced by a pair of initial-value problems. The integration of these initial-value problems goes in the opposite direction and the second problem can be solved only if the solution of the first one is known.

In this paper, we propose a mth-order asymptotic numerical method to treat the linear SPP by decomposing the numerical process into a coupled outer solution to the inner solution. The latter problem satisfies the derived boundary conditions. Inspired by the previous works in [34], a novel initial value problem method is developed which guarantees that all boundary conditions are satisfied. Consequently, we need to solve $3(m + 1)$ first-order problems with the given zero initial values and integrate them in the same direction. The method of the reduction of order is distinguished by the fact that the original problem is replaced by initial value problems, which are easy implementations to compute.

We arrange the paper as follows. The mathematical backgrounds are given in Section 2, prescribing the basic ingredients in the asymptotic analysis for a certain example. In Section 3, we decompose the SPP into finding an inner solution and an outer solution in the newly proposed boundary layer correction problem, and introduce a transformation of the independent variable, such that the second-order SPP in the new coordinate is less sharpened within the boundary layer. Here, a higher-order asymptotic expansion method is depicted. In Section 4, we derive two functions for automatically preserving the boundary conditions, and the SPP is transformed into the initial value problems (IVPs) for two new variables. A mth-order iterative algorithm is developed to determine the unknown right-end values of the new variables, and thus, the modified asymptotic solution can be successfully determined with a few iterations. Some numerical examples are solved in Section 5 by the proposed asymptotic-numerical algorithm. A special type SPP without having the spring term is considered in Section 6, where the three main results are proven and three examples are given. For a specific relation of the damping coefficient and the forcing term, a closed-form asymptotic solution can be derived. Finally, the conclusions are drawn in Section 7.

2. Mathematical Backgrounds

We consider a second-order linear SPP with variable coefficients:

$$\varepsilon u''(x) + p(x)u'(x) + q(x)u(x) = r(x), \quad 0 < x < 1, \tag{1}$$

$$u(0) = \alpha, \quad u(1) = \beta. \tag{2}$$

The exhibition of boundary layers at one or both ends of the interval depends on the property of $p(x)$. Under the assumption $p(x) > 0$, the boundary layer is attached to the left end. As customarily used in the mechanical vibration problem, $r(x)$ is a forcing term, $p(x)u'(x)$ is a damping term with $p(x)$ a damping coefficient, and $q(x)u(x)$ is a spring term with $q(x)$ as a spring coefficient.

Before embarking on the higher-order asymptotic numerical solution of Equations (1) and (2), we demonstrate some basic ingredients of the first-order asymptotic analysis demonstrated via the following example:

$$\varepsilon u''(x) + u'(x) + u(x) = 0, \tag{3}$$

$$u(0) = \alpha, \quad u(1) = \beta, \tag{4}$$

where $\varepsilon > 0$ is a sufficiently small perturbing parameter. The exact solution is

$$u_e(x) = \frac{1}{e^{a_2} - e^{a_1}} \left[(\alpha e^{a_2} - \beta)e^{a_1 x} + (\beta - \alpha e^{a_1})e^{a_2 x} \right], \tag{5}$$

where

$$a_1 = \frac{-1 + \sqrt{1 - 4\varepsilon}}{2\varepsilon}, \quad a_2 = \frac{-1 - \sqrt{1 - 4\varepsilon}}{2\varepsilon}, \tag{6}$$

and $0 < \varepsilon < 0.25$ is the admissible range of ε.

2.1. Conventional Asymptotic Match Method

We demonstrate the first-order asymptotic matched method to approximate Equations (3) and (4). The outer solution is

$$u_o(x) = y_0(x) + \varepsilon y_1(x) + \dots . \tag{7}$$

Inserting it into Equation (3) and by equating the coefficients preceding $\varepsilon^0 = 1$ and ε, we have

$$\begin{cases} y_0'(x) + y_0(x) = 0, \ y_0(1) = \beta, \\ y_1'(x) + y_1(x) = -y_0''(x), \ y_1(1) = 0. \end{cases} \tag{8}$$

Hence, we can derive the first-order outer solution:

$$u_o(x) = \beta[1 + \varepsilon(1 - x)]e^{1-x} + \mathcal{O}(\varepsilon^2). \tag{9}$$

To seek the inner solution $u_i(x)$ of Equations (3) and (4), a stretched coordinate is considered:

$$\zeta := \frac{x}{\varepsilon}, \tag{10}$$

such that

$$\frac{du(x)}{dx} = \frac{1}{\varepsilon}\frac{du(\zeta)}{d\zeta}, \quad \frac{d^2 u(x)}{dx^2} = \frac{1}{\varepsilon^2}\frac{d^2 u(\zeta)}{d\zeta^2}. \tag{11}$$

Inserting them into Equation (3) and multiplying the resultant by ε yields

$$\frac{d^2 u(\zeta)}{d\zeta^2} + \frac{du(\zeta)}{d\zeta} + \varepsilon u(\zeta) = 0. \tag{12}$$

The inner solution reads as

$$u_i(x) = w_0(x) + \varepsilon w_1(x) + \dots, \tag{13}$$

which, as it is inserted into Equation (12) and by equating the coefficients preceding $\varepsilon^0 = 1$ and ε, generates

$$\begin{cases} w_0''(\zeta) + w_0'(\zeta) = 0, \ w_0(0) = \alpha, \\ w_1''(\zeta) + w_1'(\zeta) = -w_0(\zeta), \ w_1(0) = 0. \end{cases} \tag{14}$$

Solving Equation (14), the first-order inner solution is given by

$$u_i(\zeta) = \alpha - c_1(1 - e^{-\zeta}) + \varepsilon\{c_2(1 - e^{-\zeta}) - [\alpha - c_1(1 + e^{-\zeta})]\zeta\} + \mathcal{O}(\varepsilon^2), \tag{15}$$

where c_1 and c_2 are integration constants, determined by the matching principle [35]:

$$u_i^o := \lim_{\zeta \to \infty} u_i = \lim_{x \to 0} u_o =: u_o^i, \tag{16}$$

which leads to $c_1 = \alpha - e\beta$ and $c_2 = e\beta$. Hence, the first-order inner solution is given by

$$u_i(\zeta) = e\beta + (\alpha - e\beta)e^{-\zeta} + \varepsilon\{e\beta(1 - e^{-\zeta}) - [e\beta - (\alpha - e\beta)e^{-\zeta}]\zeta\}. \tag{17}$$

Finally, the first-order uniform asymptotic solution denoted by $u_a(x)$ can be obtained by a composition technique [35]:

$$u_a(x) = u_o + u_i - u_o^i = u_o + u_i - u_i^o = \beta[1 + \varepsilon(1 - x)]e^{1-x} + [(\alpha - e\beta)(1 + x) - e\beta\varepsilon]e^{-x/\varepsilon}. \tag{18}$$

We can observe that

$$u_a(0) = \alpha, \ u_a(1) = \beta + [2(\alpha - e\beta) - e\beta\varepsilon]e^{-1/\varepsilon} \neq \beta. \tag{19}$$

This means that the asymptotic solution $u_a(x)$ does not match the right-end boundary condition in Equation (4), which has an absolute error $|2(\alpha - e\beta) - e\beta\varepsilon|e^{-1/\varepsilon}$. When ε is small, the error is negligible; however, when ε is a moderate value, the error cannot be neglected. Thus, it may induce a large error of the original asymptotic solution (18) in the entire domain.

2.2. A New Asymptotic Method

In order to improve the drawback of the conventional asymptotic method, we propose a new asymptotic method to approximate Equations (3) and (4). We express Equation (14) in terms of x with the aid of Equation (11):

$$\begin{cases} \varepsilon^2 w_0''(x) + \varepsilon w_0'(x) = 0, \\ \varepsilon^2 w_1''(x) + \varepsilon w_1'(x) = -w_0(x), \end{cases}$$

and then, we obtain

$$\varepsilon w_0''(x) + w_0'(x) = 0, \tag{20}$$
$$\varepsilon^2 w_1''(x) + \varepsilon w_1'(x) = -w_0(x), \tag{21}$$

where the prime denotes the differential with respect to x. Letting $z_j = \varepsilon^j w_j$, $j = 0, 1$, Equation (21) is changed to

$$\varepsilon z_1''(x) + z_1'(x) = -z_0(x), \tag{22}$$

and the inner solution (13) becomes

$$u_i(x) = z_0(x) + z_1(x) + \dots. \tag{23}$$

Now, we solve

$$\begin{cases} \varepsilon z_0''(x) + z_0'(x) = 0, \ z_0(0) = \alpha - u_0(0), \ z_0(1) = 0, \\ \varepsilon z_1''(x) + z_1'(x) = -z_0(x), \ z_1(0) = z_1(1) = 0, \end{cases} \tag{24}$$

and

$$u(x) = u_o(x) + u_i(x) = u_0(x) + z_0(x) + z_1(x) \tag{25}$$

represents a new first-order asymptotic solution of Equations (3) and (4), where $u_0(x)$ is still given by Equation (9) with

$$u_0(0) = \beta e(1 + \varepsilon). \tag{26}$$

Inserting it into Equation (24), $z_0(0) = \alpha - \beta e(1 + \varepsilon)$ is obtained.

Instead of considering the left-end condition in Equation (14), using the matching method to determine the integration constants c_1 and c_2 and then finding the composition solution (18), we directly subject $u_i(x)$ to the boundary conditions in Equation (24) and employ the direct sum in Equation (25) to determine the new asymptotic solution.

Through some operations on Equation (24), we can derive the new first-order asymptotic solution:

$$u(x) = \beta[1 + \varepsilon(1 - x)]e^{1-x} + A + Be^{-x/\varepsilon} - Ax + Bxe^{-x/\varepsilon} + \frac{2A[1 - e^{-x/\varepsilon}]}{1 - e^{-1/\varepsilon}}, \tag{27}$$

where

$$A := \frac{[e\beta(1 + \varepsilon) - \alpha]e^{-1/\varepsilon}}{1 - e^{-1/\varepsilon}}, \quad B := \frac{\alpha - e\beta(1 + \varepsilon)}{1 - e^{-1/\varepsilon}}. \tag{28}$$

Here, $u(x)$ in Equation (27) exactly satisfies the boundary conditions $u(0) = \alpha$ and $u(1) = \beta$ in Equation (4).

Given $\varepsilon = 0.245$, $\alpha = 0$ and $\beta = 1$, Figure 1 compares u_e, u_a and the present result u in Equation (27), where the maximum error (ME) of $|u_e - u_a|$ is 1.41×10^{-1} and the ME of $|u_e - u|$ is 6.85×10^{-2}. The present u in Equation (27) is closer to the exact solution than that of $u_a(x)$ in Equation (18). In Table 1, we compare the ME1 of $|u_e - u|$ and the ME2 of $|u_e - u_a|$ for different values of ε, which are close when $\varepsilon \leq 0.1$. For $\varepsilon \geq 0.2$, ME1 is smaller than ME2. Equations (27) and (18) possess the same asymptotic property, since

$$A \to 0, \ 1 - e^{-1/\varepsilon} \to 1, \ \text{when } \varepsilon \to 0.$$

In this situation,

$$B \to \alpha - e\beta, \ \text{or } B \to \alpha - e\beta(1 + \varepsilon),$$

and Equations (27) and (18) are the same.

Table 1. Comparing ME1 and ME2 obtained from the present solution and the original asymptotic solution to the exact one with different ε.

ε	ME1	ME2
0.24	6.566×10^{-2}	1.311×10^{-1}
0.2	4.693×10^{-2}	7.033×10^{-2}
0.1	2.485×10^{-2}	2.198×10^{-2}
0.01	5.931×10^{-4}	5.895×10^{-4}
0.001	6.664×10^{-6}	6.661×10^{-6}
0.0001	6.775×10^{-8}	6.774×10^{-8}

In summary, we can say that the new asymptotic solution (27) not only preserves the same asymptotic behavior as that of the original asymptotic solution (18), but also enhances the accuracy in the entire domain. The present method is easier to work with than the original asymptotic matching method and is suitable for the linear SPP with all the values of the perturbing parameter ε.

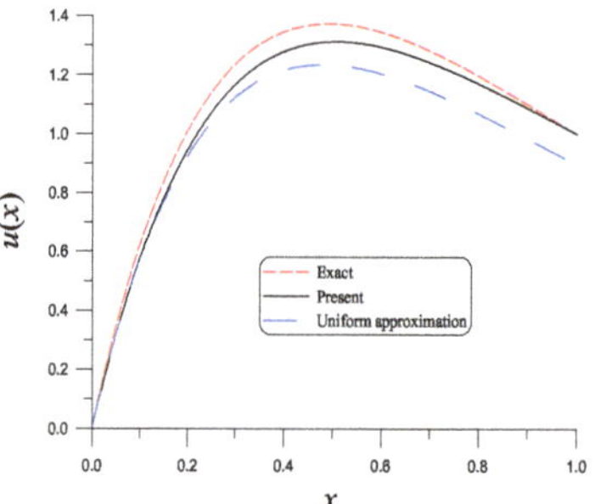

Figure 1. For a given example, comparing the exact solution, a uniform approximation and the present solution.

3. Higher-Order Asymptotic Expansion Method

Motivated by the analysis in Section 2.2, we extend it to a higher-order asymptotic expansion method by assuming

$$u(x) = u_o(x) + u_i(x) = \sum_{j=0}^{m} \varepsilon^j y_j(x) + \sum_{j=0}^{m} \varepsilon^j w_j(x) = \sum_{j=0}^{m} \varepsilon^j y_j(x) + \sum_{j=0}^{m} z_j(x), \qquad (29)$$

where m is the order of asymptotic approximation, and

$$z_j(x) := \varepsilon^j w_j(x), \ j = 0, 1, \dots, m. \qquad (30)$$

Inserting $u_o(x)$ into Equation (1) and equating the coefficients preceding ε^j, $j = 0, 1, \dots, m$, we can derive

$$\begin{cases} y_0'(x) = \frac{r(x)}{p(x)} - \frac{q(x)}{p(x)} y_0(x), \ y_0(1) = \beta, \\ y_j'(x) = -\frac{q(x) y_j(x)}{p(x)} - \frac{y_{j-1}''(x)}{p(x)}, \ y_j(1) = 0, \ j = 1, \dots, m. \end{cases} \qquad (31)$$

Then, we derive the governing equation for the inner solution $u_i(x)$ of $u(x)$. In Equation (1), the nonhomogeneous term $r(x)$ was already taken into account by Equation (31) in the outer solution and thus, we consider a homogeneous ODE for the inner solution:

$$\varepsilon u_i''(x) + p(x) u_i'(x) + q(x) u_i(x) = 0, \qquad (32)$$

$$u_i(0) = \alpha - u_o(0), \ u_i(1) = 0. \qquad (33)$$

In terms of ζ in Equation (10), Equation (32) changes to

$$u_i''(\zeta) + p(\varepsilon\zeta) u_i'(\zeta) + \varepsilon q(\varepsilon\zeta) u_i(\zeta) = 0. \qquad (34)$$

We assume

$$u_i(\zeta) = \sum_{j=0}^{m} \varepsilon^j w_j(\zeta), \qquad (35)$$

which is inserted into Equation (34) and by equating the coefficients preceding ε^j, $j = 0, 1, \dots, m$, we have

$$\begin{cases} w_0''(\zeta) + p(\varepsilon\zeta) w_0'(\zeta) = 0, \ w_0(0) = \alpha - u_o(0), \ w_0(1) = 0, \\ w_j''(\zeta) + p(\varepsilon\zeta) w_j'(\zeta) + q(\varepsilon\zeta) w_{j-1}(\zeta) = 0, \ w_j(0) = w_j(1) = 0, \ j = 1, \dots, m. \end{cases} \qquad (36)$$

Now, it is crucial that we can express Equation (36) in terms of x with the aid of Equation (11):

$$\varepsilon w_0''(x) + p(x)w_0'(x) = 0, \ w_0(0) = \alpha - u_0(0), \ w_0(1) = 0, \tag{37}$$

$$\varepsilon^2 w_j''(x) + \varepsilon p(x)w_j'(x) + q(x)w_{j-1}(x) = 0, \ w_j(0) = w_j(1) = 0, \ j = 1,\ldots,m. \tag{38}$$

Multiplying Equation (38) by ε^{j-1}, yields

$$\varepsilon^{j+1} w_j''(x) + \varepsilon^j p(x)w_j'(x) + q(x)\varepsilon^{j-1}w_{j-1}(x) = 0, \ w_j(0) = 0, \ w_j(1) = 0, \ j = 1,\ldots,m. \tag{39}$$

Then, resorting to the definition (30), Equations (37) and (39) change to

$$\begin{cases} \varepsilon z_0''(x) + p(x)z_0'(x) = 0, \ z_0(0) = \alpha - u_0(0), \ z_0(1) = 0, \\ \varepsilon z_j''(x) + p(x)z_j'(x) + q(x)z_{j-1}(x) = 0, \ z_j(0) = z_j(1) = 0, \ j = 1,\ldots,m. \end{cases} \tag{40}$$

When $0 < \varepsilon \ll 1$, the SPP (1) is very stiff within the boundary layer. In order to integrate the differential Equations (31) and (40), the following transformation between the independent variables x and t is considered:

$$x(t) = 1 - \frac{\tanh[\lambda(1-t)]}{\tanh \lambda}, \ x(0) = 0, \ x(1) = 1. \tag{41}$$

It follows from Equations (31), (40) and (41) that

$$\dot{y}_0(t) = f_0(t, y_0) := \frac{\lambda e(t)r(t)}{p(t)} - \frac{\lambda e(t)q(t)y_0}{p(t)}, \ y_0(1) = \beta, \tag{42}$$

$$\dot{y}_j(t) = f_j(t, y_j, y_{j-1}'') := -\lambda e(t)\left[\frac{q(t)y_j}{p(t)} + \frac{y_{j-1}''}{p(t)}\right], \ y_j(1) = 0, \ j = 1,\ldots,m, \tag{43}$$

$$\dot{z}_0(t) = F_0(t, z_0) := \left[2\lambda \tanh[\lambda(1-t)] - \frac{\lambda e(t)}{\varepsilon}p(t)\right]z_0(t),$$

$$z_0(0) = \alpha - u_0(0), \ z_0(1) = 0, \tag{44}$$

$$\ddot{z}_j(t) = F_j(t, \dot{z}_j, z_{j-1}) := \left[2\lambda \tanh[\lambda(1-t)] - \frac{\lambda e(t)}{\varepsilon}p(t)\right]\dot{z}_j(t) - \frac{\lambda^2 e^2(t)}{\varepsilon}q(t)z_{j-1},$$

$$z_j(0) = z_j(1) = 0, \ j = 1,\ldots,m, \tag{45}$$

where

$$e(t) := \frac{1 - \tanh^2[\lambda(1-t)]}{\tanh \lambda}. \tag{46}$$

For saving notations, $p(t)$ means that $p(x(t))$ and others are similar. The term y_{j-1}'' in Equation (31) can be expressed as a function of $y_0,\ldots,y_{j-1}$, which, however, needs a tedious work when m is increased.

Remark 1. *For the sake of comparison, the higher-order formulas developed by Kaushik et al. [36] are listed as follows:*

$$u(x) = v(x) + w(\zeta), \tag{47}$$

$$v = v_0 + \varepsilon v_1 + \ldots + \varepsilon^k v_k + \varepsilon^{k+1} V, \tag{48}$$

$$p(x)v_0' + q(x)v_0 = r(x), \ v_0(1) = \beta, \tag{49}$$

$$p(x)v_i'(x) + q(x)v_i = -v_{i-1}'', \ v_i(1) = 0, \ i = 1, \ldots, k, \tag{50}$$

$$\varepsilon V'' + p(x)V'(x) + q(x)V = -v_k'', \ V(0) = V(1) = 0, \tag{51}$$

$$w = w_0 + \varepsilon w_1 + \ldots + \varepsilon^k w_k, \tag{52}$$

$$w_0'' + p(0)w_0' = 0, \ w_0(0) = \alpha - v_0(0), \ \lim_{\zeta \to \infty} w_0(\zeta) = 0, \tag{53}$$

$$w_i'' + p(0)w_i'(x) = -\sum_{j=1}^{i}\left[\frac{p^{(j)}(0)}{j!}\zeta^j w_{i-j}' + \frac{q^{(j-1)}(0)}{(j-1)!}\zeta^{j-1} w_{i-j}\right],$$

$$w_i(0) = -v_i(0), \ \lim_{\zeta \to \infty} w_i(\zeta) = 0, \ i = 1, \ldots, k. \tag{54}$$

Equations (47)–(54) are more complicated than Equations (31) and (40). The right boundary conditions $\lim_{\zeta \to \infty} w_0(\zeta) = 0$ and $\lim_{\zeta \to \infty} w_i(\zeta) = 0$ are not easily realized by numerical method. Fortunately, Kaushik et al. [36] have derived the formulas:

$$w_0(x) = [\alpha - v_0(0)] \exp\frac{-p(0)x}{\varepsilon}, \tag{55}$$

$$w_1(x) = \left(\frac{p'(0)[\alpha - v_0(0)]}{p^2(0)} - v_1(0) + \frac{b(0)[\alpha - v_0(0)]x}{p(0)\varepsilon}\right)\exp\frac{-p(0)x}{\varepsilon}$$

$$-p'(0)[\alpha - v_0(0)]\left(\frac{x^2}{2\varepsilon^2} + \frac{x}{p(0)\varepsilon} + \frac{1}{p^2(0)}\right)\exp\frac{-p(0)x}{\varepsilon}. \tag{56}$$

Examples 5 and 7 will be given in Sections 6.2.1 and 6.2.3 to show that the accuracy of the above method is worse than the method in Equations (31) and (40). These two methods in Equations (40), (53) and (54) are different in four aspects: the coordinates x and ζ, the coefficients $p(x), q(x)$ and $p(0), q(0)$, the left boundary conditions $z_i(0) = 0$ and $w_i(0) = -v_i(0)$, and the right boundary conditions $z_i(1) = 0$ and $\lim_{\zeta \to \infty} w_i(\zeta) = 0$.

4. A Novel mth-Order Asymptotic-Numerical Method

4.1. Two Free Functions

When p and q are nonlinear functions of x, the analytic asymptotic solution is not easy to obtain from the exact solutions of Equations (31) and (40). Instead, we developed a novel numerical method to find the asymptotic-numerical solution. Before deriving a novel iterative method to solve Equations (42)–(45), we cite the following results [37,38].

Theorem 1. *For any free function $Y(t) \in C[0,1]$, the function*

$$y(t) = Y(t) - G(t) \tag{57}$$

satisfies $y(1) = b$, where

$$G(t) := e^{t-1}[Y(1) - b]. \tag{58}$$

Proof. It is obvious that

$$y(1) = Y(1) - G(1) = Y(1) - e^{1-1}[Y(1) - b] = Y(1) - [Y(1) - b] = b;$$

hence, we prove that $y(t)$ in Equation (57) satisfies the right-end boundary condition $y(1) = b$. $\square$

Theorem 2. *For any free function $Z(t) \in C[0,1]$, the function*

$$z(t) = Z(t) - H(t) \tag{59}$$

satisfies the boundary conditions $z(0) = a$ and $z(1) = 0$, where

$$H(t) := (1 - t)[Z(0) - a] + tZ(1). \tag{60}$$

Proof. In Equations (59) and (60), we insert $t = 0$ to obtain

$$z(0) = Z(0) - H(0) = Z(0) - [Z(0) - a] = a. \tag{61}$$

In Equations (59) and (60), we insert $t = 1$ to obtain

$$z(1) = Z(1) - H(1) = Z(1) - Z(1) = 0. \tag{62}$$

Thus, we end the proof. $\square$

4.2. Transforming to the Initial Value Problem

Theorems 1 and 2 can be applied in the asymptotic numerical solution of the linear SPP. For Equations (42)–(45), we consider the following transformations of variables:

$$y_j(t) = Y_j(t) - G_j(t) = Y_j(t) - e^{t-1}[Y_j(1) - b_j], \ j = 0, 1, \ldots, m, \tag{63}$$

$$z_j(t) = Z_j(t) - H_j(t) = Z_j(t) - (1 - t)[Z_j(0) - a_j] - tZ_j(1), \ j = 0, 1, \ldots, m, \tag{64}$$

where

$$b_0 = \beta, \ b_j = 0, \ j = 1, \ldots, m, \tag{65}$$

$$a_0 = \alpha - u_o(0), \ a_j = 0, \ j = 1, \ldots, m, \tag{66}$$

in which

$$u_o(0) = \sum_{j=0}^{m} \epsilon^j y_j(0) = \sum_{j=0}^{m} \epsilon^j \{Y_j(0) - e^{-1}[Y_j(1) - b_j]\}. \tag{67}$$

Letting $Y = Y_j$, $Z = Z_j$, $y = y_j$ and $z = z_j$ with $Y_j(t) \in C^1[0,1]$ and $Z_j(t) \in C^2[0,1]$ and by Theorems 1 and 2, y_j satisfies the right-end boundary condition $y_j(1) = b_j$, and z_j satisfies the boundary conditions $z_j(0) = a_j$ and $z_j(1) = 0$, automatically.

Inserting Equations (63) and (64) into Equations (42)–(45), we can derive

$$\dot{Y}_0(t) = \dot{G}_0 + f_0(t, Y_0 - G_0), \tag{68}$$

$$\dot{Y}_j(t) = \dot{G}_j + f_j(t, Y_j - G_j, \ddot{Y}_{j-1} - \ddot{G}_{j-1}), \ j = 1, \ldots, m, \tag{69}$$

$$\ddot{Z}_0(t) = F_0(t, \dot{Z}_0 - \dot{H}_0), \tag{70}$$

$$\ddot{Z}_j(t) = F_j(t, \dot{Z}_j - \dot{H}_j, Z_{j-1} - H_{j-1}), \ j = 1, \ldots, m. \tag{71}$$

In Equations (68)–(71), we take the initial values to be $Y_j(0) = Z_j(0) = \dot{Z}_j(0) = 0$, $j = 0, 1, \ldots, m$ for saving parameters, while the unknown terminal values $Y_j(1)$ and $Z_j(1)$, $j = 0, 1, \ldots, m$ are to be determined.

4.3. The Iterative Algorithm

We denote the unknown values $Y_j(1)$ and $Z_j(1)$ by

$$c_j = Y_j(1), \ d_j = Z_j(1), \ j = 0, 1, \ldots, m.$$

To find the mth-order asymptotic numerical solution of u, the current method is: (i) giving m, $c_j^0 = d_j^0 = 0$, $j = 0, 1, \ldots, m$, ϵ, and N; and (ii) repeating $k = 0, 1, 2, \ldots$ until convergence, integrating Equations (68)–(71) by using the RK4 with N steps from $t = 0$ to $t = 1$, and taking

$$c_j^{k+1} = Y_j(1), \ d_j^{k+1} = Z_j(1), \ j = 0, 1, \ldots, m.$$

If

$$\sqrt{\sum_{j=0}^{m}(c_j^{k+1} - c_j^k)^2 + \sum_{j=0}^{m}(d_j^{k+1} - d_j^k)^2} < \epsilon$$

is satisfied, then the iterations are terminated. The asymptotic numerical solution $u(t)$ is given by

$$u(t) = \sum_{j=0}^{m}[\varepsilon^j y_j + z_j] = \sum_{j=0}^{m}[\varepsilon^j(Y_j - G_j) + Z_j - H_j], \tag{72}$$

where

$$G_j = e^{t-1}[c_j^k - b_j], \ H_j = t d_j^k - (1 - t)a_j, \tag{73}$$

in which c_j^k and d_j^k are the convergent values of the sequences c_j^k and d_j^k, $k = 1, 2, \ldots$.

5. Numerical Examples

For most linear SPPs with variable coefficients, there exist no closed-form solutions. Here, we will apply the initial value problem method (IVPM) developed in [34] to compute the solutions, which are used as the referenced "exact" solutions, if the "truly exact" solution is not available.

5.1. Example 1

We consider Equations (3) and (5) again with $\varepsilon = 0.01$, $\alpha = 0$ and $\beta = 1$. Now, we solve it by using the IVPM developed in [34], and upon comparing it to the exact solution (5), the ME is found to be 7.096×10^{-10}. We give $m = 1$, $\lambda = 3.5$, $N = 1000$, and $\epsilon = 10^{-10}$ and apply the iterative algorithm in Section 4.3 to find the first-order asymptotic numerical solution of Equation (3), whose ME is 5.9305485×10^{-4}. On the other hand, the ME of the asymptotic solution (27) is 5.9305476×10^{-4}, which is very close to the asymptotic numerical solution. In Figure 2, we compare those four solutions, which are very close.

As an extension of the method in Section 2.1 to the second-order asymptotic approximation, we can derive

$$u_a(x) = \beta e^{1-x}\left[1 + \varepsilon(1 - x) + \varepsilon^2\left(\frac{1}{2}(1 - x)^2 + 2(1 - x)\right)\right]$$
$$+ \left[(\alpha - e\beta)\left(1 + x + \frac{x^2}{2}\right) - \varepsilon[e\beta - (\alpha - 2e\beta)x] - \frac{5}{2}e\beta\varepsilon^2\right]e^{-x/\varepsilon}. \tag{74}$$

On the other hand, m is raised to $m = 2$ and we apply the iterative algorithm in Section 4.3 to find the second-order asymptotic numerical solution of Equation (3), whose ME is 1.68×10^{-5}, which is comparable to the solution (74), whose ME is 1.66×10^{-5}. Upon comparison with the first-order solutions, the improvement of accuracy is one-order.

5.2. Example 2

Consider [30,32,36]

$$\varepsilon u''(x) + u'(x) - u(x) = 0, \ u(0) = 1, \ u(1) = 1, \tag{75}$$

whose solution is

$$u(x) = \frac{1}{e^{a_2} - e^{a_1}}[(e^{a_2} - 1)e^{a_1 x} + (1 - e^{a_1})e^{a_2 x}], \tag{76}$$

where

$$a_1 = \frac{-1 + \sqrt{1 + 4\varepsilon}}{2\varepsilon}, \ a_2 = \frac{-1 - \sqrt{1 + 4\varepsilon}}{2\varepsilon}. \tag{77}$$

Given $m = 2$, $\lambda = 2.9$, $N = 1000$, and $\epsilon = 10^{-7}$, the present asymptotic numerical method for the solution of Equation (75) with $\varepsilon = 0.001$ converges within 725 iterations. In Table 2, we compare the numerical results to that obtained by Reddy and Chakravarthy [30] and El-Zahar [32]. Obviously, our errors with ε^2, as expected, are smaller than other solutions by approximately two orders.

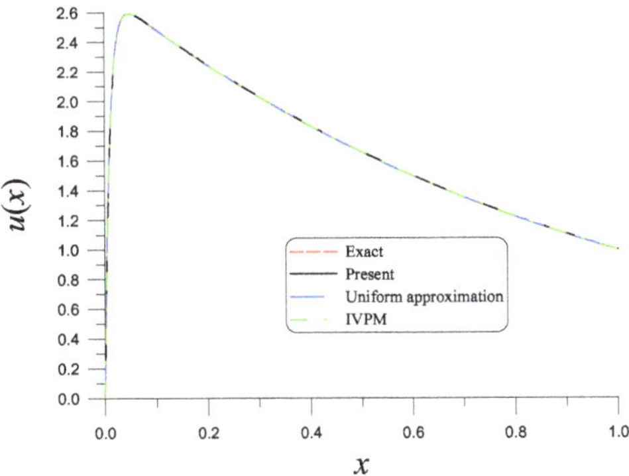

Figure 2. For example 1, comparing the exact solution, a uniform approximation, the present asymptotic-numerical solution and the IVPM solution.

Table 2. For example 2 with $\varepsilon = 0.001$, comparing the numerical solutions at different x with an exact solution and other solutions.

x	Present	[30]	[32]	Exact
0.01	0.3719750	0.3712379	0.3716054	0.3719724
0.02	0.3756809	0.3749439	0.3753111	0.3756784
0.03	0.3794527	0.3787160	0.3790831	0.3794502
0.04	0.3832624	0.3825260	0.3828929	0.3832599
0.05	0.3871104	0.3863742	0.3867410	0.38710787
0.10	0.4069374	0.4062043	0.4065697	0.4069350
0.50	0.6068350	0.6062278	0.6065307	0.6068334
0.90	0.9049277	0.9047471	0.9048374	0.9049277

5.3. Example 3

Consider a variable coefficient SPP [39]:

$$\varepsilon u''(x) + \left(1 - \frac{x}{2}\right)u'(x) - \frac{1}{2}u(x) = 0,\ u(0) = 0,\ u(1) = 1, \tag{78}$$

whose asymptotic solution is given [8]:

$$u_a(x) = \frac{1}{2-x} - \frac{1}{2}\exp\left(\frac{x^2/4 - x}{\varepsilon}\right). \tag{79}$$

It is obvious that

$$u_a(0) = 0,\ u_a(1) = 1 - \frac{1}{2}\exp\left(\frac{-3}{4\varepsilon}\right) < 1, \tag{80}$$

so that Equation (79) does not exactly satisfy the right boundary condition.

We give $\varepsilon = 0.1$, $m = 1$, $\lambda = 2$, $N = 1000$ and $\epsilon = 10^{-10}$ and apply the iterative algorithm in Section 4.3 to find the first-order asymptotic numerical solution of Equation (78), which converges within 23 iterations, as shown in Figure 3a. In Figure 3b, we compare the asymptotic numerical solution to the asymptotic solution in Equation (79). We can observe that the improvement is achieved by using the asymptotic numerical solution, where ME1: $= \max|u_e - u| = 2.62 \times 10^{-2}$ and ME2: $= |u_e - u_a| = 4.94 \times 10^{-2}$.

We give $\varepsilon = 0.01$, $m = 2$, $\lambda = 3.5$, $N = 1000$ and $\epsilon = 10^{-10}$ and apply the iterative algorithm in Section 4.3 to find the second-order asymptotic numerical solution of Equation (78), which converges with 24 iterations. We compare the second-order asymptotic numerical solution to the asymptotic solution in Equation (79), and ME1:$= \max|u_e - u| = 4.903 \times 10^{-5}$ is much smaller than ME2:$= |u_e - u_a| = 7.28 \times 10^{-3}$.

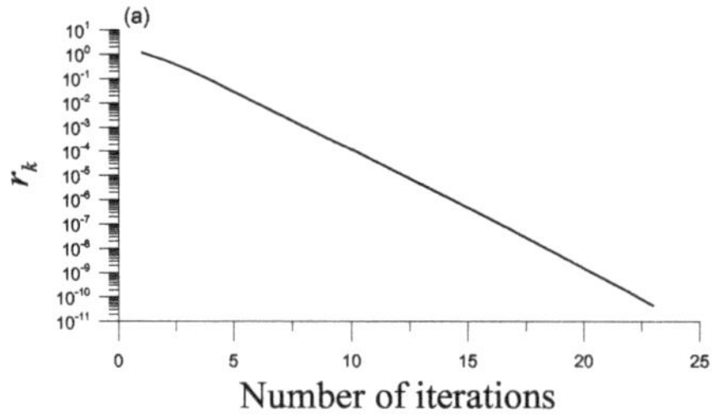

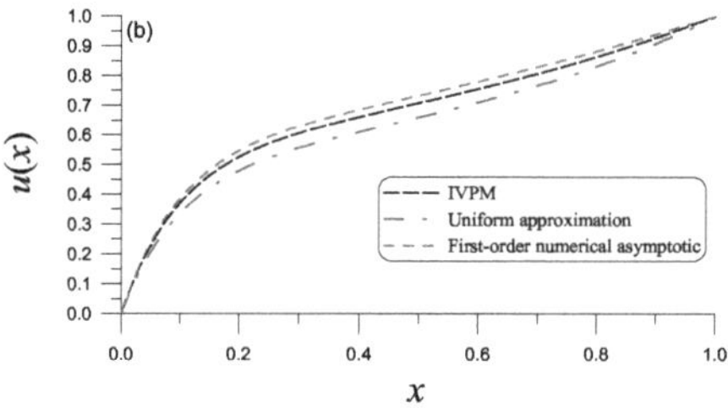

Figure 3. For example 3: (**a**) showing the convergence of iterations; and (**b**) comparing the exact solution, a uniform approximation and the present first-order solution.

5.4. Example 4

Consider

$$\varepsilon u''(x) + (2x + 1)u'(x) + 2u(x) = 0, \quad u(0) = 1, \quad u(1) = 1, \tag{81}$$

whose asymptotic solution is given by

$$u_a(x) = \frac{3}{2x + 1} - 2\exp\left(\frac{-x^2 - x}{\varepsilon}\right) + \varepsilon\left[\frac{6}{(2x + 1)^3} - \frac{2}{3(2x + 1)} - \frac{16}{3}\exp\left(\frac{-x^2 - x}{\varepsilon}\right)\right]. \tag{82}$$

We give $\varepsilon = 0.005$, $m = 1$, $\lambda = 4$, $N = 1000$ and $\epsilon = 10^{-10}$ and apply the iterative algorithm in Section 4.3 to find the first-order asymptotic numerical solution of Equation (81), which converges within 207 iterations, as shown in Figure 4a. In Figure 4b, we compare the asymptotic numerical solution to the asymptotic solution in Equation (82). We can observe that the improvement is achieved by using the asymptotic numerical solution, where ME1: $= \max|u_e - u| = 6.87 \times 10^{-4}$ and ME2: $= |u_e - u_a| = 7.34 \times 10^{-4}$.

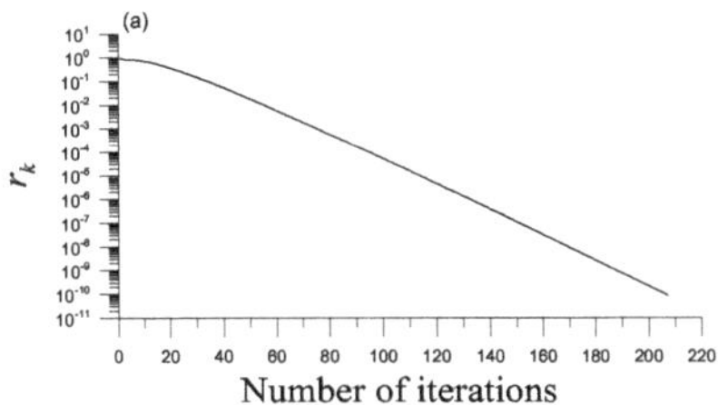

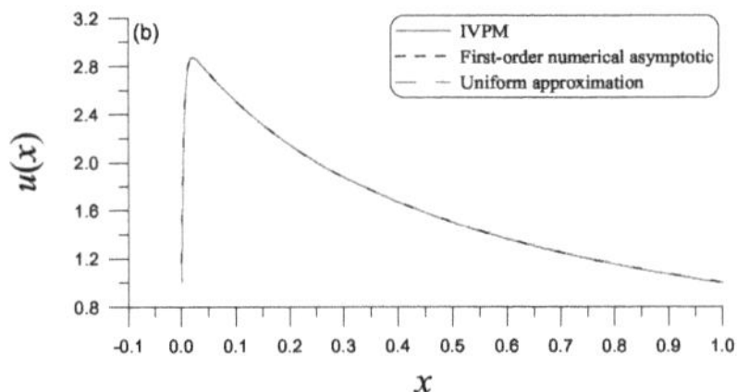

Figure 4. For example 4: (**a**) showing the convergence of iterations; and (**b**) comparing the exact solution, a uniform approximation and the present first-order solution.

6. Special Case with $q(x) = 0$

For the special case with $q(x) = 0$, Equations (1) and (2) reduce to

$$\varepsilon u''(x) + p(x)u'(x) = r(x), \ 0 < x < 1, \tag{83}$$

$$u(0) = \alpha, \ u(1) = \beta. \tag{84}$$

6.1. Main Results

Theorem 3. *For Equations (83) and (84), the series $z_j(x)$ in Equation (40) for the inner solution terminates with*

$$z_j(x) = 0, \ j \geq 1. \tag{85}$$

Proof. Inserting $q(x) = 0$ into Equation (40) yields

$$\varepsilon z_j''(x) + p(x)z_j'(x) = 0, \ j \geq 1. \tag{86}$$

Let

$$I(x) := \exp\left(\int_0^x \frac{p(\varsigma)}{\varepsilon} d\varsigma\right) \tag{87}$$

be the integrating factor. Then, Equation (86) can be written as

$$\frac{d}{dx}[I(x)z_j'(x)] = 0, \ j \geq 1, \tag{88}$$

and then we have

$$z_j(x) = k_1 \int_0^x \frac{d\varsigma}{I(\varsigma)} + k_2, \ j \geq 1, \tag{89}$$

where k_1 and k_2 are integration constants. Using the conditions $z_j(0) = z_j(1) = 0, \ j \geq 1$, we can derive $k_1 = k_2 = 0$. This ends the proof. □

Theorem 4. *For Equations (83) and (84), if $p(x)$ and $r(x)$ satisfy*

$$\frac{d}{dx}\frac{r(x)}{p(x)} = kp(x), \tag{90}$$

where $k \neq 0$ is a constant, then the series $y_j(x)$ in Equation (31) for the outer solution terminates with

$$y_j(x) = 0, \ j \geq 2. \tag{91}$$

Proof. Inserting $q(x) = 0$ into Equation (31) yields

$$y_0'(x) = \frac{r(x)}{p(x)}, \ y_1'(x) = -\frac{y_0''(x)}{p(x)} = -\frac{1}{p(x)}\frac{d}{dx}\frac{r(x)}{p(x)}. \tag{92}$$

Because of Equation (90), the latter one reduces to

$$y_1'(x) = -k. \tag{93}$$

Inserting $q(x) = 0$ and $j = 2$ into Equation (31) and using the above equation yields

$$y_2'(x) = -\frac{y_1''(x)}{p(x)} = 0, \tag{94}$$

which implies $y_2(x) = 0$ due to $y_2(1) = 0$. Then, $y_j = 0$, $j > 3$ easily follows by using

$$y_j'(x) = -\frac{y_{j-1}''(x)}{p(x)} = 0, \ y_j(1) = 0. \tag{95}$$

This ends the proof. $\square$

As a continuation of Theorem 4, we can prove the following result.

Theorem 5. *For Equations (83) and (84), if $p(x)$ and $r(x)$ satisfy Equation (90) with $k \neq 0$, then the asymptotic solution is given by*

$$u(x) = y_0(x) + \varepsilon y_1(x) + z_0(x)$$
$$= \alpha - k\varepsilon x + \int_0^x \frac{r(\xi)}{p(\xi)}d\xi + \frac{1}{B}[\beta - \alpha + k\varepsilon - A]\int_0^x \frac{d\xi}{I(\xi)}, \tag{96}$$

which is identical to the exact solution where

$$A := \int_0^1 \frac{r(\xi)}{p(\xi)}d\xi, \ B := \int_0^1 \frac{d\xi}{I(\xi)}, \tag{97}$$

and $I(x)$ is defined by Equation (87).

Proof. According to Theorems 3 and 4, we merely consider $y_0(x)$, $y_1(x)$ and $z_0(x)$ by

$$y_0'(x) = \frac{r(x)}{p(x)}, \ y_0(1) = \beta, \tag{98}$$

$$y_1'(x) = -k, \ y_1(1) = 0, \tag{99}$$

$$\varepsilon z_0''(x) + p(x)z_0'(x) = 0, \ z_0(0) = \alpha - [y_0(0) + \varepsilon y_1(0)], \ z_0(1) = 0. \tag{100}$$

The first two ODEs are derived from Equations (92) and (90), and the last ODE is derived from Equation (86) with $j = 0$.

It follows from Equations (98)–(100) that

$$y_0(x) = \int_0^x \frac{r(\xi)}{p(\xi)} d\xi + \beta - A, \tag{101}$$

$$y_1(x) = k - kx, \tag{102}$$

$$z_0(x) = c_1 \int_0^x \frac{d\xi}{I(\xi)} + c_2, \tag{103}$$

$$c_1 = \frac{1}{B}[\beta - \alpha + k\varepsilon - A], \ c_2 = \alpha - \beta - k\varepsilon + A. \tag{104}$$

Inserting $y_0(x)$, $y_1(x)$ and $z_0(x)$ into

$$u(x) = y_0(x) + \varepsilon y_1(x) + z_0(x),$$

we can derive Equation (96).

Multiplying Equation (83) by $I(x)$, it changes to

$$\frac{d}{dx}[I(x)u'(x)] = \frac{I(x)r(x)}{\varepsilon}. \tag{105}$$

Upon using $I'/p = I/\varepsilon$ in

$$\int_0^x \frac{I(\xi)r(\xi)}{\varepsilon} d\xi = \int_0^x \frac{I'(\xi)r(\xi)}{p(\xi)} d\xi = \frac{I(\xi)r(\xi)}{p(\xi)}\Big|_0^x - \int_0^x I(\xi) \frac{d}{d\xi} \frac{r(\xi)}{p(\xi)} d\xi$$

$$= \frac{I(\xi)r(\xi)}{p(\xi)}\Big|_0^x - k\int_0^x I(\xi)p(\xi)d\xi = \frac{I(\xi)r(\xi)}{p(\xi)}\Big|_0^x - k\varepsilon[I(x) - 1], \tag{106}$$

we can deduce

$$I(x)u'(x) = \frac{I(x)r(x)}{p(x)} - k\varepsilon[I(x) - 1] + k_1, \tag{107}$$

where Equation (90) was taken into account and k_1 is an integration constant. The constant $I(0)r(0)/p(0)$ was absorbed into k_1.

Further using the condition $u(0) = \alpha$ and from Equation (107), we can derive

$$u(x) = \alpha + \int_0^x \frac{r(\xi)}{p(\xi)} d\xi - k\varepsilon \int_0^x \frac{1}{I(\xi)}[I(\xi) - 1]d\xi + k_1 \int_0^x \frac{d\xi}{I(\xi)}$$

$$= \alpha + \int_0^x \frac{r(\xi)}{p(\xi)} d\xi + k_1 \int_0^x \frac{d\xi}{I(\xi)} + k\varepsilon \int_0^x \left[\frac{1}{I(\xi)} - 1\right]d\xi. \tag{108}$$

Imposing another condition $u(1) = \beta$ generates

$$\beta = \alpha + A + k_1 B + k\varepsilon(B - 1). \tag{109}$$

Solving k_1 and inserting it into Equation (108), we can again derive Equation (96). This ends the proof. $\square$

6.2. Examples

6.2.1. Example 5

Consider [40]:

$$\varepsilon u''(x) + u'(x) = 1 + 2x, \ u(0) = 0, \ u(1) = 1, \tag{110}$$

whose exact solution is

$$u_e(x) = x(x + 1 - 2\varepsilon) + (2\varepsilon - 1)\frac{1 - e^{-x/\varepsilon}}{1 - e^{-1/\varepsilon}}. \tag{111}$$

Equation (110) satisfies Equations (85) and (91) as a special case with $p = 1$ and $r = 1 + 2x$. Equations (31) and (40) lead to

$$y_0(x) = x + x^2 - 1, \ y_1(x) = 2 - 2x, \tag{112}$$

$$z_0(x) = (2\varepsilon - 1)\frac{e^{-1/\varepsilon} - e^{-x/\varepsilon}}{1 - e^{-1/\varepsilon}}. \tag{113}$$

Hence,

$$u(x) = y_0(x) + \varepsilon y_1(x) + z_0(x) = x + x^2 - 1 + \varepsilon(2 - 2x) + (2\varepsilon - 1)\frac{e^{-1/\varepsilon} - e^{-x/\varepsilon}}{1 - e^{-1/\varepsilon}}, \tag{114}$$

which is just the exact solution (111).

For this example, according to the method developed by Kaushik et al. [36], we can derive

$$u_k(x) = x + x^2 - 1 + \varepsilon(2 - 2x) + (1 - 2\varepsilon - 1)e^{-x/\varepsilon}, \tag{115}$$

which does not satisfy the right boundary condition because of $u_k(1) = 1 + (1 - 2\varepsilon - 1)e^{-1/\varepsilon} \neq 1$.

In Table 3, we compare ME1:$= \max |u_e - u|$ and ME2:$= \max |u_e - u_k|$ for different values of ε, which are close when $\varepsilon \leq 0.01$. For $\varepsilon \geq 0.05$, ME1 is smaller than ME2. Equations (114) and (115) possess the same asymptotic property, because of

$$e^{-1/\varepsilon} \to 0, \ \text{when } \varepsilon \to 0.$$

Table 3. For example 5, comparing ME1 and ME2 for different ε.

ε	0.6	0.4	0.3	0.1	0.05
ME1	0	0	0	0	0
ME2	3.78×10^{-2}	1.64×10^{-2}	1.43×10^{-2}	3.63×10^{-5}	1.86×10^{-9}

6.2.2. Example 6

Consider

$$\varepsilon u''(x) + \frac{1}{\sqrt{2x + 2}}u'(x) = 1, \ u(0) = 0, \ u(1) = 1, \tag{116}$$

which is a special case satisfying Equation (90) with $k = 1$. The exact and analytic asymptotic solution is given by

$$u_{aa}(x) = \frac{1}{3}[(2x + 2)^{3/2} - 2^{3/2}] - \varepsilon x + \frac{1}{B}[1 + \varepsilon - A]\int_0^x \frac{d\zeta}{\exp[\{\sqrt{2\zeta + 2} - \sqrt{2}\}/\varepsilon]}, \tag{117}$$

$$A = \frac{1}{3}[8 - 2^{3/2}], \ B = \int_0^1 \frac{d\zeta}{\exp[\{\sqrt{2\zeta + 2} - \sqrt{2}\}/\varepsilon]}. \tag{118}$$

We give $\varepsilon = 0.01$, $m = 1$, $\lambda = 3$, $N = 1000$, and $\epsilon = 10^{-10}$ and apply the iterative algorithm in Section 4.3 to find the first-order asymptotic numerical solution of Equation (116), which converges within 54 iterations as shown in Figure 5a. In Figure 5b, we compare the asymptotic numerical solution, the analytic asymptotic solution and the exact solution obtained from the IVPM. We can observe that they are almost coincident with ME1:$= \max |u_e - u| = 2.28 \times 10^{-10}$ and ME2:$= \max |u_e - u_{aa}| = 1.19 \times 10^{-7}$.

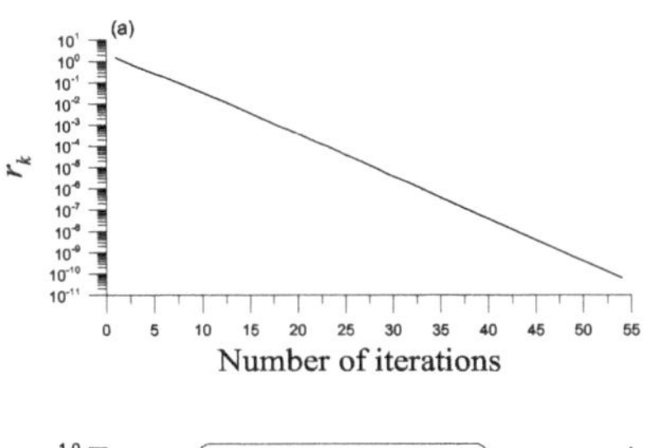

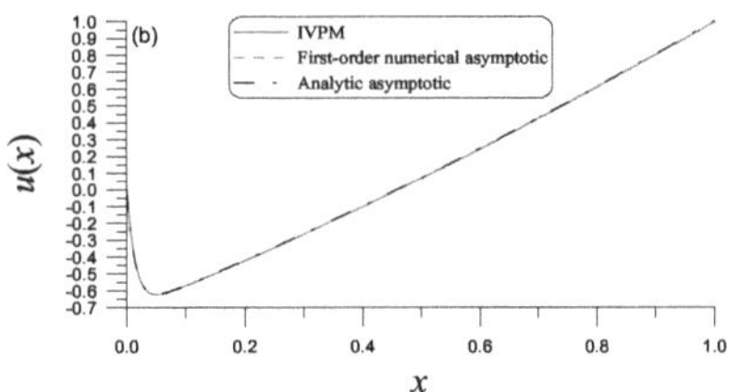

Figure 5. For example 6: (**a**) showing the convergence of iterations; and (**b**) comparing exact solution and the present first-order solution.

6.2.3. Example 7

Consider

$$\varepsilon u''(x) + (2 - \sin 2\pi x)u'(x) = (2 - \sin 2\pi x)\left(2x + \frac{1}{2\pi}\cos 2\pi x\right),$$

$$u(0) = 1, \ u(1) = 1, \tag{119}$$

which is a special case satisfying Equation (90) with $k = 1$. Then, the exact and analytic asymptotic solution is given by

$$u_{aa}(x) = 1 - \varepsilon x + \int_0^x \left(2\xi + \frac{1}{2\pi}\cos 2\pi\xi\right)d\xi + \frac{1}{B}[\varepsilon - A]\int_0^x \frac{d\xi}{\exp[\{2\xi + (\cos 2\pi\xi - 1)/(2\pi)\}/\varepsilon]}, \tag{120}$$

$$A = \int_0^1 \left(2\xi + \frac{1}{2\pi}\cos 2\pi\xi\right)d\xi, \ B = \int_0^1 \frac{d\xi}{\exp[\{2\xi + (\cos 2\pi\xi - 1)/(2\pi)\}/\varepsilon]}. \tag{121}$$

We give $\varepsilon = 0.01$, $m = 1$, $\lambda = 3$, $N = 1000$, and $\epsilon = 10^{-10}$ and apply the iterative algorithm in Section 4.3 to find the first-order asymptotic numerical solution of Equation (119), which converges within 125 iterations, as shown in Figure 6a. In Figure 6b, we compare the asymptotic numerical solution to the exact solution obtained from the IVPM, and we can observe that they are almost coincident with ME: $= \max|u_e - u| = 4.17 \times 10^{-9}$. Notice that ME: $= \max|u_e - u_{aa}| = 4.08 \times 10^{-9}$.

For this example, according to the method developed by Kaushik et al. [36], we can derive

$$u_k(x) = x^2 + \frac{1}{4\pi^2}\sin 2\pi x + \varepsilon(x - 1) + \left(1 + \varepsilon + \pi x + \frac{\pi x^2}{\varepsilon}\right)e^{-2x/\varepsilon}, \tag{122}$$

which does not satisfy the right boundary condition because of $u_k(1) = 1 + (1 + \varepsilon + \pi + \pi/\varepsilon)e^{-2/\varepsilon} > 1$.

In Table 4, we compare ME1:$= \max|u_e - u_{aa}|$ and ME2:$= \max|u_k - u_{aa}|$ for different values of ε. ME1 is much smaller than ME2.

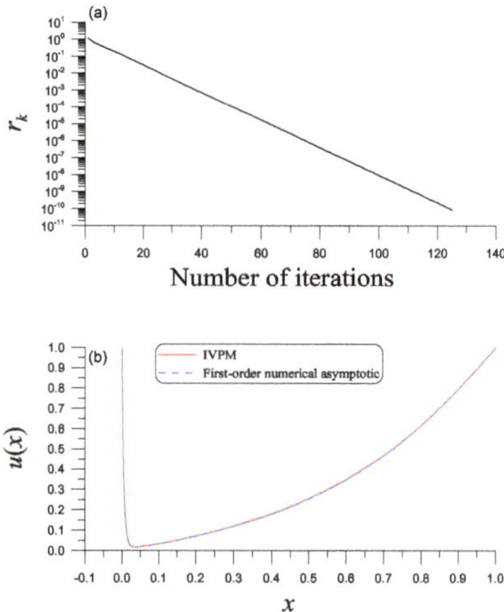

Figure 6. For example 7: (**a**) showing the convergence of iterations; and (**b**) comparing exact solution and the present first-order solution.

Table 4. For example 7, comparing ME1 and ME2 for different ε.

ε	0.2	0.1	0.05	0.03	0.01
ME1	1.79×10^{-11}	6.54×10^{-11}	2.78×10^{-11}	5.82×10^{-11}	1.19×10^{-10}
ME2	2.17×10^{-1}	1.84×10^{-1}	1.00×10^{-1}	5.95×10^{-2}	1.97×10^{-2}

7. Conclusions

It is of utmost importance that an asymptotic-numerical solution for second-order variable coefficients linear SPP can match the boundary conditions exactly. For the linear SPP, we proposed a novel boundary layer correction problem in the original coordinates which can accurately capture the asymptotic behavior within the boundary layer and at the same time preserve the boundary conditions. Therefore, the new mth-order asymptotic solution is an improvement of the conventional asymptotic solution. Resorted on the free functions in Theorems 1 and 2 as being the new variables, we exactly transformed the linear SPP to the initial value problems for the $2(m + 1)$ new variables with the given zero initial conditions and thus a newly developed iterative algorithm is converging very fast to determine the $2(m + 1)$ unknown right-end values of the new variables and to find the singularly perturbed asymptotic solution very quickly. Based on the new idea, we provided a modification for the conventional asymptotic solution of the linear SPP, such that the new asymptotic-numerical solution exactly satisfies the boundary conditions. In doing so, the accuracy of the asymptotic-numerical solution was raised and the applicable range of the perturbing parameter in the modified asymptotic solution can be extended to a moderate value. More importantly, the modified asymptotic solution possesses the same asymptotic behavior with the conventional asymptotic solution. For the special case with $q(x) = 0$, we derived the sufficient conditions for the termination of the asymptotic series solutions of outer and inner problems, and found that it may lead to the exact solution, if $d(r/p)/dx = kp$ holds for a nonzero value of k.

Author Contributions: C.-S.L.: Investigation, Methodology, Software, Data curation and Writing—Original draft preparation. C.-W.C.: Supervision, Validation, Writing—Reviewing and Editing. E.R.E.-Z.: Conceptualization and Visualization. All authors have read and agreed to the published version of the manuscript.

Funding: This research received no external funding.

Institutional Review Board Statement: Not applicable.

Informed Consent Statement: Not applicable.

Data Availability Statement: Not applicable.

Conflicts of Interest: The authors declare no conflict of interest.

References

1. Awoke, A.; Reddy, Y.N. An exponentially fitted special second-order finite difference method for solving singular perturbation problems. *Appl. Math. Comput.* **2007**, *190*, 1767–1782. [CrossRef]
2. Patidar, K.C. High order parameter uniform numerical method for singular perturbation problems. *Appl. Math. Comput.* **2007**, *188*, 720–733. [CrossRef]
3. Vigo-Aguiar, J.; Natesan, S. An efficient numerical method for singular perturbation problems. *J. Comput. Appl. Math.* **2006**, *192*, 132–141. [CrossRef]
4. Lin, T.C.; Schultza, D.H.; Zhang, W. Numerical solutions of linear and nonlinear singular perturbation problems. *Comput. Math. Appl.* **2008**, *55*, 2574–2592. [CrossRef]
5. Khuri, S.A.; Sayfy, A. A novel approach for the solution of a class of singular boundary value problems arising in physiology. *Math. Comput. Model.* **2010**, *52*, 626–636. [CrossRef]
6. Khuri, S.A.; Sayfy, A. Self-adjoint singularly perturbed boundary value problems: an adaptive variational approach. *Math. Method Appl. Sci.* **2013**, *36*, 1070–1079. [CrossRef]
7. Dogan, N.; Erturk, V.S.; Akin, O. Numerical treatment of singularly perturbed two-point boundary value problems by using differential transformation method. *Discrete Dyn. Nat. Soc.* **2012**, *2012*, 579431.
8. El-Zahar, E.R. Approximate analytical solution for singularly perturbed boundary value problems by multi-step differential transform method. *J. Appl. Sci.* **2012**, *12*, 2026–2034. [CrossRef]
9. O'Malley, R.E. *Singular Perturbation Methods for Ordinary Differential Equations*; Springer: New York, NY, USA, 1991.
10. Bender, C.M.; Orszag, S.A. *Advanced Mathematical Methods for Scientists and Engineers I*; Springer Science & Business Media: New York, NY, USA, 1999.
11. Kadalbajoo, M.K.; Gupta, V. A brief survey on numerical methods for solving singularly perturbed problems. *Appl. Math. Comput.* **2010**, *217*, 3641–3716. [CrossRef]
12. Roul, P. A fourth-order non-uniform mesh optimal B-spline collocation method for solving a strongly nonlinear singular boundary value problem describing electrohydrodynamic flow of a fluid. *Appl. Numer. Math.* **2020**, *153*, 558–574. [CrossRef]
13. Nayfeh, A.H. *Perturbation Methods*; Wiley: New York, NY, USA, 1979.
14. Roos, H.G.; Stynes, M.; Tobiska, L. *Numerical Methods for Singularly Perturbed Differential Equations*; Springer: Berlin/Heidelberg, Germany, 1996.
15. Awoke, A.; Reddy, Y.N. Terminal boundary condition for singularly perturbed two-point boundary value problems. *Neural Parallel Sci. Comput.* **2008**, *16*, 435–448.
16. Chakravarthy, P.P.; Reddy, Y.N. A cutting point technique for singular perturbation problems. *J. Math. Contr. Sci. Appl.* **2007**, *1*, 39–59.
17. Vigo-Aguiar, J.; Natesan, S. A parallel boundary value technique for singularly perturbed two-point boundary value problems. *J. Supercomput.* **2004**, *27*, 195–206. [CrossRef]
18. Andargie, A.; Reddy, Y.N. The method of asymptotic inner boundary condition for singular perturbation problems. *J. Appl. Math. Inform.* **2011**, *29*, 937–948.
19. Wang, L. A novel method for a class of nonlinear singular perturbation problems. *Appl. Math. Comput.* **2004**, *156*, 847–856. [CrossRef]
20. Valanarasu, T.; Ramanujam, N. Asymptotic initial-value method for singularly-perturbed boundary problems for second-order ordinary differential equations. *J. Optim. Theory Appl.* **2003**, *116*, 167–182. [CrossRef]
21. Kaushik, A.; Kumar, V.; Vashishth, A.K. An efficient mixed asymptotic-numerical scheme for singularly perturbed convection diffusion problems. *Appl. Math. Comput.* **2012**, *218*, 8645–8658. [CrossRef]
22. Attili, B.S. Numerical treatment of singularly perturbed two point boundary value problems exhibiting boundary layers. *Commun. Nonlinear Sci. Numer. Simul.* **2011**, *16*, 3504–3511. [CrossRef]
23. Padmaja, P.; Reddy, Y.N. A Numerical patching method for solving singular perturbation problems via Padé approximates. *Int. J. Appl. Sci. Eng.* **2013**, *11*, 51–67.
24. King, A.C.; Billinghem, A.J.; Otto, K.C. *Differential Equations, Linear, Nonlinear, Ordinary, Partial*; Cambridge University Press: Cambridge, UK, 2003.
25. Cui, M.; Lin, Y. *Nonlinear Numerical Analysis in the Reproducing Kernel Space*; Nova Science Publication: New York, NY, USA, 2009.
26. Xu, M.; Tohidib, E.; Niu, J.; Fang, Y. A new reproducing kernel-based collocation method with optimal convergence rate for some classes of BVPs. *Appl. Math. Comput.* **2022**, *432*, 127343. [CrossRef]
27. Gasparo, M.G.; Maconi, M. New initial value method for singularly perturbed boundary value problems. *J. Optim. Theo. Appl.* **1989**, *63*, 213–224. [CrossRef]

28. Gasparo, M.G.; Maconi, M. Initial value methods for second order singularly perturbed boundary value problems. *J. Optim. Theo. Appl.* **1990**, *66*, 197–210. [CrossRef]
29. Gasparo, M.G.; Maconi, M. Numerical solution of second-order nonlinear singularly perturbed boundary value problems by initial value methods. *J. Optim. Theo. App.* **1992**, *73*, 309–327. [CrossRef]
30. Reddy, Y.N.; Chakravarthy, P.P. An initial-value approach for solving singularly perturbed two-point boundary value problems. *Appl. Math. Comput.* **2004**, *155*, 95–110. [CrossRef]
31. Liu, C.-S.; El-Zahar, E.R.; Chang, C.W. A boundary shape function iterative method for solving nonlinear singular boundary value problems. *Math. Comput. Simul.* **2021**, *187*, 614–629. [CrossRef]
32. El-Zahar, E.R. Approximate analytical solution of singularly perturbed boundary value problems in MAPLE. *AIMS Math.* **2020**, *5*, 2272–2284. [CrossRef]
33. Reddy, Y.N.; Chakravarthy, P. Method of reduction of order for solving singularly-perturbed two-point boundary-value problems. *Appl. Math. Comput.* **2004**, *136*, 27–45. [CrossRef]
34. Liu, C.-S.; Chang, J.R. Boundary shape functions methods for solving the nonlinear singularly perturbed problems with Robin boundary conditions. *Int. J. Nonlinear Sci. Numer. Simul.* **2020**, *21*, 797–806. [CrossRef]
35. Nayfeh, A.H. *Introduction to Perturbation Techniques*; Wiley: New York, NY, USA, 1981.
36. Kaushik, A.; Kumar, V.; Vashishth, A.K. A higher order accurate numerical method for singularly perturbed two point boundary value problems. *Differ. Equ. Dyn. Syst.* **2017**, *25*, 267–285. [CrossRef]
37. Liu, C.-S.; Chang, C.W. Modified asymptotic solutions for second-order nonlinear singularly perturbed boundary value problems. *Math. Comput. Simul.* **2022**, *193*, 139–152. [CrossRef]
38. Liu, C.-S.; Chang, C.W. Asymptotic numerical solutions for second-order quasilinear singularly perturbed problems. *J. Marine Sci. Tech.* **2022**, *29*, 742–756. [CrossRef]
39. Kevorkian, J.; Cole, J.D. *Perturbation Methods in Applied Mathematics*; Springer Science & Business Media: New York, NY, USA, 2013.
40. Reinhardt, H.J. Singular Perturbations of difference methods for linear ordinary differential equations. *Appl. Anal.* **1980**, *10*, 53–70. [CrossRef]

Article

On the Fundamental Analyses of Solutions to Nonlinear Integro-Differential Equations of the Second Order

Cemil Tunç [1,*,†] and Osman Tunç [2,†]

[1] Department of Mathematics, Faculty of Sciences, Van Yuzuncu Yil University, Van 65080, Turkey
[2] Department of Computer Programing, Baskale Vocational School, Van Yuzuncu Yil University, Van 65080, Turkey
* Correspondence: cemtunc@yahoo.com
† These authors contributed equally to this work.

Abstract: In this article, a scalar nonlinear integro-differential equation of second order and a nonlinear system of integro-differential equations with infinite delays are considered. Qualitative properties of solutions called the global asymptotic stability, integrability and boundedness of solutions of the second-order scalar nonlinear integro-differential equation and the nonlinear system of nonlinear integro-differential equations with infinite delays are discussed. In the article, new explicit qualitative conditions are presented for solutions of both the second-order scalar nonlinear integro-differential equations with infinite delay and the nonlinear system of integro-differential equations with infinite delay. The proofs of the main results of the article are based on two new Lyapunov–Krasovskiĭ functionals. In particular cases, the results of the article are illustrated with three numerical examples, and connections to known tests are discussed. The main novelty and originality of this article are that the considered integro-differential equation and system of integro-differential equations with infinite delays are new mathematical models, the main six qualitative results given are also new.

Keywords: integro-differential equation; integro-differential system; first order; second order; infinite delay; global asymptotic stability; boundedness; integrability; LKF

MSC: 34C11; 34D05; 34D20

Citation: Tunç, C.; Tunç O. On the Fundamental Analyses of Solutions to Nonlinear Integro-Differential Equations of the Second Order. *Mathematics* **2022**, *10*, 4235. https://doi.org/10.3390/math10224235

Academic Editor: Arsen Palestini

Received: 13 October 2022
Accepted: 10 November 2022
Published: 13 November 2022

Publisher's Note: MDPI stays neutral with regard to jurisdictional claims in published maps and institutional affiliations.

1. Introduction

In the relevant literature, the global asymptotic stability, boundedness, integrability, etc., of linear and nonlinear integro-differential equations (IDEs) of the first order without delay, scalar nonlinear delay integro-differential equations (DIDEs), nonlinear delay systems of IDEs of the first order, functional differential equations (FDEs), etc., have attracted a lot of attention from researchers. For a comprehensive treatment of the subject on the stability, boundedness, integrability, etc., of solutions of first-order IDEs without delay, see, Alahmadi et al. [1], Burton [2], Furumochi and Matsuoka [3], Grimmer and Seifert [4], Jordan [5], Lakshmikantham and Rama Mohana Rao [6], Mohana Rao and Srinivas [7], Murakami [8], Rama Mohana Rao and Raghavendra [9], Sedova [10], and the bibliographies therein.

We would now like to outline some qualitative results on IDEs without delay.

In the book of Burton [2], which can be considered as a reference book of integral equations and IDEs, using the second Lyapunov method and the Lyapunov–Krasovskiĭ functional (LKF) approach, various kind of stabilities of zero solutions, integrabilities of solutions, as well as boundedness of solutions when $F(t) \neq 0$ are discussed for the systems of IDEs given by:

$$x' = A(t)x + \int_0^t C(t,s)x(s)ds,$$

$$x' = Ax + \int_0^t C(t,s)x(s)ds + F(t),$$

$$x' = Ax + \int_0^t B(t-s)x(s)ds,$$

$$x' = Ax + \int_0^t D(t-s)x(s)ds + F(t),$$

$$x' = A(t)x + \int_0^t C_1(t,s)x(s)ds + \int_0^t C_2(t,s)x(s)ds,$$

$$x' = Ax + f(t,x) + \int_0^t C(t,s)x(s)ds.$$

Next, the book of Lakshmikantham and Rama Mohana Rao [6] is also considered as a reference book of the qualitative theory of IDEs. In the book of Lakshmikantham and Rama Mohana Rao [6], using the second Lyapunov method, various qualitative behaviors of solutions such as stability, uniform stability, asymptotic stability, uniform asymptotic stability of zero solutions, as well as the integrability and boundedness of nonzero solutions when $f(t,x) \neq 0$ and $g(t,y) \neq 0$, are discussed, and some interesting results are obtained for the scalar or systems of IDEs given by:

$$u' = \alpha u + \int_0^t a(t-s)u(s)ds,$$

$$u' = \alpha(t)u + \int_0^t a(t,s)u(s)ds,$$

$$x' = A(t)x + \int_0^t K(t,s)x(s)ds,$$

$$x' = Ax + \int_0^t K(t,s)x(s)ds,$$

$$x' = A(t)x + \int_{-\infty}^t K(t,s)x(s)ds + f(t,x),$$

$$x' = Ax + \int_0^t C(t-s)x(s)ds,$$

$$y' = A(t)y + \int_0^t C(t-s)y(s)ds + g(t,y).$$

Sedova [10] considered the nonlinear system of IDEs

$$x' = G(t,x) + \int_0^t H(t,s,x(s))ds.$$

In [10], sufficient conditions for uniform asymptotic stability of the zero solution of this system are obtained using the Razumikhin method. Similar qualitative results can be found in the other sources mentioned above.

Next, for numerous results in relation to the stability, boundedness, integrability, etc., of solutions of scalar and vector DIDEs of the first order and DIDEs of fractional order, see Berezansky and Braverman [11], Berezansky et al. [12], Du [13], Tunç and Tunç [14], Funakubo et al. [15], Tunç and Tunç [16–18], Tunç [19], Tunç et al. [20], Xu [21], Wang [22], Wang [23], Wang et al. [24], and the bibliographies therein.

We would now like to outline some of these qualitative results in relation to delay integro-differential equations.

In Berezansky and Braverman [11], new explicit exponential stability conditions are obtained for the non-autonomous scalar linear DIDE:

$$x'(t) = \sum_{k=1}^{m} a_k(t)x(h_k(t)) + \int_{g(t)}^{t} K(t,s)x(s)ds,$$

$$t \in [0,\infty), x \in \mathbb{R}.$$

The proofs in the article of Berezansky and Braverman [11] are based on establishing the boundedness of solutions and exponential dichotomy.

Next, in Berezansky et al. [12], uniform exponential stability of the linear delayed integro-differential vector equation

$$x'(t) = \sum_{k=1}^{m} A_k(t)x(h_k(t)) + \sum_{k=1}^{l} \int_{g_k(t)}^{t} P_k(t,s)x(s)ds, t \in [0,\infty), x \in \mathbb{R}^n,$$

is studied. In [12], the main technique of the proofs is splitting the linear expressions in the equation (both with points and with distributed delays) into a "dominant" and a "remainder" part, which can be achieved in a number of different ways, thus providing a number of different criteria. The next important ingredient is the use of a Bohl–Perron-type result stating that a linear equation is exponentially stable if the solutions of the inhomogeneous counterpart of that equation are bounded.

In 1995, Du [13] considered the following system of linear DIDEs:

$$\frac{dx}{dt} = Ax + Bx(t - \tau(t)) + \int_{t-\tau(t)}^{t} \Omega(t,s)x(s)ds,$$

where $x \in \mathbb{R}^n$, $t \in [0,\infty)$, τ is a non-negative and differentiable variable delay, $A \in \mathbb{R}^{n \times n}$, $B \in \mathbb{R}^{n \times n}$ and $\Omega(t,s) \in C(\mathbb{R}^{n \times n}, \mathbb{R}^{n \times n})$. Du [13] is interested in constructing an LFK for this system of DIDEs, which yields uniform asymptotic stability of zero solutions of this system.

Tunç and Tunç [14] considered the nonlinear system of IDDEs with the constant time delay:

$$\dot{x}(t) = -A(t)x(t) - A_d G(x(t - h)) + C \int_{t-h}^{t} F(x(s))ds + Q(t, x(t), x(t - h)),$$

where $x \in \mathbb{R}^n$ is the sate vector, $t \in [0,\infty)$, and h is a positive constant, that is, the constant time delay. The authors [14] investigated the uniform asymptotic stability and integrability of solutions when $Q = 0$ and boundedness of solutions when $Q \neq 0$, based on the LKF approach. Similar qualitative results for the IDDEs of integer and fractional order have been obtained in [15–24].

We now outline some papers in relation to the results of this article. Additionally, for several classes of nonlinear scalar DIDEs of second order, linear and nonlinear two-dimensional systems and nonlinear n-dimensional systems, numerous qualitative results can be seen in the literature, see, e.g., Becker and Burton [25], Dishen [26], Hale and Kato [27], Berezansky and Domoshnitsky [28], Crisci et al. [29], Gözen and Tunç [30], Graef and Tunç [31], and the references of these sources. In particular, there is a scarcity of qualitative results for both scalar DIDEs of second order and system of DIDEs of first order with infinite delays, which are considered in this article.

In [25], Becker and Burton obtained a number of results on uniform stability and equi-asymptotic stability of the zero solution of the FDE:

$$x'(t) = f(t, x_t), (t \geq 0),$$

where $f : \mathbb{R} \times C \to \mathbb{R}^n$, $\mathbb{R} = (-\infty, \infty)$ is a continuous mapping with $f(t, 0) = 0$, and f takes bounded sets into bounded sets. For some $h > 0$, $C = C([-h, 0], \mathbb{R}^n)$ denotes the space of continuous functions $\phi : [-h, 0] \to \mathbb{R}^n$. For any $a \geq 0$, some $t_0 \geq 0$, and $x \in C([t_0 - h, t_0 + a], \mathbb{R}^n)$, it is assumed that $x_t = x(t + s)$ for $s \in [-h, 0]$ and $t \geq t_0$. They also found results on the uniform stability of the Volterra functional equation:

$$x'(t) = F(t, x(s); \alpha \leq s \leq t), (t \geq t_*),$$

where, for $-\infty \leq \alpha \leq t_*$, the right-hand side of this equation is a Volterra functional whose value in $\mathbb{R}^n$ is determined by $t \geq t_*$ and the values of $x(s)$ for $\alpha \leq s \leq t$. It is assumed that F is continuous in t and x for $t \geq t_*$ whenever $x \in C([\alpha, \infty), \mathbb{R}^n)$ is bounded (see [25]).

In Becker and Burton [25], the investigations are based on the Lyapunov's direct method and Jensen's inequality. Some results of Becker and Burton [25] are well illustrated by examples, including the DIDEs of second order with infinite delay. In [25], as the first application, the following DIDEs of second order with infinite delay is considered:

$$x'' + tx' + \int_{-\infty}^{t} a \exp(-(t-s))x(s)ds = 0, a > 1. \tag{1}$$

Next, in Becker and Burton [25], depending upon suitable Lyapunov–Krasovskiĭ functionals (LKFs),

$$V(t) = V(t, x(.), y(.)) = y^2 + ax^2 + \int_{-\infty}^{t} a \exp(-(t-s))y^2(s)ds, \tag{2}$$

the authors proved that the zero solution of DIDE (1) is uniformly stable for $t \geq t_*$.

In addition, in the same paper of Becker and Burton [25], as the second application, the authors considered the following non-linear DIDE of second order with infinite delay:

$$x'' + tf(x)x' + \int_{-\infty}^{t} \gamma(t-s)g(x(s))ds = 0. \tag{3}$$

Becker and Burton [25], using the following two multi-functional approaches of the LKFs:

$$U(t) = U(t, x(.), z(.)) = \left[z - \int_{-\infty}^{t} T(t-s)g(x(s))ds \right]^2 - 2 \int_{0}^{x} \tilde{g}(s)ds$$

$$+ K \int_{-\infty}^{t} \int_{t-s}^{\infty} |T(u)|du \, g^2(x(s))ds, \tag{4}$$

and

$$V(t) = V(t, x(.), z(.)) = y^2 + 2T(0)g(x) - 2\int_0^x \tilde{g}(s)ds$$

$$+ D \int_{-\infty}^{t} \int_{t-s}^{\infty} |T(u)|du\, y^2(s)ds, \tag{5}$$

where $T(t) = \int_t^{\infty} \gamma(u)du$, $F(x) = \int_0^x f(u)du$, $\tilde{g}(x) = T(0)g(x) - F(x)$, K and D are positive constants such that $|g'(x)| \leq D$ for $|x| < \delta, \delta > 0, \delta \in \mathbb{R}$, obtained sufficient conditions for both the uniform and equi-asymptotic stability of zero solution of DIDE (3).

We should note that the first reference paper for this research is the paper of Becker and Burton [25]. Motivated by Becker and Burton [25], in this article, first, we are concerned with the nonlinear DIDE of second order with infinite delay:

$$x'' + a(t)F(t, x, x') + b(t)G(x, x') + c(t)H(x') + d(t)Q(x)$$

$$+ \int_{-\infty}^{t} \exp(-(t-s))U(s, x'(s))ds = E(t, x, x'), \tag{6}$$

where $x \in \mathbb{R}$, $\mathbb{R} = (-\infty, \infty)$, $x(t) = \phi(t)$ on $(-\infty, 0]$, $s, t \in \mathbb{R}$, $t \geq s$. We suppose that $F, E \in C(\mathbb{R}^+ \times \mathbb{R}^2, \mathbb{R}), \mathbb{R}^+ = [0, \infty)$, $G, U \in C(\mathbb{R} \times \mathbb{R}, \mathbb{R}), H, Q \in C(\mathbb{R}, \mathbb{R})$, $F(t, x, 0) = 0$, $G(x, 0) = 0$, $H(0) = 0$, $Q(0) = 0$, $U(s, 0) = 0$, $a, b, c \in C(\mathbb{R}^+, (0, \infty))$ and $d \in C^1(\mathbb{R}^+, \mathbb{R}^+)$, where $C(\mathbb{R}^+, (0, \infty))$ is the space of functions defined and continuous on $\mathbb{R}^+$, taking values in $(0, \infty)$, and $C^1(\mathbb{R}^+, \mathbb{R}^+)$ is the space of functions defined and continuously differentiable on $\mathbb{R}^+$, taking values in $\mathbb{R}^+$.

We convert DIDE (6) to the following system:

$$x' = y,$$
$$y' = -a(t)F(t, x, y) - b(t)G(x, y) - c(t)H(y) - d(t)Q(x)$$

$$- \int_{-\infty}^{t} \exp(-(t-s))U(s, y(s))ds + E(t, x, y). \tag{7}$$

As for our next reference paper, Dishen [26] deals with the following linear system of DIDEs with infinite delay:

$$\begin{cases} x' = A(t)x + \int_{-\infty}^{t} C(t, s)ds + f(t), \\ y' = A(t)y + \int_{-\infty}^{t} C(t, s)ds + f(t), \end{cases} \tag{8}$$

and the author investigates the properties of this system such as the boundedness of solutions as well as the h-stability of this system. These properties of solutions are studied by using a phase space and the space C_h (which is somewhat different from the traditional phase space for infinite delay, in the sense of Hale and Kato [27]). In [26], the LKF

$$V(t, x_t, y_t) = |x(t) - y(t)| + \int_{-\infty}^{t} \int_t^{\infty} h(s - u)|x(s) - y(s)|duds. \tag{9}$$

In this article, secondly, motivated from the results of Dishen [26], instead of the linear system of DIDEs (8), we investigate the following non-linear system of DIDEs with infinite delay:

$$\begin{cases} x' = -A_1(t)f_1(x) + \int\limits_{-\infty}^{t} C_1(t,s)g_1(x(s))ds + \ell_1(t,x), \\ y' = A_2(t)f_2(y) + \int\limits_{-\infty}^{t} C_2(t,s)g_2(y(s))ds + \ell_2(t,y), \end{cases} \tag{10}$$

where x, y, s, $t \in \mathbb{R}$, $x(t) = \phi(t)$ on $(-\infty, 0]$, s, $t \in \mathbb{R}$, $t \geq s$. We suppose that A_1, $A_2 \in C(\mathbb{R}, (0, \infty))$, C_1, $C_2 \in C(\mathbb{R} \times \mathbb{R}, \mathbb{R})$, f_1, f_2, g_1, $g_2 \in C(\mathbb{R}, \mathbb{R})$, $f_1(0) = 0$, $f_2(0) = 0$, $g_1(0) = 0$, $g_2(0) = 0$, ℓ_1, $\ell_2 \in C(\mathbb{R} \times \mathbb{R}, \mathbb{R})$, $\ell_1(t, 0) = 0$ and $\ell_2(t, 0) = 0$.

In this article, we construct new sufficient qualitative conditions on the global asymptotic stability, boundedness, and integrability of solutions for both the scalar nonlinear DIDE (6) of second order and the non-linear system of DIDEs (10) with infinite delays. Defining and then using these two new LKFs, the main results of this article are proved. In special cases of (6) and (10), three examples are given as numerical applications to illustrate and verify our results. We aim to provide some new contributions to qualitative theory of FDEs and some known results in the relevant literature.

Scientific interest in both of these kinds of FDEs with infinite delays is not purely theoretical. Indeed, there are numerous and very interesting real-world applications for these kinds of FDEs with infinite delays. For example, for various real-world applications of such scalar FDEs of second order and two-dimensional systems of FDEs with infinite delays, we refer the readers to look at the books of Fridman [32], Gopalsamy [33], Hale and Verduyn Lunel [34], Hsu [35], Kolmanovskii and Myshkis [36], Rihan [37], Smith [38], Yoshizawa [39], and the bibliographies therein.

The paper is organized as follows. Section 2 contains four new qualitative results on the global asymptotic stability, the integrability of solutions of (6) and (10), and a numerical application for the particular case of (6). In Section 3, we obtain two new theorems on the bounded solutions of (6) and (10), and in particular cases for (6) and (10), two examples are given as numerical applications of these results. In Section 4, we compare qualitative results of the present paper with known ones, as well as discuss some open problems for future research.

2. Stability and Integrability

As we know from the relevant literature according to the LKF approach, to investigate the qualitative behaviors of solutions of FDEs, it is needed to construct suitable LKFs for the problems under study. The construction of LKFs for linear and nonlinear FDE still remains as an open problem in literature by this time. There is no general method to construct LKFs. When an LKF is defined or constructed, the essential question is whether the LKF has to be positive definite and its time derivative along solutions of the considered FDE has to be negative semidefinite or negative definite such that the stability or asymptotic stability of the solutions can be guaranteed, respectively. In this section, we take into consideration these facts and define two new LKFs to achieve the aim of this paper.

We define two new LKFs, $L = L(t, x_t, y_t)$ and $W = W(t, x_t, y_t)$, which are given by:

$$L(t, x_t, y_t) = d(t) \int\limits_{0}^{x} Q(\xi)d\xi + \frac{1}{2}y^2 + \gamma \int\limits_{-\infty}^{t} \exp(-(t-s))U^2(s, y(s))ds, \tag{11}$$

and

$$W(t, x_t, y_t) = |x(t)| + |y(t)| + \rho_1 \int_{-\infty}^{t} \int_{t}^{\infty} |C(u,s)| \, |g_1(x(s))| du ds$$

$$+ \rho_2 \int_{-\infty}^{t} \int_{t}^{\infty} |C(u,s)| \, |g_2(x(s))| du ds, \tag{12}$$

where γ, ρ_1 and ρ_2 are positive constants, and they will be chosen in the coming proofs. LKF (11) and LKF (12) are our basic tools in the proofs of the new results: Theorems 1, 3, 5 and Theorems 2, 4, 6, of this paper, respectively.

We now give the stability, integrability, and boundedness results of solutions of DIDE (6) and prove them using the LKF approach. At the first, we present the fundamental assumptions, called (A1)–(A4), of the main results of Theorems 1, 3, and 5 for DIDE (6):

(A1) There are positive constants F_0, G_0, H_0 and Q_0 such that:

$$a(t) \geq 1, b(t) \geq 1, c(t) \geq 1, d(t) \geq 1, d'(t) \geq 0, \forall t \in \mathbb{R}^+,$$

$$F(t, x, 0) = 0, yF(t, x, y) \geq F_0 y^2, \forall t \in \mathbb{R}^+, \forall y \neq 0 \text{ as } x, y \in \mathbb{R},$$

$$G(x, 0) = 0, yG(x, y) \geq G_0 y^2, \forall y \neq 0 \text{ as } x, y \in \mathbb{R},$$

$$H(0) = 0, yH(y \geq H_0 y^2, \forall y \neq 0 \text{ as } y \in \mathbb{R},$$

$$Q(0) = 0, xQ(x) \geq Q_0 x^2, \forall x \neq 0 \text{ as } x \in \mathbb{R}.$$

(A2) There is a positive constant U_0 such that:

$$U(t, 0) = 0, U^2(t, y) \leq U_0^2 y^2, \forall t, y \in \mathbb{R}.$$

(A3) There are positive constants F_0, G_0, H_0 from (A1) and U_0 from (A2) and ℓ_0 such that:

$$F_0 a(t) + G_0 b(t) + H_0 c(t) - 2^{-1} U_0^2 - 2^{-1} \geq \ell_0, \forall t \in \mathbb{R}^+.$$

(A4) Let λ be a continuous function such that:

$$|E(t, x, y)| \leq |\lambda(t)| \, |y|, \forall t \in \mathbb{R}^+, \forall x, y \in \mathbb{R},$$

and there are positive constants F_0, G_0, H_0 from (A1) and U_0 from (A2) and $\hbar_0$ such that:

$$F_0 a(t) + G_0 b(t) + H_0 c(t) - |\lambda(t)| - 2^{-1} U_0^2 - 2^{-1} \geq \hbar_0, \forall t \in \mathbb{R}^+.$$

As for the next step, we introduce the basic assumptions, called (C1)–(C3) of the main results, Theorems 2, 4, and 6 for the system of DIDEs (10) with infinite delay:

(C1) There are positive constants f_{10}, g_{10}, f_{20}, g_{20} and functions α_0, $\beta_0 \in C(\mathbb{R}^+, (0, \infty))$ such that

$$f_1(0) = 0, xf_1(x) \geq f_{10} x^2, g_1(0) = 0, |g_1(x)| \leq g_{10}|x|, \forall x \neq 0 \text{ as } x \in \mathbb{R},$$

$$f_2(0) = 0, yf_2(y) \geq f_{20} y^2, g_2(0) = 0, |g_2(y)| \leq g_{20}|y|, \forall y \neq 0 \text{ as } y \in \mathbb{R},$$

$$\ell_1(t, 0) = 0, |\ell_1(t, x)| \leq \alpha_0(t)|x|, \; \ell_2(t, 0) = 0, |\ell_2(t, y)| \leq \beta_0(t)|y|,$$
$$\forall t \in \mathbb{R}^+, \forall x, y \neq 0 \text{ as } x, y \in \mathbb{R}.$$

(C2)

$$\int_t^\infty |C_1(u,t)|\,du < \infty, \int_t^\infty |C_2(u,t)|\,du < \infty.$$

(C3) There are positive constants $f_{10}, g_{10}, f_{20},$ and g_{20} from (C1) and h_0, h_1 such that:

$$f_{10}A_1(t) - \alpha_0(t) - g_{10}\int_t^\infty |C_1(u,t)|\,du \geq h_0$$

and

$$f_{20}A_2(t) - \beta_0(t) - g_{20}\int_t^\infty |C_2(u,t)|\,du \geq h_1, \forall t \in \mathbb{R}^+, \mathbb{R}^+ = [0,\infty).$$

First, we give the following new global asymptotic stability theorem of (6), which is equivalent to system (7).

Theorem 1. *If (A1)–(A3) hold and $E(t,x,y) \equiv 0$, then the trivial solution of (7) is global asymptotic stable.*

Proof. We consider the LKF $L(t,x_t,y_t)$ of (11). Hence, it is obvious that

$$L(t,x_t,y_t) = 0 \text{ iff } x = y = 0.$$

By virtue of (A1), we obtain:

$$L(t,x_t,y_t) = d(t)\int_0^x \frac{Q(\xi)}{\xi}\xi\,d\xi + \frac{1}{2}y^2 + \gamma\int_{-\infty}^t \exp(-(t-s))U^2(s,y(s))\,ds$$

$$\geq d(t)\int_0^x \frac{Q(\xi)}{\xi}\xi\,d\xi + \frac{1}{2}y^2$$

$$\geq \frac{1}{2}Q_0 x^2 + \frac{1}{2}y^2,$$

i.e., we obtain:

$$L(t,x_t,y_t) \geq \frac{1}{2}Q_0 x^2 + \frac{1}{2}y^2. \tag{13}$$

By the time derivative of the LKF (11) along solutions of system (7), we obtain:

$$\frac{d}{dt}L(t,x_t,y_t) = -a(t)yF(t,x,y) - b(t)yG(x,y) - c(t)yH(y)$$

$$- d'(t)\int_0^x H(\xi)\,d\xi - y\int_{-\infty}^t \exp(-(t-s))U(s,y(s))\,ds$$

$$+ \gamma U^2(t,y) - \gamma\int_{-\infty}^t \exp(-(t-s))U^2(s,y(s))\,ds.$$

Hence, according to (A1) and (A2), we have:

$$\frac{d}{dt}L(t,x_t,y_t) \leq -F_0 a(t)y^2 - G_0 b(t)y^2 - H_0 c(t)y^2 - d'(t)\int_0^x H(\xi)\,d\xi$$

$$+ \frac{1}{2} \int_{-\infty}^{t} \exp(-(t-s)) \left[y^2(t) + U^2(s, y(s)) \right] ds$$

$$+ \gamma U^2(t, y) - \gamma \int_{-\infty}^{t} \exp(-(t-s)) U^2(s, y(s)) ds$$

$$\leq - \left[F_0 a(t) + G_0 b(t) + H_0 c(t) - 2^{-1} \right] y^2$$

$$+ \frac{1}{2} \int_{-\infty}^{t} \exp(-(t-s)) U^2(s, y(s)) ds$$

$$+ \gamma U^2(t, y) - \gamma \int_{-\infty}^{t} \exp(-(t-s)) U^2(s, y(s)) ds$$

$$\leq - \left[F_0 a(t) + G_0 b(t) + H_0 c(t) - 2^{-1} \right] y^2$$

$$+ \frac{1}{2} \int_{-\infty}^{t} \exp(-(t-s)) U^2(s, y(s)) ds$$

$$+ \left(\gamma U_0^2 \right) y^2 - \gamma \int_{-\infty}^{t} \exp(-(t-s)) U^2(s, y(s)) ds. \tag{14}$$

Let $\gamma = \frac{1}{2}$. Then, according to (A3), we obtain from (14) that:

$$\frac{d}{dt} L(t, x_t, y_t) \leq - \left[F_0 a(t) + G_0 b(t) + H_0 c(t) - 2^{-1} U_0^2 - 2^{-1} \right] y^2$$

$$\leq - (\ell_0) y^2 \leq 0. \tag{15}$$

The inequalities (13) and (15) together imply that the trivial solution of system (7) is stable, when $E(t, x, y) \equiv 0$. Next, $\frac{d}{dt} L(t, x_t, y_t) = 0$ if $y = 0$. Since $y = \frac{dx}{dt}$, then $\frac{dx}{dt} = 0$. Hence, integrating this term, we have $x(t) = \xi$, $\xi \in \mathbb{R}$, say $\xi \neq 0$. When we take $x(t) = \xi$ and $y(t) = 0$ into system (7), we derive that $Q(\xi) = 0$. It is obvious that $Q(\xi) = 0$ if $\xi = 0$. Consequently, the largest invariant set is $\{(0,0)\}$. Thus, the trivial solution of system (7) is global asymptotic stable. This is the end of proof. $\square$

Second, we present the following new global asymptotic stable theorem of (10).

Theorem 2. *If (C1)–(C3) hold, then the trivial solution of (10) is global asymptotic stable.*

Proof. According to the LKF of (12), we derive that:

$$W(t, 0, 0) = 0 \text{ and } W(t, x_t, y_t) \geq |x(t)| + |y(t)|.$$

From the LKF (12) and system (10), by the virtue of (C1)–(C3), we obtain:

$$\frac{d}{dt} W(t, x_t, y_t) \leq - A_1(t) |f_1(x)| + \int_{-\infty}^{t} |C_1(t,s)| \, |g_1(x(s))| ds + |\ell_1(t, x)|$$

$$- A_2(t) |f_2(y)| + \int_{-\infty}^{t} |C_2(t,s)| \, |g_2(y(s))| ds + |\ell_2(t, y)|$$

$$+ \rho_1 \int_t^\infty |C_1(u,t)| \, |g_1(x(t))| du - \rho_1 \int_{-\infty}^t |C_1(t,s)| |g_1(x(s))| ds$$

$$+ \rho_2 \int_t^\infty |C_2(u,t)| \, |g_2(y(t))| du - \rho_2 \int_{-\infty}^t |C_2(t,s)| \, |g_2(y(s))| ds. \tag{16}$$

Let $\rho_1 = \rho_2 = 1$. Then, (16) implies that:

$$\frac{d}{dt} W(t, x_t, y_t) \leq - A_1(t)|f_1(x)| + |\ell_1(t,x)| - A_2(t)|f_2(y)| + |\ell_2(t,y)|$$

$$+ \int_t^\infty |C_1(u,t)| \, |g_1(x(t))| du + \int_t^\infty |C_2(u,t)| \, |g_2(y(t))| du. \tag{17}$$

According to (C1)–(C3), from (17), we obtain:

$$\frac{d}{dt} W(t, x_t, y_t) \leq - f_{10} A_1(t)|x| + \alpha_0(t)|x| - f_{20} A_2(t)|y| + \beta_0(t)|y|$$

$$+ g_{10}|x| \int_t^\infty |C_1(u,t)| du + g_{20}|y| \int_t^\infty |C_2(u,t)| du$$

$$= - \left[f_{10} A_1(t) - \alpha_0(t) - g_{10} \int_t^\infty |C_1(u,t)| du \right] |x|$$

$$- \left[f_{20} A_2(t) - \beta_0(t) - g_{20} \int_t^\infty |C_2(u,t)| du \right] |y|$$

$$\leq - h_0|x| - h_1|y| < 0, (x \neq 0, \, y \neq 0).$$

Hence, we arrive at the end of the proof of Theorem 2. $\square$

We now present the following new integrability theorem of (6), which is equivalent to system (7).

Theorem 3. *If (A1)–(A3) hold and $E(t,x,y) \equiv 0$, then the square derivatives of solutions of (7) are integrable.*

Proof. According to (A1)–(A3) and $E(t,x,y) \equiv 0$, we obtain:

$$\frac{d}{dt} L(t, x_t, y_t) \leq - (\ell_0)y^2 \leq 0.$$

Taking into account that the LKF $L(t, x_t, y_t)$ is decreasing and then integrating the inequality above, we obtain:

$$\int_0^\infty y^2(\eta) d\eta < +\infty.$$

Thus, this result verifies the idea of Theorem 3. Here, the integrability concept is in the sense of Lebesgue. $\square$

We now introduce the following new integrability result of (10).

Theorem 4. *If (C1)–(C3) hold, then the solutions of (10) are integrable.*

Proof. By virtue of (C1)–(C3), we have:

$$\frac{d}{dt}W(t, x_t, y_t) \leq - h_0|x| - h_1|y| \leq 0.$$

This relation shows that the LKF $W(t, x_t, y_t)$ is decreasing. According to this information, it follows that $W(t, x_t, y_t) \leq W(0, x_0, y_0) = W_0$, $W_0 > 0$, $W_0 \in \mathbb{R}$. Integrating,

$$h_0 \int_0^t |x(s)|ds + h_1 \int_0^t |y(s)|ds \leq W(0, x_0, y_0) - W(t, x_t, y_t) \leq W(0, x_0, y_0) = W_0.$$

Consequently, we obtain:

$$\int_0^\infty |x(s)|ds \leq h_0^{-1}W_0 < \infty \text{ and } \int_0^\infty |y(s)|ds \leq h_1^{-1}W_0 < \infty,$$

where the integrability concept is in the sense of Lebesgue. This is the end of the proof. $\square$

We now give an example as numerical applications of the global asymptotic stability and integrability theorems, Theorems 1 and 3.

Example 1. *For the case $E(t, x, y) \equiv 0$ of (7), we take into consideration the following nonlinear DIDE of second order with infinite delay:*

$$x'' + (2 - \exp(-t))\left(25 + \exp(-t^2 - x^2 - (x')^2)\right)x' + \left(1 + \frac{1}{1+t^6}\right)\left(16 + x^4 + (x')^2\right)x'$$

$$+ (1 + \exp(-t))\left(4 + (x')^4\right)x' + \left(4 - \frac{3}{1 + 2\exp(t)}\right)x$$

$$+ \int_{-\infty}^t \exp(-(t - s))\frac{2x'(s)}{\sqrt{1 + s^2 + (x'(s))^2}}ds = 0. \tag{18}$$

Then, the DIDE (18) is converted to the following system:

$$x' = y,$$

$$y' = -(2 - \exp(-t))\left(25 + \exp(-t^2 - x^2 - y^2)\right)y - \left(1 + \frac{1}{1+t^6}\right)\left(16 + x^4 + y^2\right)y$$

$$- (1 + \exp(-t))\left(4 + y^4\right)y - \left(4 - \frac{3}{1 + 2\exp(t)}\right)x$$

$$- \int_{-\infty}^t \exp(-(t - s))\frac{2y(s)}{\sqrt{1 + s^2 + y^2(s)}}ds. \tag{19}$$

From the comparison of (19) and (7) and some elementary calculations, we have the following data:

$$a(t) = 2 - \exp(-t) \geq 1, t \geq 0,$$

$$b(t) = 1 + \frac{1}{1 + t^6} \geq 1,$$

$$c(t) = 1 + \exp(-t) \geq 1, t \geq 0,$$

$$d(t) = 4 - \frac{3}{1 + 2\exp(t)} \geq 1,$$

$$d'(t) = \frac{6\exp(t)}{(1 + 2\exp(t))^2} \geq 0;$$

$$F(t, x, y) = \left(25 + \exp(-t^2 - x^2 - y^2)\right)y,$$

$$F(t, x, 0) = 0,$$

$$yF(t, x, y) = y^2\left(25 + \exp(-t^2 - x^2 - y^2)\right) \geq 25y^2, \ F_0 = 25;$$

$$G(x, y) = \left(16 + x^4 + y^2\right)y, \ G(x, 0) = 0,$$

$$yG(x, y) = y^2\left(16 + x^4 + y^2\right) \geq 16y^2, \ G_0 = 16;$$

$$H(y) = \left(4 + y^4\right)y, \ H(0) = 0,$$

$$yH(y) = y^2\left(4 + y^4\right) \geq 4y^2, \ H_0 = 4;$$

$$Q(x) = x, \ Q(0) = 0,$$

$$xQ(x) = x^2, \ Q_0 = 1;$$

$$U(t, y) = \frac{2y}{\sqrt{1 + t^2 + y^2}},$$

$$U(t, 0) = 0, \ U^2(t, y) = \frac{4y^2}{1 + t^2 + y^2} \leq 4y^2, \ U_0^2 = 4;$$

$$F_0 a(t) + G_0 b(t) + H_0 c(t) - 2^{-1}U_0^2 - 2^{-1}$$

$$= 25 \times (2 - \exp(-t)) + 16 \times \left(1 + \frac{1}{1 + t^6}\right)$$

$$+4 \times (1 + \exp(-t)) - \frac{5}{2} \geq \frac{85}{2} = \ell_0 > 0.$$

According to the data above, (A1)–(A3) of Theorems 1 and 3 hold. Thus, the trivial solution of DIDE (18) is globally asymptotically stable and the square of the derivatives of its solutions are integrable.

The next section studies the boundedness of solutions of (6) and (10).

3. Boundedness

In this section, we prove two new theorems, Theorems 5 and 6, on the bounded solutions of DIDE (6), which is equivalent to system (7), and system of DIDEs (10). In particular cases of (6) and (10), two examples are given as numerical applications of Theorems 5 and 6, respectively.

The following Theorem 5 investigates the boundedness of solutions of system (7).

Theorem 5. *If (A1), (A2), and (A4) hold, then the solutions of system (7) and their derivatives are bounded.*

Proof. Clearly, by virtue of (A1), (A2), and (A4), we obtain the inequality of (13) and the following result:

$$\frac{d}{dt}L(t, x_t, y_t) \leq - \left[F_0 a(t) + G_0 b(t) + H_0 c(t) - 2^{-1} U_0^2 - 2^{-1} \right] y^2 + y E(t, x, y)$$

$$\leq - \left[F_0 a(t) + G_0 b(t) + H_0 c(t) - 2^{-1} U_0^2 - 2^{-1} \right] y^2 + |y| \, |E(t, x, y)|$$

$$\leq - \left[F_0 a(t) + G_0 b(t) + H_0 c(t) - |\lambda(t)| - 2^{-1} U_0^2 - 2^{-1} \right] y^2$$

$$\leq - (\hbar_0) y^2 \leq 0. \tag{20}$$

According to (20), the LKF $L(t, x_t, y_t)$ is decreasing, i.e.,

$$L(t, x_t, y_t) \leq L(t_0, x_{t_0}, y_{t_0}), \forall t \geq t_0.$$

Hence, from (13) and (20), we obtain:

$$\frac{1}{2} Q_0 x^2 + \frac{1}{2} y^2 \leq L(t, x_t, y_t) \leq L(t_0, x_{t_0}, y_{t_0}),$$

where $L(t_0, x_{t_0}, y_{t_0})$ is a positive constant. This inequality verifies that the solutions of system (7) are bounded. $\square$

The following Theorem 6 investigates the boundedness of solutions of system (10).

Theorem 6. *If (C1)–(C3) hold, then the solutions of system (10) are bounded.*

Proof. It is noted from Theorem 2 that

$$|x(t)| + |y(t)| \leq W(t, x_t, y_t).$$

Next, by (C1)–(C3) of Theorem 6, we obtain that:

$$\frac{d}{dt} W(t, x_t, y_t) \leq 0.$$

As a consequence of both of the results above, we can conclude that:

$$|x(t)| + |y(t)| \leq W(t, x_t, y_t) \leq W(t_0, x_{t_0}, y_{t_0}) \equiv W_0 > 0, W_0 \in \mathbb{R}, \ t \geq t_0.$$

Consequently,
$$|x(t)| \leq W_0 \text{ and } |y(t)| \leq W_0, \forall t \geq t_0.$$

Thus, clearly, the solutions of system (10) are bounded. $\square$

We now give two examples as numerical applications of Theorems 2 and 5 and Theorems 4 and 6, respectively.

Example 2. *For the case $E(t, x, y) \neq 0$, we take into consideration the following nonlinear DIDE of second order with infinite delay:*

$$x'' + (2 - \exp(-t))\left(25 + \exp(-t^2 - x^2 - (x')^2)\right)x' + \left(1 + \frac{1}{1+t^6}\right)\left(16 + x^4 + (x')^2\right)x'$$

$$+ (1 + \exp(-t))\left(4 + (x')^4\right)x' + \left(4 - \frac{3}{1 + 2\exp(t)}\right)x$$

$$+ \int_{-\infty}^{t} \exp(-(t-s))\frac{2x'(s)}{\sqrt{1 + s^2 + (x'(s))^2}}ds.$$

$$= \frac{2x'}{1 + t^2 + x^2 + (x')^2}. \tag{21}$$

Then, the DIDE (21) is converted to the following system:

$$x' = y,$$

$$y' = -(2 - \exp(-t))\left(25 + \exp(-t^2 - x^2 - y^2)\right)y - \left(1 + \frac{1}{1+t^6}\right)\left(16 + x^4 + y^2\right)y$$

$$- (1 + \exp(-t))\left(4 + y^4\right)y - \left(4 - \frac{3}{1 + 2\exp(t)}\right)x$$

$$- \int_{-\infty}^{t} \exp(-(t-s))\frac{2y(s)}{\sqrt{1 + s^2 + y^2(s)}}ds + \frac{2y}{1 + t^2 + x^2 + y^2}. \tag{22}$$

As for the next step, the discussions and the estimates relation to the functions $a(t)$, $b(t)$, $c(t)$, $d(t)$, F, G, H, Q, and U of Example 1 hold for Example 2, too. Hence, the former previous discussions will not be given here for these functions once again. As for the next step for the function E of Example 2, it is given by:

$$E(t, x, y) = \frac{2y}{1 + t^2 + x^2 + y^2}.$$

Hence, we derive:

$$|E(t, x, y)| = \frac{2|y|}{1 + t^2 + x^2 + y^2} \leq \frac{2|y|}{1 + t^2} = \lambda(t)|y|,$$

where

$$\lambda(t) = \frac{2}{1 + t^2}, t \geq 0.$$

$$F_0 a(t) + G_0 b(t) + H_0 c(t) - |\lambda(t)| - 2^{-1}U_0^2 - 2^{-1}$$

$$= 25 \times (2 - \exp(-t)) + 16 \times \left(1 + \frac{1}{1 + t^6}\right)$$

$$+ 4 \times (1 + \exp(-t)) - \frac{2}{1 + t^2} - \frac{5}{2} \geq \frac{81}{2} = \hbar_0 > 0.$$

Then, the conditions of Theorem 5 hold. Thus, the solutions of system (22) and their derivatives are bounded.

Remark 1. *It is seen from Theorems 1–3 that we do need the differentiability of the functions $a(t)$, F, $b(t)$, G, $c(t)$, H, Q, U, and E. This case is an advantage for the results of this paper, Theorems 1–3, and leads to a weaker condition for these results.*

Example 3. *We consider the following nonlinear system of DIDEs with infinite delay, which is included by (10):*

$$\begin{cases} x' = -\,(1+\exp(t^2))\left(24\pi x + \frac{x}{1+\exp(x^2)}\right) + \int_{-\infty}^{t} \frac{1}{1+t^2+s^2} \frac{x(s)}{1+x^4(s)} ds \\ \qquad + \frac{x}{(1+t^6)(1+\exp(x^2))}, \\ y' = -\,(1+\exp(t^4))\left(24\pi y + \frac{y}{1+\exp(y^2)}\right) + \int_{-\infty}^{t} \frac{1}{1+4t^2+4s^2} \frac{3y(s)}{1+y^4(s)} ds \\ \qquad + \frac{y}{(1+t^6)(1+\exp(y^2))}. \end{cases} \quad (23)$$

From the comparison of systems (23) and (10) and some elementary calculations, we have the following data:

$$A_1(t) = 1 + \exp(t^2),$$

$$A_2(t) = 1 + \exp(t^4),$$

$$f_1(x) = 24\pi x + \frac{x}{1+\exp(x^2)},$$

$$f_1(0) = 0,\, x f_1(x) = 24\pi x^2 + \frac{x^2}{1+\exp(x^2)} \geq 24\pi x^2,\ f_{10} = 24\pi;$$

$$f_2(y) = 24\pi y + \frac{y}{1+\exp(y^2)},$$

$$f_2(0) = 0,\, y f_2(y) = 24\pi y^2 + \frac{y^2}{1+\exp(y^2)} \geq 24\pi y^2,\ f_{20} = 24\pi;$$

$$C_1(t,s) = \frac{1}{1+t^2+s^2},$$

$$\int_{t}^{\infty} C_1(u,t)du = \int_{t}^{\infty} \frac{1}{1+u^2+t^2}du \leq \int_{t}^{\infty} \frac{1}{1+u^2}du$$

$$\leq \int_{0}^{\infty} \frac{1}{1+u^2}du = \frac{\pi}{2} < \infty;$$

$$C_2(t,s) = \frac{1}{1+4t^2+4s^2},$$

$$\int_{t}^{\infty} C_2(u,t)du = \int_{t}^{\infty} \frac{1}{1+4u^2+4t^2}du \leq \int_{t}^{\infty} \frac{1}{1+4u^2}du$$

$$\leq \int_{0}^{\infty} \frac{1}{1+4u^2}du = \frac{\pi}{4} < \infty;$$

$$g_1(x) = \frac{2x}{1+x^4},\, g_1(0) = 0,\, |g_1(x)| \leq 2|x|,\ g_{10} = 2;$$

$$g_2(y) = \frac{3y}{1+y^4},\, g_2(0) = 0,\, |g_2(y)| \leq 3|y|,\ g_{20} = 3;$$

$$\ell_1(t,x) = \frac{x}{(1+t^6)(1+\exp(x^2))},\, \ell_1(t,0) = 0,$$

$$|\ell_1(t,x)| \leq \frac{|x|}{1+t^6},\, \alpha_0(t) = \frac{1}{1+t^6};$$

$$\ell_2(t,y) = \frac{y}{(1+t^6)(1+\exp(y^2))}, \ell_2(t,0) = 0,$$

$$|\ell_2(t,y)| \leq \frac{|y|}{1+t^6}, \beta_0(t) = \frac{1}{1+t^6};$$

$$f_{10}A_1(t) - \alpha_0(t) - g_{10}\int_t^\infty |C_1(u,t)|du = 24\pi\left(1+\exp(t^2)\right) - \frac{1}{1+t^6} - \pi$$

$$> 23\pi = h_0;$$

$$f_{20}A_2(t) - \beta_0(t) - g_{20}\int_t^\infty |C_2(u,t)|du = 24\pi\left(1+\exp(t^4)\right) - \frac{1}{1+t^6} - \frac{3\pi}{4}$$

$$> 23\pi = h_1.$$

According the data above, (C1)–(C3) of Theorems 2, 4, and 6 hold. Thus, the trivial solution of the non-linear system of DIDEs (23) is globally asymptotically stable, and the solutions of (23) are also integrable and bounded.

4. Conclusions and Discussion

In this part, we compare Theorems 1–6 of this paper with some articles in the references of this paper.

(1) DIDEs (1) and (3) are particular cases of our DIDE (6). Next, our LKF (11) is different from the LKFs (2), (4), and (5). This is our first contribution.

(2) The system of IDEs (8) with infinite delay is linear. Our system of IDEs (10) with infinite delay is nonlinear. The system of IDEs (10) with infinite delay generalizes and improves the linear system (8). Next, our LKF (12) is different from the LKF (9). This is our second contribution.

(3) The uniform stability of solutions of DIDE (1) and the uniform and equi-asymptotic stability of the zero solution of DIDE (3) are investigated using the LKF method. In our paper, we investigate the global asymptotic stability, boundedness, and integrability of solutions of DIDE (6) using the LKF method. As it is seen our results, we established the different qualitative concepts of our solutions. Next, in the past literature, some stability concepts are discussed. In our paper, in addition to the global asymptotic stability concept, we also study boundedness and integrability of solutions, which are different from the uniform and equi-asymptotic stability concepts. These are our third contributions.

(4) h-uniformly stability, h-uniformly asymptotically stability, and h-bounded solutions of the system of IDEs (8) with infinite delay are discussed by using a phase space and the LKF method. In this paper, the global asymptotic stability of zero solution, boundedness, and integrability of solutions of (10) are discussed by the LKF method. These qualitative concepts are a bit different from the h-uniformly stability, h-uniformly asymptotically stability, and h-bounded solutions because of the defined norm. These are our next contributions.

(5) As numerical applications of the results of this paper, we provide three examples, Examples 1–3, to illustrate the applications of Theorems 1–6 of this paper. Examples 1–3 are also new contributions of this paper.

(6) To the best of our knowledge, the scalar nonlinear DIDE (6) of second order and the non-linear system of IDEs (10) with infinite delays are new mathematical models. Qualitative behaviors of solutions of these mathematical models have not been investigated in the relevant literature as of yete. Hence, the new results of this paper, Theorems 1–6, and the illustrative Examples 1–3 are complementary outcomes of this paper to the theory of FDEs.

As some open problems for future researches, we would like to suggest that qualitative properties of fractional forms of the scalar nonlinear DIDE (6) of second order with infinite delay and the non-linear system of DIDEs (10) with infinite delay can be investigated.

Author Contributions: Conceptualization, C.T. and O.T.; Data curation, O.T. and C.T.; Formal analysis, C.T. and O.T.; Methodology, C.T. and O.T.; Project administration, C.T.; Validation, C.T.; Visualization, C.T. and O.T.; Writing—original draft, O.T. All authors have read and agreed to the published version of the manuscript.

Funding: This research received no external funding.

Data Availability Statement: Not applicable.

Acknowledgments: The authors would like to thank the anonymous referees and the handling Editor for many useful comments and suggestions, leading to a substantial improvement in the presentation of this article.

Conflicts of Interest: The authors declare no conflict of interest.

References

1. Alahmadi, F.; Raffoul, Y.N.; Alharbi, S. Boundedness and stability of solutions of nonlinear Volterra integro-differential equations. *Adv. Dyn. Syst. Appl.* **2018**, *13*, 19–31.
2. Burton, T.A. *Volterra Integral and Differential Equations*, 2nd ed.; Mathematics in Science and Engineering, 202; Elsevier B.V.: Amsterdam, The Netherlands, 2005.
3. Furumochi, T.; Matsuoka, S. Stability and boundedness in Volterra integro-differential equations. *Mem. Fac. Sci. Eng. Shimane Univ. Ser. B Math. Sci.* **1999**, *32*, 25–40.
4. Grimmer, R.; Seifert, G. Stability properties of Volterra integro-differential equations. *J. Differ. Equ.* **1975**, *19*, 142–166.
5. Jordan, G.S. Asymptotic stability of a class of integro-differential systems. *J. Differ. Equ.* **1979**, *31*, 359–365.
6. Lakshmikantham, V.; Rao, M.R.M. Theory of Integro-Differential Equations. In *Stability and Control: Theory, Methods and Applications, 1*; Gordon and Breach Science Publishers: Lausanne, Switzerland, 1995.
7. Rao, M.R.M.; Srinivas, P. Asymptotic behavior of solutions of Volterra integro-differential equations. *Proc. Am. Math. Soc.* **1985**, *94*, 55–60.
8. Murakami, S. Exponential asymptotic stability for scalar linear Volterra equations. *Differ. Integral Equ.* **1991**, *4*, 519–525.
9. Rao, M.R.M.; Raghavendra, V. Asymptotic stability properties of Volterra integro-differential equations. *Nonlinear Anal.* **1987**, *11*, 475–480.
10. Sedova, N. On uniform asymptotic stability for nonlinear integro-differential equations of Volterra type. *Cybern. Phys.* **2019**, *8*, 161–166.
11. Berezansky, L.; Braverman, E. On exponential stability of linear delay equations with oscillatory coefficients and kernels. *Differ. Integral Equ.* **2022**, *35*, 559–580.
12. Berezansky, L.; Diblík, J.; Svoboda, Z.; Šmarda, Z. Uniform exponential stability of linear delayed integro-differential vector equations. *J. Differ. Equ.* **2021**, *270*, 573–595.
13. Du, X.T. Some kinds of Liapunov functional in stability theory of RFDE. *Acta Math. Appl. Sin.* **1995**, *11*, 214–224.
14. Tunç, C.; Tunç, O. On the stability, integrability and boundedness analyses of systems of integro-differential equations with time-delay retardation. *Rev. Real Acad. Cienc. Exactas Físicas Nat. Ser. A Matemáticas* **2021**, *115*, 115. [CrossRef]
15. Funakubo, M.; Hara, T.; Sakata, S. On the uniform asymptotic stability for a linear integro-differential equation of Volterra type. *J. Math. Anal. Appl.* **2006**, *324*, 1036–1049. [CrossRef]
16. Tunç, C.; Tunç, O. New results on the stability, integrability and boundedness in Volterra integro-differential equations. *Bull. Comput. Appl. Math.* **2018**, *6*, 41–58.
17. Tunç, C.; Tunç, O. New results on the qualitative analysis of integro-differential equations with constant time-delay. *J. Nonlinear Convex Anal.* **2022**, *23*, 435–448.
18. Tunç, C.; Tunç, O. Solution estimates to Caputo proportional fractional derivative delay integro–differential equations. *Rev. Real Acad. Cienc. Exactas Fis. Nat. Ser. A Mat.* **2023**, *117*, 12. [CrossRef]
19. Tunç, O. Stability, instability, boundedness and integrability of solutions of a class of integro-delay differential equations. *J. Nonlinear Convex Anal.* **2022**, *23*, 801–819.
20. Tunç, C.; Wang, Y.; Tunç, O.; Yao, J.-C. New and Improved Criteria on Fundamental Properties of Solutions of Integro-Delay Differential Equations with Constant Delay. *Mathematics* **2021**, *9*, 3317. [CrossRef]
21. Xu, D. Asymptotic behavior of Volterra integro-differential equations. *Acta Math. Appl. Sin.* **1997**, *13*, 107–110.
22. Wang, Q.Y. Stability of a class of Volterra integrodifferential equations. *J. Huaqiao Univ. Nat. Sci. Ed.* **1998**, *19*, 1–5.
23. Wang, Q.Y. Asymptotic stability of functional-differential equations with infinite time-lag. *J. Huaqiao Univ. Nat. Sci. Ed.* **1998**, *19*, 329–333.
24. Wang, L.; Du, X.T. The stability and boundedness of solutions of Volterra integro-differential equations. *Acta Math. Appl. Sin.* **1992**, *15*, 260–268.

25.   Becker, L.C.; Burton, T.A. Asymptotic stability criteria for delay-differential equations. *Proc. R. Soc. Edinb. Sect. A* **1988**, *110*, 31–44.
26.   Dishen, J. Stability and boundedness of solutions of Volterra integral differential equations with infinite delay. *Ann. Differ. Equ.* **2006**, *22*, 256–260.
27.   Hale, J.K.; Kato, J. Phase space for retarded equations with infinite delay. *Funkcial. Ekvac.* **1978**, *21*, 11–41.
28.   Berezansky, L.; Domoshnitsky, A. On stability of a second order integro-differential equation. *Nonlinear Dyn. Syst. Theory* **2019**, *19*, 117–123.
29.   Crisci, M.R.; Kolmanovskii, V.B.; Russo, E.; Vecchio, A. Stability of continuous and discrete Volterra integro-differential equations by Liapunov approach. *J. Integral Equ. Appl.* **1995**, *7*, 393–411.
30.   Gözen, M.; Tunç, C. Stability in functional integro-differential equations of second order with variable delay. *J. Math. Fundam. Sci.* **2017**, *49*, 66–89.
31.   Graef, J.R.; Tunç, C. Continuability and boundedness of multi-delay functional integro-differential equations of the second order. *Rev. Real Acad. Cienc. Exactas Fis. Nat. Ser. A Mat.* **2015**, *109*, 169–173. [CrossRef]
32.   Fridman, E. Introduction to Time-Delay Systems Analysis and Control. In *Systems & Control: Foundations & Applications*; Birkhäuser: Basel, Switzerland; Springer: Cham, Switzerland, 2014.
33.   Gopalsamy, K. Stability and oscillations in delay differential equations of population dynamics. In *Mathematics and Its Applications*, 74; Kluwer Academic Publishers Group: Dordrecht, The Netherlands, 1992.
34.   Hale, J.K.; Verduyn Lunel, S.M. Introduction to functional-differential equations. In *Applied Mathematical Sciences, 99*; Springer: New York, NY, USA, 1993.
35.   Hsu, S.B. *Ordinary Differential Equations with Applications*, 2nd ed.; Series on Applied Mathematics, 21; World Scientific Publishing Co. Pte. Ltd.: Hackensack, NJ, USA, 2013.
36.   Kolmanovskii, V.; Myshkis, A. Introduction to the Theory and Applications of Functional-Differential Equations. In *Mathematics and Its Applications, 463*; Kluwer Academic Publishers: Dordrecht, The Netherlands, 1999.
37.   Rihan, F.A. *Delay Differential Equations and Applications to Biology. Forum for Interdisciplinary Mathematics*; Springer: Singapore, 2021.
38.   Smith, H. *An Introduction to Delay Differential Equations with Applications to the Life Sciences*; Texts in Applied Mathematics, 57; Springer: New York, NY, USA, 2011.
39.   Yoshizawa, T. *Stability theory by Liapunov's Second Method*; The Mathematical Society of Japan: Tokyo, Japan, 1966.

 *mathematics*

Article

Reclamation of a Resource Extraction Site Model with Random Components

Ekaterina Gromova [1,*], Anastasiia Zaremba [2] and Nahid Masoudi [3]

[1] Transport and Telecommunication Institute, LV-1019 Riga, Latvia
[2] Faculty of Applied Mathematics and Control Processes, St. Petersburg State University, 199034 St. Petersburg, Russia
[3] Department of Economics, Memorial University of Newfoundland, St. John's, NL A1C 5S7, Canada
* Correspondence: gromova.e@tsi.lv; Tel.: +371-2057-1406

Abstract: We compute the cooperative and the Nash equilibrium solutions for the discounted optimal control problem in a two-player differential game of reclamation of a resource extraction site, where each firm's planning horizon presents the period that extraction of the resources from their site is economically viable. Hence, the planning horizon is defined by a random duration determined on the infinite time horizon. The comparison of the cooperative and Nash solutions and also the comparative statics are provided numerically. We also define the concept of "normalized value of cooperation" and explain how this concept could help us to better characterize the losses the players will face if they continue to refrain from cooperation.

Keywords: differential game; random time horizon; open-loop strategies; resource extraction; reclamation; clean-up of extraction site

MSC: 91A23; 49N70

Citation: Gromova, E.; Zaremba, A.; Masoudi, N. Reclamation of a Resource Extraction Site Model with Random Components. *Mathematics* **2022**, *10*, 4805. https://doi.org/10.3390/math10244805

Academic Editor: Mehdi Salimi

Received: 6 November 2022
Accepted: 10 December 2022
Published: 17 December 2022

Publisher's Note: MDPI stays neutral with regard to jurisdictional claims in published maps and institutional affiliations.

1. Introduction

The extraction of natural resources, i.e., the withdrawal of materials (e.g., fossil fuels, rocks, timber, fish), have great impacts on the environment. Examples of such impacts are: soil degradation, destruction of natural habitats, water contamination, air pollution, deforestation, and solid waste. Moreover, as expectations for higher standards of living and the world's population continue to grow, the demand for resources will continue to grow. Hence, reclamation and clean-up of the resource extraction sites remain a top concern and priority for environmental regulation bodies and have given rise to a growing interest in reclamation and clean-up issues, especially over the past decade (see, e.g., [1–5]).

In the extant literature, the planning horizon is always assumed to be known. However, while the lease terms are usually known to the firms, what defines an extraction site's active lifespan is the duration when extraction remains economically viable. In other words, firms abandon their extraction sites when extraction becomes economically unprofitable. Firms make economic assessments about the availability of resources in each site; however, the exact amount of the resources and their economic profitability and hence, the economically viable resource extraction period, remain uncertain both due to factors related to the market (e.g., demand and extraction cost) and also technical limitations. These uncertainties could have important implications both for the regulators and firms. In this paper, we make a first exploratory attempt to embed uncertainty in the economic extraction period into a site reclamation model. For that purpose, we extend the paper by Marsiglio and Masoudi [1] by assuming that the extraction period (firm's planning horizon) is a random variable. Moreover, in this article, we define the concept of "normalized value of cooperation" and explain how this concept could help us to better characterize the losses players will face if they continue to refrain from cooperation.

The paper proceeds as follows. Section 2 presents our model. In Section 3, we focus on the cooperative solution of the problem, while Section 4 presents the results for the non-cooperative scenario. A comparison of the two scenarios is provided in Section 5. The concept of normalized value of cooperation is introduced in Section 6. Finally, Section 7 presents concluding remarks and highlights directions for future research.

2. Model Formulation

Consider a differential game with two players (indexed by z, where $z = \{i, j\}$) [6] devoted to resource management [7,8]. The model setting follows [1], except for the fact that in our model, firms' planning horizon presents the period that extraction of the resources from each site is economically viable and not the lease duration. Hence, while in [1], the extraction period is known, in our model this is defined by a random duration determined on the infinite time horizon, denoted T^j and T^i. For the models with a random time horizon, see [9–12].

Denote the level of environmental degradation or the pollution stock as p_t, which is the state variable of the process.

Assume that firm $z, z = \{i, j\}$ extracts resources at a rate $\gamma^z > 0$. For simplicity, we assume the extraction rate is given. However, the emissions due to extraction are not constant but increasing in the pollution stock due to, e.g., the decreasing returns of the extraction technologies. In other words, emissions, e_t^z, are given by $e_t^z = \epsilon^z \gamma^z p_t$, where $\epsilon^z > 0$ is an exogenous parameter defining the environmental inefficiency of extraction activity of the firm z.

Firms engage in reclamation or abatement activities throughout the entire planning horizon. Let the reclamation efforts of the firm be $a_t^z = \alpha^z \tau_t^z$, where $\alpha^z > 0$ is the efficiency of environmental reclamation. Therefore, the environmental degradation dynamics is given by:

$$\dot{p}_t = \left(\epsilon^i \gamma^i + \epsilon^j \gamma^j - \delta \right) p_t - \alpha^i \tau_t^i - \alpha^j \tau_t^j, \tag{1}$$

where $\delta > 0$ is the natural pollution decay rate. We assume that the growth rate of pollution in the absence of abatement is positive $\epsilon^i \gamma^i + \epsilon^j \gamma^j - \delta > 0$, pollution will increase over time, leading the firms to face a substantial reclamation fee on their lease termination date.

We assume that at the closure time T^z, by regulations, the firm z is responsible to pay a reclamation cost, referred to as the abandonment reclamation fee, proportional to the environmental costs of the unclaimed pollution stock at that time, given by: $f(p_{T^z}) = \phi^z \frac{p_{T^z}^2}{2}$. Here, $\phi^z \geq 0$ is determined by the regulator and quantifies the extent to which the firm z is effectively liable for the damage caused by the unclaimed pollution at its site dismissal. For any $\phi^z > 0$ (and finite) the firm needs to account for both its instantaneous losses and abandonment reclamation fee to determine its rehabilitation efforts. For the sake of simplicity, assume also that the reclamation cost of the firm z is quadratic: $\ell(\tau_t^z) = \frac{(\tau_t^z)^2}{2}$. Thus, the cost of the firm z is the following:

$$C^z = \int_0^{T^z} \frac{(\tau_t^z)^2}{2} e^{-\rho t} dt + \phi^z \frac{p_{T^z}^2}{2} e^{-\rho T^z} \to \min_{\tau_t^z}, \tag{2}$$

where ρ is the discount rate. We assume that T^j and T^i are **random** variables defined on the infinite interval $[0, \infty)$. Let T^j and T^i correspond to the exponential distribution with the cumulative distribution function [11]

$$F(t) = 1 - e^{-rt}, t \in [0, \infty).$$

In this paper, although the model is formulated for the general case with different random terminal times, we assume that decision-makers have the same exponential distribution. Considering two different distributions would result in a problem with time inconsistent preferences, which would require a different approach to the analysis.

Thus, each firm's payoff is the sum of the mathematical expectation of the integral payoff and the mathematical expectation of the terminal part according to the considered cumulative distribution function $F(t)$, i.e., we have:

$$C^z = E\left[\int_0^{T^z} \frac{(\tau_t^z)^2}{2} e^{-\rho t} dt\right] + E\left[\phi^z \frac{p_{T^z}^2}{2} e^{-\rho T^z}\right]. \tag{3}$$

We can simplify (3) using integration by parts, provided that the probability density function (p.d.f.) $f(t)$ exists and well-defined (a similar approach has been used in [13,14]):

$$C^z = E\left[\int_0^{T^z} \frac{(\tau_t^z)^2}{2} e^{-\rho t} dt\right] + E\left[\phi^z \frac{p_{T^z}^2}{2} e^{-\rho T^z}\right] =$$

$$\int_0^\infty \int_0^t \frac{(\tau_\theta^z)^2}{2} e^{-\rho \theta} d\theta dF(t) + \int_0^\infty \phi^z \frac{p_t^2}{2} e^{-\rho t} f(t) dt = \int_0^\infty \frac{(\tau_t^z)^2}{2} e^{-\rho t} (1 - F(t)) dt + \int_0^\infty \phi^z \frac{p_t^2}{2} e^{-\rho t} f(t) dt =$$

$$\int_0^\infty \left[\frac{(\tau_t^z)^2}{2} e^{-\rho t} (1 - F(t)) + \phi^z \frac{p_t^2}{2} e^{-\rho t} f(t)\right] dt = \int_0^\infty \left[\frac{(\tau_t^z)^2}{2} e^{-(\rho+r)t} + \phi^z r \frac{p_t^2}{2} e^{-(\rho+r)t}\right] dt =$$

$$\int_0^\infty \left[\frac{(\tau_t^z)^2}{2} + \phi^z r \frac{p_t^2}{2}\right] e^{-(\rho+r)t} dt, \quad z = \overline{i,j}. \tag{4}$$

where $f(t) = F'(t)$ is a p.d.f. for T^i and T^j.

3. Cooperative Scenario

As our baseline, we first find the socially optimal levels of pollution and abatement activities of the two firms. In other words, we first solve the game assuming that the two firms cooperate with each other and minimize their joint reclamation cost. This solution gives us a benchmark to compare with the non-cooperative or the business as usual results. In the cooperative scenario, the two firms minimize their joint cost as follows:

$$C^i + C^j = \int_0^\infty \left[\frac{(\tau_t^i)^2}{2} + \phi^i r \frac{p_t^2}{2}\right] e^{-(\rho+r)t} dt + \int_0^\infty \left[\frac{(\tau_t^j)^2}{2} + \phi^j r \frac{p_t^2}{2}\right] e^{-(\rho+r)t} dt =$$

$$\int_0^\infty \left[\frac{(\tau_t^i)^2}{2} + \frac{(\tau_t^j)^2}{2} + (\phi^i + \phi^j) r \frac{p_t^2}{2}\right] e^{-(\rho+r)t} dt. \tag{5}$$

For simplicity, denote $d = (\epsilon^i \gamma^i + \epsilon^j \gamma^j - \delta)$. We then transform the problem to a maximization problem as follows:

$$\begin{cases} \int_0^\infty (-1)\left[\frac{(\tau_t^i)^2}{2} + \frac{(\tau_t^j)^2}{2} + (\phi^i + \phi^j) r \frac{p_t^2}{2}\right] e^{-(\rho+r)t} dt \to \max_{\tau_t^i, \tau_t^j}, \\ \dot{p}_t = d p_t - \alpha^i \tau_t^i - \alpha^j \tau_t^j, \\ p_0 \text{ is given.} \end{cases} \tag{6}$$

To solve the problem, we proceed by using a modification of Pontryagin's Maximum Principle [15] for an infinite interval [16]. The Hamiltonian function corresponding to our problem is defined as

$$
H = \psi_t \left[dp_t - \alpha^i \tau_t^i - \alpha^j \tau_t^j \right] - \left[\frac{(\tau_t^i)^2}{2} + \frac{(\tau_t^j)^2}{2} + (\phi^i + \phi^j) r \frac{p_t^2}{2} \right]. \tag{7}
$$

Hence,

$$
\frac{\partial H}{\partial \tau_t^z} = -\alpha^z \psi_t - \tau_t^z = 0, \quad z = \overline{i,j}. \tag{8}
$$

The optimal control of the player z is given by:

$$
\tau_t^{z*} = -\alpha^z \psi_t, \quad z = \overline{i,j}. \tag{9}
$$

The adjoint variable equation (according to maximum principle modification on infinite interval) is:

$$
\dot{\psi}_t = (\rho + r)\psi_t - d\psi_t + r(\phi^i + \phi^j)p_t. \tag{10}
$$

At the same time, using (9) we have:

$$
\dot{p}_t = dp_t + ((\alpha^i)^2 + (\alpha^j)^2)\psi_t. \tag{11}
$$

Hence, we obtain the following system of differential equations:

$$
\begin{cases} \dot{\psi}_t = (\rho + r - d)\psi_t + r(\phi^i + \phi^j)p_t, \\ \dot{p}_t = dp_t + ((\alpha^i)^2 + (\alpha^j)^2)\psi_t. \end{cases} \tag{12}
$$

In the matrix form, we have:

$$
\begin{bmatrix} \dot{p}_t \\ \dot{\psi}_t \end{bmatrix} = \begin{bmatrix} d & (\alpha^i)^2 + (\alpha^j)^2 \\ r(\phi^i + \phi^j) & \rho + r - d \end{bmatrix} \begin{bmatrix} p_t \\ \psi_t \end{bmatrix} = A^C \begin{bmatrix} p_t \\ \psi_t \end{bmatrix}. \tag{13}
$$

Note that for the optimal control problem defined on an infinite horizon, the optimal solution is a trajectory that converges to the equilibrium point (assuming there is only one equilibrium point; otherwise, more analysis is needed). If the canonical system is linear, this problem can be solved relatively easily, as a linear system has only one equilibrium point. To find a stable trajectory to this point, we need to identify all negative eigenvalues of the matrix A^C.

A^C has two eigenvalues:

$$
\Lambda(A^C) = \left\{ \sigma_1^C, \sigma_2^C \right\} = \left\{ \frac{r}{2} + \frac{\rho}{2} - \frac{\sqrt{D^C}}{2}, \ \frac{r}{2} + \frac{\rho}{2} + \frac{\sqrt{D^C}}{2} \right\},
$$

where $D^C = (\rho + r - 2d)^2 + 4r(\phi^i + \phi^j)((\alpha^i)^2 + (\alpha^j)^2) > 0$.

Since the second eigenvalue $\sigma_2^C = \frac{r}{2} + \frac{\rho}{2} + \frac{\sqrt{D^C}}{2}$ is positive, it can not produce a stable solution. However, the first eigenvalue $\sigma_1^C = \frac{r}{2} + \frac{\rho}{2} - \frac{\sqrt{D^C}}{2}$ is negative if $D^C - (r + \rho)^2 = 4r(\phi_i + \phi_j)(\alpha_i^2 + \alpha_2^2) + 4d(d - r - \rho) > 0$. Then its corresponding eigenvector is

$$
v^C = \begin{bmatrix} 1 \\ \frac{2(\phi_i + \phi_j)r}{2d - r - \rho - \sqrt{D^C}} \end{bmatrix}.
$$

Note that any trajectory that starts from $p_0 + span(v)$ will converge to the equilibrium point. There is only one stable equilibrium, so the initial value p_0 is uniquely determined.

To save in notation, let us denote $\sigma_1^C = \sigma^C$. Given the initial condition p_0, we can write the solution as follows:

$$p_t^C = p_0 e^{\sigma^C t},\tag{14}$$

$$\psi_t = -\frac{2(\phi_i + \phi_j)r}{r - 2d + \rho + \sqrt{D^C}} p_0 e^{\sigma^C t}.\tag{15}$$

and consequently, the optimal controls are:

$$(\tau_t^z)^C = \alpha^z \frac{2(\phi_i + \phi_j)r}{r - 2d + \rho + \sqrt{D^C}} p_0 e^{\sigma^C t}.\tag{16}$$

Proposition 1 summarizes this result.

Proposition 1. *The cooperative rule for the reclamation effort for firm $z = \{i, j\}$, $(\tau_t^z)^C$, and the cooperative time path of pollution, p_t^{*C}, are respectively given by:*

$$(\tau_t^z)^C = \alpha^z \frac{2(\phi^i + \phi^j)r}{r - 2d + \rho + \sqrt{D^C}} p_0 e^{\sigma t},\tag{17}$$

$$p_t^C = p_0 e^{\sigma t},\tag{18}$$

where $\sigma^C = \frac{r}{2} + \frac{\rho}{2} - \frac{\sqrt{D^C}}{2} < 0$, and $D^C = (\rho + r - 2d)^2 + 4r(\phi^i + \phi^j)((\alpha^i)^2 + (\alpha^j)^2) > 0$.

From Proposition 1 we can see that, since under the cooperative scenario firms take into account their joint abandonment reclamation fees, the only factor that differentiates their optimal reclamation efforts is their reclamation efficiency, $\alpha^z, z = \{i, j\}$, so much so that the firm with higher reclamation efficiency is asked to implement higher efforts and when $\alpha^i = \alpha^j$, regardless of any other heterogeneity among the two firms, they will implement the same levels of reclamation efforts over time. Moreover, as expected, higher initial pollution stock and abandonment reclamation fees leads to higher reclamation efforts for the two firms.

4. Nash Equilibrium

Now, we turn to solve the problem under the business as usual scenario, that is, when firms do not cooperate on their reclamation efforts and tend to focus on minimizing their own individual costs. This leads us to seek for the open-loop Nash Equilibrium, where we are facing the following optimal control problem:

$$\begin{cases} C^i = (-1)\frac{1}{2} \int_0^\infty e^{-(\rho+r)t} \left[(\tau_t^i)^2 + \phi^i r p_t^2 \right] dt \to \max_{\tau_t^i}, \\ C^j = (-1)\frac{1}{2} \int_0^\infty e^{-(\rho+r)t} \left[(\tau_t^j)^2 + \phi^j r p_t^2 \right] dt \to \max_{\tau_t^j}, \\ \dot{p}_t = dp_t - \alpha^i \tau_t^i - \alpha^j \tau_t^j, \\ p_0 \text{ is given.} \end{cases}\tag{19}$$

To find the Nash equilibrium, we define two (current state) Hamiltonian functions:

$$H^z(p, \psi_t^z, \tau_t^i, \tau_t^j) = -\frac{\phi^z r p^2}{2} - \frac{\tau_t^{z^2}}{2} + \psi_t^z \left(dp_t - \alpha^i \tau_t^i - \alpha^j \tau_t^j \right).\tag{20}$$

Note that the calculations are similar to the ones under the cooperative scenario. Hence, the optimal controls will be $\tau_i^* = -\alpha^i \psi_t^i$. The respective canonical system written for (p, ψ_t^i, ψ_t^j) is:

$$
\begin{bmatrix} \dot{p} \\ \dot{\psi}^i \\ \dot{\psi}^j \end{bmatrix} = \begin{bmatrix} d & \alpha^{i2} & \alpha^{j2} \\ \phi^i r & r-d+\rho & 0 \\ \phi^j r & 0 & r-d+\rho \end{bmatrix} \begin{bmatrix} p \\ \psi^i \\ \psi^j \end{bmatrix} = A^N \begin{bmatrix} p \\ \psi_1 \\ \psi_2 \end{bmatrix}.
\tag{21}
$$

The matrix A^N has three eigenvalues:

$$
\Lambda(A^N) = \left\{ \sigma_1^N, \sigma_2^N, \sigma_3^N \right\} = \left\{ r-d+\rho, \ \tfrac{r}{2}+\tfrac{\rho}{2}-\tfrac{\sqrt{D^N}}{2}, \ \tfrac{r}{2}+\tfrac{\rho}{2}+\tfrac{\sqrt{D^N}}{2} \right\},
$$

where $D^N = 4\phi^i(\alpha^i)^2 r + 4\phi^j(\alpha^j)^2 r + 4d^2 - 4dr - 4d\rho + r^2 + 2r\rho + \rho^2 > 0$.

The optimal solution corresponds to a stable solution to (21). To determine the stable solution, we need to analyze the eigenvalues. Note that $\sigma_3^N > 0$ is positive, so it can not produce a stable solution. However, the second one $\sigma_2^N = \tfrac{1}{2}(r+\rho-\sqrt{D})$ is negative if

$$
D^N - (r+\rho)^2 = 4\phi^i(\alpha^i)^2 r + 4\phi^j(\alpha^j)^2 r + 4d(d-r-\rho) > 0.
$$

and then its corresponding eigenvector is:

$$
v_2^N = \begin{bmatrix} \frac{2d-r-\rho-\sqrt{D}}{2r} \\ \phi_1 \\ \phi_2 \end{bmatrix}.
$$

Note that any trajectory of (21) that initiates from a point along this vector, will be described by $\dot{p} = \sigma_2 p$, and $\psi_i = p_t \frac{2r\phi^i}{2d-r-\rho-\sqrt{D^N}}$. It is important to note that $2d - r - \rho - \sqrt{D^N} < 0$, so the optimal values of the adjoint variables that correspond to $p_t > 0$ are strictly negative and hence, the respective optimal controls $\tau_t^{i*} = -\alpha_i \psi_t^{i*}$ are positive.

One special case occurs when $d > r + \rho$, i.e., the growth rate of pollution stock exceeds the depreciation rate $r + \rho$ (which is very realistic). In this case, the system (21) has 2 stable eigenvalues. Note that $d > r + \rho$ immediately implies $\sigma_2^N < 0$.

The eigenvector corresponding to $\sigma_1^N = r + \rho - d$ is:

$$
v_1^N = \begin{bmatrix} 0 \\ -(\alpha^j)^2 \\ (\alpha_i)^2 \end{bmatrix}.
$$

However, since the components corresponding to ψ_t^i and ψ_t^j are of different signs, in a neighborhood of the equilibrium point one of the adjoint variables will turn positive, which does not make sense. Thus, we dismiss this eigenvector and the respective eigenvector.

Finally, we obtain the optimal adjoint variables in the following form:

$$
\psi_t^{i*} = -\frac{2p_0\phi^i r e^{\sigma_2^N t}}{r - 2d + \rho + \sqrt{D^N}}.
$$

Now, to save in notation, let us denote $\sigma_2^N = \sigma^N$. Proposition 2 summarizes the results for the Nash Equilibrium.

Proposition 2. *The Nash rule for the reclamation effort for firm* $z = \{i, j\}$, $(\tau_t^z)^C$, *and the cooperative time path of pollution,* p_t^{*C}, *are respectively given by:*

$$(\tau_t^z)^N = \alpha^z \frac{2p_0 \phi^i r e^{\sigma^N t}}{r - 2d + \rho + \sqrt{D^N}},$$ (22)

$$p_t^N = p_0 e^{\sigma^N t},$$ (23)

where $\sigma^N = \frac{r}{2} + \frac{\rho}{2} - \frac{\sqrt{D^N}}{2} < 0$, *and* $D^N = 4\phi^i (\alpha^i)^2 r + 4\phi^j (\alpha^j)^2 r + 4d^2 - 4dr - 4d\rho + r^2 + 2r\rho + \rho^2 > 0$.

Proposition 2 suggests that, like the cooperative case, under the non-cooperative scenario, the firm with higher reclamation effort efficiency will implement higher efforts, ceteris paribus. However, unlike the cooperative scenario, in this case, since firms are taking only their private costs into account, another factor causes asymmetry in the firms' reclamation effort trajectory: their individual abandonment reclamation fees. Indeed, ceteris paribus, the firm with higher abandonment liability engages in more reclamation activities. Note that other sources of heterogeneity will not cause asymmetries in the two firms choices.

5. Comparison Analysis

In this section, we compare the results under cooperative and non-cooperative scenarios. However, due to the nature of our model, analytical comparison is not feasible and hence, we need to resort to numerical illustrations. The base parameter values we use for our numerical analysis are as follows: $p_0 = 1$, $r = 0.0001$, $\rho = 0.0001$, $d = 0.01$, $\phi_1 = 5$, $\phi_2 = 7$, $\alpha_1 = 20$, $\alpha_2 = 30$. We used these values in order to make sure we have an interior solution, but we report the results for other values in our analysis.

Figure 1 compares the trajectory of the reclamation efforts of player i under cooperative and non-cooperative scenarios. As expected, at the beginning, the reclamation efforts are considerably higher under the cooperative scenario than the non-cooperative case. However, as the gap between pollution stock under these two scenarios increases (see Figure 2), interestingly, this behavior reverses and the cooperative reclamation efforts become less than non-cooperative. Note that both reclamation efforts and pollution stock converge to zero under both scenarios, even though the rate of convergence is faster under cooperation.

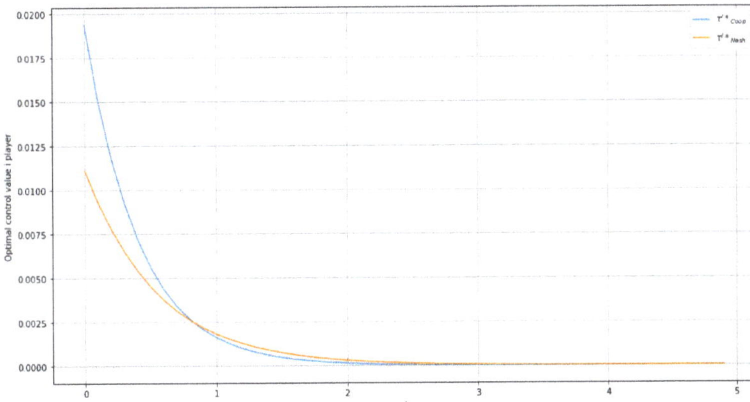

Figure 1. The optimal controls of player i under cooperation VS Nash equilibrium.

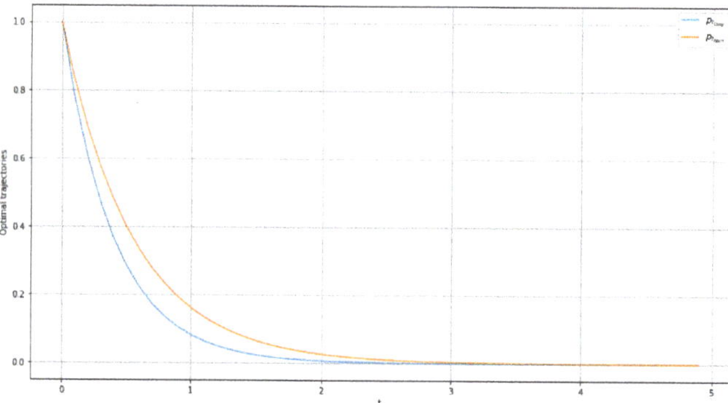

Figure 2. The optimal trajectory of pollution stock under cooperation VS Nash equilibrium.

5.1. Nash Equilibrium Analysis

Now, we turn to analyzing the impact of our key model parameters on the behavior of the players under a non-cooperative scenario. To clearly see the impact of the variables, we plot the optimal controls from two different perspectives: we show the figures for two heterogeneous players, and also we present the results for a representative player considering different values for the parameter, ceteris-paribus.

First, let us focus on the impact of the environmental reclamation efficiency, α. The analytical presentation of this impact is presented by Equation (24), which is too complicated to allow analytical comparisons. Hence, we use numerical analysis by plotting the reclamation effort trajectories under different values for α.

$$\frac{\partial(\tau_t^z)^N}{\partial \alpha^z} = \frac{2p_0\phi^z re^{\sigma^N t}}{(r - 2d + \rho + \sqrt{D^N})^2}\left[(1 - 2(\alpha^z)^2\phi^z r\frac{1}{\sqrt{D^N}})(r - 2d + \rho + \sqrt{D^N}) - 4(\alpha^z)^2\phi^z r\frac{1}{\sqrt{D^N}}\right]. \tag{24}$$

From Figure 3, we can see that, as expected, the player with higher α implements higher reclamation efforts throughout the entire non-cooperative game. However, from Figure 4, that presents the representative player i's optimal controls assuming different values of α for this player, we see a rather interesting result. That is, the impact of α on the trajectory of the optimal control of the representative player is not monotonic. In fact, while the higher α encourages the player to implement higher efforts, as the pollution stock drops quickly, the player reduces its efforts faster in compare to a situation with lower α, so much so, after some point of time, the case with lower α performs higher reclamation.

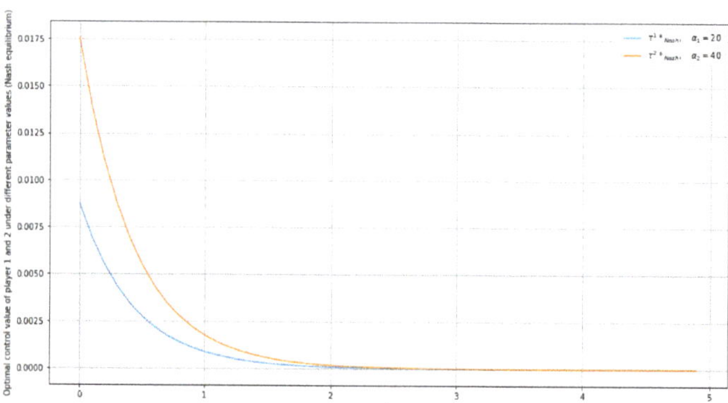

Figure 3. The optimal controls of two players under Nash equilibrium and different α.

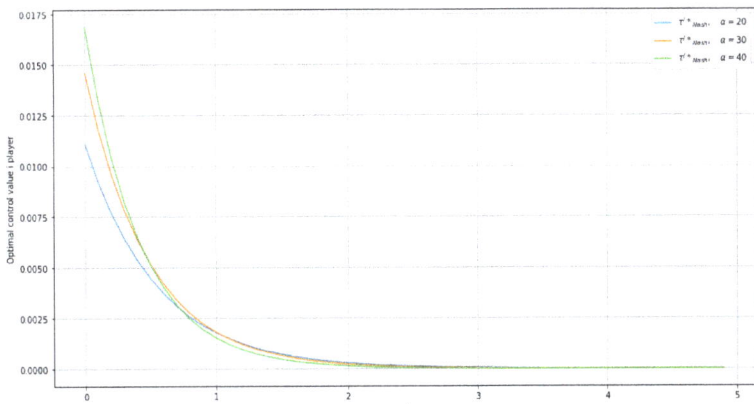

Figure 4. The optimal controls of player *i* under Nash equilibrium and different α.

Equation (25) presents the impact of the abandonment reclamation fee parameter ϕ on the players' choices. In Figures 5 and 6, we demonstrate this numerically.

$$\frac{\partial(\tau_t^z)^N}{\partial\phi^z} = \frac{2p_0\alpha^z re^{\sigma^N t}}{(r - 2d + \rho + \sqrt{D^N})^2}\left[(1 - (\alpha^z)^2\phi^z r\frac{1}{\sqrt{D^N}})(r - 2d + \rho + \sqrt{D^N}) - 2(\alpha^z)^2\phi^z r\frac{1}{\sqrt{D^N}}\right]. \tag{25}$$

From Figure 5, we can see that, again as expected, the player with higher abandonment fees puts more efforts into cleaning-up the site throughout the entire planning horizon. However, the effect of the abandonment fees remains strong and monotonically increasing, i.e., as seen in Figure 6, the higher the player's abandonment environmental obligations is, the higher is their reclamation efforts at any point of time.

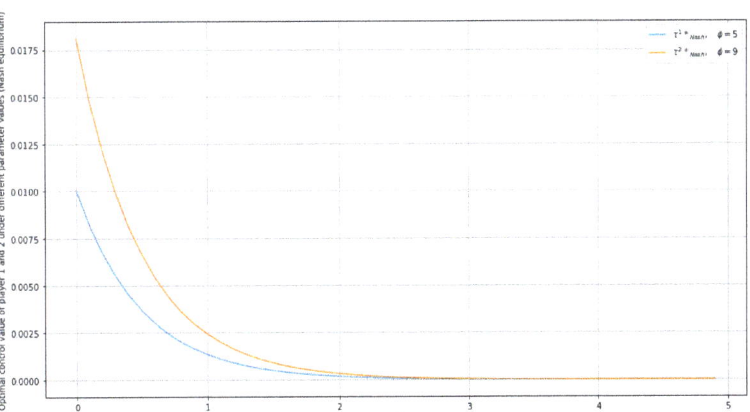

Figure 5. The optimal controls of two players under Nash equilibrium and different ϕ.

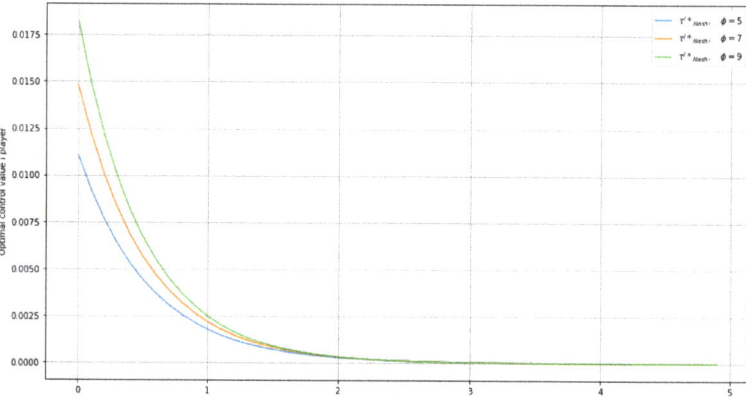

Figure 6. The optimal controls of player i under Nash equilibrium and different ϕ.

5.2. Cooperative Scenario Analysis

In this subsection, we focus on the impact of our key variables under the cooperative scenario. First, let us discuss the impact of reclamation effort efficiency parameter α, as presented in Equation (26).

$$\frac{\partial(\tau_t^z)^C}{\partial \alpha^z} = \frac{2p_0(\phi^i + \phi^j)re^{\sigma^C t}}{(r - 2d + \rho + \sqrt{D^C})^2}\left[(1 - 2(\alpha^z)^2(\phi^i + \phi^j)r\frac{1}{\sqrt{D^C}})(r - 2d + \rho + \sqrt{D^C}) - 4(\alpha^z)^2(\phi^i + \phi^j)r\frac{1}{\sqrt{D^C}}\right]. \tag{26}$$

From Figures 7 and 8, it is clear that the impact of environmental efficiency parameter on players' reclamation effort is similar to what we observed under the non-cooperative scenario. That is, higher efficiency calls for higher reclamation efforts. However, as this leads to faster fall in pollution stock (see Figure 9), this relationship reverses over time.

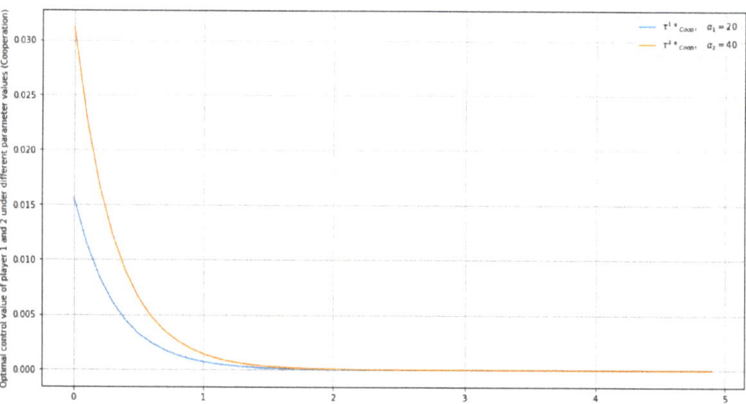

Figure 7. The optimal controls of two players under cooperative equilibrium and different ϕ.

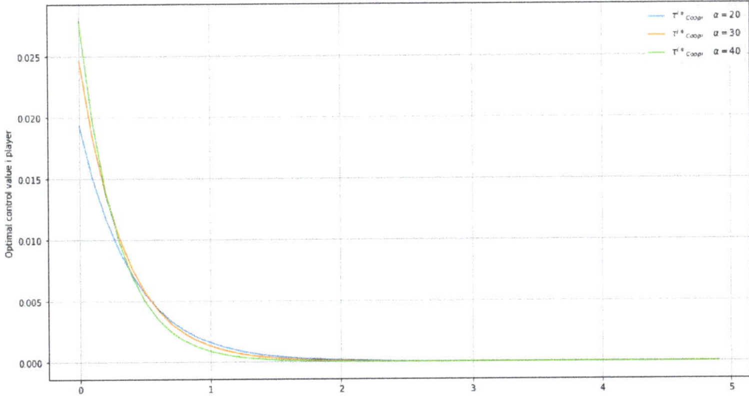

Figure 8. The optimal controls of player i under cooperative scenario and different α.

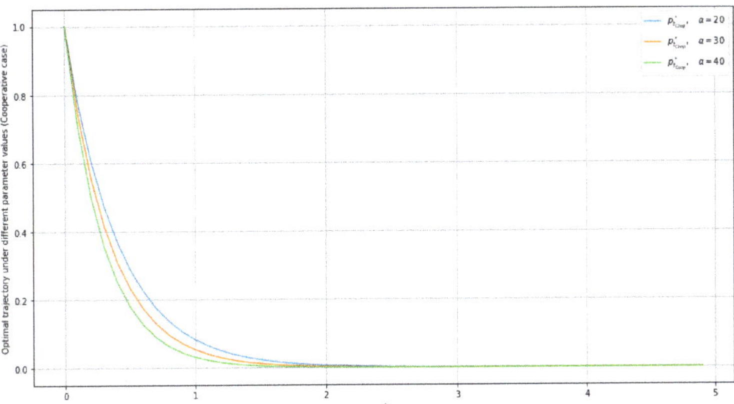

Figure 9. The optimal trajectory of pollution stock under cooperative scenario and different α.

As for the impact of abandonment fee ϕ, similar to the cooperative case, the player with higher environmental liability ϕ is asked to put more effort during the entire time horizon (see Figure 10). The same is true at the beginning of the game if we look at a representative player with different values for ϕ. However, in contrast with what we saw in the non-cooperative case (see Figure 11), here, higher ϕ does not result in a monotonic increase in reclamation effort rates at all points of time. The reason for this sharp difference between the impact of ϕ in these scenarios is that under cooperation, to minimize their joint optimal costs, both players will implement higher reclamation efforts when either player's environmental liabilities ϕ increases. However, under the non-cooperative scenario, if player i faces higher ϕ, player j may strategically lower their efforts with the knowledge that i will raise their efforts to avoid high abandonment fees. Hence, under cooperation pollution stock drops faster; consequently, the rate of cooperative reclamation efforts slow down, eventually.

$$\frac{\partial (\tau_t^z)^C}{\partial \phi^z} = \frac{2 p_0 \alpha^z r e^{\sigma^C t}}{(r - 2d + \rho + \sqrt{D^C})^2} \left[\left(1 - ((\alpha^i)^2 + (\alpha^j)^2)(\phi^i + \phi^j) r \frac{1}{\sqrt{D^C}}\right)(r - 2d + \rho + \sqrt{D^C}) - \right.$$

$$\left. 2((\alpha^i)^2 + (\alpha^j)^2)(\phi^i + \phi^j) r \frac{1}{\sqrt{D^C}} \right]. \quad (27)$$

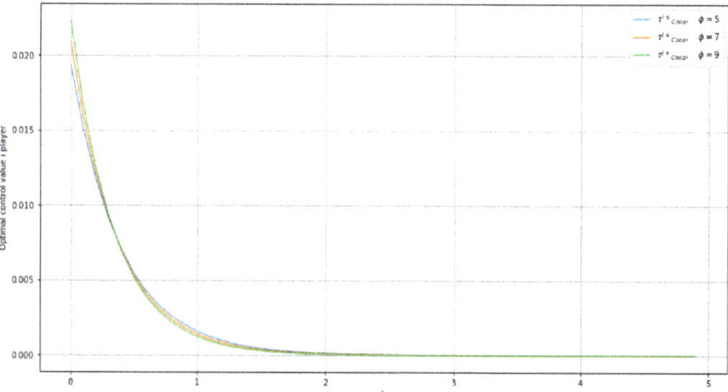

Figure 10. The optimal controls of player i under cooperative scenario and different ϕ.

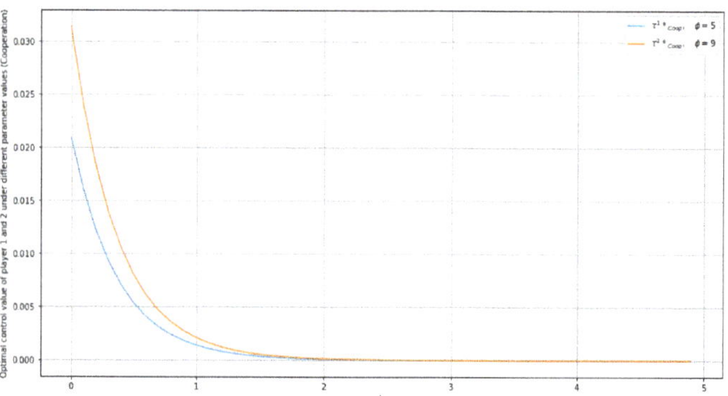

Figure 11. The optimal controls of two players under Nash equilibrium and different ϕ.

6. Normalized Value of Cooperation

In this section, we present a novel method to compare the non-cooperative and cooperative solutions based on their total costs by introducing the concept of normalized value of cooperation (NVC). A similar approach was discussed in [17]; however, in [17] the value of cooperation was computed for individual players for the entire period of the game and hence, it did not depend on a current time instant. In this paper, NVC_t is computed by taking the difference between the total cost of the two players in the Nash equilibrium and the cooperative case then dividing this value by the total cost of all players under the Nash equilibrium in the subgame of the game beginning at the time t. Note, that in this case, we consider only the subgames that start from the optimal trajectory. Hence, NVC_t takes values between 0 and 1, where 0 means that both costs coincide, i.e., there will be no difference between playing the game cooperatively or non-cooperatively from time t on, cost-wise. A value close to 1 means that the total sum of the costs corresponding to the Nash are much larger than the costs for the cooperative case. Intuitively, NVC value reveals how big the gap between cooperation and non-cooperation costs will be if players continue to play the game non-cooperatively.

$$NVC_t = \frac{\sum_{z=i,j}(C_t^z)^N - \sum_{z=i,j}(C_t^z)^C}{\sum_{z=i,j}(C_t^z)^N}.$$

(28)

Below, we illustrate the computation of the normalized value of cooperation. Consider a subgame starting at some point θ, then the life-time cost of a player z is:

$$C_\theta^z = E\left[\int_\theta^\infty \frac{(\tau_t^z)^2}{2}e^{-\rho t}dt\right] + E\left[\phi^z \frac{p_{Tz}^2}{2}e^{-\rho T^z}\right] =$$

$$\frac{1}{1-F(\theta)}\int_\theta^\infty \frac{(\tau_t^z)^2}{2}e^{-\rho t}(1-F(t))dt + \frac{1}{1-F(\theta)}\int_\theta^\infty \phi^z \frac{p_t^2}{2}e^{-\rho t}f(t)dt =$$

$$\frac{1}{1-F(\theta)}\int_\theta^\infty \left[\frac{(\tau_t^z)^2}{2}e^{-\rho t}(1-F(t)) + \phi^z \frac{p_t^2}{2}e^{-\rho t}f(t)\right]dt = e^{r\theta}\int_\theta^\infty \left[\frac{(\tau_t^z)^2}{2}e^{-(\rho+r)t} + \phi^z r \frac{p_t^2}{2}e^{-(\rho+r)t}\right]dt =$$

$$e^{r\theta}\int_\theta^\infty \left[\frac{(\tau_t^z)^2}{2} + \phi^z r \frac{p_t^2}{2}\right]e^{-(\rho+r)t}dt, \quad z = \overline{i,j}. \quad (29)$$

Thus, in cooperative case, the joint cost of the two players is:

$$C_\theta^i + C_\theta^j = e^{r\theta}\int_\theta^\infty (-1)\left[\frac{(\tau_t^i)^2}{2} + \frac{(\tau_t^j)^2}{2} + (\phi^i + \phi^j)r\frac{p_t^2}{2}\right]e^{-(\rho+r)t}dt =$$

$$(-1)\frac{1}{2}e^{r\theta}\int_\theta^\infty \left[\frac{4((\alpha^i)^2 + (\alpha^j)^2)(\phi^i + \phi^j)^2 r^2}{(r-2d+\rho+\sqrt{D^C})^2}p_0^2 e^{2\sigma^C t} + (\phi^i + \phi^j)r p_0^2 e^{2\sigma^C t}\right]e^{-(\rho+r)t}dt =$$

$$(-1)e^{r\theta}\frac{(\phi^i + \phi^j)r p_0^2}{2}\int_\theta^\infty \left[\frac{4((\alpha^i)^2 + (\alpha^j)^2)(\phi^i + \phi^j)r}{(r-2d+\rho+\sqrt{D^C})^2} + 1\right]e^{-\sqrt{D^C}t}dt =$$

$$(-1)e^{r\theta}\frac{(\phi^i + \phi^j)r p_0^2}{(-2)\sqrt{D^C}}\left[\frac{4((\alpha^i)^2 + (\alpha^j)^2)(\phi^i + \phi^j)r}{(r-2d+\rho+\sqrt{D^C})^2} + 1\right](0 - e^{-\sqrt{D^C}\theta}) =$$

$$(-1)\frac{(\phi^i + \phi^j)r p_0^2}{2\sqrt{D^C}}\left[\frac{4((\alpha^i)^2 + (\alpha^j)^2)(\phi^i + \phi^j)r}{(r-2d+\rho+\sqrt{D^C})^2} + 1\right]e^{r-\sqrt{D^C}\theta}. \quad (30)$$

Finally, the total cost of the two players for a subgame beginning from time t under cooperation is:

$$\sum_{z=i,j}(C_t^z)^C = (-1)\frac{(\phi^i + \phi^j)r p_0^2}{2\sqrt{D^C}}\left[\frac{4((\alpha^i)^2 + (\alpha^j)^2)(\phi^i + \phi^j)r}{(r-2d+\rho+\sqrt{D^C})^2} + 1\right]e^{r-\sqrt{D^C}t}. \quad (31)$$

Now, we turn to calculating the sum of the total cost of the two players for the subgame in case of Nash Equilibrium:

$$C_\theta^i + C_\theta^j = e^{r\theta}\int_\theta^\infty (-1)\left[\frac{(\tau_t^i)^2}{2} + \frac{(\tau_t^j)^2}{2} + (\phi^i + \phi^j)r\frac{p_t^2}{2}\right]e^{-(\rho+r)t}dt =$$

$$(-1)\frac{1}{2}e^{r\theta}\int_\theta^\infty \left[\frac{4((\alpha^i\phi^i)^2 + (\alpha^j\phi^j)^2)r^2}{(r-2d+\rho+\sqrt{D^N})^2}p_0^2 e^{2\sigma^N t} + (\phi^i + \phi^j)r p_0^2 e^{2\sigma^N t}\right]e^{-(\rho+r)t}dt =$$

$$(-1)e^{r\theta}\frac{r p_0^2}{2}\int_\theta^\infty \left[\frac{4((\alpha^i\phi^i)^2 + (\alpha^j\phi^j)^2)r}{(r-2d+\rho+\sqrt{D^N})^2} + (\phi^i + \phi^j)\right]e^{-\sqrt{D^N}t}dt =$$

$$(-1)e^{r\theta}\frac{r p_0^2}{(-2)\sqrt{D^N}}\left[\frac{4((\alpha^i\phi^i)^2 + (\alpha^j\phi^j)^2)r}{(r-2d+\rho+\sqrt{D^N})^2} + (\phi^i + \phi^j)\right](0 - e^{-\sqrt{D^N}\theta}) =$$

$$(-1)\frac{r p_0^2}{2\sqrt{D^N}}\left[\frac{4((\alpha^i\phi^i)^2 + (\alpha^j\phi^j)^2)r}{(r-2d+\rho+\sqrt{D^N})^2} + (\phi^i + \phi^j)\right]e^{r-\sqrt{D^N}\theta}. \quad (32)$$

Finally, the sum of the total cost of the players for a subgame commencing at the time t when they play Nash is:

$$\sum_{z=i,j}(C_t^z)^N = -1)\frac{rp_0^2}{2\sqrt{D^N}}\left[\frac{4((\alpha^i\phi^i)^2+(\alpha^j\phi^j)^2)r}{(r-2d+\rho+\sqrt{D^N})^2}+(\phi^i+\phi^j)\right]e^{r-\sqrt{D^N}t}. \tag{33}$$

In Figure 12, the normalized value of cooperation is demonstrated for our baseline parameter values. The notion of NVC can be used in many insightful ways. For example, suppose players would only continue to play non-cooperatively up to a point where the losses of continuing in that manner become too high in comparison to the cooperation. That is, when they reach such a threshold, they may find it too costly to continue to not cooperate and choose to switch to cooperation. Figure 12 presents a threshold level of 40%. So, we can find the time instant when the losses associated with Nash exceed the losses associated with cooperative case by 40%.

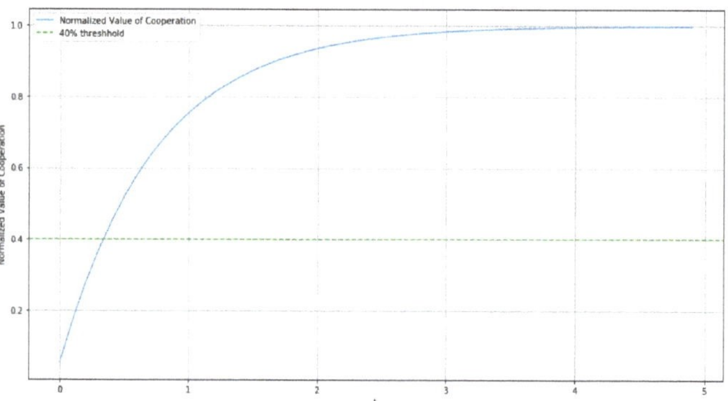

Figure 12. Normalized Value of Cooperation.

7. Conclusions

In this paper, we consider a two-player differential game of reclamation of an extraction site, where each firm's planning horizon presents the period that their extraction of the resources from each site is economically viable. Hence, in our model, the planning horizon is defined by a random duration determined on the infinite time horizon. We compute the cooperative and the Nash equilibrium solutions for the discounted optimal control problem defined on an infinite interval. The corresponding optimal solutions and the respective payoff functions are computed explicitly.

We use numerical analysis to provide insights into how the cooperative and the Nash solutions compare, and also how our key parameters affect the players' choices and the pollution stock under different scenarios. We also define the concept of "normalized value of cooperation" and explain how this concept could help us to better characterize the losses the players will face if they continue to refrain from cooperation.

Author Contributions: Conceptualization, E.G. and N.M.; formal analysis, A.Z.; investigation, A.Z. and N.M.; methodology, E.G.; project administration, A.Z.; supervision, E.G. and N.M.; validation, A.Z. and N.M.; writing—original draft, A.Z. and E.G.; writing—review and editing, E.G. and N.M. All authors have read and agreed to the published version of the manuscript.

Funding: This research was funded by RFBR and DFG, grant number 21-51-12007. This study was partially done while E. Gromova was with St. Petersburg State University.

Data Availability Statement: Not applicable.

Conflicts of Interest: The authors declare no conflict of interest.

References

1. Marsiglio, S.; Masoudi N. Reclamation of a Resource Extraction Site: A Dynamic Game Approach. *Metroeconomica* **2022**, *73*, 770–802. [CrossRef]
2. Mitchell, A.L.; Casman, E.A. Economic incentives and regulatory framework for shale gas well site reclamation in Pennsylvania. *Environ. Sci. Technol.* **2011**, *45*, 9506–9514. [CrossRef] [PubMed]
3. Lappi, P. Optimal clean-up of polluted sites. *Resour. Energy Econ.* **2018**, *54*, 53–68. [CrossRef]
4. Lappi, P. A model of optimal extraction and site reclamation. *Resour. Energy Econ.* **2020**, *29*, 101–126. [CrossRef]
5. Yang, P.; Davis, G. Non-renewable resource extraction under financial incentives to reduce and reverse stock pollution. *J. Environ. Econ. Manag.* **2018**, *92*, 282–299. [CrossRef]
6. Basar, T.; Olsder G. *Dynamic Noncooperative Game Theory*; SIAM: New York, NY, USA, 1999.
7. Dockner, E.J.; Jørgensen, S.; Long, N.V.; Sorger, G. Differential Games in Economics and Management Science. In *Cambridge Books*; Cambridge University Press: Cambridge, UK, 2000.
8. Jørgensen, S.; Zaccour, G. Developments in differential game theory and numerical methods: Economic and management applications. *Comput. Manag. Sci.* **2007**, *4*, 159–181. [CrossRef]
9. Yeung, D.; Petrosyan, L. *Cooperative Stochastic Differential Games*; Springer Science, Business Media: Berlin/Heidelberg, Germany, 2006.
10. Yaari, M. Uncertain lifetime, life insurance, and the theory of the consumer. *Rev. Econ. Stud.* **1965**, *32*, 137–150. [CrossRef]
11. Petrosyan, L.; Shevkoplyas, E. Cooperative differential games with stochastic time. *Vestn. Petersburg Univ. Math.* **2000**, *33*, 18–23.
12. Gromova, E.; Malakhova, A.; Palestini, A. Payoff Distribution in a Multi-Company Extraction Game with Uncertain Duration. *Mathematics* **2018**, *6*, 165. [CrossRef]
13. Marin-Solano, J.; Shevkoplyas, E. Non-constant discounting and differential games with random time horizon. *Automatica* **2011**, *47*, 2626–2638. [CrossRef]
14. Kostyunin, S.; Palestini, A.; Shevkoplyas, E. On a nonrenewable resource extraction game played by asymmetric firms. *J. Optim. Theory Appl.* **2014**, *163*, 660–673. [CrossRef]
15. Pontryagin, L.; Boltyanskii, V.; Gamkrelidze, R.; Mishchenko, E. *The Mathematical Theory of Optimal Processes*; Interscience: New York, NY, USA, 1962.
16. Grass, D.; Caulkins, J.P.; Feichtinger, G.; Tragler, G.; Behrens, D.A. *Optimal Control of Nonlinear Processes: With Applications in Drugs, Corruption, and Terror*; Springer: Berlin/Heidelberg, Germany, 2008.
17. Chebotareva, A.; Su, S.; Voronina, E.; Gromova, E. Value of Cooperation in a Differential Game of Pollution Control. In *International Conference on Mathematical Optimization Theory and Operations Research*; Springer: Cham, Switzerland, 2022; pp. 221–234.

 *mathematics*

Article

An Alternative Numerical Scheme to Approximate the Early Exercise Boundary of American Options

Denis Veliu [1,†], **Roberto De Marchis** [2,†], **Mario Marino** [3,†] and **Antonio Luciano Martire** [4,*,†]

[1] Departament of Finance-Banking, Metropolitan University of Tirana, 1000 Tirana, Albania
[2] MEMOTEF Department, Sapienza University of Rome, 00185 Rome, Italy
[3] DEAMS "Bruno De Finetti", University of Trieste, 34127 Trieste, Italy
[4] Department of Business Economics, Roma Tre University, 00185 Rome, Italy
* Correspondence: antonioluciano.martire@uniroma3.it
† These authors contributed equally to this work.

Abstract: This paper deals with a new numerical method for the approximation of the early exercise boundary in the American option pricing problem. In more detail, using the mean-value theorem for integrals, we provide a flexible algorithm that allows for reaching a more accurate numerical solution with fewer calculations rather than other previously described methods.

Keywords: American put pricing; nonstandard Volterra integral equations; free boundary problem

MSC: 45D05

Citation: Veliu, D.; De Marchis, R.; Marino, M.; Martire, A.L. An Alternative Numerical Scheme to Approximate the Early Exercise Boundary of American Options. *Mathematics* **2023**, *11*, 187. https://doi.org/10.3390/math11010187

Academic Editor: Panagiotis-Christos Vassiliou

Received: 25 November 2022
Revised: 21 December 2022
Accepted: 26 December 2022
Published: 29 December 2022

1. Introduction

Volterra integral equations have practical applications in many fields, including biology, medicine, finance and engineering. Although various methods are available to find analytical solutions for these integral equations, in most cases, finding a closed-form solution may be unfeasible. To this end, several numerical methods have been developed in recent years (see, e.g., [1,2]). In the present work, we deal specifically with the Volterra integral equation of the second kind, defined below

$$\phi(t) = f(t, \phi(t)) + \int_0^t k(t,s)\psi(t,s,\phi(t),\phi(s))\, ds, \tag{1}$$

with $t \in I = [0, T]$. Such an equation in which the integrand depends both on $\phi(t)$ and $\phi(s)$ is also a nonstandard Volterra integral equation ([3]).

In the field of mathematical finance, Equation (1) and its solution are a matter of interest in order to determine the value of an American financial option. More generally, a financial option is a derivative contract allowing for the holder to buy or sell an underlying financial asset at a fixed price, namely, the strike price. If the holder can buy or sell the underlying asset only at the expiration date, the option is called European; conversely, an American financial option provides the holder with the possibility to also exercise its right before the expiration date. Depending on the value of the underlying asset, it may become optimal for the holder to exercise its right before the expiration time. Such an asset value is the optimal exercise price, and by considering the optimal exercise times during the option duration, we can achieve a collection of optimal exercise prices, namely, the optimal exercise boundary. From a mathematical perspective, the definition of optimal exercise boundary identifies a free boundary problem whose solution must be determined numerically. For instance, Kim [4] showed that the early exercise boundary of an American put option is the solution of the integral equation having the form (1).

Among others, the authors in [5,6], Barone-Adesi, Whaley [7], Bunch et al. [8], Aitsahlia and Lai [9,10] considered integral equations and/or the optimal stopping problem for pricing American options. The integral representation proposed by Kim gives a suggestive economic interpretation, but a closed-form solution for these kind of problems is not available. In particular, Kim's equation ([4]) contains a double integral due to the presence of a cumulative normal distribution term. To avoid such a problem, the authors in [11,12] suggested a transformation of the original equation in order to reduce it to an one-dimensional integral equation and afterwards consider its numerical solution. The early exercise boundary shows some kind of singularity near expiration (see, e.g., [13,14]). Considering the numerical approximation problem of the early boundary exercise for the American put, there have been more efforts in recent years. The authors in[15] proposed a four-point extrapolation scheme. Bunch and Johnson [8] proposed a modified version of the two-point extrapolation scheme of Geske and Johnson. Broadie and Detemple [16] suggested a lower and upper bound approximation method. The authors in [17] showed the exponential function method combined with a three-point Richardson extrapolation. Starting from an integral equation representation for the early boundary exercise, the authors in [12] used an iteration method. The authors in [18] proposed trapezoidal formulas approximations combined with the Newton–Raphson iteration. In [19], the authors solved a variational inequality representation of the American put option pricing problem by applying the projected successive over-relaxation method. The authors in [20] suggested an analytical expression to the value of American put options and their optimal exercise boundary. The authors in [21] derived a local iterative numerical scheme based on a solution of the integral equation proposed by [13]. More recently, Nedaiasl et al. [22], starting from the cited one-dimensional reformulation of Kim's integral equations, obtained the numerical solution by using a modified version of the Nyström method in order to take into account the singularity near expiry presented by the early exercise boundary. Besides the method of Zhu [20] and others involving semianalytical approximations that are not cited for the brevity of treatment, in the American option pricing literature, numerical methods aim to numerically solve the integral equations describing the early exercise boundary. We proceed in the latter direction.

More recently, some research studies applied the integral equation approach to deal with particular financial evaluations. For instance, the authors in [23] exploited the Mellin's transform aiming to provide an integral representation for the barrier option price. In [24], the authors gave an integral equation representation for a two-free-boundaries problem arising in the American better-of option on two assets.

In the present work, using a very simplified approach, we straightforward solve the nonstandard Volterra integral equation of the form (1). In more detail, using the mean-value theorem for integrals, we provide a flexible algorithm that allows for reaching a more accurate numerical solution with fewer calculations rather than other previously described methods.

The paper is organized as follows. In Section 2, we propose our numerical method for nonstandard Volterra integral equations. In Section 3, such a method is applied to the case of the American put. In Section 4, we present some numerical results confirming the accuracy of the proposed method. Lastly, in Section 5 we show the conclusions.

2. A New Numerical Scheme for Nonstandard Volterra Integral Equations

Let us fix interval $I = [0, T]$ where $T > 0$ and consider the following nonstandard Volterra integral equation:

$$\phi(t) = f(t, \phi(t)) + \int_0^t k(t, s)\psi\Big(t, s, \phi(t), \phi(s)\Big)\, ds, \qquad (2)$$

with $t \in I = [0, T]$, where the kernel function k is continuous in $I \times I$, ψ is continuous in $I \times I \times \mathbb{R} \times \mathbb{R}$.

Let n be a positive integer, and let us consider the following partition Γ of the interval $[0, T]$ into n intervals of equal length $\Delta = T/n$:

$$0 = t_0 < t_1 < t_2 < \cdots < t_{n-1} < t_n = T. \tag{3}$$

Let us consider Equation (2). By means of the additive properties for integrals, we can rewrite for each t_i, $i = 1, 2, \ldots, n$ Equation (2) in the following way:

$$\phi(t_i) = f(t_i, \phi(t_i)) + \sum_{m=1}^{i} \int_{t_{m-1}}^{t_m} k(t_i, s)\psi\Big(t_i, s, \phi(t_i), \phi(s)\Big)\, ds. \tag{4}$$

The following result holds.

Proposition 1. *Let:*

(a)   *Function $k(t, s)$ be continuous such that it never changes sign for all $(t, s) \in I \times I$. Let $L > 0$ be a constant such that $|k(t, s)| \le L$ for each $(t, s) \in I \times I$.*
(b)   *Function $\phi(s)$ be continuous in I.*
(c)   *Function $\psi(t, s, x, y)$ be continuous in $I \times I \times \mathbb{R} \times \mathbb{R}$.*

Then, for each $m = 1, 2 \ldots, i$, the following approximation holds:

$$\int_{t_{m-1}}^{t_m} k(t_i, s)\psi\Big(t_i, s, \phi(t_i), \phi(s)\Big)\, ds =$$

$$= \frac{1}{2}\psi\Big(t_i, t_{m-1}, \phi(t_i), \phi(t_{m-1})\Big) \int_{t_{m-1}}^{t_m} k(t_i, s)\, ds +$$

$$+ \frac{1}{2}\psi\Big(t_i, t_m, \phi(t_i), \phi(t_m)\Big) \int_{t_{m-1}}^{t_m} k(t_i, s)\, ds + \epsilon_{m,i}, \tag{5}$$

where error $|\epsilon_{m,i}|$ satisfies $|\epsilon_{m,i}| \le h_m/(2n)$, with h_m a constant, and $\epsilon_{m,i} \to 0$ for $n \to \infty$.

Proof. Using the mean value theorem for integrals, it follows that

$$\int_{t_{m-1}}^{t_m} k(t_i, s)\psi\Big(t_i, s, \phi(t_i), \phi(s)\Big)\, ds = \psi\Big(t_i, \xi_m, \phi(t_i), \phi(\xi_m)\Big) \int_{t_{m-1}}^{t_m} k(t_i, s)\, ds,$$

where ξ_m is, for each m, a number belonging to the interval $[t_{m-1}, t_m]$. It follows

$$\int_{t_{m-1}}^{t_m} k(t_i, s)\psi\Big(t_i, s, \phi(t_i), \phi(s)\Big)\, ds = \frac{1}{2}\psi\Big(t_i, t_{m-1}, \phi(t_i), \phi(t_{m-1})\Big) \int_{t_{m-1}}^{t_m} k(t_i, s)\, ds +$$

$$+ \frac{1}{2}\psi\Big(t_i, t_m, \phi(t_i), \phi(t_m)\Big) \int_{t_{m-1}}^{t_m} k(t_i, s)\, ds - \frac{1}{2}\psi\Big(t_i, t_{m-1}, \phi(t_i), \phi(t_{m-1})\Big) \int_{t_{m-1}}^{t_m} k(t_i, s)\, ds +$$

$$- \frac{1}{2}\psi\Big(t_i, t_m, \phi(t_i), \phi(t_m)\Big) \int_{t_{m-1}}^{t_m} k(t_i, s)\, ds + \frac{1}{2}\psi\Big(t_i, \xi_m, \phi(t_i), \phi(\xi_m)\Big) \int_{t_{m-1}}^{t_m} k(t_i, s)\, ds +$$

$$+ \frac{1}{2}\psi\Big(t_i, \xi_m, \phi(t_i), \phi(\xi_m)\Big) \int_{t_{m-1}}^{t_m} k(t_i, s)\, ds. \tag{6}$$

Let us rearrange the elements in (6) in the following way:

$$\int_{t_{m-1}}^{t_m} k(t_i, s)\psi\Big(t_i, s, \phi(t_i), \phi(s)\Big)\, ds = \frac{1}{2}\psi\Big(t_i, t_{m-1}, \phi(t_i), \phi(t_{m-1})\Big) \int_{t_{m-1}}^{t_m} k(t_i, s)\, ds +$$

$$+ \frac{1}{2}\psi\Big(t_i, t_m, \phi(t_i), \phi(t_m)\Big) \int_{t_{m-1}}^{t_m} k(t_i, s)\, ds + \epsilon_{m,i}^{A} + \epsilon_{m,i}^{B}, \tag{7}$$

where we have set

$$\epsilon^A_{m,i} = \frac{1}{2}\left[\psi\Big(t_i, \xi_m, \phi(t_i), \phi(\xi_m)\Big) - \psi\Big(t_i, t_{m-1}, \phi(t_i), \phi(t_{m-1})\Big)\right]\int_{t_{m-1}}^{t_m} k(t_i, s)\, ds$$

and

$$\epsilon^B_{m,i} = \frac{1}{2}\left[\psi\Big(t_i, \xi_m, \phi(t_i), \phi(\xi_m)\Big) - \psi\Big(t_i, t_m, \phi(t_i), \phi(t_m)\Big)\right]\int_{t_{m-1}}^{t_m} k(t_i, s)\, ds.$$

Then, it follows that

$$|\epsilon^A_{m,i}| = \frac{1}{2}\left|\left[\psi\Big(t_i, \xi_m, \phi(t_i), \phi(\xi_m)\Big) - \psi\Big(t_i, t_{m-1}, \phi(t_i), \phi(t_{m-1})\Big)\right]\int_{t_{m-1}}^{t_m} k(t_i, s)\, ds\right| =$$

$$\frac{1}{2}\left|\psi\Big(t_i, \xi_m, \phi(t_i), \phi(\xi_m)\Big) - \psi\Big(t_i, t_{m-1}, \phi(t_i), \phi(t_{m-1})\Big)\right|\cdot\left|\int_{t_{m-1}}^{t_m} k(t_i, s)\, ds\right| \le$$

$$\frac{1}{2}\left|\psi\Big(t_i, \xi_m, \phi(t_i), \phi(\xi_m)\Big) - \psi\Big(t_i, t_{m-1}, \phi(t_i), \phi(t_{m-1})\Big)\right|\cdot\int_{t_{m-1}}^{t_m} \big|k(t_i, s)\big|\, ds \le$$

$$\frac{1}{2}\left|\psi\Big(t_i, \xi_m, \phi(t_i), \phi(\xi_m)\Big) - \psi\Big(t_i, t_{m-1}, \phi(t_i), \phi(t_{m-1})\Big)\right|\cdot\frac{TL}{n} = \frac{h^A_{m,i}}{2n},$$

where $h^A_{m,i}$ is a positive constant because the argument in modulus is a number for each m and for any fixed t_i.

As $n \to \infty$, it follows $\epsilon^A_{m,i} \to 0$, and the same considerations apply to $\epsilon^B_{m,i}$ with a positive constant $h^B_{m,i}$. If we consider the sum $\epsilon_{m,i} = \epsilon^A_{m,i} + \epsilon^B_{m,i}$, it follows $\epsilon_{m,i} \to 0$, as $n \to \infty$.

In addition, it follows easily that $|\epsilon_{m,i}| \le h_{m,i}/(2n)$, with $h_{m,i} = h^A_{m,i} + h^B_{m,i}$. $\quad\square$

Remark. *If we consider Equation (4), it follows, through Proposition 1 for each fixed t_i, that*

$$\sum_{m=1}^{i}\int_{t_{m-1}}^{t_m} k(t_i, s)\psi\Big(t_i, s, \phi(t_i), \phi(s)\Big)\, ds =$$

$$= \frac{1}{2}\sum_{m=1}^{i}\left[\psi\Big(t_i, t_{m-1}, \phi(t_i), \phi(t_{m-1})\Big)\int_{t_{m-1}}^{t_m} k(t_i, s),\, ds +\right.$$

$$\left. + \psi\Big(t_i, t_m, \phi(t_i), \phi(t_m)\Big)\int_{t_{m-1}}^{t_m} k(t_i, s),\, ds\right] + \epsilon_i,$$

where

$$\epsilon_i = \sum_{m=1}^{i}\epsilon_{m,i}.$$

From Proposition 1, it is easy to check that: $|\epsilon_i| \le H/(2n)$, with $H = \sum_{m=1}^{i} h_{m,i}$. It is straightforward to notice that $\epsilon_i \to 0$ for $n \to \infty$.

We provide the following algorithm in order to find the numerical solution.

Step 1. *Let n be a positive integer. Let us consider the following partition Γ of interval $[0, T]$ into n intervals of equal length $\Delta = T/n$:*

$$0 = t_0 < t_1 < t_2 < \cdots < t_{n-1} < t_n = T.$$

If Proposition 1 is verified, and from the additive property for integrals, for each t_i, with $i = 0, 1, 2, \ldots, n$, we can rewrite Equation (2) in the following way:

$$\phi(t_i) = f(t_i, \phi(t_i)) + \frac{1}{2}\left[\sum_{m=1}^{i} \psi\left(t_i, t_{m-1}, \phi(t_i), \phi(t_{m-1})\right) \int_{t_{m-1}}^{t_m} k(t_i, s)\, ds + \right.$$
$$\left. + \psi\left(t_i, t_m, \phi(t_i), \phi(t_m)\right) \int_{t_{m-1}}^{t_m} k(t_i, s)\, ds \right] \tag{8}$$

Step 2. *We observe that*

$$\phi(t_0) = f(t_0, \phi(t_0)) + \int_{t_0}^{t_0} k(t_0, s)\psi\left(t_0, s, \phi(t_0), \phi(s)\right) ds = f(t_0, \phi(t_0)). \tag{9}$$

Then, for $i = 0, \ldots, n$ we consider the following nonlinear system.

$$\begin{cases}
\phi(t_0) = f(t_0, \phi(t_0)), \\[4pt]
\phi(t_1) = f(t_1, \phi(t_1)) + \frac{1}{2}\left[\psi\left(t_1, t_0, \phi(t_1), \phi(t_0)\right) \int_{t_0}^{t_1} k(t_1, s)\, ds + \right. \\[4pt]
\qquad \left. + \psi\left(t_1, t_1, \phi(t_1), \phi(t_1)\right) \int_{t_0}^{t_1} k(t_1, s)\, ds \right], \\[8pt]
\phi(t_2) = f(t_2, \phi(t_2)) + \frac{1}{2}\left[\sum_{m=1}^{2} \psi\left(t_2, t_{m-1}, \phi(t_2), \phi(t_{m-1})\right) \int_{t_{m-1}}^{t_m} k(t_2, s)\, ds + \right. \\[4pt]
\qquad \left. + \psi\left(t_2, t_m, \phi(t_2), \phi(t_m)\right) \int_{t_{m-1}}^{t_m} k(t_2, s)\, ds \right], \\[4pt]
\vdots \\[4pt]
\phi(t_n) = f(t_n, \phi(t_n)) + \frac{1}{2}\left[\sum_{m=1}^{n} \psi\left(t_n, t_{m-1}, \phi(t_n), \phi(t_{m-1})\right) \int_{t_{m-1}}^{t_m} k(t_n, s)\, ds + \right. \\[4pt]
\qquad \left. + \psi(t_n, t_{m-1}, \phi(t_n), \phi(t_m)) \int_{t_{m-1}}^{t_m} k(t_n, s)\, ds \right].
\end{cases} \tag{10}$$

The above nonlinear system is solved with a numerical method that provides the approximate solution $\{\tilde{\phi}(t_0), \tilde{\phi}(t_2), \ldots, \tilde{\phi}(t_n)\}$.

3. Approaching the American Put Pricing Problem

Let us assume the asset price process $\{S(t), t \geq 0\}$ following the log-normal distribution of the form

$$dS_t = (r - \delta)S_t\, dt + \sigma S_t\, dW_t, \tag{11}$$

where W_t is the standard Wiener process, r is the constant interest rate, and δ is the dividend yield. For the aim of the present work, we follow [25] assuming that the volatility term, σ, is constant. The latter is a simplifying hypothesis, and Equation (11) can be generalized considering nonconstant volatility, as in [26]. In this case, the boundary problem is represented by a multidimensional Volterra integral equation involving more complicated integrals (see, e.g., [27]). We leave the nonconstant volatility problem to future research works.

Let us consider the interval $I = [0, T]$. We denote with $\Phi(\cdot)$ the standard cumulative normal distribution function. Let us denote with $\mathcal{B}(t)$ the early exercise boundary of an American put option, where $t \in I$. Let P the price of an American put. The authors in [28] proved the existence and uniqueness of the pair $(P, \mathcal{B})$, and the continuity and monotonic behaviour of $\mathcal{B}$. In [4], the authors showed that $\mathcal{B}(t)$, as a function of time to expiration, satisfies the following weakly singular Volterra integral equation:

$$K - \mathcal{B}(t) = Ke^{-rt}\Phi\left(-\frac{\log\left(\frac{\mathcal{B}(t)}{K}\right) + (r - \delta - \frac{\sigma^2}{2})t}{\sigma\sqrt{t}}\right) +$$

$$-\mathcal{B}(t)e^{-\delta t}\Phi\left(-\frac{\log\left(\frac{\mathcal{B}(t)}{K}\right) + (r - \delta + \frac{\sigma^2}{2})t}{\sigma\sqrt{t}}\right) +$$

$$+Kr\int_0^t e^{-r(t-s)}\Phi\left(-\frac{\log\left(\frac{\mathcal{B}(t)}{\mathcal{B}(s)}\right) + (r - \delta - \frac{\sigma^2}{2})(t-s)}{\sigma\sqrt{t-s}}\right)ds +$$

$$-\delta\mathcal{B}(t)\int_0^t e^{-\delta(t-s)}\Phi\left(-\frac{\log\left(\frac{\mathcal{B}(t)}{\mathcal{B}(s)}\right) + (r - \delta + \frac{\sigma^2}{2})(t-s)}{\sigma\sqrt{t-s}}\right)ds, \tag{12}$$

where K is the exercise price.

In Equation (12), let us consider the two integrals and in particular the two functions $k_1(t,s) = e^{-r(t-s)}$ and $k_2(t,s) = e^{-\delta(t-s)}$. It is easy to check that $k_1(t,s)$ and $k_2(t,s)$, for any $(t,s) \in I \times I$, satisfy Proposition 1 with $L = 1$.

We apply the algorithm presented in Section 2. Let us consider the following result.

Proposition 2. *Assume that the asset price, S_t, follows a log-normal distribution process of the form $dS_t = (r - \delta)S_t dt + \sigma S_t dW_t$, in which W_t is the standard Wiener process.*

Let $\mathcal{B}(t)$ be the solution of Integral Equation (12). Then, $\mathcal{B}(t)$ is a continuously differentiable function on $(0, T]$ and

- *for $r \leq \delta$:*

$$\lim_{t \to 0} \mathcal{B}(t) = K; \tag{13}$$

- *for $r > \delta$:*

$$\lim_{t \to 0} \mathcal{B}(t) = \frac{r}{\delta}K. \tag{14}$$

Proof. See [4]. □

For our purposes, let us rewrite Equation (12) in contract form:

$$\mathcal{B}(t) = K - f(t, \mathcal{B}(t)) - rK\int_0^t e^{-r(t-s)}\Phi\left(-d_2(t,s,\mathcal{B}(t),\mathcal{B}(s))\right)ds +$$
$$+\delta\mathcal{B}(t)\int_0^t e^{-\delta(t-s)}\Phi\left(-d_1(t,s,\mathcal{B}(t),\mathcal{B}(s))\right)ds, \tag{15}$$

where

- $f(t, \mathcal{B}(t)) = Ke^{-rt}\Phi\left(-\frac{\log\left(\frac{\mathcal{B}(t)}{K}\right) + (r - \delta - \frac{\sigma^2}{2})t}{\sigma\sqrt{t}}\right) - \mathcal{B}(t)e^{-\delta t}\Phi\left(-\frac{\log\left(\frac{\mathcal{B}(t)}{K}\right) + (r - \delta + \frac{\sigma^2}{2})t}{\sigma\sqrt{t}}\right);$

- $d_1(t,s,\mathcal{B}(t),\mathcal{B}(s)) = \frac{\log\left(\frac{\mathcal{B}(t)}{\mathcal{B}(s)}\right) + (r - \delta + \frac{\sigma^2}{2})(t-s)}{\sigma\sqrt{t-s}};$

- $d_2(t,s,\mathcal{B}(t),\mathcal{B}(s)) = \frac{\log\left(\frac{\mathcal{B}(t)}{\mathcal{B}(s)}\right) + (r - \delta - \frac{\sigma^2}{2})(t-s)}{\sigma\sqrt{t-s}}.$

Let n be a positive integer. Let us consider the following partition Γ of the interval $[0, T]$ into n intervals of equal length $\Delta = T/n$:

$$0 = t_0 < t_1 < t_2 < \cdots < t_{n-1} < t_n = T.$$

For each t_i, with $i = 0, 1, 2, \ldots, n$, using the additive property of integral, let us rewrite Equation (15) in this way:

$$\mathcal{B}(t_i) = K - f(t_i, \mathcal{B}(t_i)) + \sum_{m=1}^{i} \left[-rK \int_{t_{m-1}}^{t_m} e^{-r(t_i-s)} \Phi\Big(-d_2(t_i, s, \mathcal{B}(t_i), \mathcal{B}(s)) \Big) \, ds + \right.$$
$$\left. + \delta \mathcal{B}(t) \int_{t_{m-1}}^{t_m} e^{-\delta(t_i-s)} \Phi\Big(-d_1(t_i, s, \mathcal{B}(t_i), \mathcal{B}(s)) \Big) \, ds \right]. \quad (16)$$

Proposition 3. *For the two integrals appearing in Equation (16), the following equalities hold:*

$$\int_{t_{m-1}}^{t_m} e^{-r(t_i-s)} \Phi\Big(-d_2(t_i, s, \mathcal{B}(t_i), \mathcal{B}(s)) \Big) \, ds =$$
$$= \frac{1}{2} \Phi\Big(-d_2(t_i, t_{m-1}, \mathcal{B}(t_i), \mathcal{B}(t_{m-1})) \Big) \int_{t_{m-1}}^{t_m} e^{-r(t_i-s)} \, ds + \quad (17)$$
$$+ \frac{1}{2} \Phi\Big(-d_2(t_i, t_m, \mathcal{B}(t_i), \mathcal{B}(t_m)) \Big) \int_{t_{m-1}}^{t_m} e^{-r(t_i-s)} \, ds + \epsilon_{m,i}^A$$

and

$$\int_{t_{m-1}}^{t_m} e^{-\delta(t_i-s)} \Phi\Big(-d_1(t_i, s, \mathcal{B}(t_i), \mathcal{B}(s)) \Big) \, ds =$$
$$= \frac{1}{2} \Phi\Big(-d_1(t_i, t_{m-1}, \mathcal{B}(t_i), \mathcal{B}(t_{m-1})) \Big) \int_{t_{m-1}}^{\zeta_m} e^{-\delta(t_i-s)} \, ds + \quad (18)$$
$$+ \frac{1}{2} \Phi\Big(-d_1(t_i, t_m, \mathcal{B}(t_i), \mathcal{B}(t_m)) \Big) \int_{t_{m-1}}^{t_m} e^{-\delta(t_i-s)} \, ds + \epsilon_{m,i}^B,$$

where $\epsilon_{m,i}^A$ and $\epsilon_{m,i}^B$ are the errors as defined in Proposition 1.

Proof. The result follows immediately from the continuity of Φ and $\mathcal{B}$ and by means of Proposition 1. $\square$

Equation (12) represents a nonstandard Volterra integral equation of the second kind having the form (1). We solve it by using of the method described in Section 2. By applying this method, when $s = t_i$, the indeterminate form

$$\Phi\left(-\frac{\log\left(\frac{\mathcal{B}(t_i)}{\mathcal{B}(t_i)}\right) + (r - \delta - \frac{\sigma^2}{2})(t_i - t_i)}{\sigma\sqrt{t_i - t_i}} \right) = \Phi\left(\frac{0}{0} \right) \quad (19)$$

arises. Observing that

$$\lim_{s \to t^-} \Phi\left(-\frac{\log\left(\frac{\mathcal{B}(t)}{\mathcal{B}(s)}\right) + (r - \delta - \frac{\sigma^2}{2})(t - s)}{\sigma\sqrt{t - s}} \right) = \frac{1}{2}, \quad (20)$$

we can define the continuous function

$$\Phi\left(-\frac{\log\left(\frac{u(t)}{u(s)}\right) + (r - \delta - \frac{\sigma^2}{2})(t - s)}{\sigma\sqrt{t - s}} \right) = \begin{cases} \Phi\left(-\frac{\log\left(\frac{u(t)}{u(s)}\right) + (r - \delta - \frac{\sigma^2}{2})(t-s)}{\sigma\sqrt{t-s}} \right) \iff 0 \le s < t \\ \frac{1}{2} \iff t = s. \end{cases}$$

The same considerations apply to

$$\Phi\left(-\frac{\log\left(\frac{u(t)}{u(s)}\right) + (r - \delta + \frac{\sigma^2}{2})(t - s)}{\sigma\sqrt{t - s}} \right).$$

Using aforementioned notations, from the numerical approximation of the early boundary exercise, the price of the American put may be found by means of the following formula:

$$P(t, S) = f(t, S) + rK \int_0^t e^{-r(t-s)} \Phi(-d_2(t, s, S, \mathcal{B}(s))) \, ds +$$
$$- \delta S \int_0^t e^{-\delta(t-s)} \Phi(-d_1(t, s, S, \mathcal{B}(s))) \, ds. \tag{21}$$

In Equation (21), S represents the current price of the underlying asset (see [4]). The authors in [29] showed that the value of American options can be written as the sum of the corresponding European option price and the early exercise premium. Equation (21) lends itself to this interpretation being $f(t, S)$ the price of an European put.

4. Numerical Results

In this section, we present some numerical results showing the accuracy of the approximations computed by means of the pricing model presented in Sections 2 and 3. We denote by T the time expressed in year, and the interest rate, dividend yield, and volatility are expressed on an annual basis. The results were obtained using MATLAB on a MacBook Pro with a 2.6 GHz Intel Core i7 processor with 16 GB RAM. We considered $n = 110$ steps. The required computational time was about 9 s. The nonlinear system of equations of the form (10), arising in the problem discussed in Section 3, was solved applying the Broyden's method, a quasi-Newtonian method.

The obtained approximated values of $\mathcal{B}(t)$ are plotted in Figure 1 for several values of σ. We chose $S = K = 100$, $T = 2$, $r = 0.05$, $\delta = 0$ and $\sigma = 0.2, 0.40, 0.60$.

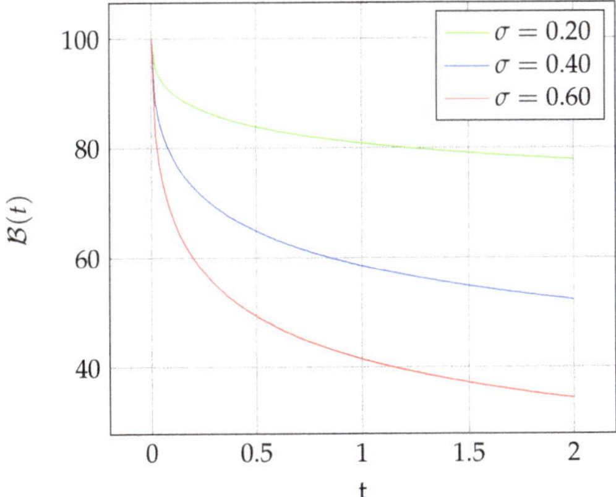

Figure 1. The numerical approximation of $\mathcal{B}(t)$: $K = 100$, $T = 2$, $r = 0.05$, $\delta = 0$ and $\sigma = 0.2, 0.40, 0.60$.

For several values of δ, the obtained values of $\mathcal{B}(t)$ are, instead, plotted in Figure 2. We chose $S = K = 100$, $T = 2$, $r = 0.05$, $\sigma = 0.2$ and $\delta = 0.05, 0.10, 0.15$.

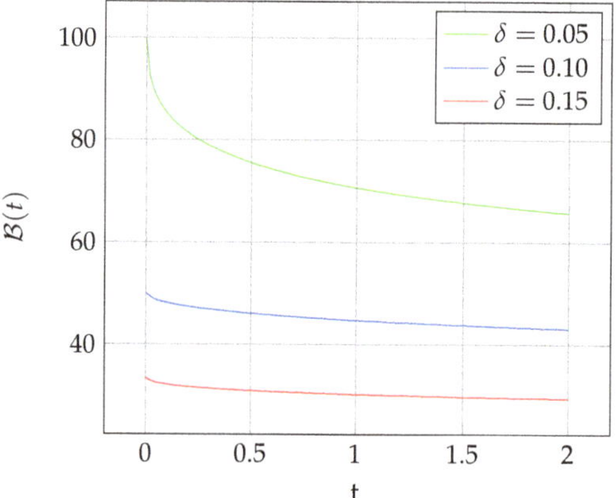

Figure 2. The numerical approximation of $\mathcal{B}(t)$: $K = 100$, $T = 2$, $r = 0.05$, $\sigma = 0.2$ and $\delta = 0.05, 0.10, 0.15$.

The numerical approximation of $\mathcal{B}(t)$ gained from our method was applied to (21); consequently, the trapezoidal numerical integration rule was engaged to calculate the price of an American put. The outcome values were compared with the benchmarks ones, stemming from a binomial tree with $n = 10{,}000$ time steps.

Table 1 displays values of the American put achieved through benchmarks methods. All the considered methods are able to produce an approximation of the boundary. In particular, the Cox, Ross and Rubenstein model ([30]), namely, C-R-R in the first column of Table 1, with $n = 10{,}000$ time steps (C-R-R), is considered. The second column contains the American put prices corresponding to different approximated values of $\mathcal{B}(t)$ using the four-point extrapolation scheme of [15], namely, G-J. The third column of Table 1 reports the modified two-point method of [8], namely, B-J. The fourth column embeds values stemming from the lower and upper bound approximation of [16], indicated as B-D. The fifth column, namely, Ju, shows the exponential functions method combined with a three-point Richardson extrapolation proposed by [17]. In addition, the iteration method proposed by [12] was considered and it is identified as K-J-K. Values within the seventh column in Table 1 represents the trapezoidal formulas approximations of [18] followed by the Newton–Raphson iteration, namely, K-K. N-B-R refers to the more recently product integration method for the approximation of the early boundary in the American option pricing problem exposed in [22]. Lastly, the last column in Table 1, indicated as D-M-M-V, represents the mean-value theorem approach that we proposed in this work.

In Table 1, we considered S as in first column, $T = 3$, $\sigma = 0.2$, $r = 0.08$, $K = 100$ and $\delta = 0.08$ and $n = 32$. The benchmark values in the first column stem from a binomial tree (C-R-R model) with $n = 10{,}000$ time steps. For ease of reading, we underlined the best approximations.

The proposed numerical approach employs about 0.66 s to compute $n = 32$ points. It is worth underlining that approximations attained with our method are coherent or even better compared to the similar stemming from benchmark methods. The only exception holds for approximations obtained by [22]. Table 2 shows results from our proposal compared to the ones [22] considering, for D-M-M-V method, $n = 110$ points.

Table 1. Numerical approximations of American put price: S as in the first column, $T = 3$, $\sigma = 0.2$, $r = 0.08$, $K = 100$, $\delta = 0.08$, and $n = 32$. For each value of S, the resulting approximation errors are displayed in the second rows within brackets. Some data in Table 1 were extracted from [22]; in addition, underlined values represent approximated prices to which the lowest error corresponds.

S	C-R-R	G-J	B-J	B-D	Ju	K-J-K	K-K	N-B-R	D-M-M-V
80	22.2050	22.2079	22.7106	22.1985	22.2084	22.1942	22.1900	<u>22.2048</u>	22.2075
	(-)	(2.9×10^{-3})	(5.1×10^{-1})	(6.5×10^{-3})	(3.4×10^{-3})	(1.1×10^{-2})	(1.5×10^{-2})	(2×10^{-4})	(2.5×10^{-3})
90	16.2071	16.1639	16.5205	16.1986	16.2106	16.1999	16.1960	<u>16.2068</u>	16.2096
	(-)	(4.3×10^{-2})	(3.6×10^{-1})	(5.9×10^{-2})	(7.2×10^{-3})	(1.1×10^{-2})	(3.9×10^{-3})	(1.1×10^{-4})	(2.5×10^{-3})
100	11.7037	11.7053	11.8106	11.6988	11.7066	11.6991	11.6958	<u>11.7037</u>	11.7061
	(-)	(1.6×10^{-3})	(1.1×10^{-1})	(4.9×10^{-3})	(2.9×10^{-3})	(4.9×10^{-3})	(7.9×10^{-3})	(1.0×10^{-5})	(4.4×10^{-3})
110	8.3671	8.3886	8.4072	8.3630	8.3695	8.3638	8.3613	<u>8.3669</u>	8.3689
	(-)	(2.1×10^{-2})	(4.0×10^{-2})	(4.1×10^{-3})	(2.4×10^{-3})	(3.3×10^{-3})	(5.8×10^{-3})	(2.0×10^{-4})	(1.8×10^{-3})
120	5.9299	5.9435	5.9310	5.9261	5.9323	5.9278	5.9258	<u>5.9298</u>	5.9314
	(-)	(1.4×10^{-2})	(1.1×10^{-3})	(3.8×10^{-3})	(2.4×10^{-3})	(2.1×10^{-3})	(4.1×10^{-3})	(1.0×10^{-4})	(1.5×10^{-3})

Table 2. Comparison between N-B-R and D-M-M-V: S as in the first column, $T = 3$, $\sigma = 0.2$, $r = 0.08$, $K = 100$ and $\delta = 0.08$. The benchmark value was obtained considering the C-R-R model with $n = 10{,}000$ time steps. For each value of S, the resulting approximation errors are displayed in the second rows within brackets.

S	C-R-R	N-B-R	D-M-M-V
80	22.2050	22.2048	22.2051
	(-)	(2.0×10^{-4})	(1.0×10^{-4})
90	16.2071	16.2068	16.2072
	(-)	(1.1×10^{-4})	(1.0×10^{-4})
100	11.7037	11.7037	11.7040
	(-)	(1.0×10^{-5})	(3.0×10^{-4})
110	8.3671	8.3669	8.3672
	(-)	(2.0×10^{-4})	(1.0×10^{-4})
120	5.9299	5.9299	5.9299
	(-)	(1.0×10^{-4})	(1.0×10^{-4})

As Table 2 shows, the approximations obtained with our method were coherent with the ones obtained by applying the method in [22]. The resulting errors in the second rows for each value of S were very small and comparable with that relative to the N-B-R method. In particular, [22] numerically solved the one-dimensional reformulation of Kim's integral equations ([11]) using a modified version of the Nyström method. Such a procedure allows for taking into account the singularity close to expiry presented by the early exercise boundary. In our method, instead, we directly dealt with Equation (15). In addition, our method may be easily extended to integral equations coming from more complicated dynamics.

In [22], taking into account $n = 32$ points, an error of range of 10^{-4} was obtained in about 14 s. Their calculations were performed on a PC with a 4.00 Intel Core i7 GHz processor with 16 GB RAM (see Figures 3–6 as reported by [22]). With our algorithm, also considering $n = 110$ points, we obtained an error of the same range in about 9 s. Moreover, our calculations were performed using a machine with a less powerful processor, a MacBook Pro with a 2.6 GHz Intel Core i7 processor with 16 GB of RAM. To test the convergence of our algorithm, we report in Table 3 some values of the American put corresponding to as many as the approximated values of $\mathcal{B}(t)$. We considered: $S = K = 100$, $T = 1$, $r = 0.08$, $\sigma = 0.2$ and $\delta = 0.08$. In Column 1, we report the time steps. The errors were computed as the difference between our values (D-D-M-V) with the ones obtained considering a binomial tree (C-R-R) model with $n = 10{,}000$ used as a benchmark. The error size of order 10^{-4} obtained when increasing the value of n proves the quality and the precision of the proposed method.

Table 3. Convergence analysis in approximating the American put price. The benchmark value, equal to 7.5009, stems from a binomial tree (C-R-R model) with $n = 10{,}000$ steps. We considered $S = K = 100$, $T = 1$, $r = \delta = 0.08$, $\sigma = 0.2$.

n	D-D-M-V	Error
10	7.5059	0.0050
20	7.5028	0.0019
30	7.5020	0.0011
40	7.5017	8.0×10^{-4}
90	7.5012	3.0×10^{-4}
110	7.5012	1.0×10^{-4}

5. Conclusions

The present work proposed a new numerical method for the approximation of the early exercise boundary of an American option. American options are financial contracts allowing for the holder to buy or sell an underlying financial asset before the contract expiration. Thus, the evaluation of an American option requires to consider that the holder may have convenience to interrupt the contract at any time depending on the value of the underlying asset; that is, a collection of optimal exercise prices, one for each optimal exercise time, must be determined. Representing such a boundary by means of a nonstandard Volterra integral equation, we propose a numerical scheme in order to approximate the solution of the free boundary problem concerning the American option. Our proposal allows for managing well-known numerical problems arising in the presence of a singularity close to expiry and of a double integral. First, we provided theoretical instruments that were at the core of the proposed method. Consequently, we compared existing pricing models with results stemming from our method, showing the accuracy of the latter. The direct solution of the integral equation suggests that our method can be applied to more complicated cases coming up in finance.

Future research works will concern the use of an asset price process characterized by a nonconstant volatility term. In particular, we aim to expand our proposal to the case of the Heston model for American options, considering the associated multidimensional Volterra integral equation for the boundary problem.

Author Contributions: Conceptualization, D.V., R.D.M., M.M. and A.L.M. The authors contributed equally to this work. All authors have read and agreed to the published version of the manuscript.

Funding: This research received no external funding.

Data Availability Statement: Not applicable.

References

1. Wazwaz, A.M. *Linear and Nonlinear Integral Equations*; Springer: Berlin, Germany, 2011.
2. Brunner, H. Volterra Integral Equations: An Introduction to Theory and Applications. In *Cambridge Monographs on Applied and Computational Mathematics*; Cambridge University Press: Cambridge, UK, 2017; No. 30.

3. Brunner, H. *Collocation Methods for Volterra Integral and Related Functional Differential Equations*; Cambridge University Press: Cambridge, UK, 2004; Volume 15.
4. Kim, I.J. The Analytic Valuation of American Options. *Rev. Financ. Stud.* **1990**, *3*, 547–572.
5. Jacka, S.D. Optimal stopping and the American Put. *Math. Financ.* **1991**, *1*, 1–14 [CrossRef]
6. Carr, P.; Jarrow, R.; Myneni, R. Alternative characterizations of American put options. *Math. Financ.* **1992**, *2*, 87–106.
7. Barone-Adesi, G.; Whaley, R.E. Efficient analytic approximation of American option values. *J. Financ.* **1987**, *81*, 301–320. [CrossRef]
8. Bunch, D.S.; Johnson, H. A simple and numerically efficient valuation method for American puts using a modified, Geske-Johnson approach. *J. Financ.* **1992**, *47*, 809–816. [CrossRef]
9. Aitsahlia, F.; Lai, T.L. A canonical optimal stopping problem for American options and its numerical solution. *J. Comput. Financ.* **1999**, *3*, 33–52. [CrossRef]
10. Aitsahlia, F.; Lai, T.L. Exercise Boundaries and Efficient Approximations to American Option Prices and Hedge Parameters. *J. Comput. Financ.* **2001**, *4*, 85–104. [CrossRef]
11. Hou, C.; Little, T.; Pant, V. A new integral representation of the early exercise boundary for American put options. *J. Comput. Financ.* **2000**, *3*, 73–96.
12. Kim, I.J.; Jang, B.-G.; Kim, K.T. A simple iterative method for the valuation of American options. *Quant. Financ.* **2013**, *13*, 885–895. [CrossRef]
13. Stamicar, R.; Ševčovič, D.; Chadam, J. The early exercise boundary for the American put near expiry: Numerical approximation. *Can. Appl. Math Q.* **1999**, *7*, 427–444.
14. Evans, J.D.; Kuske, R.; Keller J.B. American options on assets with dividends near expiry. *Math. Financ.* **2002**, *12*, 219–237. [CrossRef]
15. Geske, R.; Johnson, H.E. The American put option valued analytically. *J. Financ.* **1984**, *39*, 1511–1524. [CrossRef]
16. Broadie, M.; Detemple, J. American option valuation: New bounds, approximations, and a comparison of existing methods. *Rev. Financ. Stud.* **1996**, *9*, 1211–1250. [CrossRef]
17. Ju, N. Pricing an American option by approximating its early exercise boundary as a multipiece exponential function. *Rev. Financ. Stud.* **1998**, *11*, 627–646. [CrossRef]
18. Kallast, S.; Kivinukk, A. Pricing and hedging American options using approximations by Kim integral equations. *Eur. Financ. Rev.* **2003**, *7*, 361–383. [CrossRef]
19. Elliott, C.M.; Ockendon, J.R. *Weak and Variational Methods for Free and Moving Boundary Problems (Research Notes in Mathematics)*; Pitman: London, UK, 1982; Volume 59.
20. Zhu, S.-P. A new analytical approximation formula for the optimal exercise boundary of American put options. *Int. J. Theor. Appl. Financ.* **2006**, *9*, 1141–1177. [CrossRef]
21. Lauko, M.; Ševčovič, D. Comparison of numerical and analytical approximations of the early exercise boundary of American put options. *J. ANZIAM* **2010**, *51*, 430–448. [CrossRef]
22. Nedaiasl, K.; Bastani, A.F.; Rafiee, A. A product integration method for the approximation of the early exercise boundary in the American option pricing problem. *Math. Meth. Appl. Sci.* **2019**, *42*, 2825–2841. [CrossRef]
23. Guardasoni, C.; Rodrigo, R.M.; Sanfelici, S. A Mellin transform approach to barrier option pricing. *IMA J. Manag. Math.* **2020**, *31*, 49–67. [CrossRef]
24. Jeon, J.; Kim, G. An integral equation representation for American better-of option on two underlying assets. *Adv. Contin. Discret. Model.* **2022**, *2022*, 39. [CrossRef]
25. Black, F.; Scholes, M. The pricing of options and corporate liabilities. *J. Political Econ.* **1973**, *81*, 637–654. [CrossRef]
26. Heston, S.L. A closed-form solution for options with stochastic volatility with applications to bond and currency options. *Rev. Financ. Stud.* **1993**, *6*, 327–343. [CrossRef]
27. Chiarella, C.; Ziogas, A.; Ziveyi, J. Representation of American Option Prices Under Heston Stochastic Volatility Dynamics Using Integral Transforms. In *Contemporary Quantitative Finance*; Chiarella, C., Novikov, A., Eds.; Springer: Berlin/Heidelberg, Germany, 2010.
28. Chen, X.; Chadam, J. A mathematical analysis of the optimal exercise boundary for American put options. *SIAM J. Math. Anal.* **2006**, *38*, 1613–1641. [CrossRef]
29. Detemple, J.; Tian, W. The valuation of American options for a class of diffusion processes *Manag. Sci.* **2002**, *48*, 917–937. [CrossRef]
30. Cox, J.C.; Ross, S.A.; Rubenstein, M. Option Pricing: A Simplified Approach. *J. Financ. Econ.* **1979**, *7*, 229–263. [CrossRef]

Article

ADI Method for Pseudoparabolic Equation with Nonlocal Boundary Conditions

Mifodijus Sapagovas [1,*], **Artūras Štikonas** [2] and **Olga Štikonienė** [2]

[1] Institute of Data Science and Digital Technologies, Vilnius University, Naugarduko Str. 24, LT-03225 Vilnius, Lithuania

[2] Institute of Applied Mathematics, Vilnius University, Naugarduko Str. 24, LT-03225 Vilnius, Lithuania; arturas.stikonas@mif.vu.lt (A.Š.); olga.stikoniene@mif.vu.lt (O.Š.)

* Correspondence: mifodijus.sapagovas@mif.vu.lt

Abstract: This paper deals with the numerical solution of nonlocal boundary-value problem for two-dimensional pseudoparabolic equation which arise in many physical phenomena. A three-layer alternating direction implicit method is investigated for the solution of this problem. This method generalizes Peaceman–Rachford's ADI method for the 2D parabolic equation. The stability of the proposed method is proved in the special norm. We investigate algebraic eigenvalue problem with nonsymmetric matrices to prove this stability. Numerical results are presented.

Keywords: pseudoparabolic equation; nonlocal conditions; finite difference method; ADI method; eigenvalue problem for difference operator

MSC: 35K70; 65N06; 65N12

Citation: Sapagovas, M.; Štikonas, A.; Štikonienė, O. ADI Method for Pseudoparabolic Equation with Nonlocal Boundary Conditions. *Mathematics* **2023**, *11*, 1303. https://doi.org/10.3390/math11061303

Academic Editor: Arsen Palestini

Received: 8 February 2023
Revised: 27 February 2023
Accepted: 7 March 2023
Published: 8 March 2023

1. Introduction and Formulation of the Problem

In the past decades, the solution of the boundary-value problems with nonlocal boundary conditions has been an important and intensively investigated research area of numerical analysis and applied mathematics. We consider the third-order linear pseudoparabolic equation ($\eta > 0$) with nonlocal integral conditions in the domain $D := (0, L_x) \times (0, L_y)$

$$\frac{\partial u}{\partial t} = \frac{\partial^2 u}{\partial x^2} + \frac{\partial^2 u}{\partial y^2} + \eta \frac{\partial}{\partial t} \left(\frac{\partial^2 u}{\partial x^2} + \frac{\partial^2 u}{\partial y^2} \right) + f(x, y, t), \quad (x, y, t) \in D \times (0, T], \tag{1}$$

subject to the initial and boundary conditions (BC)

$$u(0, y, t) = \gamma_0 \int_0^{L_x} u(x, y, t)\, \mathrm{d}x + v_l(y, t), \quad (y, t) \in [0, L_y] \times [0, T], \tag{2}$$

$$u(L_x, y, t) = \gamma_1 \int_0^{L_x} u(x, y, t)\, \mathrm{d}x + v_r(y, t), \quad (y, t) \in [0, L_y] \times [0, T], \tag{3}$$

$$u(x, 0, t) = v_b(x, t), \quad u(x, L_y, t) = v_t(x, t), \quad (x, t) \in [0, L_x] \times [0, T], \tag{4}$$

$$u(x, y, 0) = u^0(x, y), \quad (x, y) \in \bar{D} := [0, L_x] \times [0, L_y]. \tag{5}$$

We have local Dirichlet BCs (4) in the y-direction and integral nonlocal boundary conditions (NBC) (2) and (3) in the x-direction.

Local and nonlocal boundary-value problems for the pseudoparabolic equations are the subject of intensive studies and a topic of great practical and theoretical interest, because many applied problems in physics, mechanics, and biology can be modelled using such equations.

For example, in the paper [1] the one-dimensional pseudoparabolic equation

$$\frac{\partial u}{\partial t} - \frac{\partial^2 u}{\partial x^2} - \eta \frac{\partial^3 u}{\partial x^2 \partial t} = F(x,t,u), \tag{6}$$

$(x,t) \in (0,1) \times [0,T]$ subject to the initial conditions

$$u(x,0) = u_0(x), \qquad 0 \le x \le 1, \tag{7}$$

and to the integral conditions

$$\int_0^1 u(x,t)dx = E(t), \qquad \int_0^1 xu(x,t)dx = G(t), \qquad 0 \le t \le T, \tag{8}$$

was considered. From a physical point of view, the problem (6)–(8) can be interpreted in the context of soil thermophysics. In this sense, (6) describes the dynamics of moisture in a subsoil layer $0 < x < 1$, while (8) represent the moisture moments [1,2].

Equations of type (6) with variable coefficients and additional terms also have many other applications in various physical situations, for example, in the theory of the two temperatures [3], in the study of the aggregation of population [4], or in the diffusion of imprisoned resonant radiation through a gas [5].

Theoretical research of pseudoparabolic equations with NBCs was started due to its applications for complex problems of science and technology. One of the first results for the third-order pseudoparabolic equations with NBCs for problems of soil dampness dynamics was considered in [6] (see also [1,7]). In the paper [8], the global existence of the weak solution for pseudoparabolic equation with the nonlocal source was considered.

A number of papers devoted to underground water flow dynamics modelled by pseudoparabolic equations with NBCs were published later, see [9,10]. Implicit finite difference schemes (FDS) for linear or nonlinear pseudoparabolic equations with Dirichlet BCs were introduced in the early 1970s [11,12]. Numerical methods for pseudoparabolic equations with NBCs have been of permanent interest for researchers during the last decades. Numerical methods for solving a one-dimensional nonlinear pseudoparabolic equation with integral conditions were introduced in [13,14]. FDS for linear 1D and 2D pseudoparabolic equations with various integral conditions were investigated in [15–21]. A separate class of pseudoparabolic equations consists of fractional pseudoparabolic equations, which were recently intensively studied [22–24].

Motivated by the works mentioned above, we study a class of two-dimensional pseudoparabolic equations with integral conditions (1)–(5). The goal of this paper is to generalize and investigate the Peaceman–Rachford alternating direction implicit (ADI) method [25] for pseudoparabolic Equation (1) with NBCs (2)–(5).

For the investigation of the stability of the ADI method, we study the structure of the spectrum of the corresponding difference operator. The structure of the spectrum of the differential and difference operators in the case of various nonlocal conditions were investigated in many papers (see, for example, [26–29]). Note that the presence of an integral term in the boundary condition can complicate the theoretical investigation of the numerical method. In this case, the matrix of the system of the difference equations is not symmetric or positive definite. The structure of the spectrum of such matrix is more complicated (and more substantive and informative) even in the case of Dirichlet or Neumann boundary value conditions. Furthermore, this structure strongly depends not only on the type of boundary conditions, but also on values of the parameters (or functions) included in the boundary conditions.

The first articles about the ADI method for the two-dimensional parabolic equations ($\eta = 0$ in (1)) with NBCs showed that this method was also quite effective [30,31] in the case of NBC. In article [32], the proof of the stability of the ADI method for a parabolic equation was based on the analysis of the structure of the spectrum for a difference operator with nonlocal conditions. That approach was also relevant for the analysis of the convergence of the ADI method for elliptic equations with NBCs [33].

The presented ADI method is also suitable for solving an inverse problem for anomalous diffusion equation with a Riemann–Liouville derivative as well as parameter identification in fractional systems [34–36].

To the best of the authors' knowledge, for the first time, a splitting method for pseudoparabolic Equation (1) with Dirichlet BCs was researched in articles [37,38].

The paper is organized as follows. In Section 2, we introduce the three-layer ADI method. Section 3 is devoted to the eigenvalue problem and in Section 4, we prove the main result of the present paper: the stability of the obtained three-layer difference scheme. In Section 5 the results of the numerical experiment are presented to demonstrate the accuracy and effectiveness of the finite difference scheme.

2. Alternating Direction Implicit (ADI) Method

Our goal is to construct a finite difference scheme for the pseudoparabolic problem and investigate its stability. The Peaceman–Rachford ADI method is used for developing a new ADI scheme for the third-order pseudoparabolic equation with NBC. The ADI method was introduced in 1955 by D.W. Peaceman and H.H. Rachford [25] and J. Douglas and H.H. Rachford [39] as a technique for the numerical solution of elliptic and parabolic differential equations. The theoretical and practical aspects of the ADI method led to extensions, generalizations, and ensuing applications far beyond the original application of a reservoir simulation. The advantage of the ADI method is that the equations that have to be solved at each step have a simpler structure and can be solved efficiently with the tridiagonal matrix algorithm. The ADI method is a predictor–corrector scheme where part of the difference operator is implicit in the initial prediction step and another part is implicit in the final correction step.

2.1. Notation

According to the standard technique of solving such problems by discretizations, we investigate finite difference schemes. We introduce grids with uniform steps ($1 < N, M, L \subset \mathbb{N}$):

$$\overline{\omega}_x^h := \{x_0 = 0,\ x_1,\ \ldots,\ x_N = L_x\},\quad h_x = x_i - x_{i-1} = L_x/N,\ i = \overline{1, N};$$

$$\overline{\omega}_y^h := \{y_0 = 0,\ y_1,\ \ldots,\ y_M = L_y\},\quad h_y = y_j - y_{j-1} = L_y/M,\ j = \overline{1, M};$$

$$\overline{\omega}^\tau := \{t_0 = 0,\ t_1,\ \ldots,\ t_L = T\},\quad \tau = t_k - t_{k-1} = T/L,\ k = \overline{1, L};$$

$$\omega_{1/2}^\tau := \{t_{1/2},\ \ldots,\ t_{L-1/2}:\ t_{k-1/2} = (t_k + t_{k-1})/2,\ k = \overline{1, L}\};$$

$$\omega_x^h := \{x_1, \ldots, x_{N-1}\};\quad \omega_y^h := \{y_1, \ldots, y_{M-1}\};\quad \omega^\tau := \{t_1, \ldots, t_L\}.$$

We use the notation $U_{ij}^k := U(x_i, y_j, t_k)$ for functions defined on the grid (or parts of this grid) $\overline{\omega} \times \overline{\omega}^\tau$ and $U_{ij}^{k-1/2} := U(x_i, y_j, t_{k-1/2})$ on the grid $\overline{\omega} \times \omega_{1/2}^\tau$, where $\overline{\omega} := \overline{\omega}_x^h \times \overline{\omega}_y^h$. We omit indices if they are the same in the whole equation.

We use notation $\mathbb{M}_{k \times l}$ for the set of $k \times l$ matrices whose elements are real numbers, $k, l \in \mathbb{N}$. For any vector $\mathbf{u} \in \mathbb{M}_{m \times 1}$ and matrix $\mathbf{A} \in \mathbb{M}_{m \times m}$, discrete ℓ_2-norms are defined as

$$\|\mathbf{u}\|_2 = \left(\sum_{i=1}^m u_i^2 \right)^{1/2},\quad \|\mathbf{A}\|_2 = \left(\max_i |\lambda_i(\mathbf{A}^* \mathbf{A})| \right)^{1/2}, \tag{9}$$

where $\mathbf{A}^*$ is an adjoint matrix and $\lambda_i(\mathbf{A})$ are eigenvalues of the matrix $\mathbf{A}$.

For functions $U_i = U(x_i)$ on the grid $\overline{\omega}_x^h$, we use the notation:

$$\delta_x^2 U_i := \frac{U_{i-1} - 2U_i + U_{i+1}}{h_x^2},\quad (U, V) := \sum_{i=1}^{N-1} U_i V_i h_x$$

$$[U, V] := U_0 V_0 h_x / 2 + (U, V) + U_n V_n h_x / 2.$$

We introduce operators δ_x^2, δ_y^2 for a function on the grid $\overline{\omega}$:

$$\delta_x^2 U_{ij} := \frac{U_{i-1,j} - 2U_{ij} + U_{i+1,j}}{h_x^2}, \quad \delta_y^2 U_{ij} := \frac{U_{i,j-1} - 2U_{ij} + U_{i,j+1}}{h_y^2},$$

and for the approximation integrals in the NBC, we define

$$[U, V]_j := U_{0j} V_{0j} h_x/2 + (U, V)_j + U_{nj} V_{nj} h_x/2, \quad (U, V)_j := \sum_{i=1}^{N-1} U_{ij} V_{ij} h_x.$$

In a space H of grid functions $U_{ij} := U(x_i, y_j)$ on the grid $\omega_x^h \times \omega_y^h$, we introduce an inner product

$$(U, V)_H := \sum_{j=1}^{M-1} (U, V)_j h_y.$$

Each such function is related to matrix $\mathcal{U} = (U_{ij}) \in \mathbb{M}_{(N-1)\times(M-1)}$. We choose one of the most obvious orderings and set a vector

$$\mathbf{U} := (U_{11}, \dots, U_{N-1,1}, U_{12}, \dots, U_{N-1,M-1})^T = \text{vec}(\mathcal{U}) \in \mathbb{M}_{(N-1)(M-1)\times 1}$$

for $U \in H$.

2.2. The ADI Method

Before writing down the solution method, we note that while using any splitting method for pseudoparabolic Equation (1), a one term with the third-order derivative u_{txx} or u_{tyy} has to be approximated in a lower layer, and for that we need at least two layers for each term. Therefore, we cannot write two-layer splitting FDS for two-dimensional pseudoparabolic equation, because the smallest number of layers is three.

Let us write the ADI method for pseudoparabolic Equation (1)

$$\frac{U^{k+1/2} - U^k}{0.5\tau} = \delta_x^2 U^{k+1/2} + \delta_y^2 U^k$$
$$+ \frac{\eta}{0.5\tau}\left(\delta_x^2 U^{k+1/2} - \delta_x^2 U^k + \delta_y^2 U^k - \delta_y^2 U^{k-1/2}\right) + F^{k+1/2}, \tag{10}$$

$$\frac{U^{k+1} - U^{k+1/2}}{0.5\tau} = \delta_x^2 U^{k+1/2} + \delta_y^2 U^{k+1}$$
$$+ \frac{\eta}{0.5\tau}\left(\delta_x^2 U^{k+1/2} - \delta_x^2 U^k + \delta_y^2 U^{k+1} - \delta_y^2 U^{k+1/2}\right) + F^{k+1/2}. \tag{11}$$

In the case $\eta = 0$, Equations (10) and (11) coincide with the classical Peaceman–Rachford method [25]. The truncation error of Equations (10) and (11) is $\mathcal{O}(\tau + h_x^2 + h_y^2)$ if the solution of the differential problem (1)–(5) is smooth enough.

In order to start the calculation with this method, it is necessary to know the values of U_{ij}^k in the two initial layers $k = 0$ and $k = 1/2$. The values of U_{ij}^0 are found from the initial condition (5). The values of $U_{ij}^{1/2}$ can be found by solving the system of difference equations written for the problem (1)–(5) using two layers. One can take $\tilde{U}_{ij}^{1/2} = U_{ij}^0$; in this case, we have error $|U_{ij}^{1/2} - \tilde{U}_{ij}^{1/2}| = \mathcal{O}(\tau)$.

Tridiagonal system (10) of order $N - 1$ is solved for $j = \overline{1, M - 1}$ with nonlocal boundary conditions

$$U^{k+1/2}|_{i=0} = \gamma_0 [1, U^{k+1/2}] + V_l^{k+1/2}, \tag{12}$$

$$U^{k+1/2}|_{i=N} = \gamma_1 [1, U^{k+1/2}] + V_r^{k+1/2}. \tag{13}$$

The truncation error of the nonlocal boundary condition is $\mathcal{O}(h_x^2)$.

After the calculation of $U^{k+1/2}$, system (11) of order $M-1$ is solved for $i = \overline{1, N-1}$ with the Dirichlet BC

$$U^{k+1}|_{j=0} = V_b^{k+1}, \qquad U^{k+1}|_{j=M} = V_t^{k+1}. \tag{14}$$

In order to investigate the stability of the ADI method (10)–(14), we rewrite this method in the most concise operator form. To this end, nonlocal conditions (12) and (13) are interpreted as a linear system with unknowns $U_{0j}^{k+1/2}$ and $U_{Nj}^{k+1/2}$ for every value of j. We express from conditions (12) and (13), the values $U_{0j}^{k+1/2}$ and $U_{Nj}^{k+1/2}$ via the remaining unknowns:

$$U^{k+1/2}|_{i=0} = \tilde{\gamma}_0(1, U^{k+1/2}) + \tilde{V}_l^{k+1/2}, \tag{15}$$

$$U^{k+1/2}|_{i=N} = \tilde{\gamma}_1(1, U^{k+1/2}) + \tilde{V}_r^{k+1/2}, \tag{16}$$

where $\tilde{\gamma}_0 := \gamma_0 d^{-1}$, $\tilde{\gamma}_1 := \gamma_1 d^{-1}$, $\tilde{V}_l := (V_l + h_x c)d^{-1}$, $\tilde{V}_r := (V_r - h_x c)d^{-1}$, $c := (\gamma_0 V_r - \gamma_1 V_l)/2$, $d := 1 - \gamma h_x/2$, $\gamma := \gamma_0 + \gamma_1$. We can write Formulas (15) and (16) in all cases when $d \neq 0$. Note, if $\gamma h_x < 2$, then $d > 0$.

Let us define square matrices $\mathbf{\Lambda}_x \in \mathbb{M}_{(N-1)\times(N-1)}$ and $\mathbf{\Lambda}_y \in \mathbb{M}_{(M-1)\times(M-1)}$ as

$$\mathbf{\Lambda}_x := \frac{1}{h_x^2}\begin{pmatrix} 2-\tilde{\gamma}_0 h_x & -1-\tilde{\gamma}_0 h_x & -\tilde{\gamma}_0 h_x & \cdots & -\tilde{\gamma}_0 h_x \\ -1 & 2 & -1 & \cdots & 0 \\ & \ddots & \ddots & \ddots & \\ & & -1 & 2 & -1 \\ -\tilde{\gamma}_1 h_x & \cdots & -\tilde{\gamma}_1 h_x & -1-\tilde{\gamma}_1 h_x & 2-\tilde{\gamma}_1 h_x \end{pmatrix},$$

$$\mathbf{\Lambda}_y := \frac{1}{h_y^2}\begin{pmatrix} 2 & -1 & & & \\ -1 & 2 & -1 & & \\ & \ddots & \ddots & \ddots & \\ & & -1 & 2 & -1 \\ & & & -1 & 2 \end{pmatrix}.$$

Let $\mathbf{I}_x \in \mathbb{M}_{(N-1)\times(N-1)}$, $\mathbf{I}_y \in \mathbb{M}_{(M-1)\times(M-1)}$ be the identity matrices and $\mathbf{I} := \mathbf{I}_y \otimes \mathbf{I}_x$, where $\mathbf{A} \otimes \mathbf{B}$ denotes the Kronecker product of matrices $\mathbf{A}$ and $\mathbf{B}$. Then, we define matrices

$$\mathbf{L}_1 := \mathbf{I}_y \otimes \mathbf{\Lambda}_x = \mathbf{diag}(\mathbf{\Lambda}_x, \ldots, \mathbf{\Lambda}_x) \in \mathbb{M}_{(M-1)(N-1)\times(M-1)(N-1)},$$

$$\mathbf{L}_2 := \mathbf{\Lambda}_y \otimes \mathbf{I}_x = \begin{pmatrix} 2\mathbf{I}_y & -\mathbf{I}_y & & & \\ -\mathbf{I}_y & 2\mathbf{I}_y & -\mathbf{I}_y & & \\ & \ddots & \ddots & \ddots & \\ & & -\mathbf{I}_y & 2\mathbf{I}_y & -\mathbf{I}_y \\ & & & -\mathbf{I}_y & 2\mathbf{I}_y \end{pmatrix} \in \mathbb{M}_{(M-1)(N-1)\times(M-1)(N-1)},$$

which will be useful to rewrite the method (10) and (11), (14)–(16) in the operator form.

Lemma 1 (see, [33]). *The matrices $\mathbf{L}_1$ and $\mathbf{L}_2$ commute:*

$$\mathbf{L}_1\mathbf{L}_2 = \mathbf{L}_2\mathbf{L}_1 = \mathbf{\Lambda}_y \otimes \mathbf{\Lambda}_x. \tag{17}$$

Proof. From the properties of the Kronecker product, we have

$$\mathbf{L}_1\mathbf{L}_2 = (\mathbf{I}_y \otimes \mathbf{\Lambda}_x)(\mathbf{\Lambda}_y \otimes \mathbf{I}_x) = (\mathbf{I}_y\mathbf{\Lambda}_y) \otimes (\mathbf{\Lambda}_x\mathbf{I}_x) = \mathbf{\Lambda}_y \otimes \mathbf{\Lambda}_x,$$

$$\mathbf{L}_1\mathbf{L}_2 = (\mathbf{\Lambda}_y \otimes \mathbf{I}_x)(\mathbf{I}_y \otimes \mathbf{\Lambda}_x) = (\mathbf{\Lambda}_y\mathbf{I}_y) \otimes (\mathbf{I}_x\mathbf{\Lambda}_x) = \mathbf{\Lambda}_y \otimes \mathbf{\Lambda}_x.$$

$\square$

Let us substitute expression (15) for $U_{0j}^{k+1/2}$ and expression (16) for $U_{nj}^{k+1/2}$ into Equation (10). Then, we can rewrite (10) in the matrix form

$$\mathbf{A}_1\mathbf{U}^{k+1/2} + \mathbf{B}_1\mathbf{U}^k + \mathbf{C}_1\mathbf{U}^{k-1/2} = 0.5\tau\widetilde{\mathbf{F}}_1^{k+1/2}, \tag{18}$$

where

$$\mathbf{A}_1 = \mathbf{I} + (\eta + 0.5\tau)\mathbf{L}_1, \quad \mathbf{B}_1 = -\mathbf{I} + (\eta + 0.5\tau)\mathbf{L}_2 - \eta\mathbf{L}_1, \quad \mathbf{C}_1 = -\eta\mathbf{L}_2. \tag{19}$$

We rewrite Equation (11) using BC (14) in the form

$$\mathbf{A}_2\mathbf{U}^{k+1} + \mathbf{B}_2\mathbf{U}^{k+1/2} + \mathbf{C}_2\mathbf{U}^k = 0.5\tau\widetilde{\mathbf{F}}_2^{k+1/2}, \tag{20}$$

where

$$\mathbf{A}_2 = \mathbf{I} + (\eta + 0.5\tau)\mathbf{L}_2, \quad \mathbf{B}_2 = -\mathbf{I} + (\eta + 0.5\tau)\mathbf{L}_1 - \eta\mathbf{L}_2, \quad \mathbf{C}_2 = -\eta\mathbf{L}_1. \tag{21}$$

We can write $\widetilde{\mathbf{F}}_1^{k+1/2}$ and $\widetilde{\mathbf{F}}_2^{k+1/2}$ in terms of known values ($F^{k+1/2}$, V_b^{k+1}, V_t^{k+1}, $\widetilde{V}_l^{k+1/2}$, $\widetilde{V}_r^{k+1/2}$), but the expressions of these functions are not important for the investigation of the stability of FDS. Each of Equations (18) and (20) separately corresponds to three-layer FDS (both together to four-layer FDS).

Lemma 2. *The matrices* $\mathbf{A}_s$, $\mathbf{B}_s$, $\mathbf{C}_s$, *and* $\mathbf{A}_s^{-1}$, $s = 1, 2$, *commute (if the inverse matrices exist).*

Proof. The matrices $\mathbf{L}_1$ and $\mathbf{L}_2$ commute (see Lemma 1). Thus, the matrices $\mathbf{A}_s$, $\mathbf{B}_s$, and $\mathbf{C}_s$, defined by (19) and (21) also commute. If $\mathbf{AB} = \mathbf{BA}$ and $\mathbf{A}^{-1}$ exists, then $\mathbf{A}^{-1}\mathbf{B} = \mathbf{A}^{-1}\mathbf{B}\mathbf{A}\mathbf{A}^{-1} = \mathbf{A}^{-1}\mathbf{A}\mathbf{B}\mathbf{A}^{-1} = \mathbf{B}\mathbf{A}^{-1}$. Therefore, it follows that matrices $\mathbf{A}_s$, $\mathbf{B}_s$, and $\mathbf{C}_s$ commute with $\mathbf{A}_s^{-1}$. $\square$

Remark 1. *We note that matrices* $\mathbf{A}_1^{-1}$ *and* $\mathbf{A}_2^{-1}$ *exist, as matrices* $\mathbf{A}_1$ *and* $\mathbf{A}_2$ *are strictly diagonally dominant.*

Corollary 1. *The matrices* $\mathbf{A}_1^{-1}\mathbf{B}_1$ *and* $\mathbf{A}_1^{-1}\mathbf{C}_1 + \mu\mathbf{I}$ *commute for all* $\mu \in \mathbb{C}$.

Lemma 3. *The following equalities*

$$\mathbf{A}_s + \mathbf{B}_s + \mathbf{C}_s = 0.5\tau(\mathbf{L}_1 + \mathbf{L}_2) = 2\mathbf{I} + \mathbf{B}_1 + \mathbf{B}_2, \quad s = 1, 2, \tag{22}$$

$$\mathbf{A}_s + \mathbf{C}_s = 2\mathbf{I} + \mathbf{B}_{3-s}, \quad \mathbf{A}_s + \mathbf{C}_{3-s} = \mathbf{I} + 0.5\tau\mathbf{L}_l, \quad s = 1, 2, \tag{23}$$

$$(\mathbf{A}_1 + \mathbf{C}_1)(\mathbf{A}_2 + \mathbf{C}_2) = \mathbf{B}_1\mathbf{B}_2 + \tau(\mathbf{L}_1 + \mathbf{L}_2) \tag{24}$$

are valid.

Proof. The equalities (22) and (23) are obvious. Finally,

$$(\mathbf{A}_1 + \mathbf{C}_1)(\mathbf{A}_2 + \mathbf{C}_2) = (2\mathbf{I} + \mathbf{B}_2)(2\mathbf{I} + \mathbf{B}_1) = 4\mathbf{I} + 2\mathbf{B}_1 + 2\mathbf{B}_2 + \mathbf{B}_2\mathbf{B}_1$$
$$= \mathbf{B}_2\mathbf{B}_1 + \tau(\mathbf{L}_1 + \mathbf{L}_2) = \mathbf{B}_1\mathbf{B}_2 + \tau(\mathbf{L}_1 + \mathbf{L}_2).$$

$\square$

Corollary 2. *The following equality*

$$-\mathbf{B}_1\mathbf{B}_2 + \mathbf{A}_1\mathbf{C}_2 + \mathbf{A}_2\mathbf{C}_1 = -\mathbf{A}_1\mathbf{A}_2 - \mathbf{C}_1\mathbf{C}_2 + \tau(\mathbf{L}_1 + \mathbf{L}_2)$$

is valid.

The methodology of the investigation of the stability of three-layer schemes for the second-order parabolic equation with Dirichlet boundary conditions is created in monograph [40]. According to that methodology, the three-layer difference scheme (18) or (20) must be rewritten in the canonical form. For example, the canonical form for (18) is

$$\widetilde{\mathbf{B}}\frac{\mathbf{U}^{k+1/2} - \mathbf{U}^{k-1/2}}{\tau} + \widetilde{\mathbf{R}}(\mathbf{U}^{k+1/2} - 2\mathbf{U}^k + \mathbf{U}^{k-1/2}) + \widetilde{\mathbf{A}}\mathbf{U}^k = \widetilde{\mathbf{F}}_1^{k+1/2},$$

where

$$\widetilde{\mathbf{B}} = \mathbf{I} + (\eta + 0.5\tau)\mathbf{L}_1 + \eta\mathbf{L}_2, \quad \tau\widetilde{\mathbf{R}} = \mathbf{I} + (\eta + 0.5\tau)\mathbf{L}_1 - \eta\mathbf{L}_2, \quad \widetilde{\mathbf{A}} = \mathbf{L}_1 + \mathbf{L}_2.$$

For the stability of difference scheme (18), the matrices $\widetilde{\mathbf{R}}$ and $\widetilde{\mathbf{A}}$ must be positive definite [40]. However, in the case of nonlocal conditions (3) and (4), these matrices are nonsymmetric because of nonsymmetrical matrix Λ_x. Furthermore, the symmetric matrix $\widetilde{\mathbf{R}}$ is not positive definite in the case of pseudoparabolic equation ($\eta \neq 0$). Thus, we investigate the stability of difference scheme (18) by using the other approach.

2.3. Reduction of the Three-Layer Scheme to a Two-Layer Scheme

In order to reduce the three-layer difference scheme to a two-layer system, we define vectors in $\mathbb{M}_{2(N-1)(M-1)\times1}$:

$$\mathbf{Y}^k = \begin{pmatrix} \mathbf{U}^k \\ \mathbf{U}^{k-1/2} \end{pmatrix}, \quad \mathbf{F}_s^{k+1/2} = \begin{pmatrix} \frac{\tau}{2}\mathbf{A}_s^{-1}\widetilde{\mathbf{F}}_s^{k+1/2} \\ 0 \end{pmatrix}, \quad s = 1, 2.$$

Then, we rewrite Equations (18) and (20) as

$$\mathbf{Y}^{k+1/2} = \mathbf{S}_1\mathbf{Y}^k + \mathbf{F}_1^{k+1/2}, \quad \mathbf{Y}^{k+1} = \mathbf{S}_2\mathbf{Y}^{k+1/2} + \mathbf{F}_2^{k+1/2},$$

where

$$\mathbf{S}_l = \begin{pmatrix} -\mathbf{A}_l^{-1}\mathbf{B}_l & -\mathbf{A}_l^{-1}\mathbf{C}_l \\ \mathbf{I} & 0 \end{pmatrix} \in \mathbb{M}_{2(N-1)(M-1)\times2(N-1)(M-1)}, \quad l = 1, 2.$$

From this, we obtain

$$\mathbf{Y}^{k+1} = \mathbf{S}\mathbf{Y}^k + \mathbf{F}^{k+1/2}, \tag{25}$$

where

$$\mathbf{S} = \mathbf{S}_2\mathbf{S}_1 = \begin{pmatrix} \mathbf{A}_2^{-1}\mathbf{B}_2\mathbf{A}_1^{-1}\mathbf{B}_1 - \mathbf{A}_2^{-1}\mathbf{C}_2 & \mathbf{A}_2^{-1}\mathbf{B}_2\mathbf{A}_1^{-1}\mathbf{C}_1 \\ -\mathbf{A}_1^{-1}\mathbf{B}_1 & -\mathbf{A}_1^{-1}\mathbf{C}_1 \end{pmatrix}, \tag{26}$$

and $\mathbf{F}^{k+1/2} = \mathbf{S}_2\mathbf{F}_1^{k+1/2} + \mathbf{F}_2^{k+1/2}$.

3. Eigenvalues of Matrix S

3.1. Eigenvalues of the Matrices Λ_x and Λ_y

It is known that the eigenvalues of Λ_y are positive and the corresponding eigenvectors are orthogonal and linearly independent:

$$\lambda_m(\Lambda_y) = \frac{4}{h_y^2}\sin^2\frac{\pi m h_y}{2L_y}, \quad \mathbf{W}^m = (W_1^m, \ldots, W_{M-1}^m)^T, \quad m = \overline{1, M-1},$$

where

$$W_j^m = \sin\frac{\pi m j h_y}{L_y}, \quad j = \overline{1, M-1}.$$

The eigenvalue problem for matrix $\mathbf{\Lambda}_x$ is equivalent to problem

$$-\delta_x^2 V_i = \lambda V_i, \quad i = \overline{1, N-1},$$
$$V_0 = \gamma_0[1, V], \quad V_n = \gamma_1[1, V].$$

All eigenvalues $\lambda_n(\mathbf{\Lambda}_y)$, $n = \overline{1, N-1}$, of this problem are real numbers and eigenvectors

$$\mathbf{V}^n = (V_1^n, \ldots, V_{N-1}^n)^T, \quad n = \overline{1, N-1},$$

are linearly independent. Furthermore, if $\gamma_0 + \gamma_1 < 2$, then all eigenvalues $\lambda_n(\mathbf{\Lambda}_x)$, $n = \overline{1, N-1}$, are positive, more precisely, $\lambda_n(\mathbf{\Lambda}_x) \in (0, 4/h_x^2)$ [28].

3.2. Eigenvalues and Eigenvectors of the Matrices $\mathbf{L}_1$ and $\mathbf{L}_2$

Vectors
$$\mathbf{U}^{m,n} = \mathbf{W}^m \otimes \mathbf{V}^n, \quad n = \overline{1, N-1}, m = \overline{1, M-1}, \tag{27}$$

are linearly independent in the vector space $\mathbb{R}^{2(N-1)(M-1)}$ according to the Kronecker product properties [41].

Since $\mathbf{L}_1 = \mathbf{I}_y \otimes \mathbf{\Lambda}_x$ and $\mathbf{L}_2 = \mathbf{\Lambda}_y \otimes \mathbf{I}_x$, we have

$$(\mathbf{I}_y \otimes \mathbf{\Lambda}_x)(\mathbf{W}^m \otimes \mathbf{V}^n) = (\mathbf{I}_y \mathbf{W}^m) \otimes (\mathbf{\Lambda}_x \mathbf{V}^n) = \lambda_n(\mathbf{\Lambda}_x) \mathbf{W}^m \otimes \mathbf{V}^n,$$
$$(\mathbf{\Lambda}_y \otimes \mathbf{I}_x)(\mathbf{W}^m \otimes \mathbf{V}^n) = (\mathbf{\Lambda}_y \mathbf{W}^m) \otimes (\mathbf{I}_x \mathbf{V}^n) = \lambda_m(\mathbf{\Lambda}_y) \mathbf{W}^m \otimes \mathbf{V}^n,$$

and we get
$$\mathbf{L}_1 \mathbf{U}^{m,n} = \lambda_n(\mathbf{\Lambda}_x) \mathbf{U}^{m,n}, \quad \mathbf{L}_2 \mathbf{U}^{m,n} = \lambda_m(\mathbf{\Lambda}_y) \mathbf{U}^{m,n}. \tag{28}$$

Therefore, matrices $\mathbf{L}_1$ and $\mathbf{L}_2$ have the same system of eigenvectors. The eigenvalues of matrix $\mathbf{L}_1$ are $\lambda_n^{(1)} = \lambda_n(\mathbf{\Lambda}_x)$, $n = \overline{1, N-1}$, and the geometric multiplicity of each eigenvalue is $M-1$; the eigenvalues of matrix $\mathbf{L}_2$ are $\lambda_m^{(2)} = \lambda_m(\mathbf{\Lambda}_y)$, $m = \overline{1, M-1}$, and the geometric multiplicity of each eigenvalue is $N-1$.

Lemma 4. *The matrices* $\mathbf{A}_s$, $\mathbf{B}_s$, $\mathbf{C}_s$, *and* $\mathbf{L}_s$, $s = 1, 2$, *commute and have a common system of linearly independent eigenvectors.*

Proof. The matrices $\mathbf{\Lambda}_1$ and $\mathbf{\Lambda}_2$ commute and have the same system of eigenvectors. Thus, according to (19) and (21), vectors $\mathbf{U}^{m,n}$ are eigenvectors of matrices $\mathbf{A}_s$, $\mathbf{B}_s$, $\mathbf{C}_s$, too. $\square$

3.3. Eigenvalues of the Matrix $\mathbf{S}$

The equation for the eigenvalues of matrix $\mathbf{S}$ is

$$\begin{vmatrix} \mathbf{A}_2^{-1}\mathbf{B}_2\mathbf{A}_1^{-1}\mathbf{B}_1 - \mathbf{A}_2^{-1}\mathbf{C}_2 - \mu\mathbf{I} & \mathbf{A}_2^{-1}\mathbf{B}_2\mathbf{A}_1^{-1}\mathbf{C}_1 \\ -\mathbf{A}_1^{-1}\mathbf{B}_1 & -\mathbf{A}_1^{-1}\mathbf{C}_1 - \mu\mathbf{I} \end{vmatrix} = 0.$$

The determinant on the left side is equal to

$$\begin{vmatrix} -\mathbf{A}_2^{-1}\mathbf{C}_2 - \mu\mathbf{I} & -\mu\mathbf{A}_2^{-1}\mathbf{B}_2 \\ -\mathbf{A}_1^{-1}\mathbf{B}_1 & -\mathbf{A}_1^{-1}\mathbf{C}_1 - \mu\mathbf{I} \end{vmatrix} = \frac{1}{\det(\mathbf{A}_1\mathbf{A}_2)} \begin{vmatrix} \mathbf{C}_2 + \mu\mathbf{A}_2 & \mu\mathbf{B}_2 \\ \mathbf{B}_1 & \mathbf{C}_1 + \mu\mathbf{A}_1 \end{vmatrix}.$$

Using Lemma 2 and Corollary 3, we get equation

$$\det\left(\mu^2\mathbf{A} + \mu\mathbf{B} + \mathbf{C}\right) = 0, \tag{29}$$

where

$$\mathbf{A} = \mathbf{A}_1\mathbf{A}_2, \quad \mathbf{C} = \mathbf{C}_1\mathbf{C}_2, \tag{30}$$

$$\mathbf{B} = -\mathbf{B}_1\mathbf{B}_2 + \mathbf{A}_1\mathbf{C}_2 + \mathbf{A}_2\mathbf{C}_1 = -\mathbf{A}_1\mathbf{A}_2 - \mathbf{C}_1\mathbf{C}_2 + \tau(\mathbf{L}_1 + \mathbf{L}_2). \tag{31}$$

The last equality follows from Corollary 2. Equation (29) is the characteristic equation of the general nonlinear eigenvalue problem

$$\mu^2\mathbf{A}\mathbf{U} + \mu\mathbf{B}\mathbf{U} + \mathbf{C}\mathbf{U} = 0. \tag{32}$$

Thus, the second order eigenvalue problem has $2(N-1)(M-1)$ eigenvalues. As a result, the next lemma is valid.

Lemma 5. *The eigenvalues of matrix* $\mathbf{S}$ *coincide with the eigenvalues of the nonlinear eigenvalue problem (32).*

The nonlinear eigenvalue problem of such type when matrices $\mathbf{A}$, $\mathbf{B}$, and $\mathbf{C}$ are symmetric is well known and has been considered in many works (see, [42]). In our case, these matrices are nonsymmetric, but it is possible to investigate nonlinear eigenvalue problem (32) using another useful property of these matrices. Namely, matrices $\mathbf{A}$, $\mathbf{B}$, and $\mathbf{C}$ have the same system of eigenvectors.

We can find the eigenvalues of nonlinear problem (32). Substituting $\mathbf{U} = \mathbf{U}^{m,n}$ into Equation (32) and taking into account that $\mathbf{U}^{m,n} \not\equiv \mathbf{0}$, we obtain

$$\mu^2\lambda_{mn}(\mathbf{A}) + \mu\lambda_{mn}(\mathbf{B}) + \lambda_{mn}(\mathbf{C}) = 0, \quad m = \overline{1, M-1}, n = \overline{1, N-1}. \tag{33}$$

The eigenvalues of matrix $\mathbf{S}$ are roots of Equation (33). We rewrite (33) as

$$a_{mn}\mu^2 + b_{mn}\mu + c_{mn} = 0, \quad m = \overline{1, M-1}, n = \overline{1, N-1}, \tag{34}$$

where

$$a_{mn} = \left(1 + (\eta + 0.5\tau)\lambda_n^{(1)}\right)\left(1 + (\eta + 0.5\tau)\lambda_m^{(2)}\right), \tag{35}$$

$$b_{mn} = -a_{mn} - c_{mn} + \tau\left(\lambda_n^{(1)} + \lambda_m^{(2)}\right), \tag{36}$$

$$c_{mn} = \eta^2\lambda_n^{(1)}\lambda_m^{(2)}. \tag{37}$$

If $\lambda_n^{(1)} > 0$, $\lambda_m^{(2)} > 0$, then taking into account $\eta > 0$, we get that $c_{mn} > 0$. From (35), we get

$$a_{mn} > c_{mn}, \quad a_{mn} > 0.5\tau\left(\lambda_n^{(1)} + \lambda_m^{(2)}\right).$$

Thus, we estimate

$$b_{mn} < -a_{mn} - c_{mn} + 2a_{mn} = a_{nm} - c_{mn} < a_{nm} + c_{mn}.$$

From (36), we have $-b_{mn} < a_{mn} + c_{mn}$. Finally, we prove

$$|c_{mn}| < a_{mn}, \quad |b_{mn}| < c_{mn} + a_{mn}.$$

Lemma 6. *If* $\gamma_0 + \gamma_1 < 2$, *then for the roots of Equation (34), we have* $|\mu| < 1$.

Proof. If $\gamma_0 + \gamma_1 < 2$, then $\lambda_n(\boldsymbol{\Lambda}_x) > 0$, $n = \overline{1, N-1}$. Eigenvalues $\lambda_m(\boldsymbol{\Lambda}_y)$, $m = \overline{1, M-1}$, are positive. Thus, we have $\lambda_n^{(1)} > 0$, $\lambda_m^{(2)} > 0$ for $m = \overline{1, M-1}$, $n = \overline{1, N-1}$. According to Hurwitz's criterion [43], the roots of polynomial $\mu^2 + b\mu + c$ satisfy condition $|\mu| < 1$ if and only if $|c| < 1$, $|b| < c + 1$. Therefore, the conditions of Hurwitz's criterion are fulfilled for $b = a_{mn}^{-1}b_{mn}$, $c = a_{mn}^{-1}c_{mn}$, and we get that $|\mu| < 1$. $\square$

Remark 2. *In the case $\eta = 0$, we have $c_{mn} = 0$, and the roots are $\mu_1 = 0$, $\mu_2 = -b_{mn}a_{mn}^{-1} = \left(1 - 0.5\tau\lambda_n^{(1)}\right)\left(1 - 0.5\tau\lambda_m^{(2)}\right)\left(1 + 0.5\tau\lambda_n^{(1)}\right)^{-1}\left(1 + 0.5\tau\lambda_m^{(2)}\right)^{-1}$, and $|\mu_2| < 1$.*

In the limit case $\tau = 0$, we have equation $a_{mn}\mu^2 - (a_{mn} + c_{mn})\mu + c_{mn} = 0$. The roots of this equation are $\mu_1 = c_{mn}a_{mn}^{-1} = \eta^2\lambda_n^{(1)}\lambda_m^{(2)}\left(1 + \eta\lambda_n^{(1)}\right)^{-1}\left(1 + \eta\lambda_m^{(2)}\right)^{-1}$, $\mu_2 = 1$, and $|\mu_1| < 1$.

4. Investigation of the Stability of Finite Difference Scheme

We examine, based on Lemma 6, the stability of the ADI method (10)–(11) or otherwise the difference scheme (25).

From Lemma 6, we can formulate the following proposition.

Proposition 1. *If $|\mu| < 1$, where μ is the eigenvalue of matrix $\mathbf{S}$, then the difference scheme $\mathbf{Y}^{n+1} = \mathbf{S}\mathbf{Y}^n + \mathbf{F}^{n+1/2}$ is stable regardless of whether the matrix $\mathbf{S}$ is symmetric or not.*

This proposition on the stability of the two-layer difference scheme for a parabolic equation has been known for a long time and was formulated before solving problems with nonlocal conditions (see, [44]). In order to understand the influence of nonlocal conditions on the stability of the difference scheme, we study in detail the case when $\mathbf{S}$ is a nonsymmetric matrix.

If $\gamma_1 = \gamma_2 = 0$ in problem (10)–(13), then matrix $\mathbf{S}$ is symmetric. In this case, all eigenvalues of $\mathbf{S}$ are real and it follows from $|\mu| < 1$ that

$$\varrho(\mathbf{S}) := \max|\mu(\mathbf{S})| < 1. \tag{38}$$

If $\mathbf{S}$ is symmetric, we have

$$\|\mathbf{S}\|_2 = \left(\max_i |\lambda_i(\mathbf{S}^2)|\right)^{1/2} = \varrho(\mathbf{S}). \tag{39}$$

Thus, the condition of the stability of the finite difference scheme (25) can be formulated as the following theorem.

Theorem 1. *If $\gamma_1 = \gamma_2 = 0$, then*

$$\|\mathbf{S}\|_2 < 1 \tag{40}$$

and ADI method (9)–(12) is stable in the discrete vector ℓ_2-norm.

Let us assume on the contrary that either γ_1 or γ_2 is nonzero in problem (1)–(5). Thus, we investigate the stability of difference scheme (10)–(13) or the system (25) with nonsymmetric matrix $\mathbf{S}$. In this case, the equality (39) does not follow from the definition of the norm (9). That is, for nonsymmetric matrix $\mathbf{S}$, the spectral radius $\varrho(\mathbf{S})$ is not the matrix norm. For this, we use the statement from linear algebra about the norm of the matrix.

Proposition 2 (see, [45], Th. 7.8). *Let $\varrho(\mathbf{A})$ be a spectral radius of an arbitrary square matrix $\mathbf{A}$. If $\varepsilon > 0$ is given, then there exists a matrix norm $\|\mathbf{A}\|_*$ for which*

$$\|\mathbf{A}\|_* \leq \varrho(\mathbf{A}) + \varepsilon. \tag{41}$$

We can formulate some corollary of this proposition.

Corollary 3. *For any square matrix $\mathbf{A}$, there exists a matrix norm $\|\mathbf{A}\|_* < 1$ if and only if $\varrho(\mathbf{A}) < 1$.*

However, the proof of Proposition 2, as well as a construction of norm $\|\mathbf{A}\|_*$, is nontrivial (see, [46] p. 12, or [47] Chapter 11.2, Section 3.4).

Now, we assume that matrix $\mathbf{S}$ has a system of linearly independent eigenvectors. In this case, we use the following proposition from linear algebra [48].

Proposition 3. *Let* $\|\mathbf{A}\|$ *and* $\|\mathbf{u}\|$ *be compatible matrix and vector norms and* $\mathbf{P}$ *be a nonsingular matrix* (det $\mathbf{P} \neq 0$). *Then,*

$$\|\mathbf{A}\|_* = \|\mathbf{P}^{-1}\mathbf{A}\mathbf{P}\| \tag{42}$$

and

$$\|\mathbf{u}\|_* = \|\mathbf{P}^{-1}\mathbf{u}\| \tag{43}$$

are also compatible matrix and vector norms.

Using the assumption that the eigenvectors of matrix $\mathbf{S}$ are linearly independent, we define matrix $\mathbf{P}$, whose columns are eigenvectors of $\mathbf{S}$. We use the ℓ_2-norm $\|\cdot\|_2$ in (42) and (43). Therefore, we get

$$\|\mathbf{u}\|_* = \|\mathbf{P}^{-1}\mathbf{u}\|_2 = (\mathbf{P}^{-1}\mathbf{u}, \mathbf{P}^{-1}\mathbf{u})^{1/2} = (\mathbf{D}\mathbf{u}, \mathbf{u})^{1/2}, \quad \mathbf{D} = (\mathbf{P}\mathbf{P}^*)^{-1}, \tag{44}$$

$$\|\mathbf{S}\|_* = \|\mathbf{P}^{-1}\mathbf{S}\mathbf{P}\|_2 = \|\mathbf{J}\|_2 = \max_i |\mu_i(\mathbf{S})| = \varrho(\mathbf{S}), \tag{45}$$

where $\mathbf{D}$ is a positive defined matrix and $\mathbf{J}$ is the Jordan form of $\mathbf{S}$.

Now, we can generalize Theorem 1.

Theorem 2. *If* $\gamma_1 + \gamma_2 < 2$, *then the ADI method (10) and (11) with nonlocal conditions (12) and (13) is stable in some vector norm. If additionally, the eigenvectors of matrix* $\mathbf{S}$ *are linearly independent, then the ADI method is stable in norm* $\|\mathbf{u}\|_* = (\mathbf{D}\mathbf{u}, \mathbf{u})^{1/2}$, *generated by the self-adjoint positive defined operator (matrix)* $\mathbf{D} = (\mathbf{P}\mathbf{P}^*)^{-1}$, *where* $\mathbf{P}$ *is a matrix whose columns are linearly independent eigenvectors of* $\mathbf{S}$.

Remark 3. *As far as the authors know, the eigenvectors of a matrix* $\mathbf{S}$ *are linearly independent if there are some additional conditions. For example, in the case when the eigenvalues of* $\mathbf{S}$ *are real. In this article, we leave this question open.*

5. Numerical Examples

One of the aims of our numerical simulations was to demonstrate the theoretical results obtained in the previous sections. Two numerical examples illustrate the effectiveness of the present ADI scheme. Another aim was to investigate numerically the influence of parameter τ, T, and η on the accuracy of the solution.

Problem 1. *We consider the model problem in the domain* $D := (0,1) \times (0,1)$

$$\frac{\partial u}{\partial t} = \frac{\partial^2 u}{\partial x^2} + \frac{\partial^2 u}{\partial y^2} + \eta \frac{\partial}{\partial t}\left(\frac{\partial^2 u}{\partial x^2} + \frac{\partial^2 u}{\partial y^2}\right) + f(x,y,t), \quad (x,y,t) \in D \times (0,T],$$

where

$$f(x,y,t) = e^{-t}\sin(\pi x)\sin(\pi y)\big(-1 + 2\pi^2(1-\eta)\big),$$

subject to the initial and boundary conditions

$$u(0,y,t) = \gamma_0 \int_0^1 u(x,y,t)\,dx - 2\frac{\gamma_0}{\pi}e^{-t}\sin(\pi y), \quad (y,t) \in [0,1] \times [0,T],$$

$$u(1,y,t) = \gamma_1 \int_0^1 u(x,y,t)\,dx - 2\frac{\gamma_1}{\pi}e^{-t}\sin(\pi y), \quad (y,t) \in [0,1] \times [0,T],$$

$$u(x,0,t) = 0, \quad u(x,1,t) = 0, \quad (x,t) \in [0,1] \times [0,T],$$

$$u(x,y,0) = \sin(\pi x)\sin(\pi y), \quad (x,y) \in [0,1] \times [0,1].$$

The right-hand side function f in the differential equation and the initial and boundary conditions were prescribed to satisfy the given exact solution

$$u^*(x,y,t) = e^{-t}\sin(\pi x)\sin(\pi y)$$

of problem (1)–(5) (see, Figure 1a).

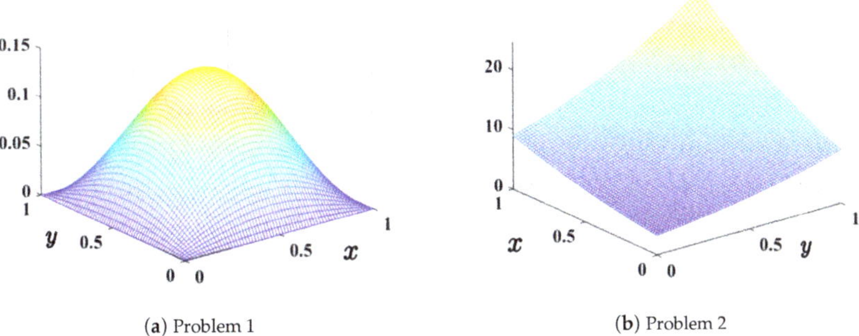

(a) Problem 1   (b) Problem 2

Figure 1. Solutions of Problems 1 and 2.

We calculated the maximum norm of the error of the numerical solution with respect to the exact solution and relative error

$$E = \max_{i=0,\cdots,M} |U_i^N - u^*(x_i,t_N)|, \quad E_r = E/|u^*(x_i,t_N)|.$$

The results of the numerical experiment are presented in Table 1. Note that the errors were $\mathcal{O}(\tau + h^2)$ with a sufficient accuracy for all τ and h. The ratio τ/h^2 was equal to 1.

The errors E for a different ratio of step sizes τ and h are given in Table 2. Now, $\tau/h^2 = 1/h$ and the error was $\mathcal{O}(\tau)$ as expected (independent of τ/h^2 which varied from 4 to 64). The plots of the error distribution at mesh points for $T = 2$ are presented in Figure 2a for the classical problem and in Figure 2b for the problem with nonlocal boundary conditions.

Problem 2. *In the second example, we considered the model problem (1)–(5) in the domain $D := (0,1) \times (0,1)$. The right-hand side function f and the initial and boundary conditions were chosen so that the function*

$$u^*(x,y,t) = e^{x+y}e^{\alpha t+1}$$

was the exact solution of the problem (see, Figure 1b), i.e.,

$$f(x,y,t) = 2\alpha e^{x+y}e^{\alpha t+1}\left(e^{x+y}e^{\alpha t+1} - \eta\right)$$

$$u(0,y,t) = \gamma_0 \int_0^1 u(x,y,t)\,\mathrm{d}x - \gamma_0(-e^{\alpha t+y+1} + e^{\alpha t+y+2}) + e^{\alpha t+y+1}, \quad (y,t) \in [0,1] \times [0,T],$$

$$u(1,y,t) = \gamma_1 \int_0^1 u(x,y,t)\,\mathrm{d}x - \gamma_1(-e^{\alpha t+y+1} + e^{\alpha t+y+2}) + e^{\alpha t+y+2}, \quad (y,t) \in [0,1] \times [0,T],$$

$$u(x,0,t) = e^{\alpha t+x+1};, \quad u(x,1,t) = e^{\alpha t+x+2}, \quad (x,t) \in [0,1] \times [0,T],$$

$$u(x,y,0) = e^{x+y}, \quad (x,y) \in [0,1] \times [0,1].$$

We set $\alpha = 0.1$.

In Table 3, E tends to $\mathcal{O}(\tau + h^2)$ as τ and h decreases but is larger for large values of τ and h. It may happen because u^* grows rapidly for large x,y,t. However, there might be other reasons.

Tables 4 and 5 show how the error depends on T and η. We can see that it should be proportional to the length of interval $[0,T]$ but does not depend too much on η. The plots of the error distribution for time $T = 2$ are presented in Figure 3a for the classical problem and in Figure 3b for the problem with nonlocal boundary conditions.

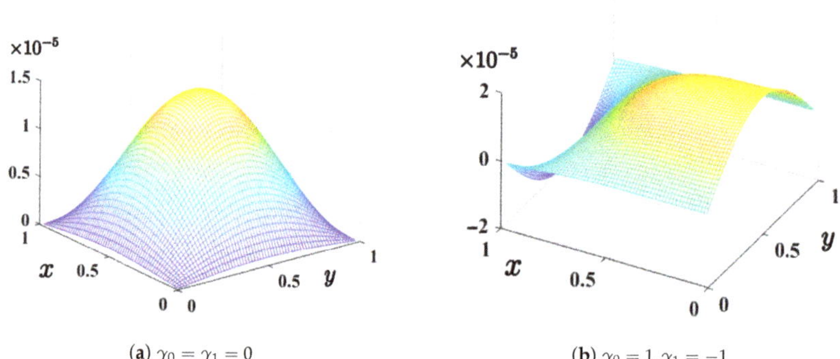

(**a**) $\gamma_0 = \gamma_1 = 0$

(**b**) $\gamma_0 = 1, \gamma_1 = -1$

Figure 2. (Problem 1) Errors for the discrete solution on the 64×64 grids for a problem solved with different values of parameters γ_0, γ_1.

Table 1. (Problem 1) The errors for different $h, \tau = h^2$ ($\eta = 1, \gamma_0 = 1, \gamma_1 = -1, T = 2$).

h	τ	E
2^{-2}	$6.2500 \cdot 10^{-2}$	$4.832 \cdot 10^{-3}$
2^{-3}	$1.5625 \cdot 10^{-2}$	$1.226 \cdot 10^{-3}$
2^{-4}	$3.9063 \cdot 10^{-4}$	$3.071 \cdot 10^{-4}$
2^{-5}	$9.7660 \cdot 10^{-5}$	$7.778 \cdot 10^{-5}$
2^{-6}	$2.4414 \cdot 10^{-5}$	$1.966 \cdot 10^{-5}$

Table 2. (Problem 1) The errors for different $h, \tau = h$ ($\eta = 1, \gamma_0 = 1, \gamma_1 = -1, T = 2$).

h	2^{-2}	2^{-3}	2^{-4}	2^{-5}	2^{-6}
E	0.0166	0.0103	0.0056	0.0028	0.0013

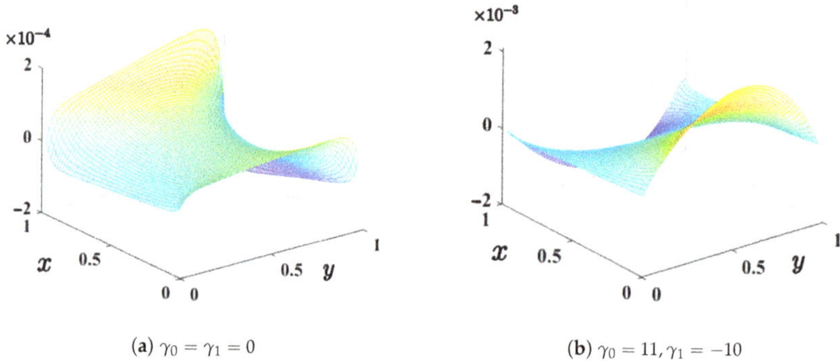

(**a**) $\gamma_0 = \gamma_1 = 0$

(**b**) $\gamma_0 = 11, \gamma_1 = -10$

Figure 3. (Problem 2) Errors for the discrete solution on the 64×64 grids for a problem solved with different values of parameters γ_0, γ_1.

Table 3. (Problem 2) The errors for different h, $\tau \neq h^2$ ($\eta = 0.1$, $\gamma_0 = 11$, $\gamma_1 = -10$, $T = 2$).

h	τ	E	E_r
0.0625	0.005	$5.044557 \cdot 10^{-2}$	$8.22822 \cdot 10^{-3}$
0.03125	0.00125	$1.40017 \cdot 10^{-2}$	$2.31612 \cdot 10^{-3}$
0.015625	0.00031250	$3.68602 \cdot 10^{-3}$	$6.1332 \cdot 10^{-4}$
0.0078125	0.00007813	$9.4561 \cdot 10^{-4}$	$1.5773 \cdot 10^{-4}$
0.00390625	0.00001953	$2.4045 \cdot 10^{-4}$	$4.011 \cdot 10^{-5}$

Table 4. (Problem 2) The errors for different T, $\alpha = 0.1$ $\eta = 1$, $\gamma_0 = 11$, $\gamma_1 = -10$, $h = 0.1$, $\tau = h^2$.

T	0.5	1	2	5	10
E	0.0011	0.0018	0.0027	0.0042	0.0069

Table 5. (Problem 2) The errors for different η, $\alpha = 0.1$ $T = 2$, $\gamma_0 = 11$, $\gamma_1 = -10$, $h = 2^{-6}$, $\tau = h^2$.

η	0.1	0.5	1	2	5	10
E	$6.10 \cdot 10^{-4}$	$5.22 \cdot 10^{-4}$	$3.82 \cdot 10^{-4}$	$1.63 \cdot 10^{-4}$	$4.78 \cdot 10^{-4}$	$8.03 \cdot 10^{-4}$

6. Conclusions and Remarks

In the article, we investigated the stability of the ADI method for the third-order 2D linear pseudoparabolic equation with boundary integral conditions (2) and (3). The ADI method defined by Formulas (10)–(13) had not been previously studied by other authors for pseudoparabolic equations.

As is well known, one of the most important properties for any numerical method to solve differential equations with boundary and initial conditions is the stability of the method. As mentioned in the introduction, for nonlocal boundary conditions, the differential problem is not self-adjoint. Therefore, the theoretical study of the method (proof of stability and convergence) usually becomes more complicated. In other words, it is not always possible to immediately apply the well-known theoretical conclusion that convergence follows from approximation and stability. In this paper, the spectrum structure of the nonsymmetric matrix $\mathbf{S}$ was used for the theoretical study of the ADI method written in (25). In Section 4, it was proved that the stability of the difference scheme in the vector norm $|| \cdot ||_*$ follows from the condition $\varrho(\mathbf{S}) < 1$. We note that the convergence of the difference method would follow from this condition, if we proved the equivalence of the norms $|| \cdot ||_*$ and $|| \cdot ||_2$, i.e., that the inequalities $C_1 || \cdot ||_* \leq || \cdot ||_2 \leq C_2 || \cdot ||_*$ were valid with constants C_1 and C_2 independent of h and τ. This approach was applied in [49]. We could not claim whether that approach was valid for pseudoparabolic 2D equations with nonlocal conditions (2) and (3).

Therefore, we chose another path. As a first step, we considered a differential equation with nonlocal conditions of a new form or a new numerical method, and we chose an approach that gave us only stability (see [21,31,49,50]). Such a methodology often works when the differential equation is with constant coefficients, and the approach is related to the spectrum structure of the differential problem.

The convergence of the ADI method is in our immediate plans but requires additional research or assumptions (see Remark 3).

Author Contributions: All Authors (M.S., A.Š. and O.Š.) have contributed as follows: Methodology, M.S.; Formal analysis, M.S. and A.Š.; Software, O.Š.; Validation, O.Š.; Writing—original draft preparation, M.S. and O.Š.; Writing—review and editing, M.S., A.Š. and O.Š. All authors have read and agreed to the published version of the manuscript.

Funding: This research received no external funding.

Institutional Review Board Statement: Not applicable.

Informed Consent Statement: Not applicable.

Data Availability Statement: No new data were created or analyzed in this study. Data sharing is not applicable to this article.

Acknowledgments: The authors would like to express their great gratitude to the referees for constructive and insightful suggestions, which helped us to greatly improve the presentation of the paper.

References

1. Bouziani, A.; Merazga, N. Solution to a semilinear pseudoparabolic problem with integral condition. *Electron. J. Differ. Equ.* **2006**, *2006*, 1–18.
2. Bouziani, A. Initial-boundary value problems for a class of pseudoparabolic equations with integral boundary conditions. *J. Math. Anal. Appl.* **2004**, *291*, 371–386. [CrossRef]
3. Ting, T. A cooling process according to two-temperature theory of heat conduction. *J. Math. Anal. Appl.* **1974**, *45*, 23–31. [CrossRef]
4. Padron, V. Effect of aggregation on population recovery modeled by a forward-backward pseudoparabolic equation. *Trans. Am. Math. Soc.* **2004**, *356*, 2739–2756. [CrossRef]
5. Sobolev, V. *A Treatise on Radiative Transfer*; D. van Nostrand Company: New York, NY, USA, 1963. [CrossRef]
6. Chudnovskij, A. *Teplofizika Pochv*; Nauka: Moscow, Russia, 1976. (In Russian)
7. Dai, D.Q.; Huang, Y. On a nonlocal boundary value problem with variable coefficients for the heat equation and the Aller equation. *Nonlinear Anal.* **2007**, *66*, 179–191. [CrossRef]
8. Yu, J.; Zhang, J. Nonlocal pseudo-parabolic equation with memory term and conical singularity: Global existence and blowup. *Symmetry* **2023**, *15*, 122. [CrossRef]
9. Nakhushev, A. On certain approximate method for boundary-value problems for differential equations and its applications in ground waters dynamics. *Differenc. Uravn.* **1982**, *18*, 72–81. (In Russian)
10. Vodakhova, V. A boundary value problem with Nakhushev nonlocal condition for a certain pseudoparabolic moisture-transfer equation. *Differenc. Uravn.* **1982**, *18*, 280–285. (In Russian)
11. Ford, W.; Ting, T. Stability and convergence of difference approximations to pseudo-parabolic partial differential equations. *Math. Comput.* **1973**, *27*, 737–743. [CrossRef]
12. Ewing, R. Numerical solution of Sobolev partial differential equations. *SIAM J. Numer. Anal.* **1975**, *12*, 345–363. [CrossRef]
13. Lin, Y.; Zhou, Y. Solving nonlinear pseudoparabolic equations with nonlocal conditions in reproducing kernel space. *Numer. Algorithms* **2009**, *52*, 173–186. [CrossRef]
14. Chattouh, A.; Saoudi, K.; Nouar, M. Rothe—Legendre pseudospectral method for a semilinear pseudoparabolic equation with nonclassical boundary condition. *Nonlinear Anal. Model. Control* **2022**, *27*, 38–53. [CrossRef]
15. Jachimavičienė, J.; Ž. Jesevičiūtė.; Sapagovas, M. The stability of finite-difference schemes for a pseudoparabolic equation with nonlocal conditions. *Numer. Funct. Anal. Optim.* **2009**, *30*, 988–1001. [CrossRef]
16. Guezane-Lakoud, A.; Belakroum, D. Time-discretization schema for an integrodifferential Sobolev type equation with integral conditions. *Appl. Math. Comput.* **2012**, *218*, 4695–4702. [CrossRef]
17. Beshtokov, M. Boundary value problems for a loaded modified fractional-order moisture transfer equation with the Bessel operator and difference methods for their solution. *Vestn. Udmurt. Univ. Mat. Mekhanika Komp'yuternye Nauk.* **2020**, *30*, 158–175. [CrossRef]
18. Beshtokov, M. A numerical method for solving the second initial-boundary value problem for a multidimensional third-order pseudoparabolic equation. *Vestn. Udmurt. Univ. Mat. Mekhanika Komp'yuternye Nauk.* **2021**, *31*, 384–408. [CrossRef]
19. Beshtokov, M. Finite-difference method for solving a multidimensional pseudoparabolic equation with boundary conditions of the third kind. *Vestn. Udmurt. Univ. Mat. Mekhanika Komp'yuternye Nauk.* **2022**, *32*, 502–527. [CrossRef]
20. Jachimavičienė, J.; Sapagovas, M.; Štikonas, A.; Štikonienė, O. On the stability of explicit finite difference schemes for a pseudoparabolic equation with nonlocal conditions. *Nonlinear Anal. Model. Control* **2014**, *19*, 225–240. [CrossRef]
21. Čiegis, R.; Tumanova, N. On construction and analysis of finite difference schemes for pseudoparabolic problems with nonlocal boundary conditions. *Math. Model. Anal.* **2014**, *19*, 281–297. [CrossRef]
22. Aitzhanov, S.; Berdyshev, A.; Bekenayeva, K. Solvability issues of a pseudo-parabolic fractional order equation with a nonlinear boundary condition. *Fractal Fract.* **2021**, *5*, 134. [CrossRef]
23. Binh, H.; Hoang, L.; Baleanu, D.; Van, H. Solvability issues of a pseudo-parabolic fractional order equation with a nonlinear boundary condition. *Fractal Fract.* **2021**, *5*, 41. [CrossRef]
24. Shi, L.; Tayebi, S.; Arqub, O.; Osman, M.; Agarwal, P.; Mahamoud, W.; Abdel-Aty, M.; Alhodaly, M. The novel cubic B-spline method for fractional Painleve' and Bagley–Trovik equations in the Caputo, Caputo–Fabrizio, and conformable fractional sense. *Alex. Eng. J.* **2023**, *65*, 413–426. [CrossRef]

25. Peaceman, D.W.; Rachford, H.H. The numerical solution of parabolic and elliptic differential equations. *J. Soc. Ind. Appl. Math.* **1955**, *3*, 28–41. [CrossRef]
26. Pečiulytė, S.; Štikonas, A. On positive eigenfunctions of Sturm–Liouville problem with nonlocal two-point boundary condition. *Math. Model. Anal.* **2007**, *12*, 215–226. [CrossRef]
27. Pečiulytė, S.; Štikonienė, O.; Štikonas, A. Investigation of negative critical points of the characteristic function for problems with nonlocal boundary conditions. *Nonlinear Anal. Model. Control* **2008**, *13*, 467–490. [CrossRef]
28. Novickij, J.; Štikonas, A. On the stability of a weighted finite difference scheme for wave equation with nonlocal boundary conditions. *Nonlinear Anal. Model. Control* **2014**, *19*, 460–475. [CrossRef]
29. Bingelė, K.; Bankauskienė, A.; Štikonas, A. Spectrum curves for a discrete Sturm–Liouville problem with one integral boundary condition. *Nonlinear Anal. Model. Control* **2019**, *24*, 755–774. [CrossRef]
30. Dehghan, M. Alternating direction implicit methods for two-dimensional diffusion with a non-local boundary condition. *Intern. J. Comput. Math.* **1999**, *72*, 349–366. [CrossRef]
31. Noye, B.; Dehghan, M. New explicit finite difference schemes for two-dimensional diffusion subject to specification of mass. *Numer. Meth. PDE* **1999**, *15*, 521–534. [CrossRef]
32. Sapagovas, M.; Kairytė, G.; Štikonienė, O.; Štikonas, A. Alternating direction method for a two-dimensional parabolic equation with a nonlocal boundary condition. *Math. Model. Anal.* **2007**, *12*, 131–142. [CrossRef]
33. Sapagovas, M.; Štikonas, A.; Štikonienė, O. Alternating direction method for the Poisson equation with variable weight coefficients in an integral condition. *Differ. Equ.* **2011**, *47*, 1163–1174. [CrossRef]
34. Brociek, R.; Wajda, A.; Sciuto, G.L.; Słota, D.; Capizzi, G. Computational methods for parameter identification in 2D fractional system with Riemann—Liouville derivative. *Sensors* **2022**, *22*, 3153. [CrossRef] [PubMed]
35. Concezzi, M.; Spigler, R. An ADI method for the numerical solution of 3D fractional reaction-diffusion equations. *Fractal Fract.* **2020**, *4*, 57. [CrossRef]
36. Yang, S.; Liu, F.; Feng, L.; Turner, I. Efficient numerical methods for the nonlinear two-sided space-fractional diffusion equation with variable coefficients. *Appl. Numer. Math.* **2020**, *157*, 55–68. [CrossRef]
37. Vabishchevich, P. On a new class of additive (splitting) operator-difference schemes. *Math. Comput.* **2012**, *81*, 267–276. [CrossRef]
38. Vabishchevich, P.; Grigor'ev, A. Splitting schemes for pseudoparabolic equations. *Differ. Equ.* **2013**, *49*, 807–814. [CrossRef]
39. Douglas, J.; Rachford, H.H. On the numerical solution of heat conduction problems in two and three space variables. *Trans. Amer. Math. Soc.* **1956**, *82*, 421–489. [CrossRef]
40. Samarskii, A. *The Theory of Difference Schemes*; Marcel Dekker: New York, NY, USA, 2001. [CrossRef]
41. Voevodin, V.; Kuznecov, Y. *Matrices and Computations*; Nauka: Moscow, Russia, 1984. (In Russian)
42. Lancaster, P. *Lambda-Matrices and Vibrating Systems*; Pergamon Press: Oxford, UK, 1966. [CrossRef]
43. Štikonas, A. The root condition for polynomial of the second order and a spectral stability of finite-difference schemes for Kuramoto-Tsuzuki equations. *Math. Model. Anal.* **1998**, *3*, 214–226. [CrossRef]
44. Varga, R. *Matrix Iteratyve Analysis*; Springer Series in Computational Mathematics; Springer: Berlin/Heidelberg, Germany, 2000. [CrossRef]
45. Atkinson, K. *An Introduction to Numerical Analysis*; John Wiley & Sons: Hoboken, NJ, USA, 1989.
46. Isaacson, E.; Keller, H. *Analysis of Numerical Methods*; John Wiley & Sons: New York, NY, USA, 1996.
47. Samarskii, A.; Gulin, A. *Numerical Methods*; Nauka: Moscow, Russia, 1989. (In Russian)
48. Collatz, L. *Functional Analysis and Numerical Mathematics*; Elsevier: Amsterdam, The Netherlands, 1966. [CrossRef]
49. Gulin, A. Stability criteria for non-self-adjoint finite differences schemes in the subspace. *Appl. Numer. Math.* **2015**, *93*, 107–113. [CrossRef]
50. Cahlon, B.; Kulkarni, D.; Shi, P. Stepwise stability for the heat equation with a nonlocal constraint. *SIAM J. Numer. Anal.* **1995**, *32*, 571–593. [CrossRef]

Article

Three-Dimensional Unsteady Mixed Convection Flow of Non-Newtonian Nanofluid with Consideration of Retardation Time Effects

Badreddine Ayadi [1,2], Kaouther Ghachem [3], Kamel Al-Khaled [4], Sami Ullah Khan [5], Karim Kriaa [6,7], Chemseddine Maatki [8,9], Nesrine Zahi [10] and Lioua Kolsi [1,*]

[1] Department of Mechanical Engineering, College of Engineering, University of Ha'il, Ha'il City 81451, Saudi Arabia
[2] Laboratory of Applied Fluid Mechanics, Environment and Process Engineering "LR11ES57", National School of Engineers of Sfax (ENIS), University of Sfax, Soukra Road Km 3.5, Sfax 3038, Tunisia
[3] Department of Industrial Engineering and Systems, College of Engineering, Princess Nourah bint Abdulrahman University, P.O. Box 84428, Riyadh 11671, Saudi Arabia
[4] Department of Mathematics & Statistics, Jordan University of Science and Technology, P.O. Box 3030, Irbid 22110, Jordan
[5] Department of Mathematics, Namal University, Mianwali 42250, Pakistan
[6] Department of Chemical Engineering, College of Engineering, Imam Mohammad Ibn Saud Islamic University (IMSIU), Riyadh 11432, Saudi Arabia
[7] Department of Chemical Engineering, National School of Engineers of Gabes, University of Gabes, Gabes 6029, Tunisia
[8] Department of Mechanical Engineering, College of Engineering, Imam Mohammad Ibn Saud Islamic University (IMSIU), Riyadh 11432, Saudi Arabia
[9] Laboratory of Metrology and Energy Systems, Energy Engineering Department, National Engineering School, University of Monastir, Monastir 5000, Tunisia
[10] Applied College, Huraymila, Imam Mohammad Ibn Saud Islamic University (IMSIU), Riyadh 11432, Saudi Arabia
* Correspondence: lioua_enim@yahoo.fr

Citation: Ayadi, B.; Ghachem, K.; Al-Khaled, K.; Khan, S.U.; Kriaa, K.; Maatki, C.; Zahi, N.; Kolsi, L. Three-Dimensional Unsteady Mixed Convection Flow of Non-Newtonian Nanofluid with Consideration of Retardation Time Effects. *Mathematics* **2023**, *11*, 1892. https://doi.org/10.3390/math11081892

Academic Editor: Arsen Palestini

Received: 8 March 2023
Revised: 12 April 2023
Accepted: 15 April 2023
Published: 17 April 2023

Abstract: The advances in nanotechnology led to the development of new kinds of engineered fluids called nanofluids. Nanofluids have several industrial and engineering applications, such as solar energy systems, heat conduction processes, nuclear systems, chemical processes, etc. The motivation of the present work is to analyze and explore the thermal and dynamic behaviors of a non-Newtonian fluid flow under time retardation effects. The flow is unsteady and caused by a bidirectional, periodically moving surface. In addition to the convective heat transfer and fluid flow, the radiation and chemical reactions have also been considered. The governing equations are established based on the modified Cattaneo–Christov heat flux formulation. It was found that the bidirectional velocities oscillate periodically, and that the magnitude of the oscillation increases with the retardation time. Higher temperatures occur when the porosity parameter is increased, and lower concentrations are encountered for higher values of the concentration relaxation parameter. The current results can be applied in thermal systems, heat transfer enhancement, chemical synthesis, solar systems, power generation, medical applications, the automotive industry, process industries, refrigeration, etc.

Keywords: heat transfer; bidirectional flow; porous medium; nanofluids; accelerating surface; chemical reaction; Oldroyd-B nanofluid

MSC: 76r05; 76r10

1. Introduction

Several studies on nanofluid applications have recently been presented. Leading to more compact systems and higher performances, nanofluids have become widely used in heat transfer systems, the production and enhancement of energy resources, the extrusion process, the nuclear industry, and many other applications. When nanoparticles are suspended in a base fluid, the suspension becomes characterized by enhanced thermophysical properties. Nanoparticles are particles with dimensions in the nanometer range, typically between 1 and 100 nanometers in size. The size of nanoparticles can vary depending on their composition, shape, and method of synthesis. In general, nanoparticles smaller than 10 nanometers tend to have unique physical and chemical properties due to their high surface-area-to-volume ratio, while those larger than 100 nanometers start to exhibit bulk-like behavior. These nanoparticles are uniformly distributed in the base liquid to enhance the thermal impact of the base materials. Such predictions were first experimentally confirmed by Choi [1]. Buongiorno [2] presented a detailed description of nanofluid convective heat transfer with a focus on the thermophoretic and Brownian motion effects. Hayat et al. [3] investigated the hydrothermal behavior of a nanofluid flow under the effect of an external magnetic field. Sui et al. [4] studied the Cattaneo–Christov double diffusive convection of a Maxwell nanofluid past a stretching sheet. Hsiao [5] presented a numerical study on the micropolar nanofluid flow by considering the MHD and viscous dissipation effects. Turkyilmazoglu [6] considered free and circular jet cooling using nanofluids. Ahmed et al. [7] presented a study on the stagnation point of nanofluid flow past a rotating disk under the effect of a heat source. Turkyilmazoglu [8] used the Buongiorno model to study the nanofluid flow in an asymmetric channel. Tlili et al. [9] studied the bioconvective non-Newtonian nanofluid flow past a stretching cylinder by considering the effect of the activation energy. Abbasi et al. [10] studied the effect of using a hybrid nanofluid on the flow over a curved channel. Kiranakumar et al. [11] presented a comprehensive review of the electrical properties of graphene oxide nanoparticles. Waqas et al. [12] studied the effect of applying an exponential heat flux on the bioconvection of a non-Newtonian nanofluid past a moving surface. Chu et al. [13] used the Keller box method to study the radiative heat transfer of various kinds of hybrid nanofluids. Habib et al. [14] investigated the combined EHD, MHD, and activation energy effects on the bioconvective, time-dependent nanofluid flow caused by an extending sheet. Xia et al. [15] studied the entropy generation caused by the natural bioconversion of Eyring–Powell nanofluids. Waqas et al. [16] studied the bioconvective micropolar nanofluid flow under the impacts of a magnetic field, radiation, and the Joule effect. Liu et al. [17] performed a molecular dynamics study on the effect of using CuO nanoparticles on the phase-change process of a PCM. Mekheimer et al. [18] studied numerically the nanoparticle drug injection in blood to detect diseased organs.

The characteristics of non-Newtonian materials are very important in industrial frameworks and engineering processes. For example, non-Newtonian polymers have several applications in manufacturing processes and chemical industries. Based on their fluid behavior, non-Newtonian liquids are classified into diverse categories. The Maxwell model describes non-Newtonian viscous flow on a long timescale. However, retardation time features are novel rheological consequences that are observed in some non-Newtonian liquids. Such characteristics are identified with the help of the Oldroyd-B fluid model. Kumar et al. [19] presented a study on the rheological behavior of Oldroyd-B fluid with consideration of viscous dissipation and the Joule and radiation effects. Sajid et al. [20] numerically investigated the mixed convection of Oldroyd-B liquid under the effects of viscous dissipation and an external magnetic field. Irfan et al. [21] tested the effect of considering a variable thermal conductivity on the double diffusive convection of Oldroyd-B nanofluid. Bai et al. [22] presented a numerical study on the transient Oldroyd-B double diffusive flow. Roy and Pop [23] conducted an investigation on the mixed convection of Oldroyd-B nanofluid past a shrinking surface. Mabood et al. [24] predicted the effect of radiation and chemical reactions on the rheological behavior of Oldroyd-B nanofluid.

The main objective of the current study is to observe the thermal and hydrodynamic behaviors of Oldroyd-B nanofluid flow caused by a bidirectionally oscillating porous surface. To perform this study, the unsteady mathematical model governing the coupled heat and mass transfer phenomena is developed using the Cattaneo–Christov thermal flux model, and HAM is used to find the semi-analytical solution. The effects of chemical reactions and radiation on the flow and heat and mass transfer are presented in terms of their velocity, temperature, and concentration profiles.

2. Problem Formulation

The Oldroyd-B nanofluid flow over a bidirectional, periodically oscillating porous surface is considered in the current study. The three-dimensional flow is caused by a moving surface with time-dependent velocity. The bidirectional surface is maintained at horizontal and vertical velocities expressed as $u = u_w = ax \sin \omega t$ and $v = v_w = by \sin \omega t$, respectively. Here, ω and b are the angular frequencies and stretching rate, respectively. Following the cartesian coordinates, x and y are being continued in the surface direction while the z axis is toward the normal direction. For oscillatory phenomena, it has been assumed that the magnitude of oscillation is small in such a manner that the flow regime is kept laminar [25–27]. The heat and concentration equations are established via the modified heat and mass flux theories. In addition, the chemical reaction effect is considered in the concentration equation. Based on the above-mentioned assumptions, the governing equations are expressed as follows [25–27]:

$$\frac{\partial v}{\partial y} + \frac{\partial u}{\partial x} + \frac{\partial w}{\partial z} = 0, \tag{1}$$

$$\left(\frac{\partial u}{\partial y}\right)v + \left(\frac{\partial u}{\partial x}\right)u + \frac{\partial u}{\partial t} + \left(\frac{\partial u}{\partial z}\right)w + \lambda_1 \left(\begin{array}{c} 2\left(w\frac{\partial^2 u}{\partial z \partial t} + vw\frac{\partial^2 u}{\partial y \partial z}\right) + 2\left(uv\frac{\partial^2 u}{\partial x \partial y}\right) \\ + \frac{\partial^2 u}{\partial t^2} + v^2\frac{\partial^2 u}{\partial y^2} + u^2\frac{\partial^2 u}{\partial x^2} + w^2\frac{\partial^2 u}{\partial z^2} \\ + 2\left(v\frac{\partial^2 u}{\partial y \partial t}\right) + 2\left(uw\frac{\partial^2 u}{\partial x \partial z} + u\frac{\partial^2 u}{\partial x \partial t}\right) \end{array} \right) - \nu\frac{\partial^2 u}{\partial z^2}$$

$$+\nu\lambda_2\left(\frac{\partial^2 v}{\partial z^2}\frac{\partial u}{\partial y} + \frac{\partial^2 w}{\partial z^2}\frac{\partial u}{\partial z} + \frac{\partial^2 u}{\partial z^2}\frac{\partial u}{\partial x}\right)$$

$$-\nu\lambda_2\left(\frac{\partial^3 u}{\partial z^2 \partial t} + v\frac{\partial^3 u}{\partial y \partial z^2} + u\frac{\partial^3 u}{\partial x \partial z^2} + w\frac{\partial^3 u}{\partial z^3}\right) - \frac{\nu u}{k_p}, \tag{2}$$

$$u\left(\frac{\partial v}{\partial x}\right) + v\left(\frac{\partial v}{\partial y}\right) + w\left(\frac{\partial v}{\partial z}\right) + \frac{\partial v}{\partial t} + \lambda_1 \left(\begin{array}{c} 2\left(w\frac{\partial^2 v}{\partial z \partial t}\right) + 2\left(uv\frac{\partial^2 v}{\partial x \partial y} + vw\frac{\partial^2 v}{\partial y \partial z}\right) \\ + \frac{\partial^2 v}{\partial t^2} + v^2\frac{\partial^2 v}{\partial y^2} + w^2\frac{\partial^2 v}{\partial z^2} + u^2\frac{\partial^2 v}{\partial x^2} \\ + 2\left(v\frac{\partial^2 v}{\partial y \partial t}\right) + 2\left(uw\frac{\partial^2 v}{\partial x \partial z} + u\frac{\partial^2 v}{\partial x \partial t}\right) \end{array} \right) - \nu\frac{\partial^2 v}{\partial z^2}$$

$$+\nu\,\lambda_2\left(\frac{\partial v}{\partial y}\frac{\partial^2 v}{\partial z^2} + \frac{\partial^2 w}{\partial z^2}\frac{\partial v}{\partial z} + \frac{\partial v}{\partial x}\frac{\partial^2 u}{\partial z^2}\right) = \nu\,\lambda_2\left(\frac{\partial^3 v}{\partial z^2 \partial t} + w\frac{\partial^3 v}{\partial z^3} + v\frac{\partial^3 v}{\partial y \partial z^2} + u\frac{\partial^3 v}{\partial x \partial z^2}\right) - \frac{\nu u}{k_p}, \tag{3}$$

$$u\frac{\partial T}{\partial x} + v\frac{\partial T}{\partial y} + w\frac{\partial T}{\partial z} + \frac{\partial T}{\partial t} + \delta_2 \left[\begin{array}{c} 2u\frac{\partial^2 T}{\partial x \partial t} + w^2\frac{\partial^2 T}{\partial z^2} + v^2\frac{\partial^2 T}{\partial y^2} + u^2\frac{\partial^2 T}{\partial x^2} + 2w\frac{\partial^2 T}{\partial z \partial t} + w\frac{\partial u}{\partial z}\frac{\partial T}{\partial x} \\ +v\left(\frac{\partial T}{\partial z}\frac{\partial w}{\partial y} + \frac{\partial T}{\partial y}\frac{\partial v}{\partial y}\right) + \frac{\partial w}{\partial t}\frac{\partial T}{\partial z} + u\left(\frac{\partial T}{\partial y}\frac{\partial v}{\partial x} + \frac{\partial T}{\partial x}\frac{\partial u}{\partial x} + \frac{\partial T}{\partial z}\frac{\partial w}{\partial x}\right) \\ +\frac{\partial u}{\partial t}\frac{\partial T}{\partial x} + \frac{\partial v}{\partial t}\frac{\partial T}{\partial y} + \frac{\partial^2 T}{\partial t^2} + v\frac{\partial u}{\partial y}\frac{\partial T}{\partial x} + w\frac{\partial v}{\partial z}\frac{\partial T}{\partial y} \\ +2v\left(u\frac{\partial^2 T}{\partial x \partial y} + w\frac{\partial^2 T}{\partial y \partial z} + \frac{\partial^2 T}{\partial y \partial t}\right) + w\left(2u\frac{\partial^2 T}{\partial x \partial z} + \frac{\partial w}{\partial z}\frac{\partial T}{\partial z}\right) \end{array} \right]$$

$$= \left(\alpha_m + \frac{16\sigma_s T_\infty^3}{3k^*(\rho c)_f}\right)\frac{\partial^2 T}{\partial z^2} + \sigma_*\left[\frac{D_T}{T_\infty}\left(\frac{\partial T}{\partial z}\right)^2 + D_B\frac{\partial C}{\partial z}\frac{\partial T}{\partial z}\right], \tag{4}$$

$$
\left(\frac{\partial C}{\partial y}\right)v + \left(\frac{\partial C}{\partial x}\right)u + \frac{\partial C}{\partial t} + \left(\frac{\partial C}{\partial z}\right)w + \delta_2
\begin{bmatrix}
2u\frac{\partial^2 C}{\partial x\partial t} + w^2\frac{\partial^2 C}{\partial z^2} + v^2\frac{\partial^2 C}{\partial y^2} + u^2\frac{\partial^2 C}{\partial x^2} \\[4pt]
+2w\frac{\partial^2 C}{\partial z\partial t} + w\frac{\partial u}{\partial z}\frac{\partial C}{\partial x} + v\frac{\partial v}{\partial y}\frac{\partial C}{\partial y} \\[2pt]
+v\frac{\partial w}{\partial y}\frac{\partial C}{\partial z} + \frac{\partial v}{\partial t}\frac{\partial C}{\partial y} \\[4pt]
+u\left(\frac{\partial C}{\partial y}\frac{\partial v}{\partial x} + \frac{\partial u}{\partial x}\frac{\partial C}{\partial x} + \frac{\partial C}{\partial z}\frac{\partial w}{\partial x}\right) \\[4pt]
+\frac{\partial u}{\partial t}\frac{\partial C}{\partial x} + \frac{\partial^2 C}{\partial t^2} + v\frac{\partial u}{\partial y}\frac{\partial C}{\partial x} \\[2pt]
+\frac{\partial w}{\partial t}\frac{\partial C}{\partial z} + w\frac{\partial v}{\partial z}\frac{\partial C}{\partial y} \\[4pt]
+2v\left(u\frac{\partial^2 C}{\partial x\partial y} + w\frac{\partial^2 C}{\partial y\partial z} + \frac{\partial^2 C}{\partial y\partial t}\right) \\[4pt]
+w\left(2u\frac{\partial^2 C}{\partial x\partial z} + \frac{\partial w}{\partial z}\frac{\partial C}{\partial z}\right)
\end{bmatrix}
\tag{5}
$$

$$
= \left(\frac{D_T}{T_\infty}\right)\frac{\partial^2 T}{\partial z^2} + D_B\frac{\partial^2 C}{\partial z^2} - k_*(C - C_\infty).
$$

The boundary conditions are [25–27]:

$$
u = u_w = ax\sin\omega t,\ w = 0, \quad C = C_w,\ v = v_w = by\,\sin\omega t,\ T = T_w,\ z = 0,
\tag{6}
$$

$$
u \to 0,\ C \to C_\infty,\ T \to T_\infty,\ v \to 0, \quad as\ z \to \infty.
\tag{7}
$$

The used dimensionless variables are [25,27]:

$$
\left.
\begin{aligned}
&v = yag_\xi(\xi,\tau),\ \mathrm{w} = -\sqrt{va}(+g(\xi,\tau) + f(\xi,\tau)), u = xaf_\xi(\xi,\tau) \\[6pt]
&\xi = \sqrt{\tfrac{a}{v}}z,\ \tau = t\omega,\ \theta(\xi,\tau) = \tfrac{T-T_\infty}{T_w-T_\infty},\ \phi(\xi,\tau) = \tfrac{C-C_\infty}{C_w-C_\infty}.
\end{aligned}
\right\}
\tag{8}
$$

Using these new variables, the governing equations become:

$$
f_{\xi\xi\xi} + ff_{\xi\xi} + gf_{\xi\xi} - \left(f_\xi^2 + Sf_{\xi\tau}\right) - Haf_\xi - \beta_1
\begin{bmatrix}
S^2 f_{\xi\tau\tau} + 2Sf_\xi f_{\xi\tau} + (f+g)^2 f_{\xi\xi\xi} \\[4pt]
-2(f+g)(Sf_{\xi\xi\tau} + f_\xi f_{\xi\xi})
\end{bmatrix}
+ \beta_2
\begin{bmatrix}
Sf_{\xi\xi\xi\tau} + f_{\xi\xi}(g_{\xi\xi} + f_{\xi\xi}) \\[4pt]
-(f+g)f_{\xi\xi\xi\xi}
\end{bmatrix},
\tag{9}
$$

$$
\begin{aligned}
g_{\xi\xi\xi} + (g+f)g_{\xi\xi} - Haf_\xi - (g_\xi^2 + Sg_{\xi\tau}) + \beta_2
&\begin{bmatrix}
g_{\xi\xi}(f_{\xi\xi} + g_{\xi\xi}) \\[4pt]
+Sg_{\xi\xi\xi\tau} - (g+f)g_{\xi\xi\xi\xi}
\end{bmatrix} \\[8pt]
-\beta_1
&\begin{bmatrix}
S^2 g_{\xi\tau\tau} + g_{\xi\xi\xi}(f+g)^2 + 2Sg_\xi g_{\xi\tau} \\[4pt]
-2(Sg_{\xi\xi\tau} + g_\xi g_{\xi\xi})(f+g)
\end{bmatrix} = 0,
\end{aligned}
\tag{10}
$$

$$
\frac{(1+Rd)}{\mathrm{Pr}}\theta_{\xi\xi} + \left(Nb\theta_\xi\phi_\xi - S\theta_\tau + Nt\theta_\xi^2 + (g+f)\theta_\xi\right) - \delta_T
\begin{pmatrix}
S^2\theta_{\tau\tau} - S(f_\tau\theta_\xi + g_\tau\theta_\xi) \\[4pt]
-2S(g+f)\theta_{\tau\xi} + (g+f)^2\theta_{\xi\xi} \\[4pt]
+(f_\xi + g_\xi)(f+g)\theta_\xi
\end{pmatrix} = 0,
\tag{11}
$$

$$
\phi_{\xi\xi} + Le\mathrm{Pr}\left[(g+f)\phi_\xi - S\phi_\tau - Kr\phi\right] + \frac{Nt}{Nb}\theta_{\xi\xi} - Sc\delta_c
\begin{pmatrix}
S^2\phi_{\tau\tau} - S(f_\tau\phi_\xi + g_\tau\phi_\xi) \\[4pt]
-2S(g+f)\phi_{\tau\xi} + (g+f)^2\phi_{\xi\xi} \\[4pt]
+(f_\xi + g_\xi)(f+g)\phi_\xi
\end{pmatrix} = 0.
\tag{12}
$$

The dimensionless boundary conditions are as follows:

$$g(0,\tau) = 0,\, f(0,\tau) = 0,\, f_\zeta(0,\tau) = \sin\tau,\, g_\zeta(0,\tau) = \gamma\sin\tau,\, \theta(0,\tau) = 1 \left.\right\}$$
$$\phi(0,\tau) = 1,\, g_\zeta(\infty,\tau) = 0,\, f_\zeta(\infty,\tau) = 0,\, \theta(\infty,\tau) = 0,\, \phi(\infty,\tau) = 0. \quad (13)$$

The dimensionless parameters β_1, β_2 (Deborah numbers), Nb (Brownian motion), Le (Lewis number), Kr (chemical reaction), γ (stretching ratio constant), Kr (reaction constant), δ_T (thermal relaxation constant), δ_c (concentration relaxation constant), S (ratio of frequency to stretching rate), Pr (Prandtl number), and Nt (thermophoresis) are defined as:

$$Le = \frac{\alpha_m}{D_B},\, Kr = \frac{k_*}{a},\, \beta_1 = \lambda_1 a,\, \beta_2 = \lambda_2 a,\, \mathrm{Pr} = \frac{\nu}{\alpha_m},\, S = \frac{\omega}{a},\, Nb = \frac{\sigma_* D_B(C_w - C_\infty)}{\nu},$$
$$R = \frac{16\sigma_s T_\infty^3}{3kk^*},\, \delta_c = \delta_2 a,\, \gamma = \frac{b}{a}\, Nt = \frac{\sigma_* D_T(T_w - T_\infty)}{\nu T_\infty},\, Ha = \frac{\nu}{ak_p},\, \delta_T = \delta_1 a. \quad (14)$$

The local Sherwood and Nusselt numbers are expressed by the following relations [27]:

$$(\mathrm{Re}_x)^{-1/2} Nu_x = -(1+R)\theta_\zeta(0,\tau),\, Sh_x(\mathrm{Re}_x)^{-1/2} = -\phi_\zeta(0,\tau). \quad (15)$$

where Re_x is the local Reynolds number.

3. Homotopy Analytical Method

The resolutions of the formulated model are performed analytically with the implementation of the homotopy analysis scheme. The motivations for using the homotopy analysis method are justified, as this scheme provides high accuracy and little error. It should also be mentioned that the HAM method does not have any limitations related to the fixation of any small or large parameters [28–30]. The initial guesses for performing simulations are:

$$f_0(\zeta,\tau) = \left(1 - e^{-\zeta}\right)\sin\tau,\, g_0(\zeta,\tau) = \gamma\left(1 - e^{-\zeta}\right)\sin\tau,$$
$$\theta_0(\zeta,\tau) = e^{-\zeta},\, \phi_0(\zeta,\tau) = e^{-\zeta}. \quad (16)$$

The use of the linear operators (Υ):

$$\Upsilon_f = \frac{\partial^3}{\partial\zeta^3} - \frac{\partial}{\partial\zeta},\quad \Upsilon_g = \frac{\partial^3}{\partial\zeta^3} - \frac{\partial}{\partial\zeta},\quad \Upsilon_\theta = \frac{\partial^2}{\partial\zeta^2} - 1,\quad \Upsilon_\phi = \frac{\partial^2}{\partial\zeta^2} - 1. \quad (17)$$

gives the following equations:

$$l_f\left[\kappa_1 + \kappa_2 e^\zeta + \kappa_3 e^{-\zeta}\right] = 0,\quad l_g\left[\kappa_4 + \kappa_5 e^\zeta + \kappa_6 e^{-\zeta}\right] = 0,$$
$$l_\theta\left[\kappa_7 e^\zeta + \kappa_8 e^{-\zeta}\right] = 0,\quad l_\phi\left[\kappa_9 e^\zeta + \kappa_{10} e^{-\zeta}\right] = 0. \quad (18)$$

4. Convergence of HAM

The convergence regime is estimated with the proper values of auxiliary factors h_f, h_θ, h_g and h_ϕ. The feasible region for ensuring the solution validity is highlighted with plotted h-curves. Figure 1 is presented to predict this convergence region. The convergence regime is defined by $-1.4 \leq h_f \leq 0.2$, $-1.4 \leq h_\theta \leq -0.2$, $-1.3 \leq h_g \leq -0.1$ and $-1.3 \leq h_\phi \leq -0.35$.

This section is dedicated to exploring the effects of the governing parameters on the flow, temperature, and concentration fields. The formulated mathematical problem is associated with the theoretical flow assumptions instead of any experimental data. Therefore, physical analysis is performed for ranges of governing parameters as follows: $0 \leq Ha \leq 0.3$, $0 \leq \beta_2 \leq 1.4$, $0.1 \leq \delta_T \leq 1.2$, $0.1 \leq \mathrm{Pr} \leq 1.2$, $0.1 \leq Nb \leq 1.2$, $0.1 \leq Rd \leq 1.2$, and $0.2 \leq \delta_C \leq 0.8$, $0.0 \leq Kr \leq 0.5$. Figure 2a,b illustrate the velocity component profiles f_ζ and g_ζ for various values of the porosity parameter Ha. A declining behavior in both velocity components is observed when Ha is increased. Physically, this reduction is due to the reduced permeability of the porous media. Figure 3a,b present the effects of the retardation time factor β_2 on f_ξ and g_ξ. Both velocity components have larger values for higher values of β_2. This increase is due to the intensification of the flow caused by the retardation time. In fact, the retardation time is associated with the rest position attained by fluid particles. Figure 4a,b show the effect of the retardation parameter β_2 on f_ξ and g_ξ. The increase in β_2, leads to an increase in velocity. In both graphs, a phase shift of smaller magnitude is noticed.

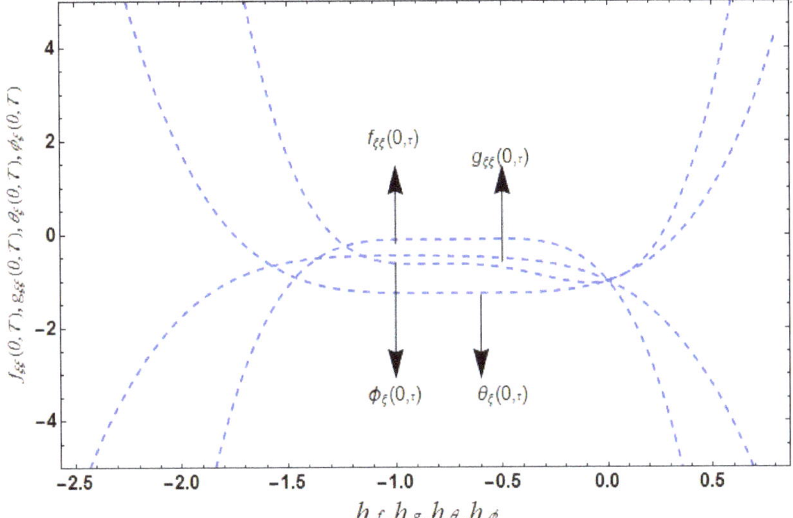

Figure 1. h-curves for all profiles.

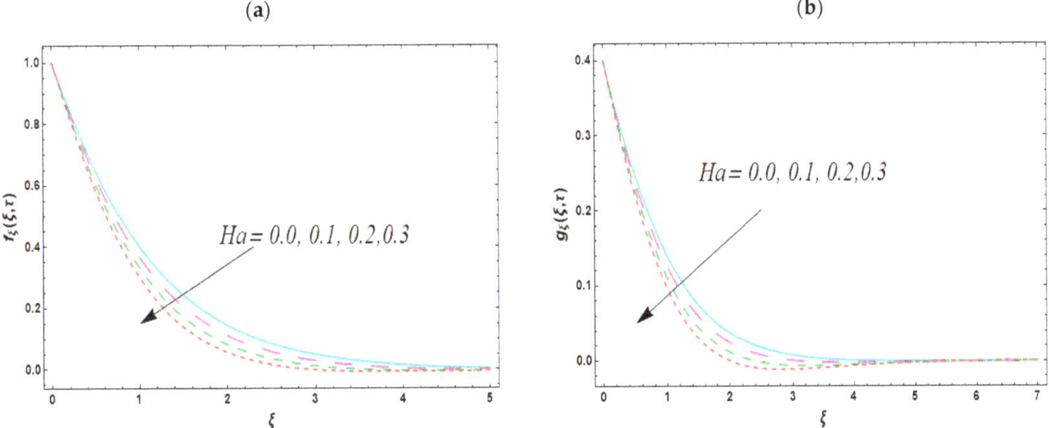

Figure 2. (**a**) Profiles of f_ξ for various Ha values; (**b**) profiles of g_ξ for various Ha values.

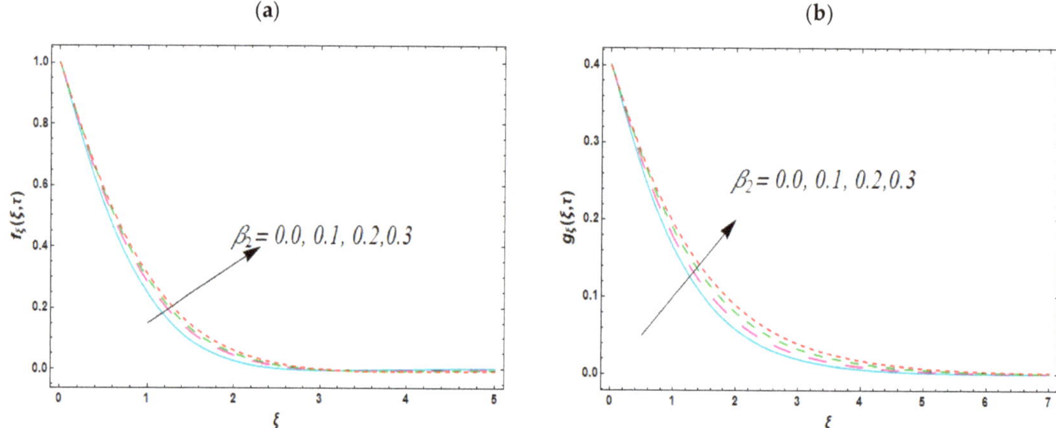

Figure 3. (**a**) Profiles of f_ξ for various β_2 values; (**b**) profiles of g_ξ for various β_2 values.

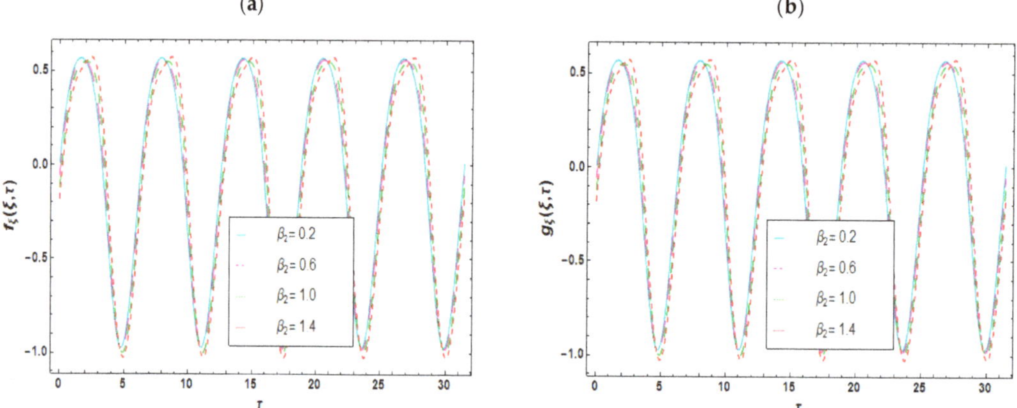

Figure 4. (**a**) Temporal variations in f_ξ for various β_2 values and (**b**) temporal variations in g_ξ for various β_2 values.

The results illustrated in Figure 5a report the effects of δ_T on the behavior of the temperature profile θ. Lower temperatures are encountered when the thermal relaxation factor δ_T is increased. This decrease leads to a lower heat transfer rate. Figure 5b illustrates the temperature profile θ for various Prandtl number Pr values. The Prandtl number is inversely proportional to the thermal diffusivity. Thus, the increase in Pr values, leads to a reduction in temperature. In Figure 5c, the effect of increasing the Brownian motion constant N_b on the temperature field is presented. Higher temperatures occur for larger values of N_b. Physically, Brownian motion is based on the random movement of heated particles, some of which collide with each other. This collision enhances thermal transport. The effect of the radiation parameter Rd on the temperature θ profile is exposed in Figure 5d. The increase in Rd leads to higher temperature values. This is due to the enhancement of heat transfer by the combined effects of convective and radiative heat transfers. Figure 6a–e illustrate the changes in concentration profile ϕ caused by the variation in the porosity parameter Ha, the Lewis number Le, the concentration relaxation parameter δ_C, the reaction parameter Kr, and the Brownian parameter Nb. As presented in Figure 6a, due to the change in the porosity parameter, an increase in the concentration is exhibited. Physically, such observations are due to the permeability of the porous space. From Figure 6b, it is concluded that the increase in Le reduces the concentration value ϕ. The results presented in Figure 6c–e demonstrate that the increases in δ_C, Kr, and Nb lead to lower values of concentration. Table 1 presents the effect of the governing parameters on the Nusselt number. It is noticed that the increase in Pr leads to an enhancement of the heat transfer rate, while the opposite occurs for Nb and Nt. Similarly, Table 2 shows the effects of the governing parameters on the Sherwood number. An important enhancement of the mass transfer is noticed for higher values of Le and N_b.

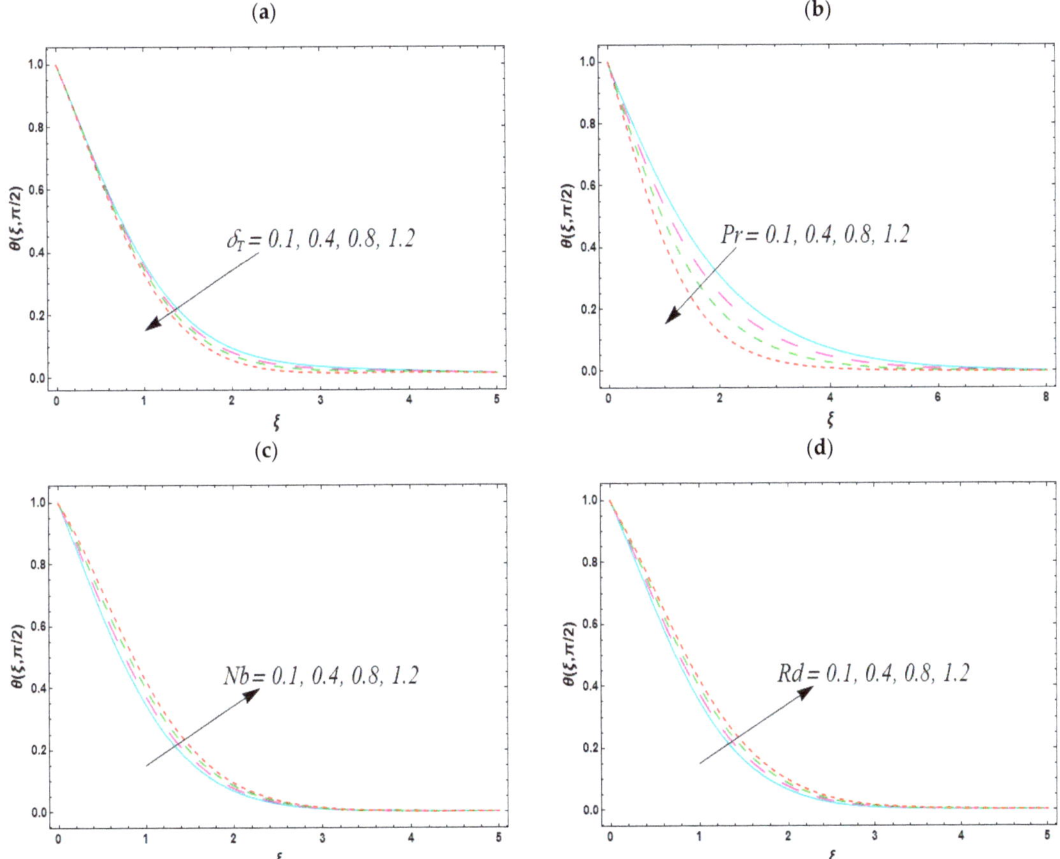

Figure 5. Temperature profiles for various values of (**a**) δ_T, (**b**) Pr, (**c**) N_b and (**d**) Rd.

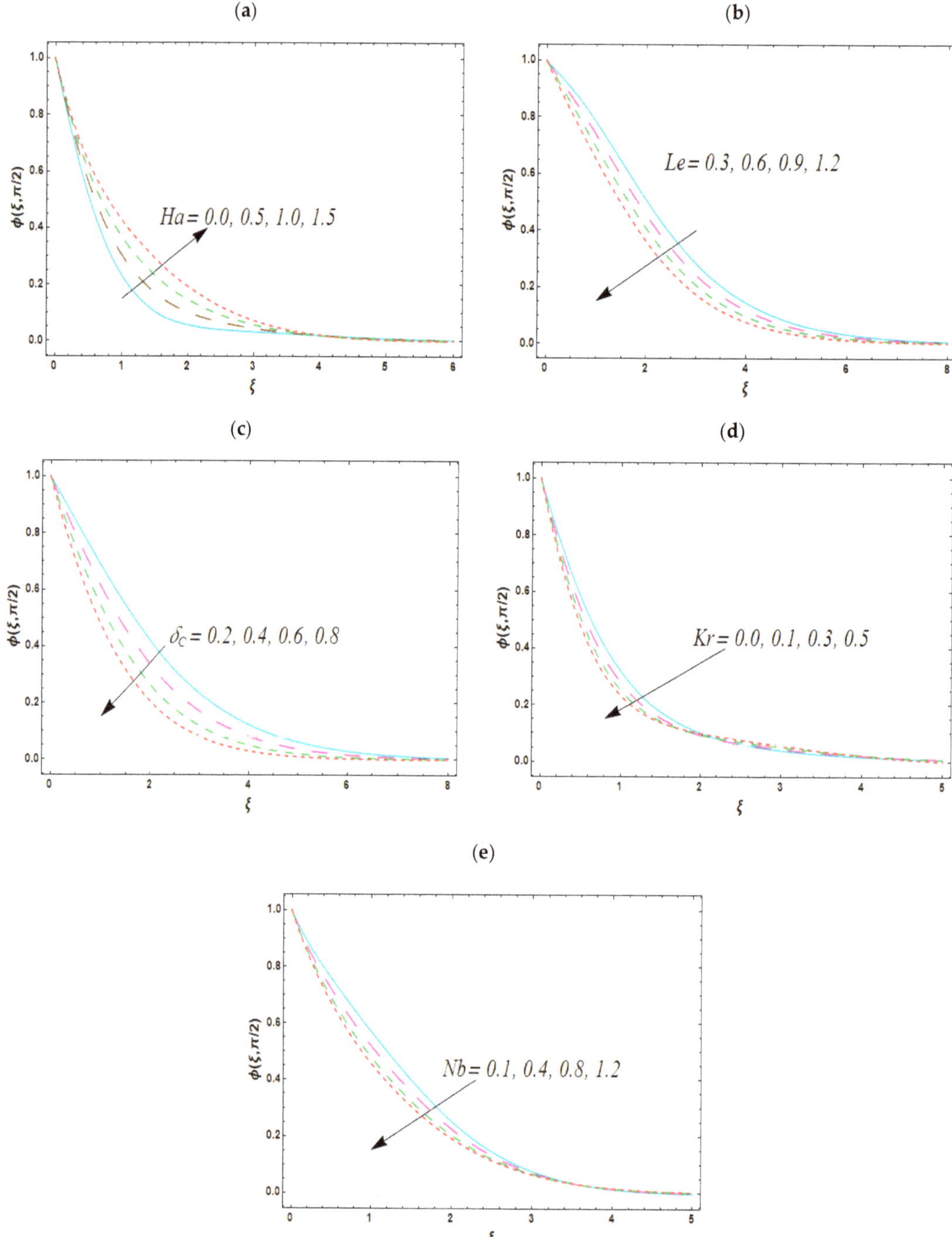

Figure 6. Concentration profiles for various values of (**a**) *Ha*, (**b**) *Le*, (**c**) δ_C, (**d**) *Kr* and (**e**) *Nb*.

Table 1. Evaluation of Nusselt number at various governing parameters.

Pr	Le	N_b	N_t	$\dfrac{Nu_x}{(\mathrm{Re}_x)^{1/2}}$
0.2	0.1	0.3	0.3	0.51425
0.4				0.56789
0.8				0.60670
0.3	0.4			0.62317
	0.6			0.64209
	0.8			0.66324
		0.2		0.48359
		0.4		0.4556
		0.6		0.427857
			0.2	0.48053
			0.6	0.46475
			0.8	0.428857

Table 2. Evaluation of Sherwood number at various governing parameters.

Le	N_b	N_t	$\dfrac{Sh_x}{(\mathrm{Re}_x)^{1/2}}$
0.2	0.3		0.754231
0.6			0.83544
0.8			0.93567
0.3	0.2		0.64567
	0.6		0.72675
	0.8		0.74534
		0.2	0.63556
		0.4	0.58324
		0.6	0.53677

5. Conclusions

The heat and mass transfer characteristics of Oldroyd-B nanofluid are analyzed in consideration of chemical reactions and thermal radiation effects. The flow is generated by the bidirectional periodic oscillating surface. The HAM computations are performed for solution assessment. The main findings can be summarized as follows:

- ❖ A reduction in the flow intensity due to the increase in the porosity parameter is noticed.
- ❖ No phase shift of the oscillating velocity is encountered for all the considered parameters.
- ❖ An augmentation of the velocity magnitude occurs when the oscillation frequency ratio is increased.
- ❖ The retardation parameter causes an increase in velocity.
- ❖ The increase in the thermal relaxation factor causes a reduction in temperature.
- ❖ The porosity parameters enhance the thermal and concentration profiles.
- ❖ An augmentation of the heat transfer occurs when the radiative parameter is increasing.
- ❖ Lower concentrations are encountered for higher values of the Prandtl and Lewis numbers.
- ❖ The local Nusselt number increases with the Lewis and Prandtl numbers.
- ❖ The current analysis can be extended by modifying the model, evaluating the entropy generation, performing a sensitivity analysis, considering hybrid nanofluids, using an artificial neural network, etc.

Author Contributions: Conceptualization, B.A., K.G. and L.K.; Methodology, K.A.-K., S.U.K., K.K. and L.K.; Software, B.A., K.G. and N.Z.; Formal analysis, K.G., S.U.K., C.M. and L.K.; Investigation, B.A., K.G. and S.U.K.; Writing—original draft, B.A., K.G., K.A.-K., S.U.K., K.K., C.M., N.Z. and L.K.; Writing—review & editing, B.A., K.G., K.A.-K., S.U.K., K.K., C.M., N.Z. and L.K.; Project administration, K.G.; Funding acquisition, K.G. All authors have read and agreed to the published version of the manuscript.

Funding: Princess Nourah bint Abdulrahman University Researchers Supporting Project number (PNURSP2023R41), Princess Nourah bint Abdulrahman University, Riyadh, Saudi Arabia.

Data Availability Statement: Not available.

Conflicts of Interest: The authors declare no conflict of interest.

Nomenclature

(u, v, w)	velocity components
ω	frequency
t	time
λ_1	relaxation time
λ_2	retardation time
D_B	Brownian diffusion
v	kinematic viscosity
K_r	chemical reaction rate
D_T	thermal expression coefficient
α_m	thermal diffusivity
δ_1	thermal relaxation coefficient
δ_2	concentration relaxation coefficient
σ_s	Stefan–Boltzmann constant
k^*	mean absorption coefficient
β_2	retardation time
Nb	Brownian motion
Le	Lewis number
K_r	chemical reaction
γ	stretching ratio constant
Kr	reaction constant
δ_T	thermal relaxation constant
δ_c	concentration relaxation constant
S	ratio of frequency to stretching rate
Pr	Prandtl number
Nt	thermophoresis

References

1. Choi, S.U.S. *Enhancing Thermal Conductivity of Fluids with Nanoparticles. 231*; American Society of Mechanical Engineers: New York, NY, USA, 1995; pp. 99–106.
2. Buongiorno, J. Convective Transport in Nanofluids. *J. Heat Transfer.* **2006**, *128*, 240–250. [CrossRef]
3. Hayat, T.; Kiyani, M.; Ahmad, I.; Ahmad, B. On analysis of magneto Maxwell nano-material by surface with variable thickness. *Int. J. Mech. Sci.* **2017**, *131–132*, 1016–1025. [CrossRef]
4. Sui, J.; Zheng, L.; Zhang, X. Boundary layer heat and mass transfer with Cattaneo–Christov double-diffusion in upper-convected Maxwell nanofluid past a stretching sheet with slip velocity. *Int. J. Therm. Sci.* **2016**, *104*, 461–468. [CrossRef]
5. Hsiao, K.-L. Micropolar nanofluid flow with MHD and viscous dissipation effects towards a stretching sheet with multimedia feature. *Int. J. Heat Mass Transf.* **2017**, *112*, 983–990. [CrossRef]
6. Turkyilmazoglu, M. Free and circular jets cooled by single phase nanofluids. *Eur. J. Mech.—B/Fluids* **2019**, *76*, 1–6. [CrossRef]
7. Ahmed, J.; Khan, M.; Ahmad, L. Stagnation point flow of Maxwell nanofluid over a permeable rotating disk with heat source/sink. *J. Mol. Liq.* **2019**, *287*, 110853. [CrossRef]
8. Turkyilmazoglu, M. Buongiorno model in a nanofluid filled asymmetric channel fulfilling zero net particle flux at the walls. *Int. J. Heat Mass Transf.* **2018**, *126*, 974–979. [CrossRef]
9. Tlili, I.; Waqas, H.; Almaneea, A.; Khan, S.U.; Imran, M. Activation Energy and Second Order Slip in Bioconvection of Oldroyd-B Nanofluid over a Stretching Cylinder: A Proposed Mathematical Model. *Processes* **2019**, *7*, 914. [CrossRef]

10. Abbasi, A.; Farooq, W.; Tag-ElDin, E.S.M.; Khan, S.U.; Khan, M.I.; Guedri, K.; Elattar, S.; Waqas, M.; Galal, A.M. Heat Transport Exploration for Hybrid Nanoparticle (Cu, Fe_3O_4)—Based Blood Flow via Tapered Complex Wavy Curved Channel with Slip Features. *Micromachines* **2022**, *13*, 1415. [CrossRef]

11. Kiranakumar, H.V.; Thejas, R.; Naveen, C.S.; MIjaz Khan Prasanna, G.D.; Reddy, S.; Oreijah, M.; Guedri, K.; Bafakeeh, O.T.; Jameel, M. A review on electrical and gas-sensing properties of reduced graphene oxide-metal oxide nanocomposites. *Biomass Convers. Biorefin.* **2022**, 1–11. [CrossRef]

12. Waqas, H.; Oreijah, M.; Guedri, K.; Khan, S.U.; Yang, S.; Yasmin, S.; Khan, M.I.; Bafakeeh, O.T.; Tag-ElDin, E.S.M.; Galal, A.M. Gyrotactic Motile Microorganisms Impact on Pseudoplastic Nanofluid Flow over a Moving Riga Surface with Exponential Heat Flux. *Crystals* **2022**, *12*, 1308. [CrossRef]

13. Chu, Y.-M.; Khan, M.I.; Abbas, T.; Sidi, M.O.; Alharbi, K.A.M.; Alqsair, U.F.; Khan, S.U.; Malik, M. Radiative thermal analysis for four types of hybrid nanoparticles subject to non-uniform heat source: Keller box numerical approach. *Case Stud. Therm. Eng.* **2022**, *40*, 102474. [CrossRef]

14. Habib, D.; Salamat, N.; Abdal, S.; Siddique, I.; Ang, M.C.; Ahmadian, A. On the role of bioconvection and activation energy for time dependent nanofluid slip transpiration due to extending domain in the presence of electric and magnetic fields. *Ain Shams Eng. J.* **2021**, *13*, 101519. [CrossRef]

15. Xia, W.-F.; Haq, F.; Saleem, M.; Khan, M.I.; Khan, S.U.; Chu, Y.-M. Irreversibility analysis in natural bio-convective flow of Eyring-Powell nanofluid subject to activation energy and gyrotactic microorganisms. *Ain Shams Eng. J.* **2021**, *12*, 4063–4074. [CrossRef]

16. Waqas, M.; Sadiq, M.A.; Bahaidarah, H.M. Gyrotactic bioconvection stratified flow of magnetized micropolar nanoliquid configured by stretchable radiating surface with Joule heating and viscous dissipation. *Int. Commun. Heat Mass Transf.* **2022**, *138*, 106229. [CrossRef]

17. Liu, X.; Adibi, M.; Shahgholi, M.; Tlili, I.; Sajadi, S.M.; Abdollahi, A.; Li, Z.; Karimipour, A. Phase change process in a porous Carbon-Paraffin matrix with different volume fractions of copper oxide Nanoparticles: A molecular dynamics study. *J. Mol. Liq.* **2022**, *366*, 120296. [CrossRef]

18. Mekheimer, K.S.; Abo-Elkhair, R.E.; Abdelsalam, S.I.; Ali, K.K.; Moawad, A.M.A. Biomedical simulations of nanoparticles drug delivery to blood hemodynamics in diseased organs: Synovitis problem. *Int. Commun. Heat Mass Transfer* **2022**, *130*, 105756. [CrossRef]

19. Kumar, K.G.; Ramesh, G.; Gireesha, B.; Gorla, R. Characteristics of Joule heating and viscous dissipation on three-dimensional flow of Oldroyd B nanofluid with thermal radiation. *Alex. Eng. J.* **2018**, *57*, 2139–2149. [CrossRef]

20. Sajid, M.; Ahmed, B.; Abbas, Z. Steady mixed convection stagnation point flow of MHD Oldroyd-B fluid over a stretching sheet. *J. Egypt. Math. Soc.* **2015**, *23*, 440–444. [CrossRef]

21. Irfan, M.; Khan, M.; Khan, W.A.; Sajid, M. Thermal and solutal stratifications in flow of Oldroyd-B nanofluid with variable conductivity. *Appl. Phys. A* **2018**, *124*, 674. [CrossRef]

22. Bai, Y.; Tang, Q.; Zhang, Y. Unsteady MHD oblique stagnation slip flow of Oldroyd-B nanofluids by coupling Cattaneo-Christov double diffusion and Buongiorno model. *Chin. J. Phys.* **2022**, *79*, 451–470. [CrossRef]

23. Roy, N.C.; Pop, I. Dual solutions of magnetohydrodynamic mixed convection flow of an Oldroyd-B nanofluid over a shrinking sheet with heat source/sink. *Alex. Eng. J.* **2021**, *61*, 5939–5948. [CrossRef]

24. Mabood, F.; Abbasi, A.; Farooq, W.; Hussain, Z.; Badruddin, I. Effects of non-linear radiation and chemical reaction on Oldroyd-B nanofluid near oblique stagnation point flow. *Chin. J. Phys.* **2022**, *77*, 1197–1208. [CrossRef]

25. Aziz, S.; Ahmad, I.; Ali, N.; Khan, S.U. Magnetohydrodynamic mixed convection 3-D simulations for chemically reactive couple stress nanofluid over periodically moving surface with thermal radiation. *J. Therm. Anal. Calorim.* **2020**, *146*, 435–448. [CrossRef]

26. Ahmad, I.; Aziz, S.; Khan, S.U.; Ali, N. Periodically moving surface in an Oldroyd-B fluid with variable thermal conductivity and Cattaneo-Christov heat flux features. *Heat Transf.* **2020**, *49*, 3246–3266. [CrossRef]

27. Ahmad, I.; Aziz, S.; Ali, N.; Khan, S.U. Radiative unsteady hydromagnetic 3D flow model for Jeffrey nanofluid configured by an accelerated surface with chemical reaction. *Heat Transf.* **2020**, *50*, 942–966. [CrossRef]

28. Liao, S.J. *Homotopy Analysis Method in Nonlinear Differential Equations*; Springer: Berlin/Heidelberg, Germany, 2012.

29. Al-Qudah, A.; Odibat, Z.; Shawagfeh, N. A linearization-based computational algorithm of homotopy analysis method for nonlinear reaction–diffusion systems. *Math. Comput. Simul.* **2021**, *194*, 505–522. [CrossRef]

30. Yang, Y.; Liao, S. Comparison between homotopy analysis method and homotopy renormalization method in fluid mechanics. *Eur. J. Mech.—B/Fluids* **2023**, *97*, 187–198. [CrossRef]

Article

A Bimodal Model for Oil Prices

Joanna Goard [1,*] and Mohammed AbaOud [2]

[1] School of Mathematics and Applied Statistics, University of Wollongong, Wollongong, NSW 2522, Australia
[2] Department of Mathematics and Statistics, Imam Mohammad Ibn Saud Islamic University (IMSIU), Riyadh 11564, Saudi Arabia; maabaoud@imamu.edu.sa
* Correspondence: joanna@uow.edu.au

Abstract: Oil price behaviour over the last 10 years has shown to be bimodal in character, displaying a strong tendency to congregate around one range of high oil prices and one range of low prices, indicating two distinct peaks in its frequency distribution. In this paper, we propose a new, single nonlinear stochastic process to model the bimodal behaviour, namely, $dp = \alpha(p_1 - p)(p_2 - p_(p_3 - p)dt + \sigma p^\gamma dZ, \ \gamma = 0, 0.5$. Further, we find analytic approximations of oil price futures under this model in the cases where the stable fixed points of the corresponding deterministic model are (a) evenly spaced about the unstable fixed point and (b) are spaced in the ratio 1:2 about the unstable fixed point. The solutions are shown to produce accurate prices when compared to numerical solutions.

Keywords: futures on oil valuation; analytical approximations

MSC: 35R35; 91G50; 91-10

Citation: Goard, J.; AbaOud, M. A Bimodal Model for Oil Prices. *Mathematics* **2023**, *11*, 2222. https://doi.org/10.3390/math11102222

Academic Editor: Arsen Palestini

Received: 7 March 2023
Revised: 25 April 2023
Accepted: 27 April 2023
Published: 9 May 2023

1. Introduction

Crude oil is one of the world's most important commodities, not just for consumption but also as a financial asset. Futures contracts on oil are traded by financial institutions and investors for investment and risk management purposes. Successful hedging and risk management techniques, though, depend upon the accurate pricing of the contracts. In order to value financial contracts on oil, one needs to understand and develop a stochastic process that describes oil price dynamics. There are many complex factors affecting oil prices, including net demand in the market, geopolitical events, interest rates, the weather, the cost of extracting and producing oil and even market sentiment. In recent years, the corona virus pandemic saw many governments restricting travel, and businesses were forced to shut down. This led to the fall in demand for oil. In the first three months of 2020, oil consumption was down 5.6 million barrels per day to 94.4 million barrels per day. This in turn led to a drop in oil prices. In April 2020, the price for a barrel of oil fell to $-$USD 37.68 in the US for West Texas Intermediate (WTI) and USD 9 per barrel worldwide for Brent oil. When Russia attacked Ukraine on 24 February 2022, investors saw the potential for sanctions on Russian oil exports, which saw oil prices rocket. Large price changes over short periods are not new—they are an inherent part of the oil market. Observing the data set of oil prices over the last 10 years, it is obvious that the data are bimodal in nature (other commodities such as natural gas and food grains may also exhibit the same price pattern over this period). There is a strong tendency for prices to stay around one range of high prices and then a range of low prices before going back to the high prices and so on.

In this paper, we model the bimodal nature of oil with a nonlinear one-factor stochastic model. One-factor models are of the form $dp = A(p,t)dt + B(p,t)dZ$, where $p \ (= p_t)$ is the price of oil at time t, $A(p,t)$ is the drift term, $B(p,t)$ is the diffusion term, and where here and in the rest of this paper, dZ is an increment in a Wiener process Z under a real probability measure. The main advantages of using one-factor models are simplicity and tractability—i.e., they can lead to closed formulae for futures prices.

An early model used to define the behaviour of commodity prices was the GBM model—i.e., Geometric Brownian Motion, in which $A(p,t) = \mu p$ and $B(p,t) = \sigma p$, where μ and σ are constant. Using this model, Brennan and Schwartz [1] identified a relationship between spot and futures prices that included known constant convenience yields and interest rates. Using a GBM model, Gabillon [2] established a closed-form solution for futures prices of oil that depended only on the spot price of oil and a constant cost of carry of physical oil. He did, however, observe that with this formula, the term structure in backwardation could not be explained. So Gabillon extended his formula to include convenience yield. This formula could now describe both backwardation and contango states. Unfortunately, however, the formula implies a discontinuity when changing between the backwardation and contango states. Gabillon noted that use of the GBM model to value oil futures could lead to unreasonable over- or under-valuations.

Other authors suggested including mean reversion in the oil price model to capture the effect of net demand of the commodity. Using this property, Bjerksund and Ekern [3] derived the price of a European call option when the spot price follows the Ornstein–Uhlenbeck process: $A(p,t) = \eta(\mu - p)$, $B(p,t) = \sigma$. This process can, however, generate negative prices, which, although can happen with oil prices, is very rare. In a well-known paper on futures pricing of oil, Schwartz [4] derived an analytic solution for futures prices under the mean-reverting model: $dp = \eta p(\mu - \ln(p))dt + \sigma p dZ$. Pindyck [5] also added a mean-reversion term to a deterministic linear trend model. AbaOud and Goard [6] proposed two one-factor models for oil prices with $B(p,t) = \sigma p^{\frac{3}{4}}$ and empirically showed they outperformed some well-known models in capturing the behaviour of oil prices. They also derived futures prices based on their mean-reverting models.

A number of extensions have been proposed to the one-factor model for oil prices. These include two- and three-factor models. In the two-factor models, the convenience yield and long-run mean seem to be the popular choices for the second factor. Gibson and Schwartz [7] assumed that the underlying oil price follows the GBM process and the short convenience yield follows the Ornstein–Uhlenbeck (OU) process. This was later modified by Schwartz [4], who modelled the spot price using the Geometric Ornstein–Uhlenbeck process. Some authors who considered the long-term price as a second state variable include Gabillon [2], Pilipovic [8] and Schwartz and Smith [9].

The addition of factors to the model can add complexity to the model. However, Schwartz [4] derived a futures prices under a three-factor model for oil that included the spot price, convenience yield and interest rate. In this model, the spot price follows the GBM, and the convenience yield and interest rate follow OU processes. Hilliard and Reis [10] also used the three-factor model proposed by Schwartz [2] but added jumps into the spot price process. Cortazar and Schwartz [11] proposed a three-factor model that includes spot price, convenience yield and long-term spot price return. Abadie and Chamorro [12] use mean-reverting spot price and volatility and a long-term equilibrium price that follows a GBM.

Various other modifications to the one-factor model can be found in the literature. This includes the paper by Cortazar and Naranjo [13], who used n-factor Gaussian models, and Ogbogbo [14], who considers a Levy market and uses a Levy process to model oil prices.

Examination of oil price data sets over a span of 10 years, and even just the past 5 years, shows that they are bimodal in character, showing a strong inclination to aggregate around one range of high prices and one range of low prices. No system of affine equations could lead to a finite number of non-unique fixed point solutions. Therefore, to model bimodal oil price data, we require a nonlinear model. In order to achieve this, we require only a single nonlinear equation with two stable fixed points at high and low values of oil prices, respectively. Obviously, we also need the additional external stochastic driving force, representing the unpredictable effect of many neglected influences that will enable transitions to occur between the two basins of attraction. The simplest such single-factor model is

$$dp = \alpha(p_1 - p)(p_2 - p)(p_3 - p)dt + B(p,t)dZ, \tag{1}$$

with $\alpha > 0$, p_1 the stable low fixed point, p_3 the stable high fixed point and p_2 an unstable intermediate fixed point. In the neighbourhood of $p = p_1$, oil prices revert to p_1 as

$$p = p_1 e^{-\alpha(p_2-p_1)(p_3-p_1)t} \tag{2}$$

with time scale $1/[\alpha(p_2 - p_1)(p_3 - p_1)]$. Similarly, in the neighbourhood of $p = p_3$, oil prices revert to p_3 exponentially with a time scale $1/[\alpha(p_3 - p_2)(p_3 - p_1)]$.

For an initial value p_0 strictly between p_1 and p_2, the full solution to the nonlinear deterministic model (i.e., (1) with $B(p, t) = 0$) is

$$t = -\frac{1}{\alpha} \ln\left([\frac{p - p_1}{p_0 - p_1}]^{a_1} [\frac{p - p_3}{p_0 - p_3}]^{a_3} [\frac{p - p_2}{p_0 - p_2}]^{-a_2} \right),$$

where

$$a_1 = \frac{p_3 - p_2}{(p_2 - p_1)p_3^2 - (p_3 - p_1)p_2^2 + (p_3 - p_2)p_1^2},$$

$$a_2 = \frac{p_1 - p_3}{(p_2 - p_1)p_3^2 - (p_3 - p_1)p_2^2 + (p_3 - p_2)p_1^2},$$

$$a_3 = \frac{p_2 - p_1}{(p_2 - p_1)p_3^2 - (p_3 - p_1)p_2^2 + (p_3 - p_2)p_1^2}.$$

Similar solutions can be found for other initial conditions simply by separation of variables and integration by partial fractions.

The occasional switching between the zone of low oil price, with interval of attraction $[0, p_2)$, and the zone of high oil price, with interval of attraction (p_2, ∞), occurs because of the random excursion $B(p, t)dZ$. This simple device for modelling bimodal oil price dynamics is to be compared with the device of deterministic chaos, which requires at least three coupled autonomous differential equations, two coupled non-autonomous equations or two coupled difference equations.

The goal of this paper is two-fold:

1. To model oil prices, we want to demonstrate the significance of the cubic term in Equation (1) with $B(P, t) = \sigma p^\gamma$ (which we call our unrestricted model). To do this, in Section 2, we compare the ability to capture oil price behaviour of several existing one-factor stochastic models for oil prices that are subsets of the unrestricted model. The estimation technique that we use to compare these models is the statistical method of the Generalized Method of Moments (GMM). This method combines the observed data with the information in population moment conditions to generate estimates of the unknown parameters in the given model. Using 10 years of data, we empirically test the nested models and explain the results.

2. Having justified the need for a cubic drift term, in Section 3, we formulate analytic approximate solutions to futures prices under (1) with $B(p, t) = \sigma$ and $B(p, t) = \sigma p^{\frac{1}{2}}$.

We present our conclusion in Section 4.

2. Motivation for the Bimodal Model—An Empirical Study

In this section, we empirically test ten oil price models that are nested within our unrestricted model for their ability to capture the dynamics of oil price movements. The estimation technique that we use to compare these models is the Generalized Method of Moments (GMM), which is a method used to find efficient estimates of parameters when the number of moment conditions is larger than the number of parameters being estimated. The method is summarised in Appendix A, but for a more detailed explanation, the reader is referred to Hayashi [15], Mackinlay and Richardson [16] and also Ferson and Foerster [17].

2.1. The Models to Be Tested

Table 1 lists the ten stochastic models of the form $dp = A(p,t)dt + B(p,t)dZ$ that were examined for their capability of fitting oil prices. They can each be nested within the unrestricted model

$$dp = (k_1 + k_2 p + k_3 p^2 + k_4 p^3)dt + \sigma p^\gamma dZ, \tag{3}$$

where k_1, k_2, k_3, k_4, M and γ are constants, by placing restrictions on certain parameters as given in Table 2.

Table 1. Models to be tested in the form $dp = A(p,t)dt + B(p,t)dZ$.

Model	$A(p,t)$	$B(p,t)$
1	$(k_1 + k_2 p + k_3 p^2 + k_4 p^3)$	$\sigma p^{1/2}$
2	$(k_1 + k_2 p)$	$\sigma p^{1/2}$
3	$(k_2 p + k_3 p^2)$	$\sigma p^{1/2}$
4	$k_2 p$	σp
5	$k_2 p$	$\sigma p^{1/2}$
6	$(k_1 + k_2 p + k_3 p^2 + k_4 p^3)$	σ
7	$(k_1 + k_2 p)$	σ
8	$(k_2 p + k_3 p^2)$	σ
9	$k_2 p$	σ
10	$(k_2 p + k_3 p^2)$	$\sigma p^{3/2}$

Table 2. Parameter restrictions on unrestricted models (3).

Model	k_1	k_2	k_3	k_4	γ
1					0.5
2			0	0	0.5
3	0			0	0.5
4	0		0	0	1
5	0		0	0	0.5
6					0
7			0	0	0
8	0			0	0
9	0		0	0	0
10	0			0	1.5

In Models 1–3 and 5, the diffusion term follows the square-root process, which is the type used by Heston [18] to model volatility. This implies that the volatility of the percentage change in price is a decreasing function of p. The diffusion term in Models 6–9 means that the volatility of p is constant in absolute terms.

Model 4 is the Geometric Brownian Motion used by Black and Scholes [19] to value European options. It infers an instantaneous growth rate of k_2 and presumes that the volatility of percentage changes and the expected percentage change in prices are constant. It was also used to value oil by Brennan and Schwarz [1], McDonald and Siegel [20] and Gabillon [2].

The drift term in Models 2 and 7 can be written as $-k_2(\frac{-k_1}{k_2} - p)$. With $k_1 > 0, k_2 < 0$, the models are mean-reverting in nature, where the price reverts to the constant $\frac{-k_1}{k_2}$ with reversion rate $-k_2$. Larger values of $|k_2|$ mean faster reversion to the long-run mean $\frac{-k_1}{k_2}$. These models are then referred to as the Heston model and the Mean-Reverting Gaussian, respectively.

In Models 3, 8 and 10, we can write the nonlinear drift term as $-k_3 p(\frac{-k_2}{k_3} - p)$. If $k_2 > 0, k_3 < 0$, then these models are also mean-reverting in nature, where the price reverts to the constant $\frac{-k_2}{k_3}$ with a reversion rate that depends on p. Model 10 was used by Goard to model interest rates [21] and volatility [22,23]. The 3/2 power in the diffusion term proved useful to reduce the heteroskedasticity (heteroskedasticity means that the variance of the errors varies widely across the observations) of interest rates and volatility.

2.2. The Data

For our GMM analysis, Brent crude oil spot prices (sampled both weekly and monthly) between January 2013 and December 2022 were collected from the U.S. Energy Information Administration. The prices are plotted in Figure 1. From this figure, it can be seen that in the period 2013–2016 (from 0 to 37 in (a) and 0 to 159 in (c)) prices decreased and reached about USD 28 per barrel. In this time, the demand for oil was low, but at the same time there was overproduction of oil. As a result, the Organization of the Petroleum Exporting Countries (OPEC) aimed to support oil prices by agreeing to reduce crude supply. This decision can be considered to be the most important factor that caused the increase in oil prices over the period 2016–2020 (from 38–86 in (a) and from 160–374 in (c)). However, the global pandemic (COVID-19) had a detrimental impact on the oil market as most countries enforced strict social distancing and lockdowns to control virus expansion. This caused a dive in oil demand and a historical low spot price was recorded (below USD 20 per barrel). Since then (from mid 2020 to 2022), oil prices have seen an increasing trend due to many factors, but most importantly, OPEC's reduction of crude supply and the Russian invasion of Ukraine in February 2022.

Table 3 shows the standard statistics for Brent crude oil (weekly and monthly) spot prices 2013–2022. We see that the mean price in our period of study is about USD 70 and the standard deviation is about USD 25. The minimum and maximum are very close to the same distance from the mean, while the mean is close to the median. Both of these observations are consistent with low skewness. Further, both the minimum and maximum are just over two standard deviations from the mean, which is consistent with slightly negative kurtosis.

From Figure 1, we can see the bimodal nature of the data with the stable low fixed point in the interval [44, 50] and the stable high point in the interval [104, 110]. The histograms confirm the bimodality of the data.

Table 3. Standard statistics for Brent crude oil (weekly and monthly) spot prices 2013–2022.

Standard Statistics	Weekly Data	Monthly Data
Mean	70.61	70.64
Median	64.82	64.56
Standard Deviation	24.95	24.87
Sample Variance	622.44	618.30
Kurtosis	−0.86	−0.88
Skewness	0.40	0.41
Range	113.16	104.33
Minimum	14.24	18.38
Maximum	127.40	122.71
number of observation	520	120

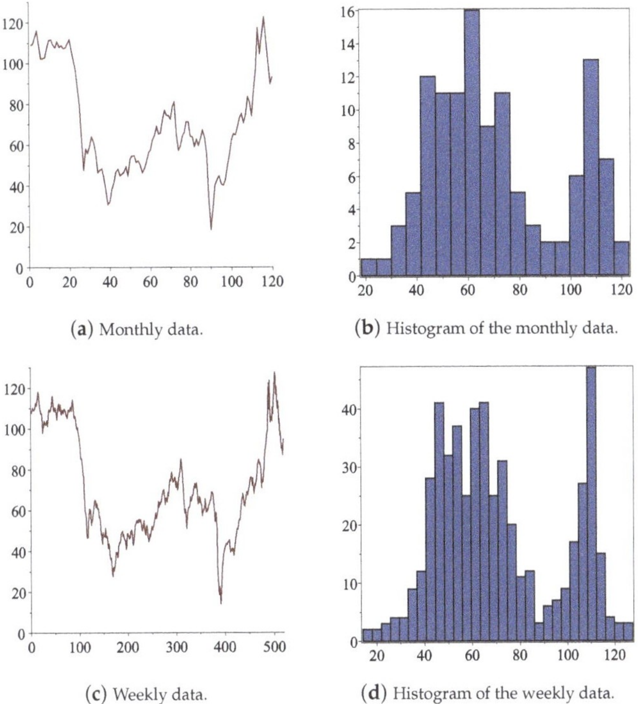

(**a**) Monthly data.

(**b**) Histogram of the monthly data.

(**c**) Weekly data.

(**d**) Histogram of the weekly data.

Figure 1. Brent crude oil prices 2011–2022.

2.3. Performance of Nested Models

We now compare Models 1–10, which are listed in Table 1, for their ability to capture the behaviour of Brent crude oil prices in the 10 years between 2012 and 2022. As mentioned in Section 2.1, each model can be nested within the unrestricted model (3), which we use as a benchmark to compare the performances of each of the nested models.

In particular, GMM was used to estimate the parameters of the continuous-time model for $\eta = \frac{p}{100}$, whereby Itô's Lemma, η follows

$$d\eta = (c_1 + c_2\eta + c_3\eta^2 + c_4\eta^3)dt + M\eta^\gamma dZ \tag{4}$$

where

$$\begin{aligned}
c_1 &= k_1/100, \\
c_2 &= k_2, \\
c_3 &= 100k_3, \\
c_4 &= 100^2 k_4, \\
M &= \sigma 100^{\gamma-1}.
\end{aligned}$$

Tables A1 and A2 in Appendix B present the results from the GMM analysis using 10 years of monthly and 10 years of weekly data, respectively. In the tables, 'DF' stands for degrees of freedom.

Table A1 presents the results from the 10 years of monthly data. The tables provide very strong evidence of the importance of the cubic drift term when explaining variation in oil prices. Every coefficient in the cubic drift term is statistically significantly different from zero at the 1% level of significance. The χ^2 p-values indicate that only Models 1 and 6, which include all the cubic terms, are acceptable at the 5% level of significance, with Model 6 (which has $\gamma = 0$) not being able to be rejected even at the 50% level of significance. All the other models are rejected or misspecified in terms of their overidentifying restrictions. In other words, the restrictions on these models are unreasonable.

Table A2 has the results from the 10 years of weekly data. Every coefficient in the cubic drift term is statistically significantly different from zero at the 10% level of significance. However, it is clear that the value of γ is also an important parameter differentiating the models. The χ^2 p-values of models with $\gamma = 1, 1.5$ (Models 4 and 10) indicate that these models are rejected at the 1% level of significance. It is interesting that in Models 2, 3, 5, 7, 8 and 9, the coefficients in the drift term are individually not statistically significantly different from zero, but jointly they are statistically significantly different from zero. Model 1, with all nonzero coefficients in the cubic drift term and with $\gamma = 0.5$, has the highest p-values of the overidentification tests and cannot be rejected even at the 25% level of significance.

We note that we also did a similar analysis with the 5 years of data from 2017 and 2022 and found very similar results. As a further note, from the GMM results, the data infer that the p_i values are generally such that $|p_3 - p_2| = 2|p_2 - p_1|$. However, when $\gamma = 0$, we could also use the approximation $|p_3 - p_2| = |p_2 - p_1|$. We simulated the oil price data over 10 years, both monthly and weekly, with the parameter values provided by the GMM results. See Figures A1 and A2, where in Figure A1 we have monthly simulations and in Figure A2 we have weekly simulations. Comparing these with the plots of the true data in Figure 1, we see that they can mimic the essential features of the true oil price movement. For example, they have values congregating around p_1 and p_3, and the prices switch between these two regions. The range of values are also the same, staying in the interval $[18, 125]$. Note that in Figure A1a,c we have $|p_1 - p_2| = |p_2 - p_3|$ with $\gamma = 0$ and 1.5, respectively, and in Figure A1b,d we have $|p_1 - p_2| = 2|p_2 - p_3|$ with $\gamma = 0$ and 1.5, respectively. Similarly, in Figure A2a,c we have $|p_1 - p_2| = |p_2 - p_3|$ with $\gamma = 0$ and 1.5, respectively, and in Figure A2b,d we have $|p_1 - p_2| = 2|p_2 - p_3|$ with $\gamma = 0$ and 1.5, respectively.

3. Analytic Futures Prices Under Model (3)

Given that the real process for $p(= p_t)$ is of the form

$$dp = \alpha(p_1 - p)(p_2 - p)(p_3 - p)dt + \sigma p^\gamma dZ, \tag{5}$$

then allowing for the possibility of a nonzero market price of risk, $\lambda(p, t)$, associated with oil prices, the risk-neutral process will be

$$dp = [\alpha(p_1 - p)(p_2 - p)(p_3 - p) - \lambda(p,t)\sigma p^\gamma]dt + \sigma p^\gamma d\bar{Z}, \tag{6}$$

where $\bar{Z}$ is a Wiener process under an equivalent risk-neutral probability measure under which p becomes a martingale. One way $\lambda(p, t)$ can be found is by implying it from market futures prices, i.e., choosing a λ^* that minimises the error between market and model prices. This usually involves assuming a form for the market price of risk (see, e.g., Egloff et al. [24]). Here, like many other authors (e.g., Stein and Stein [25] and Grünbichler and Longstaff [26]), we assume that the market price of risk $\lambda(p, t)$ is such that the forms of the real and risk-neutral processes are alike. This means that when $\gamma = 0$, then $\lambda(p,t) = d_0 + d_1 p + d_2 p^2 + d_3 p^3$, and when $\gamma = 0.5$, then $\lambda(p,t) = f_0 p^{-0.5} + f_1 p^{0.5} + f_2 p^{3/2} + f_3 p^{5/2}$, where $d_i, f_i, i = 0, 1, 2, 3$ are constants. Without loss of generality, for convenience we will still use the same notation for the constants.

The partial differential equation (PDE) that governs futures prices under the risk-neutral process

$$dp = \alpha(p_1 - p)(p_2 - p)(p_3 - p)dt + \sigma p^\gamma d\bar{Z}, \tag{7}$$

is given by (see [27])

$$F_\tau = \frac{\sigma^2 p^{2\gamma}}{2} F_{pp} + \alpha(p_1 - p)(p_2 - p)(p_3 - p)F_p, \tag{8}$$

where $F(p,0) = p$. From the GMM analysis of Section 2.3, we choose to consider only the cases $\gamma = 0$ and $\gamma = 1/2$. We start by non-dimensionalising the problem. This ensures that the relative sizes of different variables are obvious and signifies the important variables and constants in the equation. Hence, we let $z = \frac{F}{p_1}$, $y = \frac{p}{p_1}$ and $\tau_b = \tau \alpha p_1^2$. This reduces the problem to

$$z_{\tau_b} = \epsilon y^{2\gamma} z_{yy} + (1 - y)(q_2 - y)(q_3 - y)z_y, \quad \text{where } \epsilon = \frac{\sigma^2 p_1^{2\gamma-4}}{2\alpha}, \tag{9}$$

and $q_2 = \frac{p_2}{p_1}$, $q_3 = \frac{p_3}{p_1}$, to be solved subject to $z(y,0) = y$. Hence, once $z(y, \tau_b)$ is calculated, we then have $F = p_1 z\left(\frac{p}{p_1}, \tau \alpha p_1^2\right)$. However, to the best of the authors' knowledge, PDE (9) has no analytic solution, and so we look for a good analytic approximation.

Given that p_1 is large and we are considering $\gamma = 0, 0.5$, then ϵ is assumed small ($\ll 1$). Hence, we seek a perturbation solution of the form

$$z = z_0 + \epsilon z_1 + \epsilon^2 z_2 + \dots \tag{10}$$

where $z_0(y,0) = y$, $z_i(y,0) = 0$ for $i = 1, 2, 3 \dots$ Substituting (10) into (9) and collecting the coefficients of ϵ^0, we get that z_0 needs to satisfy

$$(z_0)_{\tau_b} = (1 - y)(q_2 - y)(q_3 - y)(z_0)_y \tag{11}$$

subject to $z_0(y,0) = y$. Note, this equation is independent of γ.

Solving (11) by the method of characteristics gives

$$z_0 = \bar{\phi}\left[\frac{e^{-\tau_b}(1 - y)^{\frac{1}{(q_2-1)(q_3-1)}}(q_3 - y)^{\frac{1}{(q_3-1)(q_3-q_2)}}}{(q_2 - y)^{\frac{1}{(q_2-1)(q_3-q_2)}}} \right], \tag{12}$$

where we need $z_0 = y$ when $\tau_b = 0$. This is hard to solve for the function $\bar{\phi}$ for arbitrary q_1, q_2, q_3. However, we recall from the GMM analysis that if we let $q_2 = 1 + \epsilon_2$, $q_3 = 1 + \epsilon_2 + \epsilon_3$, then we can well approximate ϵ_3 by ϵ_2 or $2\epsilon_2$. Hence, we will study these two cases and will get solutions for futures prices of the form

$$F = p_1 z\left(\frac{p}{p_1}, \tau \alpha p_1^2\right)$$

where $z = z_0 + \epsilon z_1$ with
1. $\epsilon_3 = \epsilon_2$ when (a) $\gamma = 0$ and (b) $\gamma = 0.5$ and
2. $\epsilon_3 = 2\epsilon_2$ when (a) $\gamma = 0$ and (b) $\gamma = 0.5$.

As explained further in the paper, if higher-order approximations $z_2, z_3, \dots$ are needed, then they can be found in a similar way to z_1.

3.1. Case $\epsilon_3 = \epsilon_2$

Here we assume $\epsilon_3 = \epsilon_2$, so we have $q_2 = 1 + \epsilon_2$ and $q_3 = 1 + 2\epsilon_2$. We now approximate z under this assumption by finding z_0 and z_1 as in (10).

3.1.1. The O(1) Term z_0

With $\epsilon_3 = \epsilon_2$, without loss of generality, from (12) we may write

$$z_0 = \phi\left[\frac{e^{-2\epsilon_2^2 \tau_b}(1 - y)(q_3 - y)}{(q_2 - y)^2} \right],$$

for some function ϕ so that $z_0(y, 0) = y$.

By letting $Y = 1 - y$ at $\tau_b = 0$, we need to find ϕ so that

$$1 - Y = \phi\left[\frac{Y(Y + 2\epsilon_2)}{(Y + \epsilon_2)^2}\right].$$

We let

$$\tilde{\zeta} = \frac{Y(Y + 2\epsilon_2)}{(Y + \epsilon_2)^2} \tag{13}$$

and solve for Y (and hence y) in terms of $\tilde{\zeta}$. This gives us

$$Y = -\epsilon_2 \pm \epsilon_2 \frac{\sqrt{1 - \tilde{\zeta}}}{1 - \tilde{\zeta}}. \tag{14}$$

Hence, $\phi(\tilde{\zeta}) = 1 + \epsilon_2\left(1 \mp \frac{1}{\sqrt{1-\tilde{\zeta}}}\right)$. However, to satisfy the initial condition, we must use the positive sign when $y > q_2$, and when $y < q_2$ we must use the negative sign. This then leads to the solution for all y:

$$z_0 = 1 + \epsilon_2\left(1 + \frac{y - q_2}{\sqrt{(q_2 - y)^2 - e^R(1 - y)(q_3 - y)}}\right), \quad \text{where } R = -2\epsilon_2^2\tau_b. \tag{15}$$

[Note that in terms of the original variables we get $F = p_1 z\left(\frac{p}{p_1}, \tau\alpha p_1^2\right)$, and, hence,

$$F(p, \tau) = p_2 + \frac{(p_2 - p_1)(p - p_2)}{\sqrt{(p_2 - p)^2 - e^{\bar{R}}(p_1 - p)(p_3 - p)}}, \quad \text{where } \bar{R} = -2\tau\alpha\epsilon_2^2 p_1^2.$$

We also note that we can simplify $p_2 - p_1 = p_1\epsilon_2$.]

Figure 2 illustrates the solution z_0, in which q_2 and q_3 are approximately 1.52 and 2.04, respectively. We see that when $y < 1$, the solution increases with τ_b (contango). When $1 < y < q_2$, the solution decreases with τ_b (backwardation), and then, when $q_2 < y < q_3$, the solution again increases with τ_b. This is to be expected, as p_1 and p_3 are the stable fixed points.

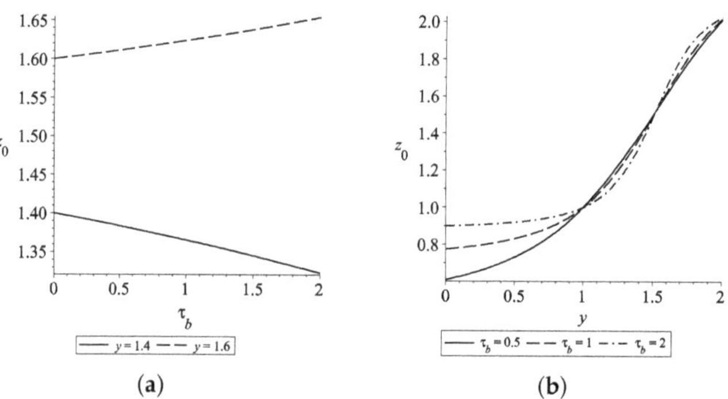

Figure 2. Plot of z_0 when $\epsilon_3 = \epsilon_2 = 25/48$.

3.1.2. The $O(\epsilon)$ Term z_1

We now consider two cases for the approximation z_1: when $\gamma = 0$, so $\epsilon = \frac{\sigma^2}{2\alpha p_1^4}$, and when $\gamma = 0.5$, so $\epsilon = \frac{\sigma^2}{2\alpha p_1^3}$, in (9).

Subcase $\gamma = 0$ in (9)

Substituting (10) into (9) and collecting the coefficients of ϵ^1, we get that with $\gamma = 0$, z_1 needs to satisfy

$$(z_1)_{\tau_b} = (z_0)_{yy} + (1-y)(q_2 - y)(q_3 - y)(z_1)_y \tag{16}$$

subject to $z_1(y,0) = 0$. Solving (16) by the method of characteristics (see [28]), we get

$$z_1 = \psi(\xi) - Q, \text{ where } \xi = e^{-2\epsilon_2^2 \tau_b} \frac{(1-y)(q_3 - y)}{(q_2 - y)^2}, \text{ and } Q = \int \frac{f(y)}{(1-y)(q_2 - y)(q_3 - y)} dy,$$

where $f(y) = (z_0)_{yy}$ with $e^{-2\epsilon_2^2 \tau_b}$ replaced by $\dfrac{A(1 + \epsilon_2 - y)^2}{(1-y)(1 + 2\epsilon_2 - y)}$ with A constant.

After integration, we then replace A with $\dfrac{e^{-2\epsilon_2^2 \tau_b}(1-y)(1 + 2\epsilon_2 - y)}{(1 + \epsilon_2 - y)^2}$.

This gives

$$\begin{aligned}
Q = {} & \frac{X(q_2 - y)}{\epsilon_2 [(q_2 - y)^2 - X(1-y)(q_3 - y)]^{\frac{5}{2}}} \, * \\
& \left\{ -\frac{3X}{16}((1-y)^2 + (q_3 - y)^2) + \frac{3}{2}(1-y)(q_3 - y) \right. \\
& + \frac{15X}{8}(1-y)(q_3 - y) + \frac{3}{2}(q_2 - y)^2 \\
& + \frac{3}{\epsilon_2^2}(1-y)(q_3 - y)(q_2 - y)^2 \ln\left(\frac{(1-y)(q_3 - y)}{(q_2 - y)^2} \right) \\
& \left. + \frac{3X}{2\epsilon_2^2}(1-y)^2(q_3 - y)^2 \ln\left(\frac{(1-y)(q_3 - y)}{(q_2 - y)^2} \right) \right\},
\end{aligned} \tag{17}$$

where $X = \exp(-2\epsilon_2^2 \tau_b)$. To find $\psi(\xi)$, we use the initial condition at $\tau = 0$ that $z_1 = 0$, so we need

$$\psi(\bar{\xi}) = Q(\bar{\xi}) \text{ where } \bar{\xi} = \frac{(1-y)(q_3 - y)}{(q_2 - y)^2} \text{ (i.e } \xi \text{ at } \tau_b = 0).$$

Hence, to find $\psi(\xi)$, we need to first write Q as a function of $\bar{\xi}$ when $\tau_b = 0$. This can be done easily by using (14) and considering the cases $y > q_2$, $y < q_2$ separately. This gives $\psi(\bar{\xi})$. Replacing $\bar{\xi}$ by ξ, we get $\psi(\xi)$.

After much simplification, we get $\psi(\xi)$ in terms of y and τ_b for all y as:

$$\begin{aligned}
\psi(\xi) = {} & \frac{(q_2 - y)}{\epsilon_2^3((q_2 - y)^2 - X(1-y)(q_3 - y))^{\frac{5}{2}}} \\
& * \left[\ln\left(\frac{X(1-y)(q_3 - y)}{(q_2 - y)^2} \right) \left(3X(1-y)(q_3 - y)(q_2 - y)^2 + \frac{3}{2}X^2(1-y)^2(q_3 - y)^2 \right) \right. \\
& + (27/8)X(1-y)(q_3 - y)[(q_2 - y)^2 - X(1-y)(q_3 - y)] \\
& + 3/2[(q_2 - y)^4 - X(1-y)(q_3 - y)(q_2 - y)^2] \\
& \left. - \frac{3}{8}[(q_2 - y)^2 - X(1-y)(q3 - y)][2(q_2 - y)^2 - X(1-y)(q_3 - y)] \right].
\end{aligned} \tag{18}$$

Then $z_1 = \psi(\xi) - Q$. The above reasoning serves to prove the following proposition:

Proposition 1. *An analytic approximation of (9) with $\epsilon_2 = \epsilon_3$ and $\gamma = 0$ is $z = z_0 + \epsilon z_1$, where z_0 is given in (15) and z_1 is given by $\psi(\xi) - Q$ using (17) and (18). Then the futures price is given by $F = p_1 z\left(\frac{p}{p_1}, \tau \alpha p_1^2 \right)$.*

The $O(\epsilon)$ term z_1 when $\gamma = 0$ is plotted in Figure 3. When $y < q_2$, z_1 is increasing in τ_b, and it is decreasing in τ_b when $q_2 < y < q_3$. This is the opposite behaviour to that of z_0 when $y > 1$. The difference between the curves in z_1 are also larger than those for z_0.

In Table 4 we compare the approximate $O(1)$ and $O(\epsilon)$ results for z_0 and $z = z_0 + \epsilon z_1$ with those obtained numerically using an implicit finite difference (FD) scheme in Maple [29] with increments of y and τ_b, respectively, of $\delta y = 10^{-3}$ and $\delta\tau_b = 10^{-3}$. We use the numerical results as the proxy for the true solution. The table also lists the root mean square error (RMSE) $\sqrt{\frac{\sum(x_i - \hat{x}_i)^2}{N}}$ and the mean absolute error (MAE) $\frac{\sum|x_i - \hat{x}_i|}{N}$, where x_i are the FD values, $\hat{x}_i$ are our estimated values and N is the number of data points.

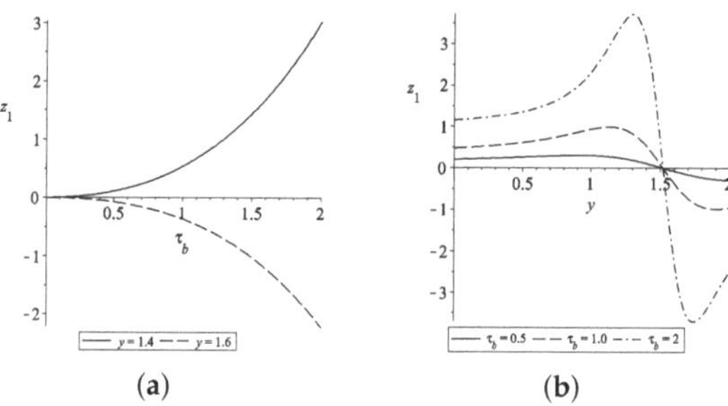

Figure 3. Plot of z_1 when $\epsilon_3 = \epsilon_2$ and $\gamma = 0$.

Table 4. $\epsilon_2 = \epsilon_3, \gamma = 0, \epsilon_2 = \frac{25}{48}$.

y	$(\tau_b, \epsilon) = (0.05523, 0.25)$			$(\tau_b, \epsilon) = (0.07732, 0.247)$		
	z_0	$z = z_0 + \epsilon z_1$	FD	z_0	$z = z_0 + \epsilon z_1$	FD
0.8511	0.8574	0.8589	0.8589	0.8599	0.8626	0.8626
1.0638	1.0623	1.0633	1.0633	1.0617	1.0636	1.0636
1.2766	1.2737	1.2743	1.2743	1.2726	1.2737	1.2737
1.4894	1.4889	1.4890	1.4890	1.4887	1.4888	1.4888
1.7021	1.7045	1.7041	1.7041	1.7055	1.7047	1.7047
1.9149	1.9174	1.9165	1.9165	1.9184	1.9167	1.9167
RMSE	8.75×10^{-4}	0		1.62×10^{-3}	0	
MAE	7.5×10^{-4}	0		1.38×10^{-3}	0	

y	$(\tau_b, \epsilon) = (0.1105, 0.25)$			$(\tau_b, \epsilon) = (0.1546, 0.2474)$		
	z_0	$z = z_0 + \epsilon z_1$	FD	z_0	$z = z_0 + \epsilon z_1$	FD
0.8511	0.8634	0.8688	0.8688	0.8680	0.8780	0.8778
1.0638	1.0607	1.0648	1.0647	1.0595	1.0673	1.0670
1.2766	1.2709	1.2731	1.2731	1.2685	1.2730	1.2729
1.4894	1.4884	1.4887	1.4887	1.4880	1.4886	1.4886
1.7021	1.7069	1.7052	1.7053	1.7089	1.7055	1.7056
1.9149	1.9199	1.9163	1.9163	1.9219	1.9150	1.9152
RMSE	3.31×10^{-3}	5.77×10^{-5}		6.16×10^{-3}	1.78×10^{-4}	
MAE	2.85×10^{-3}	3.33×10^{-5}		5.38×10^{-3}	1.5×10^{-4}	

y	$(\tau_b, \epsilon) = (0.2209, 0.25)$			$(\tau_b, \epsilon) = (0.9941, 0.0385)$		
	z_0	$z = z_0 + \epsilon z_1$	FD	z_0	$z = z_0 + \epsilon z_1$	FD
0.8511	0.8745	0.8937	0.8929	0.9271	0.9584	0.9575
1.0638	1.0577	1.0734	1.0725	1.0402	1.0771	1.0742
1.2766	1.2651	1.2745	1.2739	1.2235	1.2568	1.2519
1.4894	1.4874	1.4887	1.4886	1.4797	1.4853	1.4842
1.7021	1.7118	1.7047	1.7052	1.7486	1.7207	1.7253
1.9149	1.9248	1.9108	1.9110	1.9555	1.9180	1.9216
RMSE	1.20×10^{-2}	5.93×10^{-4}		2.41×10^{-2}	3.38×10^{-3}	
MAE	1.06×10^{-2}	5.17×10^{-4}		2.12×10^{-2}	3.00×10^{-3}	

The tables clearly show the excellent results from using z_0 and $z_0 + \epsilon z_1$ as compared to the numerical FD method. The results are displayed to four decimal places in terms of the dimensionless parameters τ_b and ϵ. The first-order approximation z_0 results on their own yield relatively good results. However, it is obvious that the results from using $z_0 + \epsilon z_1$ are an improvement on the z_0 alone. We have excellent results, especially for smaller values of τ_b and ϵ, with the RMSE ranging from 0 (when $\tau_b = 0.0552$) to 0.0034 (when τ_b is almost one). Similarly, the MAEs are of comparable order.

If higher degrees of accuracy are ever needed, then the next approximation z_2 can be found using the same technique we used here to find z_1.

Subcase $\gamma = 0.5$ in (9)

We now look to approximate z_1 when $\epsilon_3 = \epsilon_2$ and $\gamma = \frac{1}{2}$. The PDE in this case is

$$(z_1)_{\tau_b} = y(z_0)_{yy} + (1 - y)(q_2 - y)(q_3 - y)(z_1)_y \tag{19}$$

to be solved subject to $z_1(y, 0) = 0$ and where $q_2 = 1 + \epsilon_2$, $q_3 = 1 + 2\epsilon_2$. Solving (19) by the method of characteristics, we get $z_1 = \psi(\xi) - Q$, where $\xi = e^{-2\epsilon_2^2 \tau_b} \dfrac{(1 - y)(q_3 - y)}{(q_2 - y)^2}$, and $Q = \displaystyle\int \frac{f(y)}{(1 - y)(q_2 - y)(q_3 - y)} dy$, where $f(y) = y(z_0)_{yy}$ with $e^{-2\epsilon_2^2 \tau_b}$ replaced by $\dfrac{K(q_2 - y)^2}{(1 - y)(q_3 - y)}$ with K constant.

After integration, we then replace K with $\xi = \dfrac{e^{-2\epsilon_2^2 \tau_b}(1 - y)(q_3 - y)}{(q_2 - y)^2}$.

We thus find

$$
\begin{aligned}
Q = {} & \frac{(y - 1 - \epsilon_2)}{\left[(1 + \epsilon_2 - y) - X(1 - y)(1 + 2\epsilon_2 - y)\right]^{\frac{5}{2}}} \\
& * \left[-\frac{3}{2}X(1 - y)(1 + 2\epsilon_2 - y)\left(1 + \frac{1}{\epsilon_2}\right) \right. \\
& + \frac{3}{8}X^2(1 - y)^2 \\
& + \frac{3}{2\epsilon_2}X(1 - y)(1 + \epsilon_2 - y)^2 \\
& - \frac{3}{\epsilon_2}X(1 - y)(1 + 2\epsilon_2 - y)(y - 1 - \epsilon_2) \\
& + \frac{3X^2}{16\epsilon_2}\left[(1 + 2\epsilon_2 - y)^2 + (1 - y)^2\right] \\
& - \frac{3}{2\epsilon_2}X(1 + \epsilon_2 - y)^2 \\
& - \frac{15}{8\epsilon_2}X^2(y - 1)(y - 1 - 2\epsilon_2) \\
& + \frac{3}{8\epsilon_2}X^2(y - 1)(1 + 2\epsilon_2 - y)^2 \\
& - \frac{3}{2\epsilon_2}X^2(1 - y)^2(y - 1 - 2\epsilon_2) \\
& - \frac{3}{\epsilon_2^3}X(1 - y)(1 + 2\epsilon_2 - y)(1 + \epsilon_2 - y)^2 \ln\left(\frac{(1 - y)(1 + 2\epsilon_2 - y)}{(1 + \epsilon_2 - y)^2}\right) \\
& - \frac{3}{4\epsilon_2^2}X(1 - y)(1 + 2\epsilon_2 - y)(1 + \epsilon_2 - y)^2 \ln\left(\frac{(1 - y)(1 + 2\epsilon_2 - y)^7}{(1 + \epsilon_2 - y)^8}\right) \\
& - \frac{3}{2\epsilon_2^3}X^2(1 - y)^2(1 + 2\epsilon_2 - y)^2 \ln\left(\frac{(1 - y)(1 + 2\epsilon_2 - y)}{(1 + \epsilon_2 - y)^2}\right) \\
& \left. - \frac{1}{16\epsilon_2^2}X^2(1 - y)^2(1 + 2\epsilon_2 - y)^2 \ln\left(\frac{(1 - y)^{15}(1 + 2\epsilon_2 - y)^{33}}{(1 + \epsilon_2 - y)^{48}}\right) \right].
\end{aligned}
\tag{20}
$$

To find $\psi(\xi)$, we use the initial condition at $\tau = 0$, i.e., $z_1(y, 0) = 0$. Hence, we need

$$\psi(\bar{\xi}) = Q \ \text{ where } \ \bar{\xi} = \frac{(1-y)(q_3 - y)}{(q_2 - y)^2}.$$

So to find $\psi(\xi)$, we need to first write Q as a function of $\bar{\xi}$ when $\tau_b = 0$. This gives $\psi(\bar{\xi})$. Replacing $\bar{\xi}$ by ξ, we get $\psi(\xi)$.

After much simplification, we get:

- for $y > q_2$

$$
\begin{aligned}
\psi(\xi) \ = \ & \frac{1}{(1-\xi)^{5/2}}\left[-\frac{15}{4}\xi(1-\xi)(\frac{1}{\epsilon_2^2} + \frac{1}{\epsilon_2^3}) - \frac{3\sqrt{1-\xi}}{4\epsilon_2^2} \right. \\
& -\left(\frac{39}{8\epsilon_2^2}\right)\xi\sqrt{1-\xi} + (1-\xi)\left(\frac{-3(1+\epsilon_2)}{4\epsilon_2^3}\right) \\
& -\frac{3\xi\ln(\xi)}{\epsilon_2^3} - \frac{3\xi^2\ln(\xi)}{2\epsilon_2^3} \\
& \left. -\frac{3\xi}{4\epsilon_2^2}\ln\left[\xi(\sqrt{1-\xi}-1)^6\right] - \frac{\xi^2}{16\epsilon_2^2}\ln\left[\xi^{15}(\sqrt{1-\xi}-1)^{18}\right] \right]
\end{aligned}
\tag{21a}
$$

- for $y < q_2$

$$
\begin{aligned}
\psi(\xi) \ = \ & \frac{-1}{(1-\xi)^{5/2}}\left[-\frac{15}{4}\xi(1-\xi)(\frac{1}{\epsilon_2^2} + \frac{1}{\epsilon_2^3}) + \frac{3\sqrt{1-\xi}}{4\epsilon_2^2} \right. \\
& +\left(\frac{39}{8\epsilon_2^2}\right)\xi\sqrt{1-\xi} - \frac{3}{4\epsilon_2^3}(1-\xi)(\epsilon_2 + 1) \\
& -\frac{3\xi\ln(\xi)}{\epsilon_2^3} - \frac{3\xi^2\ln(\xi)}{2\epsilon_2^3} \\
& \left. -\frac{3\xi}{4\epsilon_2^2}\ln\left[\xi(\sqrt{1-\xi}+1)^6\right] - \frac{\xi^2}{16\epsilon_2^2}\ln\left[\xi^{15}(\sqrt{1-\xi}+1)^{18}\right] \right]
\end{aligned}
\tag{21b}
$$

- for $y = q_2$

$$z_1 = 0 \text{ and } Q = \psi(\xi) = 0. \tag{21c}$$

Then $z_1 = \psi(\xi) - Q$. The work in the current section and in Section 3.1.1 provides the proof for the following proposition:

Proposition 2. *An analytic approximation of (9) with $\epsilon_2 = \epsilon_3$ and $\gamma = 0.5$ is $z = z_0 + \epsilon z_1$, where z_0 is given in (15) and z_1 is given by $\psi(\xi) - Q$ using (20) and (21a)–(21c). Then the futures price is given by $F = p_1 z\left(\frac{p}{p_1}, \tau \alpha p_1^2\right)$.*

In Figure 4, we plot z_1 when $\gamma = 0.5$. Compared with Figure 5 when $\gamma = 0$, we see that although the figures have the same shape, the magnitudes of the values with $\gamma = 0.5$ tend to be larger, especially as τ_b increases.

In Table 5 we list the values obtained for $z = z_0$, $z = z_0 + \epsilon z_1$ and those obtained using an implicit finite difference method in Maple [29], with the dimensionless parameters as given in the table. We see that the $O(1)$ solutions z_0 are by themselves fairly accurate, but the $O(\epsilon)$ approximations $z = z_0 + \epsilon z_1$ are clearly better, with RMSE ranging from 4.08×10^{-5} and five-significant-figure accuracy (with $\tau_b = 0.0506$) to RMSE of 0.00169 and three-significant-figure accuracy (with $\tau_b = 0.663$).

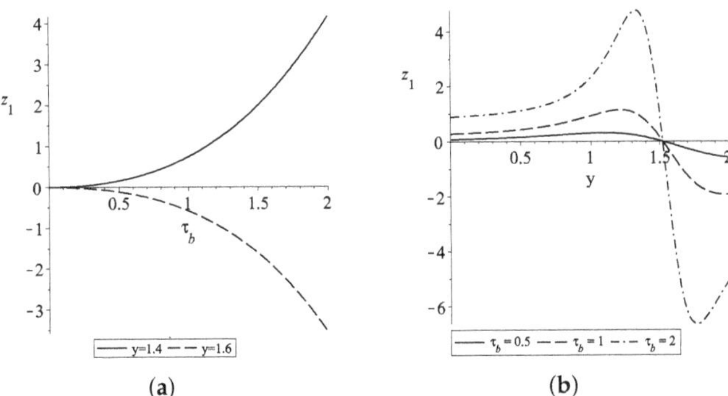

Figure 4. Plot of z_1 when $\epsilon_3 = \epsilon_2 = 25/48$ and $\gamma = 0.5$.

Table 5. $\epsilon_2 = \epsilon_3, \gamma = 0.5, \epsilon_2 = \frac{25}{48}$.

| y | $(\tau_b, \epsilon) = (0.05063, 0.2469)$ | | FD | y | $(\tau_b, \epsilon) = (0.07732, 0.1548)$ | | FD |
	z_0	$z = z_0 + \epsilon z_1$			z_0	$z = z_0 + \epsilon z_1$	
0.8	0.8929	0.8939	0.8939	0.8511	0.8599	0.8613	0.8613
1.1	1.1090	1.1098	1.1098	1.0638	1.0617	1.0630	1.0629
1.3	1.3311	1.3316	1.3315	1.2766	1.2726	1.2735	1.2734
1.5	1.5560	1.5559	1.5559	1.4894	1.4887	1.4888	1.4888
1.7	1.7805	1.7796	1.7796	1.7021	1.7055	1.7046	1.7046
2	2.0010	1.9992	1.9992	1.9149	1.9184	1.9163	1.9163
RMSE	9.88×10^{-4}	4.08×10^{-5}		RMSE	1.24×10^{-3}	5.77×10^{-5}	
MAE	8.33×10^{-4}	1.67×10^{-5}		MAE	1.08×10^{-3}	3.33×10^{-5}	

| y | $(\tau_b, \epsilon) = (0.1013, 0.2469)$ | | FD | y | $(\tau_b, \epsilon) = (0.1546, 0.1548)$ | | FD |
	z_0	$z = z_0 + \epsilon z_1$			z_0	$z = z_0 + \epsilon z_1$	
0.8	0.8967	0.9006	0.9005	0.8511	0.8680	0.8734	0.8732
1.1	1.1069	1.1103	1.1101	1.0638	1.0595	1.0647	1.0644
1.3	1.3288	1.3307	1.3306	1.2766	1.2685	1.2721	1.2718
1.5	1.5565	1.5561	1.5559	1.4894	1.4880	1.4886	1.4883
1.7	1.7831	1.7796	1.7796	1.7021	1.7089	1.7053	1.7051
2	2.0020	1.9950	1.9950	1.9149	1.9219	1.9136	1.9136
RMSE	3.86×10^{-3}	1.29×10^{-4}		RMSE	4.92×10^{-3}	2.42×10^{-4}	
MAE	3.32×10^{-3}	1.0×10^{-4}		MAE	4.3×10^{-3}	2.17×10^{-4}	

| y | $(\tau_b, \epsilon) = (0.2025, 0.2469)$ | | FD | y | $(\tau_b, \epsilon) = (0.6627, 0.3612)$ | | FD |
	z_0	$z = z_0 + \epsilon z_1$			z_0	$z = z_0 + \epsilon z_1$	
0.8	0.9039	0.9180	0.9171	0.8511	0.9088	0.9234	0.9231
1.1	1.1027	1.1160	1.1145	1.0638	1.0471	1.0654	1.0644
1.3	1.3242	1.3323	1.3305	1.2766	1.2415	1.2583	1.2560
1.5	1.5575	1.5557	1.5544	1.4894	1.4832	1.4862	1.4847
1.7	1.7885	1.7741	1.7738	1.7021	1.7324	1.7142	1.7155
2	2.0039	1.9770	1.9780	1.9149	1.9431	1.9107	1.9133
RMSE	1.44×10^{-2}	1.23×10^{-3}		RMSE	1.77×10^{-2}	1.69×10^{-3}	
MAE	1.25×10^{-2}	1.13×10^{-3}		MAE	1.57×10^{-2}	1.5×10^{-3}	

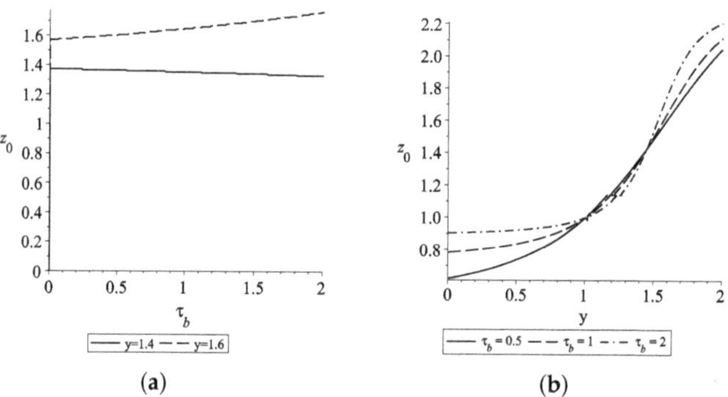

Figure 5. Plot of z_0 when $\epsilon_2 = 25/48$ and $\epsilon_3 = 2\epsilon_2$.

3.2. Case $\epsilon_3 = 2\epsilon_2$

We now assume $\epsilon_3 = 2\epsilon_2$ so that $q_2 = 1 + \epsilon_2$ and $q_3 = 1 + 3\epsilon_2$. We approximate z under this assumption by finding z_0 and z_1 as in Equation (10).

3.2.1. The O(1) Term z_0

The PDE for z_0 is given in (11), but we now have $q_3 = 1 + 3\epsilon_2$ as well as $q_2 = 1 + \epsilon_2$. By the method of characteristics, the solution to this is

$$z_0 = \phi(\xi) \quad \text{where } \xi = e^{-6\epsilon_2^2 \tau_b} \frac{(1-y)^2(q_3-y)}{(q_2-y)^3}. \tag{22}$$

To find the function ϕ, we use the initial condition $z_0(y,0) = y$.

Letting $Y = 1 - y$, we need to solve the cubic equation

$$Y^3(\bar{\xi} - 1) + Y(3\epsilon_2\bar{\xi} - 3\epsilon_2) + Y(3\epsilon_2\bar{\xi}) + \bar{\xi}\epsilon_2^3 = 0, \tag{23}$$

where

$$\bar{\xi} = \frac{(1-y)^2(q_3-y)}{(q_2-y)^3}, \tag{24}$$

i.e., ξ when $\tau_b = 0$.

We let $X = e^{-6\epsilon_2^2\tau_b}$ and consider three cases:

(a) $\xi = X\bar{\xi} < 0$;
(b) $\xi = X\bar{\xi} > 1$;
(c) $0 < X\bar{\xi} < 1$.

In Cases (a) and (b), (23) has only one real solution for Y, namely

$$Y = \epsilon_2 \left[\frac{\left[\left(1 + \sqrt{\frac{\bar{\xi}}{\bar{\xi}-1}}\right)(\bar{\xi}-1)^2\right]^{1/3}}{\bar{\xi}-1} - \frac{1}{\left[\left(1 + \sqrt{\frac{\bar{\xi}}{\bar{\xi}-1}}\right)(\bar{\xi}-1)^2\right]^{1/3}} - 1 \right]. \tag{25}$$

Hence, for **Case (a)** $\xi = X\bar{\xi} < 0 \Rightarrow q_2 < y < q_3$, we can find

$$z_0 = 1 + \epsilon_2 + \epsilon_2 \left[\frac{Q^{\frac{1}{3}}}{(1 - X\xi)} + \frac{1}{Q^{\frac{1}{3}}} \right], \tag{26}$$

where $Q = (1 - X\xi)^2 + \sqrt{-X\xi}(1 - X\xi)^{3/2}$.

This leads to

$$z_0 = 1 + \epsilon_2 + \epsilon_2 \left[\frac{(Y + \epsilon_2)\tilde{R}^{2/3} - R(Y + \epsilon_2)^2}{-R\tilde{R}^{1/3}} \right], \tag{27}$$

where

$$
\begin{aligned}
R &= XY^2(Y + 3\epsilon_2) - (Y + \epsilon_2)^3 > 0, \\
\tilde{R} &= R^{\frac{3}{2}}[R^{\frac{1}{2}} - \sqrt{X}Y(Y + 3\epsilon_2)^{\frac{1}{2}}].
\end{aligned}
$$

For **Case (b)** $\zeta = X\tilde{\zeta} > 1 \Rightarrow 1 - k_0^*\epsilon_2 < y < q_2$

where $k_0^* = -1 + X^{1/3}\left\{ \left(\frac{1}{1-X} + \frac{1}{(1-X)^{3/2}} \right)^{\frac{1}{3}} + \left(\frac{1}{1-X} - \frac{1}{(1-X)^{3/2}} \right)^{\frac{1}{3}} \right\}$, we find

$$z_0 = 1 + \epsilon_2 - \epsilon_2 \left[\frac{Q_1^{\frac{1}{3}}}{(X\zeta - 1)} - \frac{1}{Q_1^{\frac{1}{3}}} \right], \tag{28}$$

where $Q_1 = (X\zeta - 1)^2 + \sqrt{X\tilde{\zeta}}(X\zeta - 1)^{3/2}$.

However, upon simplification, this leads to the same solution for z_0 as in (27).

For **Case (c)** $0 < \zeta = X\tilde{\zeta} < 1$

Equation (23) has three real solutions, which we can write as

$$
\begin{aligned}
Y &= k_i\epsilon_2, \quad i = 0, 1, 2 \quad \text{where} \\
k_0 &= -1 + 2r^{1/3}\cos\left(\frac{\pi - \theta}{3} \right), \\
k_1 &= -1 - r^{1/3}\cos\left(\frac{\pi - \theta}{3} \right) + \sqrt{3}r^{1/3}\sin\left(\frac{\pi - \theta}{3} \right), \\
k_2 &= -1 - r^{1/3}\cos\left(\frac{\pi - \theta}{3} \right) - \sqrt{3}r^{1/3}\sin\left(\frac{\pi - \theta}{3} \right),
\end{aligned}
$$

where $r = \dfrac{1}{(1 - \tilde{\zeta})^{3/2}}$, $\theta = \tan^{-1}\sqrt{\dfrac{\tilde{\zeta}}{1 - \tilde{\zeta}}}$.

From this, we get z_0 in the intervals $0 \leq y < 1$, $1 \leq y < 1 - k_0^*\epsilon_2$ and $y \geq q_3$.

Putting all the solutions together, we have

$$z_0 = \begin{cases}
1 + (1 - 2\tilde{r}^{\frac{1}{3}}\cos(\frac{\pi - \tilde{\theta}}{3}))\epsilon_2 & \text{if } 0 \leq y < 1, \\
1 + (1 + \tilde{r}^{\frac{1}{3}}\cos(\frac{\pi - \tilde{\theta}}{3}) - \sqrt{3}\tilde{r}^{\frac{1}{3}}\sin(\frac{\pi - \tilde{\theta}}{3}))\epsilon_2 & \text{if } 1 \leq y \leq 1 - k_0^*\epsilon_2, \\
1 + \epsilon_2 - \epsilon_2(\frac{(Y + \epsilon_2)\tilde{R}^{\frac{2}{3}} - (Y + \epsilon_2)^2 R}{R\tilde{R}^{\frac{1}{3}}}) & \text{if } 1 - k_0^*\epsilon_2 < y < q_2, \\
1 + \epsilon_2 - \epsilon_2(\frac{(Y + \epsilon_2)\tilde{R}^{\frac{2}{3}} - (Y + \epsilon_2)^2 R}{R\tilde{R}^{\frac{1}{3}}}) & \text{if } q_2 \leq y < q_3, \\
1 + (1 + \tilde{r}^{\frac{1}{3}}\cos(\frac{\pi - \tilde{\theta}}{3}) + \sqrt{3}\tilde{r}^{\frac{1}{3}}\sin(\frac{\pi - \tilde{\theta}}{3}))\epsilon_2 & \text{if } y \geq q_3.
\end{cases} \tag{29}$$

where

$$Y = 1 - y \tag{30}$$

$$\tilde{r} = \frac{1}{(1 - \zeta)^{\frac{3}{2}}}, \tag{31}$$

$$\tilde{\theta} = \tan^{-1}\left(\sqrt{\frac{\zeta}{1 - \zeta}} \right), \tag{32}$$

$$k_0^* = -1 + X^{\frac{1}{3}}\left\{ \left(\frac{1}{1-X} + \frac{1}{(1-X)^{\frac{3}{2}}}\right)^{\frac{1}{3}} + \left(\frac{1}{1-X} - \frac{1}{(1-X)^{\frac{3}{2}}}\right)^{\frac{1}{3}} \right\}, \tag{33}$$

$$\tilde{R} = R^2 - \sqrt{X}Y(Y + 3\epsilon_2)^{\frac{1}{3}}R^{\frac{3}{2}} \tag{34}$$

$$R = XY^2(Y + 3\epsilon_2) - (Y + \epsilon_2)^3 > 0, \tag{35}$$

$$X = \exp(-6\epsilon_2^2 \tau_b). \tag{36}$$

Note that the solutions match at the endpoints of their intervals, and we have that when $y = 1, z_0 = 1$; when $y = q_2, z_0 = q_2$; and when $y = q_3, z_0 = q_3$.

The solution is plotted in Figure 5. Compared with Figure 2 where $\epsilon_3 = \epsilon_2$, the shapes of the figures are very similar. However, the magnitudes of the values here when $\epsilon_3 = 2\epsilon_2$ are larger, especially when $y > q_2 \approx 1.52$.

3.2.2. The $O(\epsilon)$ Term z_1

We now find the $O(\epsilon)$ approximation z_1 for two cases: when $\gamma = 0$ and when $\gamma = 0.5$.

Subcase: $\gamma = 0$

We now approximate z_1 when $\epsilon_3 = 2\epsilon_2$ and $\gamma = 0$.

By substituting (10) into (9) and collecting the coefficients of ϵ^1, we get

$$(z_1)_{\tau_b} = (z_0)_{yy} + (1 - y)(q_2 - y)(q_3 - y)(z_1)_y. \tag{37}$$

Solving (37) by the method of characteristics, we have

$$\frac{dy}{d\tau_b} = -(1 - y)(q_2 - y)(q_3 - y) \Rightarrow e^{-6\epsilon_2^2 \tau_b}\frac{(1 - y)^2(q_3 - y)}{(q_2 - y)^3} = A,$$

where A is constant. Further, we have

$$\frac{dz_1}{dy} = -\frac{(z_0)_{yy}}{(1 - y)(q_2 - y)(q_3 - y)} \Rightarrow z_1 = -\int \frac{f(y, \tau_b)}{(1 - y)(q_2 - y)(q_3 - y)}dy + \psi(\zeta) \tag{38}$$

where $f(y, \tau_b) = (z_0)_{yy}$ with $X = e^{-6\epsilon_2^2 \tau_b}$ replaced by $\frac{A(q_2-y)^3}{(1-y)^2(q_3-y)}$, and where $\zeta = e^{-6\epsilon_2^2 \tau_b}\frac{(1-y)^2(q_3-y)}{(q_2-y)^3}$.

First, we simplify the integrand in (38) before integrating, and then after the integration we replace A with $\frac{X(1-y)^2(q_3-y)}{(q_2-y)^3}$. We write the solution to (38) as $-Q(y, \tau_b) + \psi(\zeta)$.

For $(z_0)_{yy}$, we use z_0 in Equation (29).

To find $\psi(\zeta)$, we use the initial condition $z_1(y, 0) = 0$. So at $\tau = 0$ (i.e., $X = 1$), we write

$$z_1(y, 0) = -Q(y, 0) + \psi(\bar{\zeta}) = 0, \quad \text{where } \bar{\zeta} = \zeta|_{\tau=0}$$

Hence, $\psi(\bar{\zeta}) = Q(y, 0)$. So we write $Q(y, 0)$ as a function of $\bar{\zeta}$ using Equation (38) to get $Q(\bar{\zeta})$. Then $\psi(\zeta) = Q(\zeta)$. The above reasoning serves to prove the following proposition:

Proposition 3. *An analytic approximation of (9) with $\epsilon_2 = 2\epsilon_3$ and $\gamma = 0$ is $z = z_0 + \epsilon z_1$, where z_0 is given in (29) and z_1 is given by $\psi(\zeta) - Q$ as explained above in this section. Then the futures price is given by $F = p_1 z\left(\frac{p}{p_1}, \tau\alpha p_1^2\right)$.*

Unfortunately, the integral Q cannot be obtained explicitly. However, excellent approximations of the integral can be found using series representations of the integrand. Here, we obtain results using Maple [29] for the most relevant interval, namely

$$lowb < y < q_3, \quad \text{where } lowb = 1 - k_0^*\epsilon_2.$$

We first split the integral into two, namely

(a) $lowb < y < q_2$ where $\zeta > 1$;
(b) $q_2 < y < q_3$ where $\zeta < 0$.

In (a), we write the integrand as a series in $q_2 - y$. In (b), we write the integrand for $y < 1 + 2\epsilon_2$ as a series in $y - q_2$ and otherwise as a series in $q_3 - y$. The results obtained are listed in Table 6.

As in the previous section, we tabulate in Table 6 the values obtained for $z = z_0$ and $z = z_0 + \epsilon z_1$ and those obtained using an implicit finite difference method in Maple [29] using the dimensionless parameters as stated in the table. Again, the $O(1)$ solutions z_0 are relatively accurate, but the $O(\epsilon)$ approximations $z = z_0 + \epsilon z_1$ are certainly an improvement, with RMSE ranging from 8×10^{-5} and mostly five-significant-figure accuracy (with $\tau_b = 0.0552$) to RMSE of 2.33×10^{-3} and mostly three-significant-figure accuracy (with $\tau_b = 0.3093$).

Table 6. $\epsilon_3 = 2\epsilon_2, \gamma = 0, \epsilon_2 = \frac{25}{48}$.

y	$(\tau_b, \epsilon) = (0.0552, 0.25)$			$(\tau_b, \epsilon) = (0.0773, 0.2474)$		
	z_0	$z = z_0 + \epsilon z_1$	FD	z_0	$z = z_0 + \epsilon z_1$	FD
1.5	1.4994	1.4998	1.4998	1.4991	1.5000	1.5000
1.6	1.6026	1.6028	1.6028	1.6036	1.6040	1.6040
1.7	1.7061	1.7061	1.7061	1.7086	1.7085	1.7085
1.8	1.8096	1.8093	1.8093	1.8135	1.8129	1.8129
2.1	2.1163	2.1152	2.1154	2.1229	2.1215	2.1210
2.2	2.2162	2.2151	2.2151	2.2227	2.2204	2.2204
RMSE	6.2×10^{-4}	8.0×10^{-5}		1.31×10^{-3}	2.0×10^{-4}	
MAE	4.8×10^{-4}	3.0×10^{-5}		1.03×10^{-3}	8.0×10^{-5}	

y	$(\tau_b, \epsilon) = (0.1105, 0.25)$			$(\tau_b, \epsilon) = (0.1546, 0.2474)$		
	z_0	$z = z_0 + \epsilon z_1$	FD	z_0	$z = z_0 + \epsilon z_1$	FD
1.5	1.4987	1.5006	1.5006	1.4982	1.5020	1.5019
1.6	1.6052	1.6061	1.6061	1.6074	1.6092	1.6091
1.7	1.7124	1.7122	1.7122	1.7176	1.7172	1.7172
1.8	1.8194	1.8182	1.8183	1.8267	1.8250	1.8253
2.1	2.1327	2.1292	2.1289	2.1459	2.1382	2.1383
2.2	2.2323	2.2276	2.2277	2.2451	2.2359	2.2361
RMSE	2.62×10^{-3}	1.4×10^{-4}		5.12×10^{-3}	1.6×10^{-4}	
MAE	2.08×10^{-3}	8.0×10^{-5}		3.97×10^{-3}	1.3×10^{-4}	

y	$(\tau_b, \epsilon) = (0.2209, 0.25)$			$(\tau_b, \epsilon) = (0.3093, 0.2474)$		
	z_0	$z = z_0 + \epsilon z_1$	FD	z_0	$z = z_0 + \epsilon z_1$	FD
1.5	1.4974	1.5055	1.5049	1.4963	1.5127	1.5107
1.6	1.6108	1.6145	1.6142	1.6156	1.6228	1.6219
1.7	1.7256	1.7247	1.7248	1.7344	1.7344	1.7347
1.8	1.8402	1.8342	1.8350	1.8577	1.8443	1.8471
2.1	2.1657	2.1493	2.1500	2.1920	2.1589	2.1621
2.2	2.2638	2.2449	2.2458	2.2882	2.2517	2.2548
RMSE	1.05×10^{-2}	6.3×10^{-4}		1.99×10^{-2}	2.33×10^{-3}	
MAE	8.43×10^{-3}	5.7×10^{-4}		1.58×10^{-2}	2.05×10^{-3}	

In Figure 6, z_1 is plotted as a function of τ_b in [0,2] for various values of y with $\epsilon_2 = 25/48$. We see that when $y \leq 1.55$, z_1 increases as a function of τ_b; when $y = 1.6$, z_1 initially slowly increases before turning to decrease; then, for $1 \leq \tau_b \leq 2$ when $y \geq 1.65$, z_1 decreases before turning. The larger y is in this last range, the smaller the magnitude of the turning point. Compared with z_1 when $\epsilon_3 = \epsilon_2$ and $\gamma = 0$, z_1 generally increases/decreases more quickly but mostly maintains the same shape.

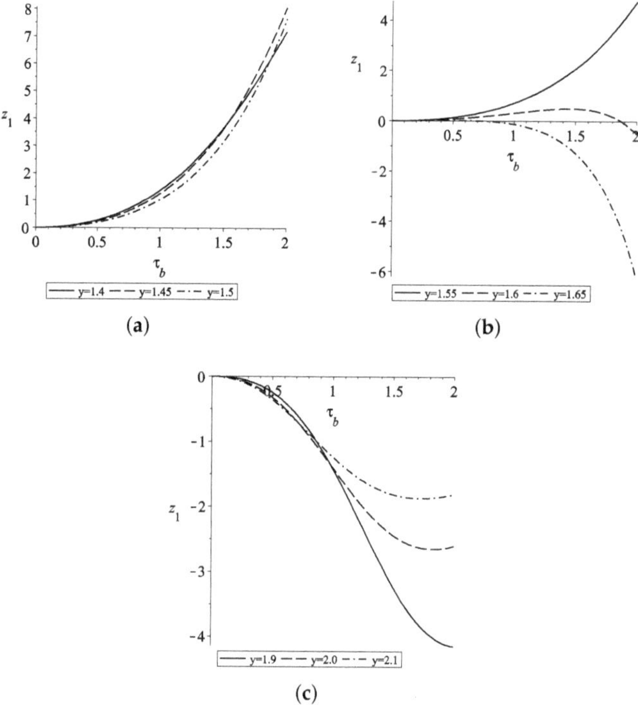

Figure 6. Plot of z_1 when $\epsilon_3 = 2\epsilon_2$ and $\gamma = 0$.

Subcase $\gamma = 0.5$

For z_1 when $\epsilon_3 = 2\epsilon_2$ and $\gamma = \frac{1}{2}$, we solve

$$(z_1)_{\tau_b} = y(z_0)_{yy} + (1-y)(q_2 - y)(q_3 - y)(z_1)_y, \tag{39}$$

where $q_2 = 1 + \epsilon_2$ and $q_3 = 1 + 3\epsilon_2$.

Hence,

$$z_1 = -\int \frac{f(y, \tau_b)}{(1-y)(q_2 - y)(q_3 - y)} dy + \psi(\xi),$$

where $f(y, \tau_b) = y(z_0)_{yy}$ with $X = e^{-6\epsilon_2^2 \tau_b}$ replaced by $\frac{A(q_2 - y)^3}{(1-y)^2(q_3 - y)}$ (after $(z_0)_{yy}$ has been determined). The solution process is then the same as in the previous section. Hence, the above work provides the proof for the following proposition:

Proposition 4. *An analytic approximation of (9) with $\epsilon_2 = 2\epsilon_3$ and $\gamma = 0.5$ is $z = z_0 + \epsilon z_1$, where z_0 is given in (29) and z_1 is as given above. Then the futures price is given by $F = F = p_1 z\left(\frac{p}{p_1}, \tau \alpha p_1^2\right)$.*

In Figure 7, z_1 when $\gamma = 0.5$ is plotted as a function of τ_b in [0,2] for various values of y with $\epsilon_2 = 25/48$. Compared to the case when $\gamma = 0$, z_1 displays the same behaviour but the magnitude of the values is greater.

In Table 7 we present the results obtained for $z = z_0$ and $z = z_0 + \epsilon z_1$ and those obtained using an implicit finite difference method in Maple [29]. The dimensionless parameters used are given in the table. The results are very similar to those of Tables 4–6, with the $O(\epsilon)$ approximations $z = z_0 + \epsilon z_1$ outperforming the $O(1)$ solutions z_0. The RMSE from the $O(\epsilon)$ approximations ranges from 6.0×10^{-5} with mostly five-significant-figure accuracy (with $\tau_b = 0.0773$) to RMSE of 5.57×10^{-3} and mostly three-significant-figure accuracy with ($\tau_b = 0.6627$).

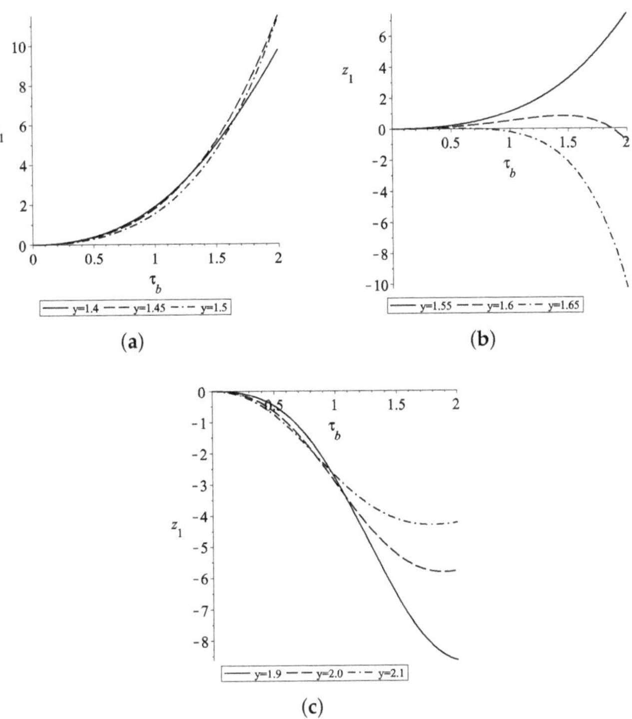

Figure 7. Plot of z_1 when $\epsilon_3 = 2\epsilon_2$ and $\gamma = 0.5$.

Table 7. $\epsilon_3 = 2\epsilon_2, \gamma = 0.5, \epsilon_2 = \frac{25}{48}$.

y	$(\tau_b, \epsilon) = (0.0506, 0.2469)$			$(\tau_b, \epsilon) = (0.0773, 0.1548)$		
	z_0	$z = z_0 + \epsilon z_1$	FD	z_0	$z = z_0 + \epsilon z_1$	FD
1.5	1.4994	1.5000	1.5000	1.4991	1.5000	1.4999
1.6	1.6024	1.6026	1.6026	1.6036	1.6040	1.6040
1.7	1.7056	1.7055	1.7055	1.7086	1.7085	1.7085
1.8	1.8088	1.8083	1.8083	1.8135	1.8128	1.8128
2.1	2.1150	2.1130	2.1133	2.1229	2.1205	2.1204
2.2	2.2149	2.2127	2.2127	2.2227	2.2195	2.2195
RMSE	1.18×10^{-3}	1.2×10^{-4}		1.72×10^{-3}	6.0×10^{-5}	
MAE	8.8×10^{-4}	5.0×10^{-5}		1.28×10^{-3}	3.0×10^{-5}	

y	$(\tau_b, \epsilon) = (0.1013, 0.2469)$			$(\tau_b, \epsilon) = (0.1546, 0.1548)$		
	z_0	$z = z_0 + \epsilon z_1$	FD	z_0	$z = z_0 + \epsilon z_1$	FD
1.5	1.4988	1.5012	1.5009	1.4982	1.5017	1.5014
1.6	1.6048	1.6059	1.6057	1.6074	1.6092	1.6088
1.7	1.7113	1.7111	1.7109	1.7176	1.7172	1.7169
1.8	1.8178	1.8160	1.8159	1.8276	1.8247	1.8246
2.1	2.1300	2.1231	2.1231	2.1459	2.1356	2.1357
2.2	2.2297	2.2210	2.2210	2.2451	2.2323	2.2325

Table 7. *Cont.*

RMSE	4.70×10^{-3}	1.7×10^{-4}		6.89×10^{-3}	2.6×10^{-4}	
MAE	3.48×10^{-3}	1.3×10^{-4}		5.18×10^{-3}	2.3×10^{-4}	
y	$(\tau_b, \epsilon) = (0.2025, 0.2469)$			$(\tau_b, \epsilon) = (0.6627, 0.0361)$		
	z_0	$z = z_0 + \epsilon z_1$	FD	z_0	$z = z_0 + \epsilon z_1$	FD
1.5	1.4976	1.5076	1.5053	1.4913	1.5115	1.5074
1.6	1.6100	1.6147	1.6126	1.6374	1.6456	1.6427
1.7	1.7234	1.7221	1.7205	1.7889	1.7811	1.7807
1.8	1.8366	1.8282	1.8276	1.9368	1.9034	1.9149
2.1	2.1602	2.1313	2.1325	2.2928	2.2440	2.2482
2.2	2.2587	2.2237	2.2255	2.3755	2.3267	2.3300
RMSE	1.84×10^{-2}	1.70×10^{-3}		2.86×10^{-2}	5.57×10^{-3}	
MAE	1.39×10^{-2}	1.60×10^{-3}		2.36×10^{-2}	4.40×10^{-3}	

4. Conclusions

There are many stochastic models that can be found in the literature that aim to model oil prices. Most have mean-reverting drifts that imply reversion to one mean value. However, examination of historical oil prices points to two basins of attraction. In this paper, we have addressed this fact and modelled the oil price process with a single one-factor nonlinear model that can capture this property. GMM analysis comprehensively indicated that a cubic term was necessary in the drift term in the oil price process, as in our bimodal model. Pricing futures contracts under our model requires solving a partial differential equation for which an exact analytic solution is not available. However, we were able to find analytic approximations for the futures prices that provide fast and accurate solutions. We first non-dimensionalised the governing PDE and found perturbation expansions for the new non-dimensional dependent variable z. The results showed that—while the leading-order approximation $z = z_0$ yielded good results—using the next-order approximation $z = z_0 + \epsilon z_1$ provided even better approximations. Higher-order approximations can be found routinely if necessary, as indicated in Section 3.1.2. There are definite advantages to having an analytic approximation over a numerical answer as it gives faster answers and insight into the general properties of the solution, but, more importantly here, we would be able to calibrate it to oil price data to find the best parameter values to fit the model to price and forecast futures prices. This will be the subject of our next paper: calibration of oil price models to real data and comparing their performance in valuing and forecasting oil price futures. Given that crude oil is, at the moment, the main source of energy production in the world, and given the reliance many investors around the world have on oil futures for the purposes of speculation and management of their portfolios' risk, we feel that the current paper could provide a better understanding and guidance to investors.

Author Contributions: Writing—review and editing, J.G. and M.A. All authors have read and agreed to the published version of the manuscript.

Funding: The authors extend their appreciation to the Deanship of Scientific Research at Imam Mohammad Ibn Saud Islamic University for funding this work through Research Group no. RG-21-09-19.

Data Availability Statement: The data used in this research are available from the U.S. Energy Information Administration (EIA) via https://www.eia.gov/ accessed on 6 March 2023.

Appendix A. Methodology

The Generalized Method of Moments (GMM) of Hansen [30] is used in this paper to estimate the parameters of the continuous-time model for $\eta = \frac{p}{100}$. GMM was chosen as the estimation technique as it does not need the distribution of oil price changes to be normal and the GMM estimators and their standard errors are consistent even if distributions are heteroskedastic. (Heteroskedasticity means that the variance of the errors varies widely across the observations. It can make coefficient estimates less precise using some techniques.) Further, GMM is often used in empirical finance tests to compare continuous-time models for different underlying assets (see, e.g., Rajet et al. [31] and Hamisultane [32]). By Itô's Lemma, η follows

$$d\eta = (c_1 + c_2\eta + c_3\eta^2 + c_4\eta^3)dt + M\eta^\gamma dZ \tag{A1}$$

where

$$
\begin{aligned}
c_1 &= k_1/100, \\
c_2 &= k_2, \\
c_3 &= 100k_3, \\
c_4 &= 100^2 k_4, \\
M &= \sigma 100^{\gamma-1}.
\end{aligned}
$$

Note that if we write (3) as $dp = \alpha(p_1 - p)(p_2 - p)(p_3 - p)dt + \sigma p^\gamma dZ$, then $k_1 = \alpha p_1 p_2 p_3$, $k_2 = -\alpha(p_2 p_3 + p_1 p_2 + p_1 p_3)$, $k_3 = \alpha(p_1 + p_2 + p_3)$ and $k_4 = -\alpha$.

We use the discrete-time econometric specification corresponding to (A1), namely:

$$\eta_{t+1} - \eta_t = c_1 + c_2\eta_t + c_3\eta_t^2 + c_4\eta_t^3 + \varepsilon_{t+1} \tag{A2a}$$

$$\text{where } E[\varepsilon_{t+1}] = 0 \tag{A2b}$$

$$\text{and } E[\varepsilon_{t+1}^2] = M^2 \eta_t^{2\gamma} \Delta t. \tag{A2c}$$

We define θ to be the parameter vector with components c_1, c_2, c_3, c_4, M and γ and let $f_t(\theta)$ be the vector:

$$f_t(\theta) = \begin{bmatrix} \varepsilon_{t+1} \otimes [1, \eta_t, \eta_t^2, \sqrt{\eta_t}]^T \\ (\varepsilon_{t+1}^2 - M^2 \eta_t^{2\gamma} \Delta t) \otimes [1, \eta_t]^T \end{bmatrix}$$

Subject to the null hypothesis that conditions (A2a)–(A2c) are correct, then the orthogonality conditions, $E[f_t] = 0$, apply. The technique of GMM firstly replaces $E[f_t(\theta)] = 0$ with its sample counterpart, $g(\theta) = \frac{1}{n} \sum_{t=1}^{n} f_t(\theta)$, which uses n observations. It then considers the quadratic form $q(\theta) = g(\theta)^T W g(\theta)$, where W is a positive definite weighting matrix (the matrix W has the sample estimate adjusted for serial correlation and heteroskedasticity using the method of Newey and West [33] with Bartlett weights) and estimates the parameters in the vector θ that minimise this quadratic form. The optimal choice for the matrix W has been found to be (see Hansen [30]) the inverse of the covariance matrix of the sample moment, $[Var(g(\theta))]^{-1} = [E[f_t(\theta)f_t(\theta)^T]]^{-1}$.

In the unrestricted model (A1), the number of parameters that are not known is equal to the number of orthogonality conditions. This means the system is exactly identified and there exists a unique solution θ for which $q(\theta) = 0$ with any choice of W. For Models 1–10. which are nested within the unrestricted model, the number of the parameters that are unknown is less than that of the orthogonality conditions. Hence, in this case, the system is overidentified and there is no solution for θ. GMM then uses the same weighting matrix that was found to estimate the parameters in the unrestricted model (A1).

For each of the nested models, we can test the validity of the restrictions imposed on the parameters using the hypothesis test Hypothesis A1 versus Hypothesis A2 where

Hypothesis A1. *The nested model does not enforce/impose overidentified restrictions. In other words, the nested model is not misspecified.*

Hypothesis A2. *The nested model does enforce/impose overidentified restrictions. That is, the nested model is misspecified.*

The following test statistic, known as the Hansen test (see Newey and West [33]), can be used:

$$S = n(q(\hat{\theta}_0) - q(\hat{\theta})),$$

where $q(\hat{\theta})$ and $q(\hat{\theta}_0)$ are the objective functions for the unrestricted model and for the restricted model, respectively. If the null hypothesis, Hypothesis A1, is true, then the test statistic S is asymptotically distributed with χ^2_{j-k}, where j and k are the number of parameters in the unrestricted model and restricted model, respectively. With a specified level of significance α, if $\chi^2_{j-k;\alpha}$ is less than the calculated test statistic S, then we need to reject the null hypothesis and conclude that the restricted model is invalid (in other words, the restrictions are unfounded and unreasonable) at the $100(1-\alpha)\%$ level of significance. Hence, if the p-value is less than the set level of significance α, then we conclude that at the $100\alpha\%$ level of significance, the restricted model is invalid.

Appendix B.

Appendix B.1. GMM Results

Table A1. Empirical Results for Nesting Models 1–10 within (3) using 10 years of monthly data.

Model	c_1	c_2	c_3	c_4	M	γ	χ^2 p-Value	DF
Unrestricted	3.221 [0.001]	−14.544 [0.002]	20.796 [0.005]	−9.382 [0.008]	−0.2329 [<0.001]	0.1277 [0.520]	N/A	N/A
1	3.448 [<0.001]	−14.818 [0.002]	20.628 [0.005]	−9.170 [0.009]	−0.2426 [<0.001]	0.5	0.09	1
2	0.502 [0.009]	−0.6844 [0.011]	0	0	0.2415 [<0.001]	0.5	0.005	3
3	0	0.6214 [0.040]	−0.7370 [0.027]	0	0.2404 [<0.001]	0.5	0.001	3
4	0	0.3878 [0.329]	0	0	−0.500 [<0.001]	1	0	4
5	0	0.111 [0.779]	0	0	−0.5302 [<0.001]	0.5	0	4
6	3.086 [0.002]	−14.275 [0.004]	20.711 [0.006]	−9.427 [0.009]	0.2242 [<0.001]	0	0.514	1
7	0.2878 [0.165]	−0.4651 [0.102]	0	0	0.2262 [<0.001]	0	0.030	3
8	0	0.2641 [0.394]	−0.4071 [0.230]	0	0.2291 [<0.001]	0	0.016	3
9	0	−0.096 [0.289]	0	0	0.2392 [<0.001]	0	0.017	4
10	0	0.9125 [0.001]	−1.006 [0.001]	0	0.2023 [<0.001]	1.5	0	3

Table A2. Empirical Results for Nesting Models 1–10 within (3) using 10 years of weekly data.

Model	c_1	c_2	c_3	c_4	M	γ	χ^2 p-Value	DF
Unrestricted	2.696 [0.091]	−12.825 [0.074]	19.137 [0.063]	−8.895 [0.056]	0.2284 [<0.001]	0.3140 [0.064]	N/A	N/A
1	2.9398 [0.061]	−13.897 [0.049]	20.774 [0.040]	−9.682 [0.034]	0.2390 [<0.001]	0.5	0.282	1
2	0.1993 [0.272]	−0.255 [0.316]	0	0	−0.234 [<0.001]	0.5	0.122	3
3	0	0.3238 [0.255]	−0.3769 [0.252]	0	−0.2346 [<0.001]	0.5	0.125	3
4	0	0.0717 [0.378]	0	0	−0.2464 [<0.001]	1	0	4
5	0	0.014 [0.864]	0	0	−0.2389 [<0.001]	0.5	0.134	4
6	2.167 [0.175]	−10.343 [0.150]	15.316 [0.135]	−7.081 [0.125]	0.201 [<0.001]	0	0.065	1
7	0.0987 [0.593]	−0.1804 [0.483]	0	0	−0.1990 [<0.001]	0	0.116	3
8	0	0.1199 [0.681]	−0.2020 [0.547]	0	−0.1991 [<0.001]	0	0.121	3
9	0	−0.052 [0.526]	0	0	−0.2014 [<0.001]	0	0.185	4
10	0	0.7269 [0.009]	−0.7831 [0.015]	0	−0.2290 [<0.001]	1.5	0	3

Appendix B.2. Simulations

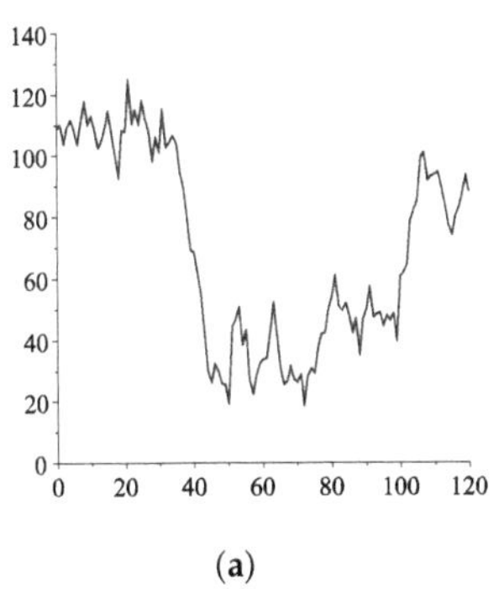

(**a**)

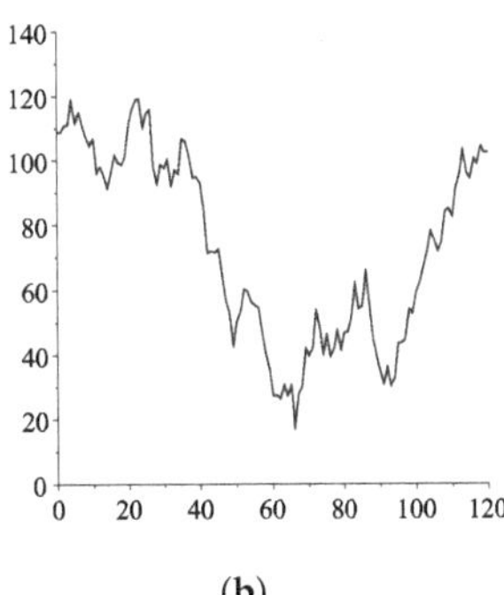

(**b**)

Figure A1. *Cont.*

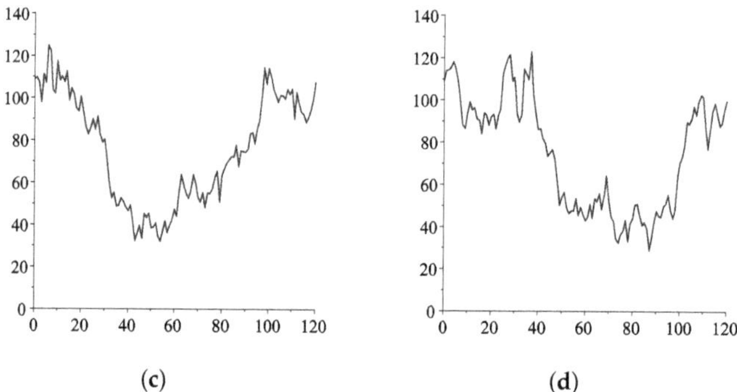

(c)   (d)

Figure A1. Monthly simulations: (**a**) monthly over 10 years with $p_1 = 44, p_2 = 74, p_3 = 104$, $\gamma = 0, \sigma = 24$; (**b**) monthly over 10 years with $p_1 = 47, p_2 = 67, p_3 = 107, \gamma = 0, \sigma = 22$; (**c**) monthly over 10 years with $p_1 = 44, p_2 = 74, p_3 = 104, \gamma = 0.5, \sigma = 2.59$; (**d**) monthly over 10 years with $p_1 = 47, p_2 = 67, p_3 = 107, \gamma = 0.5, \sigma = 2.59$.

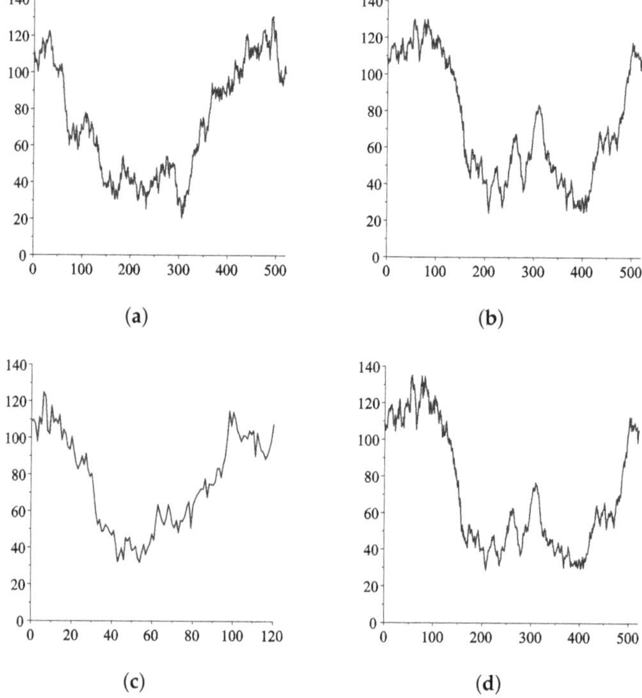

(a)   (b)

(c)   (d)

Figure A2. Weekly simulations: (**a**) weekly over 10 years with $p_1 = 42, p_2 = 73, p_3 = 104$, $\gamma = 0, \sigma = 22$; (**b**) weekly over 10 years with $p_1 = 47, p_2 = 67, p_3 = 107, \gamma = 0, \sigma = 22$; (**c**) weekly over 10 years with $p_1 = 42, p_2 = 73, p_3 = 104, \gamma = 0.5, \sigma = 2.4$; (**d**) weekly over 10 years with $p_1 = 47, p_2 = 67, p_3 = 107, \gamma = 0.5, \sigma = 2.59$.

References

1. Brennan, M.; Schwartz, E. Evaluating Natural Resource Investments. *J. Bus.* **1985**, *58*, 135–157. [CrossRef]
2. Gabillon, J. *The Term Structures of Oil Futures Prices*; Oxford Institute for Energy Studies: Oxford, UK, 1991.
3. Bjerksund, P.; Ekern, S. Contingent claims evaluation of mean-reverting cash flows in shipping. In *Real Options in Capital Investment: Models, Strategies, and Applications*; Trigeorgis, L., Ed.; Praeger: Westport, Ireland, 1995.
4. Schwartz, E. The stochastic behaviour of commodity prices: Implications for valuation and hedging. *J. Financ.* **1997**, *3*, 923–973. [CrossRef]
5. Pindyck, R. The Long-Run evolutions of energy prices. *Energy J.* **1999**, *20*, 1–27. [CrossRef]
6. AbaOud, M.; Goard, J. Stochastic Models for Oil Prices and the Pricing of Futures on Oil. *Appl. Math. Financ.* **2015**, *22*, 189–206. [CrossRef]
7. Gibson, R.; Schwartz, E. Stochastic Conveience Yield And The Pricing of Oil Continget Claims. *J. Financ.* **1999**, *3*, 959–976.
8. Pilipovic, D. *Energy Risk: Valuing and Managing Energy Derivatives*; McGraw Hill: New York, NY, USA, 1997.
9. Schwartz, E.; Smith, J. Short-Term Variation And Long-Trem Dyanamics in Commodity Prices. *Manag. Sci.* **2000**, *46*, 893–911. [CrossRef]
10. Hilliard, J.; Reis, J. Valuation of Commodity Futures and Options Under Stochastic Convenience Yield, Interest Rates, and Jump Diffusions in The Spot. *J. Financ. Quant. Anal.* **1998**, *33*, 61–86. [CrossRef]
11. Cortazar, G.; Schwartz, E. Implementing a Stochastic Model For Oil Futures Prices. *Energy Econ.* **2003**, *25*, 215–238. [CrossRef]
12. Abadie, L.; Chamorro, J. Valuation of Real Options in Crude Oil Production. *Energies.* **2017**, *10*, 1218. [CrossRef]
13. Cortazar, J.; Naranjo, L. An N-factor Gaussian model of oil futures prices. *J. Futures Mark.* **2006**, *26*, 243–268. [CrossRef]
14. Ogbogbo, C. Stochastic Model of Crude Oil Spot Price Process as a Jump-Diffusion Process. *Appl. Math. Inf. Sci.* **2009**, *13*, 1029–1037.
15. Hayashi, F. *Econometrics*; Princeton University Press: Princeton, NJ, USA, 2000.
16. Mackinlay, A.; Richardson, M. Using Generalized Method of Moments to Test Mean-Variance Efficiency. *J. Financ.* **1991**, *46*, 511–526. [CrossRef]
17. Ferson, W.; Foerster, S. Finite Sample Properties of the Generalized Method of Moments in Tests of Conditional Asset Pricing Models. *J. Financ. Econ.* **1994**, *36*, 29–55. [CrossRef]
18. Heston, S. *A Simple New Formula for Options with Stochastic Volatility*; Olin, J.M., Ed.; School of Business, Washington University: St. Louis, MI, USA, 1997.
19. Black, F.; Scholes, M. The Valuation of Option Contracts And a Test of Market Efficiency. *J. Financ.* **1972**, *27*, 399–417. [CrossRef]
20. McDonald, R.; Siegel, D. Investment and The Valuation of Firms When There Is An Option to Shut Down. *Int. Econ. Rev.* **1985**, *26*, 331–349. [CrossRef]
21. Goard, J.; Hansen, N. Comparison of the performance of a time-dependent short-interest rate model with time-independent models. *Appl. Math. Financ.* **2004**, *11*, 147–164. [CrossRef]
22. Goard, J.; Mazur, M. Stochastic volatility models and the pricing of vix options. *Math. Financ.* **2013**, *23*, 439–458. [CrossRef]
23. Goard, J. A time-dependent variance model for pricing variance and volatility swaps. *Appl. Math. Financ.* **2011**, *18*, 51–70. [CrossRef]
24. Egloff, D.; Leippold, M.; Wu, L. The Term Structure of Variance Swap Rates and Optimal Variance Swap Investments. *J. Fin. Quant. Anal.* **2010**, *45*, 1279–1310. [CrossRef]
25. Stein, E.; Stein, J. Stock Price Distributions with Stochastic Volatility: An Analytical Approach. *Rev. Finan. Stud.* **1991**, *4*, 727–752. [CrossRef]
26. Grünbichler, A.; Longstaff, F. Valuing Futures and Options on Volatility. *J. Bank. Financ.* **1996**, *20*, 985–1001. [CrossRef]
27. Wilmott, P. *Derivatives: The Theory and Practice of Financial Engineering*; John Wiley & Sons: Chichester, UK, 1998.
28. Debnath, L. *Nonlinear Partial Differential Equations for Scientists and Engineers*; Birkhäuser: Boston, MA, USA, 2005.
29. Maple. *Maplesoft*; A Division ofWaterloo Maple Inc.: Waterloo, ON, Canada, 2018.
30. Hansen, L. Large Sample Properties of Generalized Method of Moments Estimators. *Econometrica* **1982**, *50*, 1029–1054. [CrossRef]
31. Raj, M.; Sim, A.; Thurston, D. A generalized method of moments comparison of the cox-ingersoll-ross and heath-jarrow-morton models. *J. Bus. Econ.* **1997**, *49*, 169–192. [CrossRef]
32. Hamisultane, H. Utility-based pricing of weather derivatives. *Eur. J. Financ.* **2009**, *16*, 503–525. [CrossRef]
33. Newey, W.; West, K. A Simple, Positive Semi-Definite, Heteroskedasticity and Autocorrelation Consistent Covariance Matrix. *Econometrica* **1982**, *55*, 703–708. [CrossRef]

 *mathematics*

Article

Compactness of Commutators for Riesz Potential on Generalized Morrey Spaces

Nurzhan Bokayev [1,†], Dauren Matin [2,*,†], Talgat Akhazhanov [2] and Aidos Adilkhanov [1]

[1] Department of Fundamental Mathematics, Faculty of Mechanics and Mathematics, L.N. Gumilyov Eurasian National University, Astana 010000, Kazakhstan; bokayev2011@yandex.ru (N.B.); adilkhanov_kz@mail.ru (A.A.)

[2] Higher Mathematics Department, Faculty of Mechanics and Mathematics, L.N. Gumilyov Eurasian National University, Astana 010000, Kazakhstan; talgat_a2008@mail.ru

* Correspondence: d.matin@mail.kz; Tel.: +7-777-36-999-66

† These authors contributed equally to this work.

Abstract: In this paper, we give the sufficient conditions for the compactness of sets in generalized Morrey spaces $M_p^{w(\cdot)}$. This result is an analogue of the well-known Fréchet–Kolmogorov theorem on the compactness of a set in Lebesgue spaces L_p, $p > 0$. As an application, we prove the compactness of the commutator of the Riesz potential $[b, I_\alpha]$ in generalized Morrey spaces, where $b \in VMO$ ($VMO(\mathbb{R}^n)$ denote the BMO-closure of $C_0^\infty(\mathbb{R}^n)$). We prove auxiliary statements regarding the connection between the norm of average functions and the norm of the difference of functions in the generalized Morrey spaces. Such results are also of independent interest.

Keywords: commutator; Riesz potential; compactness; generalized Morrey space; VMO

MSC: 42B20; 42B25

1. Introduction

Morrey spaces M_p^λ, named after C. Morrey, were introduced by him in 1938 in [1] and defined as follows: For $1 \leq p \leq \infty$, $n \geq 1$, $0 < \lambda < n$, $f \in M_p^\lambda$ if $f \in L_p^{loc}$ and

$$\|f\|_{M_p^\lambda} \equiv \|f\|_{M_p^\lambda(\mathbb{R}^n)} = \sup_{x \in \mathbb{R}^n, r > 0} \left(r^{-\lambda} \|f\|_{L_p(B(x,r))} \right) < \infty,$$

where $B(x, r)$ is a ball with center at the point x and of radius $r > 0$.

For $\lambda = 0$ and $\lambda = n$, the Morrey spaces $M_p^0(\mathbb{R}^n)$ and $M_p^n(\mathbb{R}^n)$ coincide (with equality of norms) with the spaces $L_p(\mathbb{R}^n)$ and $L_\infty(\mathbb{R}^n)$, respectively.

Later, the Morrey spaces were found to have many important applications to the Navier–Stokes equations (see [2,3]), the Shrodinger equations (see [4,5]) and the potential analysis (see [6,7]).

Generalized Morrey spaces $M_p^{w(\cdot)}$ were first considered by T. Mizuhara [8], E. Nakai [9] and V.S. Guliyev [10].

Let $1 \leq p \leq \infty$ and let w be a measurable non-negative function on $(0, \infty)$ that is not equivalent to zero. The generalized Morrey space $M_p^{w(\cdot)} \equiv M_p^{w(\cdot)}(\mathbb{R}^n)$ is defined as the set of all functions $f \in L_p^{loc}(\mathbb{R}^n)$ with $\|f\|_{M_p^{w(\cdot)}} < \infty$, where

$$\|f\|_{M_p^{w(\cdot)}} = \sup_{x \in \mathbb{R}^n, \ r > 0} \left(w(r) \|f\|_{L_p(B(x,r))} \right).$$

The space $M_p^{w(\cdot)}$ coincides with the Morrey space M_p^λ if $w(r) = r^{-\lambda}$, where $0 \leq \lambda \leq \frac{n}{p}$.

Citation: Bokayev, N.; Matin, D.; Akhazhanov, T.; Adilkhanov, A. Compactness of Commutators for Riesz Potential on Generalized Morrey Spaces. *Mathematics* **2024**, *12*, 304. https://doi.org/10.3390/math12020304

Academic Editor: Arsen Palestini

Received: 6 December 2023
Revised: 13 January 2024
Accepted: 15 January 2024
Published: 17 January 2024

By $\Omega_{p\infty}$ we denote the set of all non-negative, measurable on $(0,\infty)$ functions, not equivalent to 0 and such that for some $t > 0$,

$$\|w(r)r^{\frac{n}{p}}\|_{L_\infty(0,t)} < \infty, \quad \|w(r)\|_{L_\infty(t,\infty)} < \infty.$$

The space $M_p^{w(\cdot)}$ is non-trivial if and only if $w \in \Omega_{p\infty}$ [11,12].

The Riesz potential I_α of order $\alpha(0 < \alpha < n)$ is defined by

$$I_\alpha f(x) = \int_{\mathbb{R}^n} \frac{f(y)}{|x-y|^{n-\alpha}} dy.$$

For the function $b \in L_{loc}(\mathbb{R}^n)$, let M_b denote the multiplication operator $M_b f = bf$, where f is a measurable function. Then, the commutator for the Riesz potential I_α and the operator M_b is defined by

$$[b, I_\alpha](f)(x) = M_b(I_\alpha(f(x))) - I_\alpha(M_b f)(x) = \int_{\mathbb{R}^n} \frac{[b(x) - b(y)]f(y)}{|x-y|^{n-\alpha}} dy.$$

The function $b \in L_\infty(\mathbb{R}^n)$ is said to belong to the space $BMO(\mathbb{R}^n)$ if

$$\|b\|_* = \sup_{Q \subset \mathbb{R}^n} \frac{1}{|Q|} \int_Q |b(x) - b_Q| dx < \infty,$$

where Q is a ball in $\mathbb{R}^n$ and $b_Q = \frac{1}{|Q|} \int_{\mathbb{R}^n} b(y) dy$.

By $VMO(\mathbb{R}^n)$, we denote the BMO-closure of the space $C_0^\infty(\mathbb{R}^n)$, where $C_0^\infty(\mathbb{R}^n)$ is the set of all functions from $C^\infty(\mathbb{R}^n)$ with compact support.

The boundedness of the Riesz potential on the Morrey spaces was investigated by S. Spanne, J. Peetre [13] and D. Adams. [14]. T. Mizuhara [8], E. Nakai [9] and V.S. Guliyev [10] generalized the results of D. Adams and obtained sufficient conditions for the boundedness of I_α on the generalized Morrey spaces. Boundedness of the commutator for the Riesz potential on the Morrey spaces and on the generalized Morrey spaces was considered in [15,16], respectively. The compactness of the commutator for the Riesz potential on the Morrey spaces and on the Morrey spaces with non-doubling measures was considered in [17,18], respectively. The pre-compactness of sets on the Morrey spaces and on variable exponent Morrey spaces was considered in [17,19,20]. The compactness of the commutator for the Riesz potential $[b, I_\alpha]$ on the Morrey-type spaces was also considered in [21,22].

The boundedness and compactness of integral operators and their commutators on various function spaces play an important role in harmonic analysis, in potential theory and PDE [23,24] and in some important physical properties and physical structures [25,26]. Moreover, the interest in the compactness of operator $[b, T]$, where T is the classical Calderón–Zygmund singular integral operator, in complex analysis is from the connection between the commutators and the Hankel-type operators. The compactness of $[b, T]$ attracted attention among researchers in PDEs. For example, with the aid of the compactness of $[b, T]$, one easily derives a Fredholm alternative for equations with VMO coefficients in all L_p spaces for $1 < p < \infty$ (see [27]). Hence, it is possible that the compactness of $[b, I_\alpha]$ on generalized Morrey spaces will be applied to discuss some local problems of PDEs with VMO coefficients (see also [28]).

The main goal of this paper is to find the conditions for the pre-compactness of sets on generalized Morrey spaces and to find sufficient conditions for the compactness of the commutator of the Riesz potential $[b, I_\alpha]$ on the generalized Morrey spaces $M_p^{w(\cdot)}(\mathbb{R}^n)$, namely, to find conditions for parameters p, q, α and functions w_1 and w_2 ensuring the compactness of operators $[b, I_\alpha]$ from $M_p^{w_1(\cdot)}$ to $M_q^{w_2(\cdot)}$.

This paper is organized as follows: In Section 2, we present results on the pre-compactness of a set in generalized Morrey spaces. To do this, we will establish some auxiliary lemmas. In Section 3, we give sufficient conditions for the compactness of the commutator for the Riesz potential $[b, I_\alpha]$ on the generalized Morrey space $M_p^{w(\cdot)}(\mathbb{R}^n)$. We will also recall some theorems and establish some auxiliary lemmas. Finally, we draw conclusions in Section 4.

We make some conventions on notation. Throughout this paper, we always use C to denote a positive constant that is independent of the main parameters involved but whose value may differ from line to line. Constants with subscripts, such as C_p, are dependent on the subscript p. We denote $f \lesssim g$ if $f \leq Cg$. By $C(\mathbb{R})$, we denote the set of all continuous bounded functions on $\mathbb{R}$ with the uniform norm, by χ_A we denote the characteristic function of the set $A \subset \mathbb{R}^n$ and by ^cA we denote the complement of A.

2. On the Pre-Compactness of a Set in Generalized Morrey Spaces

In this section, we give sufficient conditions for the pre-compactness of sets in generalized Morrey spaces.

Theorem 1. *Let $1 \leq p < \infty$ and $w \in \Omega_{p\infty}$. Suppose that the set $S \subset M_p^{w(\cdot)}$ satisfies the following conditions:*

$$\sup_{f \in S} \|f\|_{M_p^{w(\cdot)}} < \infty, \tag{1}$$

$$\lim_{u \to 0} \sup_{f \in S} \|f(\cdot + u) - f(\cdot)\|_{M_p^{w(\cdot)}} = 0, \tag{2}$$

$$\lim_{r \to \infty} \sup_{f \in S} \|f\chi_{^cB(0,r)}\|_{M_p^{w(\cdot)}} = 0. \tag{3}$$

Then S is a pre-compact set in $M_p^{w(\cdot)}$.

For the Morrey space M_p^λ, an analogue of Theorem 1 was proved in [17,19]. If $\lambda = 0$, it coincides with the well-known Fréchet–Kolmogorov theorem (see [29]). Theorem 1 is formulated in terms of the difference of a function (see condition (2)). The conditions for the pre-compactness of sets in the global and local Morrey-type spaces were given in terms of the average functions

$$(M_r f)(x) = \frac{1}{|B(x,r)|} \int_{B(x,r)} f(y)dy, \quad f \in M_p^{w(\cdot)},$$

in [30–32]. Here, $|A|$ is the Lebesgue measure of the set $A \subset \mathbb{R}^n$.

To prove Theorem 1, we will need the following auxiliary statements.

Lemma 1. *Let $1 \leq p < \infty$ and $w \in \Omega_{p\infty}$. Then, for all $f \in M_p^{w(\cdot)}$ and $r > 0$*

$$\|M_r f - f\|_{M_p^{w(\cdot)}} \leq \sup_{u \in B(0,r)} \|f(\cdot + u) - f(\cdot)\|_{M_p^{w(\cdot)}}. \tag{4}$$

Proof. Let $z \in \mathbb{R}^n$ and $\rho > 0$. Using the Hölder inequality, we have

$$\|M_r f - f\|_{L_p(B(z,\rho))} =$$

$$= \left(\int_{B(z,\rho)} \left| \frac{1}{|B(x,r)|} \int_{B(x,r)} f(y)dy - f(x) \right|^p dx \right)^{\frac{1}{p}}$$

$$
= \left(\int\limits_{B(z,\rho)} \left| \frac{1}{|B(x,r)|} \int\limits_{B(x,r)} (f(y) - f(x))dy \right|^p dx \right)^{\frac{1}{p}}
$$

$$
\leq \left(\int\limits_{B(z,\rho)} \left(\frac{1}{|B(x,r)|} \int\limits_{B(x,r)} |f(y) - f(x)|^p dy \right) dx \right)^{\frac{1}{p}}.
$$

Next, using the change of variables $y = x + u$ and the Fubini theorem, we obtain

$$
\|M_r f - f\|_{L_p(B(z,\rho))} \leq \left(\int\limits_{B(z,\rho)} \left(\frac{1}{|B(0,r)|} \int\limits_{B(0,r)} |f(x + u) - f(x)|^p du \right) dx \right)^{\frac{1}{p}}
$$

$$
= \left(\frac{1}{|B(0,r)|} \int\limits_{B(0,r)} \left(\int\limits_{B(z,\rho)} |f(x + u) - f(x)|^p dx \right) du \right)^{\frac{1}{p}}
$$

$$
= \left(\frac{1}{|B(0,r)|} \int\limits_{B(0,r)} \|f(\cdot + u) - f(\cdot)\|^p_{L_p(B(z,\rho))} du \right)^{\frac{1}{p}}.
$$

Hence,

$$
\|M_r f - f\|_{M_p^{w(\cdot)}} = \sup_{z \in \mathbb{R}^n,\, \rho > 0} w(\rho) \|M_r f - f\|_{L_p(B(z,\rho))}
$$

$$
\leq \sup_{z \in \mathbb{R}^n,\, \rho > 0} w(\rho) \left(\frac{1}{|B(0,r)|} \int\limits_{B(0,r)} \|f(\cdot + u) - f(\cdot)\|^p_{L_p(B(z,\rho))} du \right)^{\frac{1}{p}}
$$

$$
\leq \left(\frac{1}{|B(0,r)|} \int\limits_{B(0,r)} \sup_{z \in \mathbb{R}^n,\, \rho > 0} w(\rho) \|f(\cdot + u) - f(\cdot)\|^p_{L_p(B(z,\rho))} du \right)^{\frac{1}{p}}.
$$

$$
= \left(\frac{1}{|B(0,r)|} \int\limits_{B(0,r)} \|f(\cdot + u) - f(\cdot)\|^p_{M_p^{w(\cdot)}} du \right)^{\frac{1}{p}}
$$

$$
\leq \sup_{u \in B(0,r)} \|f(\cdot + u) - f(\cdot)\|_{M_p^{w(\cdot)}}.
$$

Lemma 1 is proved. $\square$

Lemma 2. *Let* $1 \leq p < \infty$, $w \in \Omega_{p\infty}$. *Then, for all* $f \in M_p^{w(\cdot)}$ *and* $r > 0$

$$
\|M_r f\|_{M_p^{w(\cdot)}} \leq \|f\|_{M_p^{w(\cdot)}}. \tag{5}
$$

Proof. Using the change of variables $y = x + u$, the Hölder inequality and the Fubini theorem, we obtain

$$\|M_r f\|_{L_p(B(z,\rho))} = \left(\int_{B(z,\rho)} \left| \frac{1}{|B(x,r)|} \int_{B(x,r)} f(y)dy \right|^p dx \right)^{\frac{1}{p}}$$

$$\leq \left(\int_{B(z,\rho)} \left(\frac{1}{|B(x,r)|} \int_{B(x,r)} |f(y)|^p dy \right) dx \right)^{\frac{1}{p}}$$

$$= \left(\int_{B(z,\rho)} \left(\frac{1}{|B(0,r)|} \int_{B(0,r)} |f(x+u)|^p du \right) dx \right)^{\frac{1}{p}}$$

$$= \left(\frac{1}{|B(0,r)|} \int_{B(0,r)} \left(\int_{B(z,\rho)} |f(x+u)|^p dx \right) du \right)^{\frac{1}{p}}$$

$$= \left(\frac{1}{|B(0,r)|} \int_{B(0,r)} \left(\int_{B(z+u,\rho)} |f(v)|^p dv \right) du \right)^{\frac{1}{p}}$$

$$= \left(\frac{1}{|B(0,r)|} \int_{B(0,r)} \|f\|^p_{L_p(B(z+u,\rho))} du \right)^{\frac{1}{p}} .$$

Therefore,

$$\|M_r f\|_{M_p^{w(\cdot)}} = \sup_{z\in\mathbb{R}^n,\, \rho>0} \left(w(\rho)\|M_r f\|_{L_p(B(z,\rho))} \right)$$

$$\leq \sup_{z\in\mathbb{R}^n,\, \rho>0} \left(\frac{1}{|B(0,r)|} \int_{B(0,r)} \left(w(\rho)\|f\|_{L_p(B(z+u,\rho))} \right)^p du \right)^{\frac{1}{p}}$$

$$\leq \left(\frac{1}{|B(0,r)|} \int_{B(0,r)} \left(\sup_{z\in\mathbb{R}^n,\, \rho>0} w(\rho)\|f\|_{L_p(B(z+u,\rho))} \right)^p du \right)^{\frac{1}{p}}$$

$$= \left(\frac{1}{|B(0,r)|} \int_{B(0,r)} \left(\sup_{x\in\mathbb{R}^n,\, \rho>0} w(\rho)\|f\|_{L_p(B(x,\rho))} \right)^p du \right)^{\frac{1}{p}} = \|f\|_{M_p^{w(\cdot)}} .$$

Lemma 2 is proved. $\square$

Lemma 3. *Let* $1 \leq p < \infty$, $w \in \Omega_{p\infty}$. *Then, there exists* $r_0 > 0$ *and for any* $0 < r \leq r_0$ *there is* $C_1 > 0$, *depending only on* r, n, p, w, *such that*
(1) for any $f \in M_p^{w(\cdot)}$

$$\|M_r f\|_{C(\mathbb{R}^n)} \leq C_1 \|f\|_{M_p^{w(\cdot)}(\mathbb{R}^n)}. \tag{6}$$

(2) for any $\delta > 0$

$$\sup_{u \in B(0,\delta)} \|M_r f(\cdot + u) - M_r f(\cdot)\|_{C(\mathbb{R}^n)} \le C_1 \sup_{u \in B(0,\delta)} \|f(\cdot + u) - f(\cdot)\|_{M_p^{w(\cdot)}(\mathbb{R}^n)}. \tag{7}$$

Proof. (1) Since the function $w \in \Omega_{p\infty}$ is not equivalent to 0, then there exists $r_0 > 0$ such that $\sup\limits_{r_0 < \rho < \infty} w(\rho) > 0$. Let $0 < r \le r_0$. Using the Hölder inequality, for any $x \in \mathbb{R}^n$, we have

$$|M_r f(x)| \le \frac{1}{|B(x,r)|^{\frac{1}{p}}} \|f\|_{L_p(B(x,r))}.$$

Hence,

$$|M_r f(x)| w(\rho) \le \frac{1}{(v_n r^n)^{\frac{1}{p}}} \left(w(\rho) \|f\|_{L_p(B(x,r))} \right),$$

where v_n is the volume of the unit ball in $\mathbb{R}^n$, and

$$|M_r f(x)| \sup_{r < \rho < \infty} w(\rho) \le \frac{1}{(v_n r^n)^{\frac{1}{p}}} \left(\sup_{r < \rho < \infty} w(\rho) \|f\|_{L_p(B(x,r))} \right)$$

$$\le \frac{1}{(v_n r^n)^{\frac{1}{p}}} \left(\sup_{r < \rho < \infty} w(\rho) \|f\|_{L_p(B(x,\rho))} \right) \le \frac{1}{(v_n r^n)^{\frac{1}{p}}} \left(\sup_{\rho > 0} w(\rho) \|f\|_{L_p(B(x,\rho))} \right).$$

Therefore, for any $x \in \mathbb{R}^n$

$$|M_r f(x)| \le C_1 \|f\|_{M_p^{w(\cdot)}}, \tag{8}$$

where $C_1 = \left(\left(\sup\limits_{r < \rho < \infty} w(\rho) \right) (v_n r^n)^{\frac{1}{p}} \right)^{-1} < \infty$, since $w \in \Omega_{p\infty}$.

(2) For any $x_1, x_2 \in B(0,r)$, by Hölder's inequality, we have

$$|(M_r f)(x_1) - (M_r f)(x_2)| = \frac{1}{v_n r^n} \left| \int_{B(x_1,r)} f(y)dy - \int_{B(x_2,r)} f(y)dy \right|$$

$$= (v_n r^n)^{-1} \left| \int_{B(0,r)} f(z + x_1)dz - \int_{B(0,r)} f(z + x_2)dz \right|$$

$$\le (v_n r^n)^{-1} \int_{B(0,r)} |f(z + x_1) - f(z + x_2)| dz$$

$$= (v_n r^n)^{-1} \int_{B(x_2,r)} |f(s + x_1 - x_2) - f(s)| ds$$

$$\le (v_n r^n)^{-\frac{1}{p}} \|f(\cdot + x_1 - x_2) - f(\cdot)\|_{L_p(B(x_2,r))}.$$

Therefore, similar to the first part of the proof, we obtain

$$|(M_r f)(x_1) - (M_r f)(x_2)| \le C_1 \|f(\cdot + x_1 - x_2) - f(\cdot)\|_{M_p^{w(\cdot)}}.$$

Hence,

$$\sup_{x_1,x_2 \in \mathbb{R}^n, \, |x_1 - x_2| \le \delta} |(M_r f)(x_1) - (M_r f)(x_2)|$$

$$\le C_1 \sup_{x_1,x_2 \in \mathbb{R}^n, \, |x_1 - x_2| \le \delta} \|f(\cdot + x_1 - x_2) - f(\cdot)\|_{M_p^{w(\cdot)}}$$

$$= C_1 \sup_{u \in B(0,\delta)} \|f(\cdot + u) - f(\cdot)\|_{M_p^{w(\cdot)}}.$$

Lemma 3 is proved. □

Lemma 4. *Let $1 \le p < \infty$, $w \in \Omega_{p\infty}$. Then, there exists $C_2 > 0$, depending only on n, p, w, such that for any $r, R > 0$ and for any $f, g \in M_p^{w(\cdot)}$*

$$\|M_r f - M_r g\|_{M_p^{w(\cdot)}} \le C_2 (1 + R^{\frac{n}{p}}) \|M_r f - M_r g\|_{C(\overline{B(0,R)})}$$

$$+ \sup_{u \in B(0,r)} \|f(\cdot + u) - f(\cdot)\|_{M_p^{w(\cdot)}} + \sup_{u \in B(0,r)} \|g(\cdot + u) - g(\cdot)\|_{M_p^{w(\cdot)}}$$

$$+ \left\| f \chi_{^cB(0,R)} \right\|_{M_p^{w(\cdot)}} + \left\| g \chi_{^cB(0,R)} \right\|_{M_p^{w(\cdot)}}.$$

Proof. Indeed,

$$\|M_r f - M_r g\|_{M_p^{w(\cdot)}}$$

$$\le \left\| (M_r f - M_r g)\chi_{B(0,R)} \right\|_{M_p^{w(\cdot)}} + \left\| (M_r f - M_r g)\chi_{^cB(0,R)} \right\|_{M_p^{w(\cdot)}} := I_1 + I_2.$$

First, we will estimate I_1. By using $B(x,\rho) \cap B(0,R) \subset B(0,R)$, $B(x,\rho) \cap B(0,R) \subset B(x,\rho)$, for any $\rho > 0, R > 0$, we have

$$I_1 = \sup_{x \in \mathbb{R}^n, \, \rho > 0} \left(w(\rho)\|M_r f - M_r g\|_{L_p(B(x,\rho)\cap B(0,R))} \right)$$

$$\le \sup_{x \in \mathbb{R}^n, \, 0 < \rho < 1} \left(w(\rho)\|M_r f - M_r g\|_{L_p(B(x,\rho)\cap B(0,R))} \right)$$

$$+ \sup_{x \in \mathbb{R}^n, \, 1 \le \rho < \infty} \left(w(\rho)\|M_r f - M_r g\|_{L_p(B(x,\rho)\cap B(0,R))} \right)$$

$$\le \|M_r f - M_r g\|_{C(\overline{B(0,R)})} \cdot \left(\sup_{0 < \rho < 1} w(\rho)(v_n \rho^n)^{\frac{1}{p}} + \sup_{1 \le \rho < \infty} w(\rho)(v_n R^n)^{\frac{1}{p}} \right)$$

$$\le \|M_r f - M_r g\|_{C(\overline{B(0,R)})} \cdot v_n^{\frac{1}{p}} \left(\sup_{0 < \rho < 1} w(\rho)\rho^{\frac{n}{p}} + \sup_{1 \le \rho < \infty} w(\rho) R^{\frac{n}{p}} \right).$$

Therefore,

$$I_1 \le \|M_r f - M_r g\|_{C(\overline{B(0,R)})} \cdot v_n^{\frac{1}{p}} \left(\sup_{0 < \rho < 1} w(\rho)\rho^{\frac{n}{p}} + \sup_{1 \le \rho < \infty} w(\rho) \right) \times$$

$$\times \left(\frac{\sup_{0 < \rho < 1} w(\rho)\rho^{\frac{n}{p}}}{\sup_{0 < \rho < 1} w(\rho)\rho^{\frac{n}{p}} + \sup_{1 < \rho < \infty} w(\rho)} + \frac{\sup_{1 \le \rho < \infty} w(\rho)}{\sup_{0 < \rho < 1} w(\rho)\rho^{\frac{n}{p}} + \sup_{1 \le \rho < \infty} w(\rho)} \cdot R^{\frac{n}{p}} \right)$$

$$\le C_2 \left(1 + R^{\frac{n}{p}} \right) \|M_r f - M_r g\|_{C(\overline{B(0,R)})},$$

where

$$C_2 = v_n^{\frac{1}{p}} \left(\sup_{0 < \rho < 1} w(\rho)\rho^{\frac{n}{p}} + \sup_{1 \le \rho < \infty} w(\rho) \right) < \infty,$$

since, by $w \in \Omega_{p\infty}$.

For estimate I_2, using Lemma 1, we have

$$I_2 = \left\| (M_r f - M_r g)\chi_{^c B(0,R)} \right\|_{M_p^{w(\cdot)}}$$

$$\leq \left\| (M_r f - f)\chi_{^c B(0,R)} \right\|_{M_p^{w(\cdot)}} + \left\| (f - g)\chi_{^c B(0,R)} \right\|_{M_p^{w(\cdot)}} + \left\| (M_r g - g)\chi_{^c B(0,R)} \right\|_{M_p^{w(\cdot)}}$$

$$\leq \left\| M_r f - f \right\|_{M_p^{w(\cdot)}} + \left\| (f - g)\chi_{^c B(0,R)} \right\|_{M_p^{w(\cdot)}} + \left\| M_r g - g \right\|_{M_p^{w(\cdot)}}$$

$$\leq \sup_{u \in B(0,r)} \left\| f(\cdot + u) - f(\cdot) \right\|_{M_p^{w(\cdot)}} + \sup_{u \in B(0,r)} \left\| g(\cdot + u) - g(\cdot) \right\|_{M_p^{w(\cdot)}}$$

$$+ \left\| f\chi_{^c B(0,R)} \right\|_{M_p^{w(\cdot)}} + \left\| g\chi_{^c B(0,R)} \right\|_{M_p^{w(\cdot)}}.$$

From estimates of I_1 and I_2, we obtain the inequality of Lemma 4.

Lemma 4 is proved. $\square$

Lemma 5. *Let $1 \leq p < \infty$, $w \in \Omega_{p\infty}$. Then, for any $r, R > 0$ and for any $f, g \in M_p^{w(\cdot)}$*

$$\| f - g \|_{M_p^{w(\cdot)}} \leq C_2 \left(1 + R^{\frac{n}{p}} \right) \| M_r f - M_r g \|_{C(\overline{B(0,R)})}$$

$$+ 2 \sup_{u \in B(0,r)} \| f(\cdot + u) - f(\cdot) \|_{M_p^{w(\cdot)}} + 2 \sup_{u \in B(0,r)} \| g(\cdot + u) - g(\cdot) \|_{M_p^{w(\cdot)}} \qquad (9)$$

$$+ \left\| f\chi_{^c B(0,R)} \right\|_{M_p^{w(\cdot)}} + \left\| g\chi_{^c B(0,R)} \right\|_{M_p^{w(\cdot)}},$$

where $C_2 > 0$ is the same as in Lemma 4.

Proof. It is sufficient to note that

$$\| f - g \|_{M_p^{w(\cdot)}} \leq \| M_r f - f \|_{M_p^{w(\cdot)}} + \| M_r f - M_r g \|_{M_p^{w(\cdot)}} + \| M_r g - g \|_{M_p^{w(\cdot)}}$$

and use Lemmas 1 and 4. $\square$

Proof of Theorem 1. Let $S \subset M_p^{w(\cdot)}$ and let conditions (1)–(3) hold.

Step 1. First, we show that the set $S_r = \{ M_r f : f \in S \}$ is a strongly pre-compact set in $C\big(\overline{B(0,R)}\big)$.

Let $0 < r < r_0$, where r_0 is defined in Lemma 3 and $R > 0$ is fixed. Due to inequality (6) and condition (1), it follows that

$$\sup_{f \in S} \| M_r f \|_{C(\overline{B(0,R)})} \leq \sup_{f \in S} \| M_r f \|_{C(\mathbb{R}^n)} \leq C_1 \sup_{f \in S} \| f \|_{M_p^{w(\cdot)}} < \infty.$$

In addition, due to inequality (7) and condition (2), it follows that

$$\sup_{u \in B(0,\delta)} \| M_r f(\cdot + u) - M_r f(\cdot) \|_{C(\overline{B(0,R)})} \leq \sup_{u \in B(0,\delta)} \| M_r f(\cdot + u) - M_r f(\cdot) \|_{C(\mathbb{R}^n)}$$

$$\leq C_1 \sup_{u \in B(0,\delta)} \| f(\cdot + u) - f(\cdot) \|_{M_p^{w(\cdot)}}.$$

Therefore, by using condition (2), we have

$$\lim_{u \to 0} \sup_{f \in S} \| M_r f(\cdot + u) - M_r f(\cdot) \|_{C(\overline{B(0,R)})} = 0.$$

As such, we obtained that the set S_r is uniformly bounded and equicontinuous in $C(\overline{B(0,R)})$.

Therefore, by the Ascoli–Arzela theorem, the set S_r is pre-compact in $C(\overline{B(0,R)})$, then the set S_r is totally bounded in $C(\overline{B(0,R)})$. Hence, for any $\varepsilon > 0$, there exists $f_1, ..., f_m \in S$ (depending on ε, r and R) such that $\{M_r f_1, M_r f_2, ..., M_r f_m\}$ is a finite ε-net in S_r with respect to norm of $C(\overline{B(0,R)})$. Therefore, for any $f \in S$, there is $1 \le j \le m$ such that

$$\left\| M_r f - M_r f_j \right\|_{C(\overline{B(0,R)})} < \varepsilon.$$

Hence,

$$\min_{j=1,...,m} \left\| M_r f - M_r f_j \right\|_{C(\overline{B(0,R)})} < \varepsilon.$$

Step 2. Let us show that the set S is a relative compact set in $M_p^{w(\cdot)}$. Let $\{\varphi_1, ..., \varphi_m\}$ be an arbitrary finite subset of S. By inequality (9) for any $f \in S$ and any $j = 1, ..., m$ we have

$$\left\| f - \varphi_j \right\|_{M_p^{w(\cdot)}} \le C_2(1 + R^{\frac{n}{p}}) \left\| M_r f - M_r \varphi_j \right\|_{C(\overline{B(0,R)})}$$

$$+ 2 \sup_{u \in B(0,r)} \left\| f(\cdot + u) - f(\cdot) \right\|_{M_p^{w(\cdot)}} + 2 \sup_{u \in B(0,r)} \left\| \varphi_j(\cdot + u) - \varphi_j(\cdot) \right\|_{M_p^{w(\cdot)}}$$

$$+ \left\| f \chi_{{}^c B(0,R)} \right\|_{M_p^{w(\cdot)}} + \left\| \varphi_j \chi_{{}^c B(0,R)} \right\|_{M_p^{w(\cdot)}}$$

$$\le C_2(1 + R^{\frac{n}{p}}) \left\| M_r f - M_r \varphi_j \right\|_{C(\overline{B(0,R)})}$$

$$+ 4 \sup_{g \in S} \sup_{u \in B(0,r)} \left\| g(\cdot + u) - g(\cdot) \right\|_{M_p^{w(\cdot)}} + 2 \sup_{g \in S} \left\| g \chi_{{}^c B(0,R)} \right\|_{M_p^{w(\cdot)}},$$

where C_2 is the same as in Lemma 4, $C_2 = v_n^{\frac{1}{p}} \left(\sup_{0 < \rho < 1} w(\rho) \rho^{\frac{n}{p}} + R^{\frac{n}{p}} \sup_{1 \le \rho < \infty} w(\rho) \right)$.

Hence, for any $f \in S$:

$$\min_{j=1,...,m} \left\| f - \varphi_j \right\|_{M_p^{w(\cdot)}} \le C_2(1 + R^{\frac{n}{p}}) \min_{j=1,...,m} \left\| M_r f - M_r \varphi_j \right\|_{C(\overline{B(0,R)})}$$

$$+ 4 \sup_{g \in S} \sup_{u \in B(0,r)} \left\| g(\cdot + u) - g(\cdot) \right\|_{M_p^{w(\cdot)}} + 2 \sup_{g \in S} \left\| g \chi_{{}^c B(0,R)} \right\|_{M_p^{w(\cdot)}}. \tag{10}$$

Let $\varepsilon > 0$. First, using condition (3) we find $R(\varepsilon) > 0$ such that

$$\sup_{g \in S} \left\| g \chi_{{}^c B(0,R(\varepsilon))} \right\|_{M_p^{w(\cdot)}} < \frac{\varepsilon}{6}.$$

Next, using condition (2), we find $r(\varepsilon)$ such that

$$\sup_{u \in B(0,r(\varepsilon))} \sup_{g \in S} \left\| g(\cdot + u) - g(\cdot) \right\|_{M_p^{w(\cdot)}} < \frac{\varepsilon}{12}.$$

Finally, by the pre-compactness of the set $S_{r(\varepsilon)}$ in $C(\overline{B(0, R(\varepsilon))})$, there exist $m(\varepsilon) \in \mathbb{N}$ and $f_{1,\varepsilon}, ..., f_{m(\varepsilon),\varepsilon} \in S$, such that for any $f \in S$

$$\min_{j=1,...,m(\varepsilon)} \left\| M_{r(\varepsilon)} f - M_{r(\varepsilon)} f_{j,\varepsilon} \right\|_{C(\overline{B(0,R(\varepsilon))})} < \frac{\varepsilon}{3 C_2(1 + R^{\frac{n}{p}})}.$$

Therefore, setting $\varphi_j = f_{j,\varepsilon}, j = 1, ..., m(\varepsilon)$, by inequality (10), for any $f \in S$ we obtain

$$\min_{j=1,...,m(\varepsilon)} \left\| f - f_{j,\varepsilon} \right\|_{M_p^{w(\cdot)}} < \frac{\varepsilon}{3} + \frac{\varepsilon}{3} + \frac{\varepsilon}{3} = \varepsilon.$$

Then, we have that $\varphi_j = f_{j,\varepsilon}, j = 1, ..., m(\varepsilon)$ is a finite ε-net in S in the norm of $M_p^{w(\cdot)}$.

Therefore, the set S is a pre-compact set in $M_p^{w(\cdot)}$. Theorem 1 is proved. $\square$

3. Compactness of the Commutator for the Riesz Potential on Generalized Morrey Spaces

The main goal of this section is to find sufficient conditions for the compactness of the commutator $[b, I_\alpha]$ from $M_p^{w_1(\cdot)}$ to $M_q^{w_2(\cdot)}$.

The Riesz potential I_α of order $\alpha (0 < \alpha < n)$ is defined by

$$I_\alpha f(x) = \int_{\mathbb{R}^n} \frac{f(y)}{|x - y|^{n-\alpha}} dy.$$

The boundedness of I_α on Morrey spaces was investigated in [13,14].

The sufficient conditions for the boundedness of I_α from $M_p^{w_1(\cdot)}$ to $M_q^{w_2(\cdot)}$ were obtained by T. Mizuhara [8], E. Nakai [9], and V.S. Guliyev [10].

The following theorems give sufficient conditions for the boundedness of the Riesz potential and its commutator in generalized Morrey spaces.

Theorem 2 ([10]). *Let $1 < p < q < \infty$ and $\alpha = n\left(\frac{1}{p} - \frac{1}{q}\right)$. Moreover, let functions $w_1 \in \Omega_{p,\infty}$, $w_2 \in \Omega_{q,\infty}$ satisfy the condition*

$$\left\| w_1^{-1}(r) r^{-\frac{n}{q}-1} \right\|_{L_1(t,\infty)} \lesssim w_2^{-1}(t) t^{-\frac{n}{p}} \tag{11}$$

uniformly in $t \in (0, \infty)$. Then, the operator I_α is bounded from $M_p^{w_1(\cdot)}$ to $M_q^{w_2(\cdot)}$.

Theorem 3 ([16]). *Let $1 < p < q < \infty$, $0 < \alpha < \frac{n}{p'}$, $\frac{1}{q} = \frac{1}{p} - \frac{\alpha}{n}$, $b \in BMO(\mathbb{R}^n)$ and $w_1(\cdot), w_2(\cdot)$ satisfy the following condition*

$$\int_r^\infty \ln\left(e + \frac{l}{r}\right) \frac{\underset{t<s<\infty}{ess\ inf}\ w_1(s) dt}{t} \lesssim w_2(r). \tag{12}$$

Then, the operator $[b, I_\alpha]$ is bounded from $M_p^{w_1(\cdot)}$ to $M_q^{w_2(\cdot)}$.

Theorem 4. *Let $1 < p < q < \infty$, $0 < \alpha < n(1 - \frac{1}{q})$, $\frac{1}{q} = \frac{1}{p} - \frac{\alpha}{n}$, $b \in VMO(\mathbb{R}^n)$ and functions $w_1 \in \Omega_{p,\infty}$, $w_2 \in \Omega_{q,\infty}$ satisfy conditions (11) and (12). Then, the commutator $[b, I_\alpha]$ is a compact operator from $M_p^{w_1(\cdot)}$ to $M_q^{w_2(\cdot)}$.*

To prove Theorem 4, we need the following auxiliary statements.

Lemma 6. *Let $n \in \mathbb{N}$, $1 < p < q < \infty$, $0 < \alpha < n\left(1 - \frac{1}{q}\right)$, $\beta > 0$, $\frac{1}{q} = \frac{1}{p} - \frac{\alpha}{n}$. Then, there is $C_5 > 0$, depending only on n, p, q, α, such that for some $f \in L_p(B(0, \beta))$ satisfying the condition $supp f \subset \overline{B(0, \beta)}$, and for some $\gamma \geq 2\beta, t \in \mathbb{R}^n, r > 0$*

$$\left\| (I_\alpha f) \chi_{{}^c B(0,\gamma)} \right\|_{L_q(B(t,r))} \leq C_5 \gamma^{\alpha-n} (min\{\gamma, r\})^{\frac{n}{q}} \|f\|_{L_p(B(0,\beta))}. \tag{13}$$

Proof. Let $f \in L_p(B(t, r))$. By definition of the operator I_α, we have

$$I := \left\| (I_\alpha f) \chi^c_{B(0,\gamma)} \right\|_{L_q(B(t,r))}$$

$$= \left(\int_{B(t,r) \cap {}^cB(0,\gamma)} \left| \int_{\mathbb{R}^n} \frac{f(y)}{|x-y|^{n-\alpha}} dy \right|^q dx \right)^{\frac{1}{q}}$$

$$\le \left(\int_{B(t,r) \cap {}^cB(0,\gamma)} \left| \int_{B(0,\beta)} \frac{f(y)}{|x-y|^{n-\alpha}} dy \right|^q dx \right)^{\frac{1}{q}}.$$

Since $\beta \le \frac{\gamma}{2}$ for $x \in {}^cB(0,\gamma), y \in B(0,\beta)$, we have

$$|x-y| \ge |x| - |y| \ge |x| - \beta = \frac{|x|}{2} + \frac{|x|}{2} - \beta \ge \frac{|x|}{2}. \tag{14}$$

By $(n-\alpha)q - n > 0$, we have

$$I \le 2^{n-\alpha} \left(\int_{{}^cB(0,\gamma)} \frac{dx}{|x|^{(n-\alpha)q}} \right)^{\frac{1}{q}} \int_{B(0,\beta)} |f(y)| dy$$

$$\le 2^{n-\alpha} \left(\int_{\gamma}^{\infty} \rho^{-(n-\alpha)q+n-1} d\rho \right)^{\frac{1}{q}} (v_n \beta^n)^{1-\frac{1}{p}} \|f\|_{L_p(B(0,\beta))}$$

$$\equiv C_6 \gamma^{\alpha - n(1-\frac{1}{q})} \|f\|_{L_p(B(0,\beta))}. \tag{15}$$

Since $\beta \le \frac{\gamma}{2}$ for $x \in {}^cB(0,\gamma), y \in B(0,\beta)$, by (14) $|x-y| \ge \frac{|x|}{2}$.
Therefore,

$$I \le 2^{n-\alpha} \gamma^{\alpha-n} \left(\int_{B(t,r)} dx \right)^{\frac{1}{q}} \int_{B(0,\beta)} |f(y)| dy$$

$$\le 2^{n-\alpha} \gamma^{\alpha-n} (v_n r^n)^{\frac{1}{q}} (v_n \beta^n)^{1-\frac{1}{p}} \|f\|_{L_p(B(0,\beta))}$$

$$= C_4 \gamma^{\alpha-n} r^{\frac{n}{q}} \|f\|_{L_p(B(0,\beta))}. \tag{16}$$

Inequalities (15) and (16) imply inequality (13), where $C_5 = \max\{C_6, C_4\}$ $\square$

Lemma 7. *Let $n \in \mathbb{N}, 1 < p < q < \infty, 0 < \alpha < n\left(1 - \frac{1}{q}\right), \frac{1}{q} = \frac{1}{p} - \frac{\alpha}{n}, \beta > 0$. Then, there is $C_7 > 0$ depending only on n, p, q, α such that for some $f \in L_p(B(0,\beta)), b \in L_\infty(\mathbb{R}^n)$ satisfying the condition supp $b \subset \overline{B(0,\beta)}$, and for some $\gamma \ge 2\beta, t \in \mathbb{R}^n, r > 0$*

$$\left\| ([b, I_\alpha]f) \chi_{{}^cB(0,\gamma)} \right\|_{L_q(B(t,r))} \le C_7 \gamma^{\alpha-n} (min\{\gamma, r\})^{\frac{n}{q}} \|b\|_{L_\infty(\mathbb{R}^n)} \|f\|_{L_p(B(0,\beta))}. \tag{17}$$

Proof. Let $\gamma > \beta, supp\, b \subset B(0,\beta)$, for $x \in {}^cB(0,\gamma), b(x) = 0$. Then

$$\left\| [b, I_\alpha] f \chi_{{}^cB(0,\gamma)} \right\|_{L_q(B(t,r))}$$

$$= \left(\int_{B(t,r) \cap {}^cB(0,\gamma)} \left| \int_{\mathbb{R}^n} \frac{(b(x)-b(y))f(y)}{|x-y|^{n-\alpha}} dy \right|^q dx \right)^{\frac{1}{q}}$$

$$\leq \left(\int_{B(t,r) \cap {}^c B(0,\gamma)} \left| \int_{\mathbb{R}^n} \frac{b(y)f(y)}{|x-y|^{n-\alpha}} dy \right|^q dx \right)^{\frac{1}{q}}$$

$$\leq \left(\int_{B(t,r) \cap {}^c B(0,\gamma)} \left| \int_{B(0,\beta)} \frac{|b(y)| \cdot |f(y)|}{|x-y|^{n-\alpha}} dy \right|^q dx \right)^{\frac{1}{q}}$$

$$\leq \left(\int_{B(t,r) \cap {}^c B(0,\gamma)} \left| \int_{B(0,\beta)} \frac{|f(y)|}{|x-y|^{n-\alpha}} dy \right|^q dx \right)^{\frac{1}{q}} \|b\|_{L_\infty(\mathbb{R}^n)}.$$

Finally, by proof of Lemma 6, we obtain estimate (17). $\square$

Proof of Theorem 4. Let us prove that for $[b, I_\alpha]f$, conditions (1)–(3) of Theorem 1 are satisfied.

Let F be an arbitrary bounded set in $M_p^{w_1(\cdot)}$. Due to the density, it is sufficient to prove the statement of the theorem under the condition $b \in C_0^\infty(\mathbb{R}^n)$; i.e., under this condition, the set $G = \{[b, I_\alpha]f : f \in F\}$ is pre-compact in $M_q^{w_2(\cdot)}$.

Let

$$\|f\|_{M_p^{w_1(\cdot)}} \leq D, \quad \text{for} \quad f \in F.$$

By Theorem 3, we have

$$\|[b, I_\alpha]f\|_{M_q^{w_2(\cdot)}} \leq C_8 \cdot \sup_{f \in F} \|f\|_{M_p^{w_1(\cdot)}} \leq C_8 \cdot D < \infty.$$

This implies condition (1) of Theorem 1.

Now let us prove that condition (3) of Theorem 1 holds for $[b, I_\alpha]$. On the other hand, suppose that $supp\, b \subset \{x : |x| \leq \beta\}$. For any $0 < \varepsilon < 1$, we take $\gamma > \beta + 1$ such that $(\gamma - \beta)^{-(n-\alpha)+n/q} < \varepsilon$. Below, we show that for every $t \in \mathbb{R}^n$ and $r > 0$,

$$\|[b, I_\alpha]f \chi_{{}^c B(0,\gamma)}\|_{M_q^{w_2(\cdot)}} < C_9 \cdot D \cdot \varepsilon,$$

hence

$$\lim_{\gamma \to \infty} \left\| ([b, I_\alpha]f) \chi_{{}^c B(0,\gamma)} \right\|_{M_q^{w_2(\cdot)}} = 0.$$

By Lemma 7, we have

$$\left\| ([b, I_\alpha]f) \chi_{{}^c B(0,\gamma)} \right\|_{M_q^{w_2(\cdot)}} = \sup_{x \in (\mathbb{R}^n)} \left\| w_2(r) \|([b, I_\alpha]f) \chi_{{}^c B(0,\gamma)}\|_{L_p(B(x,r))} \right\|_{L_\infty(0,\infty)}$$

$$\leq C_5 \gamma^{\alpha - n} \sup_{x \in (\mathbb{R}^n)} \left\| w_2(r)(min\{\gamma, r\})^{\frac{n}{q}} \right\|_{L_\infty(0,\infty)} \|b\|_{L_\infty(\mathbb{R}^n)} \|f\|_{L_p(B(0,\beta))}.$$

For $r < t < \gamma$, we have $(min\{\gamma, r\})^{\frac{n}{q}} = r^{\frac{n}{q}}$. Using condition $w_2 \in \Omega_{q,\infty}$, we obtain

$$\|w_2(r) r^{\frac{n}{q}}\|_{L_\infty(0,t)} < \infty.$$

For $\gamma < t < r$, we have $(min\{\gamma, r\})^{\frac{n}{q}} = \gamma^{\frac{n}{q}}$. Using condition $w_2 \in \Omega_{q,\infty}$, we obtain

$$\|w_2(r) \gamma^{\frac{n}{q}}\|_{L_\infty(t,\infty)} = \gamma^{\frac{n}{q}} \|w_2(r)\|_{L_\infty(t,\infty)} < \infty.$$

$$\lim_{\gamma \to \infty} \left\| ([b, I_\alpha] f) \chi_{{}^c B(0,\gamma)} \right\|_{M_q^{w_2(\cdot)}} = 0.$$

Consequently, we have the required condition (3) of Theorem 1.

Now, let us prove that condition (2) of Theorem 1 holds for the set $[b, I_\alpha]$, where $f \in F$. That is, we will show that for all $\varepsilon > 0$ and for all $f \in F$, the inequality

$$\left\| [(b, I_\alpha f)(\cdot + z)] - [b, I_\alpha] f(\cdot) \right\|_{M_q^{w_2(\cdot)}} \leq C_{10} \cdot \varepsilon,$$

is satisfied for sufficiently small $|z|$.

Let ε be an arbitrary number such that $0 < \varepsilon < \frac{1}{2}$. For $|z| \in \mathbb{R}^n$, we have

$$[b, I_\alpha] f(x + z) - [b, I_\alpha] f(x) = \int\limits_{|x-y| > \frac{|z|}{\varepsilon}} \frac{[b(x+z) - b(x)] f(y)}{|x - y|^{n-\alpha}} \, dy$$

$$+ \int\limits_{|x-y| > \frac{|z|}{\varepsilon}} \left(\frac{1}{|x - y|^{n-\alpha}} - \frac{1}{|x + z - y|^{n-\alpha}} \right) \cdot [b(y) - b(x + z)] f(y) \, dy$$

$$+ \int\limits_{|x-y| \leq \frac{|z|}{\varepsilon}} \frac{[b(y) - b(x)] f(y)}{|x - y|^{n-\alpha}} \, dy - \int\limits_{|x-y| \leq \frac{|z|}{\varepsilon}} \frac{[b(y) - b(x + z)] f(y)}{|x + z - y|^{n-\alpha}} \, dy$$

$$= J_1 + J_2 + J_3 - J_4.$$

Due to $b \in C_0^\infty(\mathbb{R}^n)$, we have

$$|b(x) - b(x + z)| \leq |\nabla f(x)| \cdot |z| \leq C_{11}|z|.$$

Then,

$$|J_1| \leq C_{11}|z| I_\alpha(|f|)(x).$$

By Theorem 2,

$$\|J_1\|_{M_q^{w_2(\cdot)}} \leq C_{11}|z| \|I_\alpha(f)\|_{M_q^{w_2(\cdot)}} \leq C_{11}|z| \|f\|_{M_p^{w_1(\cdot)}} \leq C_{11} D|z|.$$

For J_2, we have that

$$(b(x + z) - b(y)) \leq 2\|b\|_\infty \leq C_{10}.$$

Therefore,

$$|J_2| \leq C_{12}|z| \int\limits_{|x-y| > \frac{|z|}{\varepsilon}} \frac{f(y)}{|x - y|^{n-\alpha}} \, dy \leq C_{12}\varepsilon I_\alpha(|f|)(x).$$

Again, based on Theorem 2, we obtain

$$\|J_2\|_{M_q^{w_2(\cdot)}} \leq C_{12}\varepsilon \|I_\alpha(f)\|_{M_p^{w_1(\cdot)}} \leq C_{12}\varepsilon \|f\|_{M_p^{w_1(\cdot)}} \leq C_{12} \cdot D \cdot \varepsilon.$$

Now, consider J_3. Since $b \in C_0^\infty$, we have $|b(x) - b(y)| \leq C_{13}|x - y|$.

Then, for $|J_3|$, we have

$$|J_3| \leq C_{13} \int\limits_{|x-y| \leq \frac{|z|}{\varepsilon}} \frac{f(y)}{|x - y|^{n-\alpha-1}} \, dy$$

$$\leq C_{13}\varepsilon^{-1}|z| \int\limits_{|x-y| \leq \frac{|z|}{\varepsilon}} \frac{f(y)}{|x - y|^{n-\alpha}} \, dy$$

$$\leq C_{13} \cdot \frac{|z|}{\varepsilon} I_\alpha(|f|)(x).$$

Therefore, by Theorem 2

$$\|J_3\|_{M_q^{w_2(\cdot)}} \leq C_{13} \cdot \varepsilon^{-1}|z| \|I_\alpha(f)\|_{M_q^{w_2(\cdot)}} \leq C_{13} \cdot \varepsilon^{-1}|z| \|f\|_{M_p^{w_1(\cdot)}} \leq \varepsilon^{-1}|z|.$$

Similarly, using the estimate

$$|b(x+z) - b(y)| \leq C_{14}|x+z-y|,$$

we obtain

$$|J_4| \leq C_{14} \int_{|x-y|\leq\varepsilon^{-1}|z|} |x+z-y|^{-n+\alpha+1}|b(y)|dy \leq C_{14}(\varepsilon^{-1}|z|+|z|)I_\alpha|f|(x+z).$$

Therefore,

$$\|J_4\|_{M_q^{w_2(\cdot)}} \leq C_{14} \cdot (\varepsilon^{-1}|z|+|z|)\|f\|_{M_p^{w_1(\cdot)}} \leq C_{14} \cdot D \cdot (\varepsilon^{-1}|z|+|z|).$$

Here, the constants do not depend on z and ε.
Taking $|z|$ small enough, we finally obtain

$$\|[b, I_\alpha(f)(\cdot+z)] - [b, I_\alpha]f(\cdot)\|_{M_q^{w_2(\cdot)}}$$

$$\leq \|J_1\|_{M_q^{w_2(\cdot)}} + \|J_2\|_{M_q^{w_2(\cdot)}} + \|J_3\|_{M_q^{w_2(\cdot)}} + \|J_4\|_{M_q^{w_2(\cdot)}} \leq C_{15} \cdot D \cdot \varepsilon,$$

that is, the set $[b, I_\alpha](f)$, $f \in F$ also satisfies condition (2) of Theorem 1. Then, according to Theorem 1, the set $[b, I_\alpha](f)$, $f \in F$ is compact in $M_q^{w_2(\cdot)}$. Theorem 4 is proved.
$\square$

Remark 1. *When proving Theorem 4, we used the method from [19], taking into account the specifics of the generalized Morrey space.*

4. Conclusions

In this paper we have obtained the sufficient conditions for the compactness of sets in generalized Morrey spaces . Moreover, we have obtained the sufficient conditions for the compactness of the commutator $[b, I_\alpha]$ for the Riesz potential operator on generalized Morrey spaces $M_p^{w(\cdot)}(R^n)$. More precisely, we prove that if $b \in VMO(R^n)$, then $[b, I_\alpha]$ is a compact operator from $M_p^{w_1(\cdot)}$ to $M_q^{w_2(\cdot)}$.

Author Contributions: Conceptualization, N.B., T.A. and A.A.; Writing—original draft and editing, D.M.; Validation and formal analysis, N.B. All authors have read and agreed to the published version of the manuscript.

Funding: This work is funded by the Science Committee of the Ministry of Science and Higher Education of the Republic of Kazakhstan (grant no. AP14869887).

Data Availability Statement: Data is contained within the article.

Acknowledgments: The authors would like to express their gratitude to the referees for numerous very constructive comments and suggestions.

Conflicts of Interest: All of authors in this article declare no conflicts of interest. All of the funders in this article support the article's publication.

References

1. Morrey, C. On the solutions of quasi-linear elleptic partial diferential equations. *Trans. Am. Math. Soc.* **1938**, *1*, 126–166. [CrossRef]
2. Kato, T. Strong solutions of the Navier-Stokes equation in Morrey spaces. *Bol. Soc. Brasil. Mat.* **1992**, *22*, 127–155. [CrossRef]
3. Taylor, M. Analysis on Morrey spaces and applications to Navier-Stokes and other evolution equations. *Commun. Part. Differ. Equ.* **1992**, *17*, 1407–1456 [CrossRef]
4. Shen, Z. The periodic Schrödinger operators with potentials in the Morrey class. *J. Funct. Anal.* **2002**, *193*, 314–345. [CrossRef]
5. Guliyev, V.S.; Guliyev, R.V.; Omarova, M.N.; Ragusa, M.A.; Schrodinger type operators on local generalized Morrey spaces related to certain nonnegative potentials. *Discret. Contin. Dyn. Syst. Ser. B* **2020**, *5*, 671–690. [CrossRef]
6. Di Fazio, G.; Ragusa, M. Interior estimates in Morrey spaces for strong solutions to nondivergence form equations with dicontinuous coefficients. *J. Funct. Anal.* **1993**, *112*, 241–256. [CrossRef]
7. Huang, Q. Estimates on the generalized Morrey spaces $L_\phi^{2,\lambda}$ and BMO_ψ for linear elliptic systems. *Indiana Univ. Math. J.* **1996**, *45*, 397–439. [CrossRef]
8. Mizuhara, T. Boundedness of some classical operators on generalized Morrey spaces. In Proceedings of the Harmonic Analisis, ICM 90 Satellite Proceedings, Sendai, Japan, 14–18 August 1990; Igari, S., Ed.; Springer: Tokyo, Japan , 1991; pp. 183–189. [CrossRef]
9. Nakai, E. Hardy—Littlewood maximal operator, singular integral operators and Riesz potentials on generalized Morrey spaces. *Math. Nachr.* **1994**, *166* , 95–103. [CrossRef]
10. Guliyev, V.S. Integral Operators on Function Spaces on the Homogeneous Groups and on Domains in Rn. DSci Dissertation, Moscow Mathematical Institute Steklov, Russia, Moscow , 1994; pp. 1–329. (In Russian)
11. Burenkov, V.I. Recent progress in studying the boundedness of classical operators of real analysis in general Morrey-type spaces. I. *Eurasian Math. J.* **2012**, *3*, 11–32.
12. Burenkov, V.I. Recent progress in studying the boundedness of classical operators of real analysis in general Morrey-type spaces. II. *Eurasian Math. J.* **2013**, *1*, 21–45.
13. Peetre, J. On the theory of $L^{p,\lambda}$ spaces. *J. Funct. Anal.* **1969**, *4*, 71–87. [CrossRef]
14. Adams, D.R. Lectures on L_p-Potential Theory. *Umea Univ.* **1981**, *2*, 1–74.
15. Ding, Y. A characterization of BMO via commutators for some operators. *Northeast. Math. J.* **1997**, *13*, 422–432.
16. Guliyev, V.S. Generalized weighted Morrey spaces and higher order commutators of sublinear operators. *Eurasian Math. J.* **2012**, *3*, 33–61.
17. Chen, Y.; Ding, Y.; Wang, X. Compactness of commutators of Riesz potential on Morrey space. *Potential Anal.* **2009**, *4*, 301–313. [CrossRef]
18. Sawano, Y.; Shiai, S. Compact commutators on Morrey spaces with non-doubling measures. *Georgian Math. J.* **2008**, *2*, 353–376. [CrossRef]
19. Chen, Y.; Ding, Y.; Wang, X. Compactness of Commutators for singular integrals on Morrey spaces. *Can. J. Math.* **2012**, *64*, 257–281. [CrossRef]
20. Bandaliyev, R.A.; Górka, P.; Guliyev, V.S.; Sawano, Y. Relatively Compact Sets in Variable Exponent Morrey Spaces on Metric Spaces. *Mediterr. J. Math.* **2021**, *6*, 1–23. [CrossRef]
21. Bokayev, N.A.; Matin, D.T.; Baituyakova, Z.Z. A sufficient condition for compactness of the commutators of Riesz potential on global Morrey-type space. *AIP Conf. Proc.* **2018**, *1997*, 020008. [CrossRef]
22. Matin, D.T.; Akhazhanov, T.B.; Adilkhanov, A. Compactness of Commutators for Riesz Potential on Local Morrey-type spaces. *Bull. Karagand. Univ. Math. Ser.* **2023**, *110*, 93–103. [CrossRef]
23. Stein, E.M. *Singular Integral and Differentiability Properties of Functions*; Princeton University Press: Princeton, NJ, USA, 1971. [CrossRef]
24. Stein, A.M.; Weiss, G. *Introduction to Fourier Analysis on Euclidean Spaces*; Princeton University Press: Princeton, NJ, USA, 1971.
25. Yang, X.; Zhang, Q.; Yuan, G.; Sheng, Z. On positivity preservation in nonlinear finite volume method for multi-term fractional subdiffusion equation on polygonal meshes. *Nonlinear Dyn.* **2018**, *92*, 595–612. [CrossRef]
26. Yang, X.; Zhang, Z. On conservative, positivity preserving, nonlinear FV scheme on distorted meshes for the multi-term nonlocal Nagumo-type equations. *Appl. Math. Lett.* **2024**, *150*, 108972. [CrossRef]
27. Iwaniec, T.; Sboedone, C. Riesz treansform and elliptic PDE's with VMO-coefficients. *J. D'Anal. Math.* **1998**, *74*, 183–212. [CrossRef]
28. Palagachev, D.; Softova, L. Singular integral operators, Morrey spaces and fine regularity of solutions to PDE's. *Potential Anal.* **2004**, *20*, 237–263. [CrossRef]
29. Yosida, K. *Functional Analysis*; Springer: Berlin/Heidelberg, Germany, 1978. [CrossRef]
30. Bokayev, N.A.; Burenkov, V.I.; Matin, D.T. On pre-compactness of a set in general local and global Morrey-type spaces. *Eurasian Math. J.* **2017**, *3*, 109–115.

31. Matin, D.T.; Baituyakova, Z.Z.; Adilkhanov, A.N.; Bostanov, B.O. Sufficient conditions for the pre-compactness of sets in Local Morrey-type spaces. *Bull. Karagand. Univ. Math. Ser.* **2018**, *92*, 54–63. [CrossRef]
32. Bokayev, N.A.; Burenkov, V.I.; Matin, D.T. Sufficient conditions for the pre-compactness of sets in global Morrey-type spaces. *AIP Conf. Proc.* **2017**, *1980*, 030001. [CrossRef]

 *mathematics*

Article

Qualitative Properties of the Solutions to the Lane–Emden Equation in the Cylindrical Setup

Arsen Palestini [1,*,†] and Simone Recchi [2,†]

1   Dipartimento di Metodi e Modelli per l'Economia il Territorio e la Finanza MEMOTEF, Sapienza University of Rome, Via del Castro Laurenziano 9, 00161 Rome, Italy

2   Independent Researcher, Urbangasse 6/3/41, 1170 Wien, Austria; recchisimo@outlook.com

*   Correspondence: arsen.palestini@uniroma1.it

†   These authors contributed equally to this work.

Abstract: We analyze the Lane–Emden equations in the cylindrical framework. Although the explicit forms of the solutions (which are also called polytropes) are not known, we identify some of their qualitative properties. In particular, possible critical points and zeros of the polytropes are investigated and discussed, leading to possible improvements in the approximation methods which are currently employed. The cases when the critical parameter is odd and even are separately analyzed. Furthermore, we propose a technique to evaluate the distance between a pair of polytropes in small intervals.

Keywords: Lane–Emden equation; polytrope; ODEs

MSC: 45J05; 44A45; 76E20; 85A99

Citation: Palestini, A.; Recchi, S. Qualitative Properties of the Solutions to the Lane–Emden Equation in the Cylindrical Setup. *Mathematics* **2024**, *12*, 542. https://doi.org/10.3390/math12040542

Academic Editor: Dongfang Li

Received: 26 December 2023
Revised: 2 February 2024
Accepted: 4 February 2024
Published: 9 February 2024

1. Introduction

One of the most fascinating open problems in Applied Mathematics is the Lane–Emden equation, together with its variation, the Emden–Fowler equation, which was initially proposed in 1870 by Jonathan Homer Lane [1] and subsequently extended by Robert Emden [2] in 1907, who aimed to model the dynamic behaviour of a non-rotating fluid subject to internal pressure and self-gravity. In order to briefly introduce the physical setting, the Lane–Emden equation originates from the combination of Poisson's equation and a generic polytropic equation of state, $P = K_N \rho^\gamma$, where P and ρ, respectively, are the pressure and the density of a fluid, K_N is a positive constant, and $\gamma = 1 + \frac{1}{N}$ is the ratio of specific heats (see [3,4] for more details). After some simple manipulations, the Lane–Emden equation is derived as having $\theta(x) = \left(\dfrac{\rho(x)}{\rho_c} \right)^{1/N}$, where ρ_c is the central density.

The Lane–Emden equation has encountered wide success, especially in the 1930s, both in physics, where Sir Ralph Howard Fowler [5,6] found and generalized further results and gave birth to the Emden–Fowler equation, and in astrophysics, where Chandrasekhar established the related spherical solutions in [7], the first edition of which was published in 1939 and then subsequently reprinted in 1967. Furthermore, Chandrasekhar and Fermi applied the Lane–Emden equation to isothermal filaments [8], some years later.

Successively, many contributions have been published on the equation, its several modified versions, and its applications. Christodoulou and Kazanas [9] derived exact asymmetric solutions of the Lane–Emden equation under rotation. A major result had already been provided by Jeremiah Paul Ostriker [10] in 1964; he was able to determine the solutions to the equation in closed form for cylindrical polytropes for the parameters $N = 0$ (i.e., liquid cylinders), $N = 1$, and $N = \infty$ (i.e., cylinders with an isothermal perfect gas). In the astrophysics literature, a solution to the Lane–Emden equation is often called a polytrope. We will also use this denomination throughout this paper. For those who are willing to develop an extensive knowledge of polytropes, the main textbook on this subject was published by Horedt [11] in 2004.

The present study focuses on Lane–Emden equations in the cylindrical setup. The reason for this focus is that quite recent astronomical observations, particularly the ones obtained by the Herschel space observatory (see [12]), show that star-forming regions occur preferentially in long thin cylindrical filaments of gas. The radial density distribution within the filaments can be well approximated with the solutions of appropriate Lane–Emden equations, but the specific profiles differ considerably from the expected profile for the isothermal case mentioned above. There seems to also be clear evidence that the polytropic index, N, can change within a single filament. Theoretical studies show that this behaviour could be due to temperature gradients within a filament (see [3]). Moreover, star-forming regions are highly dynamic, and, hence, the properties of star-forming filaments change over time. These arguments show, on the one hand, the relevance of analytical solutions for the Lane–Emden equations, and, on the other hand, show that differences between analytical solutions with different values of N are important tools to obtain insights about real-world phenomena. We would like to outline, however, that a detailed comparison with astrophysical observations is out of the scope of this work. We wish here to lay down purely mathematical ideas, which will be further developed in follow-up papers (see Section 6).

In recent years, the Lane–Emden equation has been widely studied in several versions, although it can be solved in closed form in only a few cases. An approach based on operational calculus, initially introduced by Adomian [13], was outlined by Bengochea et al. in some recent works [14–16]. In particular, in [14], a procedure is derived which is based on a linear operator acting on the set of all formal series, which turns out to be helpful in solving several kinds of differential equations with variable coefficients, fractional differential equations, and difference equations as well. Such an approach is adopted in [15], to determine an algebraic solution to a specific version of the Lane–Emden equation. More recently, a numerical approximation algorithm was proposed by [17]. Furthermore, some novel computational strategies were implemented by [18,19].

Our approach is substantially different from the ones adopted in the above-mentioned literature. Firstly, we focus only on the cylindrical setup, which can be identified by the use of the following class of equations for each integer $N \in \mathbb{Z}$:

$$\theta''(x) + \frac{\theta'(x)}{x} + \theta^N(x) = 0$$

Actually, we might also extend this analysis to $N \in \mathbb{R}$, although the most intuitive application of Lane–Emden theory is to integer numbers. We are trying to establish a number of qualitative properties of the related solutions, in order to better visualize their behaviour. In our analysis, what emerges about these solutions is a slight difference between the cases where N is odd and where N is even. To the best of our knowledge, no previous study has ever captured such a qualitative distinction. The most recent studies, such as [17–19], rely on well-structured numerical methods for approximation or on novel techniques that are implemented in wider classes of problems (see [14–16,20]). We stress that our attempt is somewhat more specific, because a deep qualitative analysis may lead to new ideas to refine the search for the closed form solutions that are still unknown.

The following is a basic summary of the present work.

- We reconstruct the extended derivations of the basic Lane–Emden equations in the basic scenarios;
- We outline the current state of the art, including explicit solutions, solution methods, and cases in which the Lane–Emden equation is still unsolved;
- We identify a sequence of qualitative properties of the solutions in the cylindrical scenario. In particular, two distinct analyses are carried out, depending on whether the critical exponent, M, is either odd or even;
- Finally, we expose a relation which may be helpful in evaluating the distance between a pair of solutions in a small interval.

The remainder of this paper is structured as follows. In Section 2, we introduce the Lane–Emden differential equation, together with some of its variations, and in Section 3 we present an overview of some known solutions, emphasizing the cases where $N = 0$ and $N = 1$. Our main analytical results are collected in Section 4, where some qualitative properties are stated and demonstrated. In Section 5, the results are summarized and discussed. Finally, our concluding remarks and some ideas regarding future developments can be read in Section 6.

2. The Standard Lane–Emden Equation

Firstly, we introduce the Lane–Emden equation in its well-known form, as follows:

$$\theta''(x) + k\frac{\theta'(x)}{x} + \theta^N(x) = 0, \tag{1}$$

Based on the value of k, either we have the following cylindrical setting, if $k = 1$:

$$\theta''(x) + \frac{\theta'(x)}{x} + \theta^N(x) = 0, \tag{2}$$

or we have the following spherical setting, if $k = 2$:

$$\theta''(x) + 2\frac{\theta'(x)}{x} + \theta^N(x) = 0. \tag{3}$$

2.1. Initial Conditions and an Analysis of the Singularity

The standard boundary conditions that form a Cauchy problem with a Lane–Emden equation are the specifications of the values of θ and θ' at 0, i.e., $\theta(0) = 1$ and $\theta'(0) = 0$. Namely, the value of θ at 0 is due to its definition, whereas the vanishing of its derivative at 0 indicates the absence of gravity in the cylinder's axis (see [10,21] for more explanation on the related physical motivations).

It is worthwhile to discuss the singularity topic, because the initial conditions of the Lane–Emden problem are typically taken to be $x = 0$. In (1), there seems to be a singularity at 0; hence, a specific strategy is necessary to overcome such a critical characteristic of the equation. Namely, (1) can be also written as follows:

$$\frac{\theta''(x) + \theta^N(x)}{k} = -\frac{\theta'(x)}{x}.$$

Since the initial condition of the related Cauchy problem is $\theta'(0) = 0$, meaning that we are analysing the problem in the neighbourhood of 0, we can note that an indeterminate form appears in the right-hand side of the above expression. By applying De L'Hospital's Theorem (as we will also do when carrying out the qualitative analysis in Section 4), we deduce that the limit is finite, i.e.,

$$\lim_{x \longrightarrow 0}\left(-\frac{\theta'(x)}{x}\right) = -\lim_{x \longrightarrow 0}\theta''(x).$$

A further result is established as well; taking the limits for x and tending to 0 on both sides also provides the value of the second order derivative at 0, i.e., $\theta''(0) = -\dfrac{1}{k+1}$, which can be easily verified based on the form of the known exact solutions in Section 3. Additionally, the results that we will expose in Section 4 will clarify that such a singularity always disappears when computing the limits at $x = 0$, and that, consequently, the analysis of the Lane–Emden equation does not suffer from this critical aspect.

2.2. Modified Versions of the Lane–Emden Equation

Some researchers extend the form of (1) to establish the definitions of other classes of Lane–Emden equations. For example, in [22], (1) is referred to as a Lane–Emden equation of the first kind (see [20]), whereas the Lane–Emden equation of the second kind has the following formulation:

$$\theta''(x) + k\frac{\theta'(x)}{x} + e^{\theta(x)} = 0. \tag{4}$$

Moreover, in [20], a further version is mentioned, originating from a change of variable in (4), whose form is

$$\theta''(x) + k\frac{\theta'(x)}{x} + e^{-\theta(x)} = 0$$

and whose initial conditions are replaced with $\theta(0) = \theta'(0) = 0$, which turns out to be the profile of isothermal cylinders (see [10] for the derivation of the hydrostatic problem).

A whole class of Lane–Emden problems can be established by employing the most general form, as follows:

$$\theta''(x) + k\frac{\theta'(x)}{x} + f(\theta(x)) = 0, \tag{5}$$

where $f(\cdot)$ is a sufficiently regular function of $\theta(x)$.

It is also interesting to remark that (5) can be reformulated as an integro-differential equation. By multiplying the left hand side by x^k, we have

$$x^k \theta''(x) + kx^{k-1}\theta'(x) + x^k f(\theta(x)) = 0,$$

which is equivalent to the equation

$$\left(x^k \theta'(x)\right)' = -x^k f(\theta(x)),$$

which can be integrated on both sides, entailing

$$\theta'(x) = -\frac{1}{x^k}\int_0^x t^k f(\theta(t))dt, \tag{6}$$

where the initial condition turns out to be

$$\lim_{x \to 0}\frac{1}{x^k}\int_0^x t^k f(\theta(t))dt = 0,$$

which holds if and only if

$$\lim_{x \to 0} x f(\theta(x)) = 0,$$

by De L'Hospital's Theorem.

Form (6) is commonly used for numerical approximations of the solutions (see, for example, [22]). Perhaps the most relevant modification of the Lane–Emden equation is the Emden–Fowler equation, as follows (see Chandrasekhar [7] or Fowler's contributions [5,6]):

$$\frac{d}{dx}\left(x^\rho \frac{dy}{dx}\right) + x^\alpha y^\tau(x) = 0, \qquad x \geq 0, \tag{7}$$

where $\rho, \alpha \in \mathbb{R}$, $\tau \in \mathbb{R}_+$. Many papers contain a number of results for (7); a survey outlining the results found up to 1975 is discussed in [23], whereas subsequent relevant papers include [24–26], as well as many others.

Such equations can be transformed into the following modified form:

$$y''(x) - h(x)y^\tau(x) = 0, \qquad x \geq 0, \tag{8}$$

where $h(x)$ is a continuous and non-negative function.

3. Exact Solutions

In the literature, the known solutions to (2) in closed forms are only available for $N = 0$, $N = 1$, and $N = \infty$. In particular, since our main interest lies in the solution of the Lane–Emden equations for specific values of N (see Section 4), the case of $N = \infty$ must, necessarily, be neglected. Physically, as we mentioned in the introduction, the case $N = \infty$ does not fit astrophysical observations of star-forming filaments.

We will proceed to briefly outlining the related polytropes and solution procedures for $N = 0$ and $N = 1$.

3.1. Polytropes for N = 0

The easiest case occurs when $N = 0$, and we can trivially solve this via the separation of the variables (this case is far from reality, in that $N = \frac{1}{\gamma-1}$. Despite this, we will outline the polytropes for completeness). In fact, in this case, a generalization of (3) and (2) can be solved as well.

Proposition 1. *All generalized Lane–Emden equations of the following kind:*

$$
\begin{cases}
\dfrac{1}{x^k}\dfrac{d}{dx}\left(x^k\dfrac{d\theta}{dx}\right) + \theta^N(x) = 0 \\
\theta(0) = 1 \\
\theta'(0) = 0
\end{cases}
\tag{9}
$$

can be solved for all $k \geq 0$ when $N = 0$, and the solution is the following family of parabolas:

$$
\theta_k^*(x) = 1 - \frac{x^2}{2(k+1)}.
\tag{10}
$$

Proof. When $N = 0$, (9) amounts to:

$$
\frac{d}{dx}\left(x^k\frac{d\theta}{dx}\right) = -x^k.
$$

Then, after integrating both sides, we have:

$$
x^k\frac{d\theta}{dx} = -\frac{x^{k+1}}{k+1} + C_0 \iff \cdots \iff \theta(x) = -\frac{x^2}{2(k+1)} + \frac{C_0}{(-k+1)x^{k-1}} + C_1
$$

Then, applying the boundary conditions yields $C_0 = 0$ and $C_1 = 1$, leading to the following family of parabolas, indexed by k: $\theta_k^*(x) = 1 - \dfrac{x^2}{2(k+1)}.$ $\quad\square$

The respective polytropes for (2) and (3) are as follows:

$$
\theta_1^*(x) = 1 - \frac{x^2}{4}, \qquad\qquad \theta_2^*(x) = 1 - \frac{x^2}{6}.
$$

3.2. Polytropes for N = 1

When $N = 1$, the polytrope of (3) is known as well. Expanding Equation (3) yields the following:

$$
\frac{1}{x^2}\left(2x\theta'(x) + x^2\theta''(x)\right) + \theta(x) = 0 \iff \theta''(x) + \frac{2}{x}\theta'(x) + \theta(x) = 0.
\tag{11}
$$

On the other hand, expanding the form (2) yields the following:

$$\frac{1}{x}\left(\theta'(x) + x\theta''(x)\right) + \theta(x) = 0 \iff \theta''(x) + \frac{1}{x}\theta'(x) + \theta(x) = 0. \tag{12}$$

In order to solve these, we assume a power series solution of the following kind (where $a_0 = 1$ because $\theta(0) = 1$):

$$\theta(x) = 1 + \sum_{j=1}^{\infty} a_j x^j. \tag{13}$$

Plugging (13) into (11) leads to

$$\sum_{j=2}^{\infty}(j-1)ja_j x^{j-2} + 2\sum_{j=1}^{\infty} ja_j x^{j-2} + 1 + \sum_{j=1}^{\infty} a_j x^j = 0 \iff$$

$$\iff \frac{2a_1}{x} + 2a_2 + 4a_2 + 1 + \sum_{j=3}^{\infty}[((j-1)j + 2j)a_j + a_{j-2}]x^{j-2} = 0,$$

whose coefficients are supposed to verify

$$a_1 = 0, \qquad a_2 = -\frac{1}{6}, \qquad a_j = -\frac{a_{j-2}}{j(j+1)};$$

hence, the polytrope is as follows:

$$\theta^*(x) = 1 + \sum_{j=1}^{\infty} \frac{(-1)^j x^{2j}}{(2j+1)!} = \frac{\sin x}{x}. \tag{14}$$

An analogous procedure can be carried out to solve (12). Plugging (13) into (12) yields

$$\sum_{j=2}^{\infty}(j-1)ja_j x^{j-2} + \sum_{j=1}^{\infty} ja_j x^{j-2} + 1 + \sum_{j=1}^{\infty} a_j x^j = 0 \iff$$

$$\iff \frac{a_1}{x} + 2a_2 + 2a_2 + 1 + \sum_{j=3}^{\infty}[((j-1)j + j)a_j + a_{j-2}]x^{j-2} = 0,$$

whose coefficients are

$$a_1 = 0, \qquad a_2 = -\frac{1}{4}, \qquad a_j = -\frac{a_{j-2}}{j^2},$$

leading to the following polytrope:

$$\theta^*(x) = 1 + \sum_{j=1}^{\infty} \frac{(-1)^j x^{2j}}{((2j)!!)^2}. \tag{15}$$

The next proposition intends to generalize the above findings, as in Proposition 1.

Proposition 2. *All generalized Lane–Emden equations of the following kind:*

$$\begin{cases} \dfrac{1}{x^k}\dfrac{d}{dx}\left(x^k \dfrac{d\theta}{dx}\right) + \theta^N(x) = 0 \\ \theta(0) = 1 \\ \theta'(0) = 0 \end{cases}$$

can be solved for all $k \geq 0$ when $N = 1$, and the solution is the following family of power series:

$$\theta_k^*(x) = 1 + \sum_{j=1}^{\infty} \frac{(-1)^j x^{2j}}{(2j)!!(2j-1+k)!!}. \tag{16}$$

Proof. Expanding the equation leads to the following:

$$\theta''(x) + \frac{k}{x}\theta'(x) + \theta(x) = 0. \tag{17}$$

Employing the above method, we obtain the following:

$$\frac{ka_1}{x} + 2a_2 + 2ka_2 + 1 + \sum_{j=3}^{\infty}[((j-1)j + kj)a_j + a_{j-2}]x^{j-2} = 0.$$

By exploiting the above relation, all the coefficients can be calculated explicitly. For example, the three terms not containing x yield $2a_2 + 2ka_2 + 1 = 0$ imply that $a_2 = -1/(2(k+1))$. Considering all the terms in the identity, we can also obtain a recurrence relation to generate all coefficients for $j \geq 3$, as follows:

$$a_1 = 0, \qquad a_2 = -\frac{1}{2+2k}, \qquad a_j = -\frac{a_{j-2}}{j(j+k-1)},$$

Consequently, the polytrope is (16). $\square$

4. Analytical Properties in the Cylindrical Scenario

In this Section, we will establish some qualitative properties of the solutions to (2). We begin from some elementary analytical results, and then proceed to provide some insights regarding the graph of the involved functions. From now on, we will indicate, with $\theta_M^*(x)$, the solution to the cylindrical Lane–Emden equation for $N = M$.

Proposition 3. *For all $M \geq 0$, we have that $(\theta_M^*)''(0) = -\dfrac{1}{2}$.*

Proof. It is elementary to collect the terms in (2) as follows:

$$(\theta_M^*)''(x) + \frac{(\theta_M^*)'(x)}{x} + (\theta_M^*)^M(x) = 0 \qquad \Longleftrightarrow \qquad \frac{((\theta_M^*)'(x)x)'}{x} = -(\theta_M^*)^M(x).$$

Now we call $F_M(x) = (\theta_M^*)'(x)x$, whose derivatives, respectively, are as follows:

$$F_M'(x) = (\theta_M^*)''(x)x + (\theta_M^*)'(x), \qquad F_M''(x) = (\theta_M^*)'''(x)x + 2(\theta_M^*)''(x).$$

Since $F_M'(0) = (\theta_M^*)'(0) = 0$, and by the initial condition $\theta_M^*(0) = 1$, we can deduce the following:

$$\lim_{x \to 0} \frac{F_M'(x)}{x} = -1$$

However, the above limit is equal to $F_M''(0)$ by De L'Hospital's Theorem, hence the following:

$$F_M''(0) = 2(\theta_M^*)''(0) = -1,$$

which implies that $(\theta_M^*)''(0) = -\dfrac{1}{2}$. $\square$

It is simple to check that the same procedure illustrated in Proposition 3 can be extended to calculate the higher order derivatives of the solution at zero. Although we will not be further developing this argument in this paper, the implementation of this method might provide an approximation series of the solution in a neighbourhood of the origin.

As an illustrative example of the method, we can check the value of the third derivative at 0.

Since $F''(x) = x(\theta_M^*)'''(x) + 2(\theta_M^*)''(x)$, differentiating the right-hand side as well yields the following:

$$x(\theta_M^*)'''(x) + 2(\theta_M^*)''(x) = -(\theta_M^*)^M(x) - Mx(\theta_M^*)^{M-1}(x)(\theta_M^*)'(x)$$

which can be reformulated as follows:

$$(\theta_M^*)'''(x) = -\frac{2(\theta_M^*)''(x) + (\theta_M^*)^M(x)}{x} - M(\theta_M^*)^{M-1}(x)(\theta_M^*)'(x).$$

Subsequently, evaluating both sides at 0 entails the following:

$$(\theta_M^*)'''(0) = \lim_{x \longrightarrow 0} \left(-\frac{2(\theta_M^*)''(x) + (\theta_M^*)^M(x)}{x} - M(\theta_M^*)^{M-1}(x)(\theta_M^*)'(x) \right)$$

Then, by De L'Hospital's Theorem, we obtain $(\theta_M^*)'''(0) = -2(\theta_M^*)'''(0)$, implying that $(\theta_M^*)'''(0) = 0$.

Furthermore, Proposition 3 establishes that all M, $\theta_M^*(x)$ is concave in a neighbourhood of 0. As a matter of fact, the solution that we explicitly know for $M = 0$ is a parabola, with decreasing and concave behaviour for $x > 0$. As is well-known, if the function admits no inflection points for $x > 0$, this is a sufficient condition to guarantee the existence of a zero x_M^*. When $M = 0$, $x_0^* = 2$.

The following results intend to establish some further qualitative properties of $\theta_M^*(x)$, which are verified for all $M \geq 1$.

Proposition 4. *If $\theta_M^*(x)$ admits at least a positive zero for $M \geq 1$, and x_M is the smallest zero of $\theta_M^*(x)$, then one of the following conditions holds:*

1. $\theta_M^*(x_M) = (\theta_M^*)'(x_M) = (\theta_M^*)''(x_M) = \cdots = (\theta_M^*)^{(k)}(x_M) = 0$ *for all* $k \in \mathbb{Z}_+$;
2. *The function $\theta_M^*(x)$ admits at least one inflection point $F(x_F, y_F)$, such that $0 < x_F < x_M$.*

Proof. If we call $F_M(x) = (\theta_M^*)'(x)x$, it is easy to note that $F_M'(x_M) = 0$ by construction. Since $F_M'(x_M) = (\theta_M^*)''(x_M)x_M + (\theta_M^*)'(x_M) = 0$, two cases may occur. In the first case, both the first and second derivatives of $\theta_M^*(x)$ vanish at x_M, but this, necessarily, implies that all the derivatives of any order vanish at x_M, which is the least interesting scenario for qualitative analysis. In the second case, we have that $x_M = -\dfrac{(\theta_M^*)'(x_M)}{(\theta_M^*)''(x_M)}\theta_M^*(x_M)$, which can only hold if the second order derivative changed its sign in the interval $(0, x_M)$, meaning that the graph has an inflection point at $x_F < x_M$. $\quad\square$

Now, we will provide further insights on the behaviour of the solution by separating two circumstances, specifically where M is odd and where M is even, because some relevant differences occur. The role of possible inflection points, zeros, and stationary points will be analysed in detail.

4.1. Qualitative Behaviour if M Is Odd

The presence of a stationary point, i.e., either a maximum or a minimum point when M is odd, is an interesting issue. If we suppose that $\theta_M^*(x)$ admits one stationary point, x^*, such that $(\theta_M^*)'(x^*) = 0$, in the main equation we would have the following:

$$(\theta_M^*)''(x^*) = -(\theta_M^*)^M(x^*).$$

If $\theta_M^*(x^*) > 0$, this point can only be a local maximum, by the negativity of the second order derivative. Vice versa, if $\theta_M^*(x^*) < 0$, it is a local minimum, and clearly $x_F < x_M < x^*$.

The above considerations establish that, if M is odd, $(\theta_M^*)(x)$ can only have a maximum point by having both positive coordinates. On the other hand, any local minimum has a negative image; hence, there is always at least one inflection point and a zero between each maximum and minimum point.

4.2. Qualitative Behaviour if M Is Even

If M is even, i.e., a positive integer greater than or equal to 2, the results are slightly different, with respect to the previous case. Suppose that $x^* > 0$ is the first stationary point for $\theta_M^*(x)$. If $\theta_M^*(x^*) > 0$, the negativity of the second order derivative implies that such a point is a local maximum, but this holds true even if $\theta_M^*(x^*) < 0$. A stationary point can only be a maximum point; therefore, there can only be one maximum point, after which the solution decreases asymptotically. No oscillating behaviour is feasible in this case, unlike in the easiest case we have seen, where $M = 0$ and the polytrope is monotonically decreasing. There may be some changes in the convexity/concavity form of the graph, but the behaviour is unambiguously decreasing.

4.3. Evaluation of the Difference between the Two Solutions

If we call θ_M^* and θ_P^* the solutions for any $M, P \in \mathbb{Z}_+$, where $M \neq P$, we posit that $k = 1$; i.e., we are in the cylindrical setup. With (1), we have the following:

$$\begin{cases} (\theta_M^*)''(x) + \dfrac{(\theta_M^*)'(x)}{x} + (\theta_M^*)^M(x) = 0 \\[2ex] (\theta_P^*)''(x) + \dfrac{(\theta_P^*)'(x)}{x} + (\theta_P^*)^P(x) = 0 \end{cases} \Longleftrightarrow$$

$$\Longleftrightarrow \begin{cases} \dfrac{\left((\theta_M^*)'(x)x\right)'}{x} = -(\theta_M^*)^M(x) \\[2ex] \dfrac{\left((\theta_P^*)'(x)x\right)'}{x} = -(\theta_P^*)^P(x) \end{cases}.$$

Now, if we call $F_M(x) = (\theta_M^*)'(x)x$ and $F_P(x) = (\theta_P^*)'(x)x$, we obtain the following dynamic system:

$$\begin{cases} F_M'(x) = -x(\theta_M^*)^M(x) \\[2ex] F_P'(x) = -x(\theta_P^*)^P(x) \end{cases}$$

which is endowed with the initial conditions $F_M(0) = 0$ and $F_P(0) = 0$. By subtracting the left-hand sides, we obtain the following:

$$(F_M(x) - F_P(x))' = x\left[(\theta_P^*)^P(x) - (\theta_M^*)^M(x)\right]$$

from which we then obtain, after integrating both sides, the following:

$$F_M(x) - F_P(x) = \int_0^x t\left[(\theta_P^*)^P(t) - (\theta_M^*)^M(t)\right] dt,$$

i.e.,

$$(\theta_M^*(x) - \theta_P^*(x))' = \frac{\int_0^x t\left[(\theta_P^*)^P(t) - (\theta_M^*)^M(t)\right] dt}{x};$$

then, by integrating both sides again, we obtain the following:

$$\theta_M^*(x) - \theta_P^*(x) = \int_0^x \left[\frac{\int_0^t s\left[(\theta_P^*)^P(s) - (\theta_M^*)^M(s)\right] ds}{t}\right] dt. \tag{18}$$

In (18), the difference between solutions is on the left-hand side, whereas the difference between their powers is in the double integral on the right-hand side. This relation can be employed to identify an approximation method for the polytropes, with the help of the above considerations on the qualitative behaviour of the solutions.

5. Summary of the Main Results

In this paper, we identified some properties of the solutions of the Lane–Emden equation (i.e., the polytropes) in a cylindrical framework, especially taking into account the critical points and their possible positions in the graph of the functions. The qualitative properties that we exposed may be helpful in either constructing possible new explicit forms for the polytropes or implementing methods for approximation. Moreover, the results obtained in this paper (in particular in Section 4) can help shed light on the properties of important astrophysical objects, such as filamentary star-forming regions.

Such results can potentially be extended and improved. Eventually, important follow-up work will be devoted to an accurate study of the relevance of our mathematical analysis and the results of the study of star-forming filaments. In particular, our method for approximating solutions with different polytropic indices, as in Equation (18), can be used to study the temporal evolution of the density profile of filaments in specific regions. Since star formation changes the thermal properties of a filament, this, in turn, leads to temporal variations of the polytropic index, which can be described by our solutions if we can identify P and M in (18) as values of N at different moments in time.

Finally, some new elements for a better understanding of the behaviour of the solutions may emerge from the comparison between polytropes, which can also be viewed as a double integral and can, therefore, be numerically approximated by traditional methods.

6. Concluding Remarks and Discussion

The findings in the present work can be further extended in several different ways. A future development of the present work may concern the realization and computational optimization of a suitable algorithm to constructively approximate the real solutions in their explicit forms.

Moreover, we will also use existing numerical schemes, in follow-up papers, to approximate the solution of the Lane–Emden equations in relevant cases. One simple method that can be employed is a Runge–Kutta scheme (see [4]), but we will also employ modern techniques based in higher order Haar wavelet methods, tailored to the Lane–Emden equations [18,19].

Another possible extension of this work might specifically be focused on Emden–Fowler equations of several kinds. In this respect, some studies may be carried out in future that are based on the recent methodology introduced by Rufai and Ramos for third-order Emden–Fowler equations [25] in 2023.

More generally, the qualitative analysis of the Emden–Fowler equations' solutions is a complex and stimulating issue.

Author Contributions: Conceptualization, A.P. and S.R.; methodology, A.P. and S.R.; software, A.P. and S.R.; validation, A.P. and S.R.; formal analysis, A.P. and S.R.; investigation, A.P. and S.R.; resources, A.P. and S.R.; data curation, A.P. and S.R.; writing—original draft preparation, A.P. and S.R.; writing—review and editing, A.P. and S.R.; visualization, A.P. and S.R.; supervision, A.P. and S.R.; project administration, A.P. and S.R.; funding acquisition, A.P. and S.R. All authors have read and agreed to the published version of the manuscript.

Funding: This research received no external funding.

Data Availability Statement: Data are contained within the article.

Conflicts of Interest: The authors declare no conflicts of interest.

References

1. Lane, H.J. On the Theoretical Temperature of the Sun, Under the Hypothesis of A Gaseous Mass Maintaining Its Volume by Its Internal Heat, and Depending on the Laws of Gases as Known to Terrestrial Experiment. *Am. J. Sci.* **1870**, *148*, 57–74. [CrossRef]
2. Emden, R. *Gaskugeln*; BG Teubner: Stuttgart, Germany, 1907.
3. Recchi, S.; Hacar, A.; Palestini, A. Nonisothermal filaments in equilibrium. *Astron. Astroph.* **2013**, *558*, 27. [CrossRef]
4. Recchi, S.; Hacar, A.; Palestini, A. On the equilibrium of rotating filaments. *Month. Not. R. Astron. Soc.* **2014**, *444*, 1775–1782. [CrossRef]
5. Fowler, R.H. The form near infinity of real continuous solutions of a certain differential equation of second order. *Quart. J. Math.* **1914**, *45*, 289–350.
6. Fowler, R.H. Further studies of Emden's and similar differential equations. *Quart. J. Math.* **1931**, *1*, 259–288. [CrossRef]
7. Chandrasekhar, S. *An Introduction to the Study of Stellar Structure*; University of Chicago Press: Chicago, IL, USA, 1939; pp. 84–103.
8. Chandrasekhar, S.; Fermi, E. Problems of Gravitational Stability In The Presence of A Magnetic Field. *Astroph. J.* **1953**, *118*, 115–141. [CrossRef]
9. Christodoulou, D.M.; Kazanas, D. Exact Axisymmetric Solutions of The 2-D Lane-Emden Equations with Rotation. *J. Mod. Phys.* **2016**, *7*, 2177–2187. [CrossRef]
10. Ostriker, J. The equilibrium of polytropic and isothermal cylinders. *Astroph. J.* **1964**, *140*, 1056. [CrossRef]
11. Horedt, G.P. *Polytropes: Applications in Astrophysics and Related Fields*; Springer Science & Business Media: Berlin, Germany, 2004; Volume 306.
12. Hacar, A.; Tafalla, M.; Kauffmann, J.; Kovács, A. Cores, filaments, and bundles: Hierarchical core formation in the L1495/B213 Taurus region. *Astron. Astroph.* **2013**, *554*, A55. [CrossRef]
13. Adomian, G. A new approach to nonlinear partial differential equations. *J. Math. Anal. Appl.* **1984**, *102*, 420–434. [CrossRef]
14. Bengochea, G.; Verde-Star, L. Linear algebraic foundations of the operational calculi. *Adv. Appl. Math.* **2011**, *47*, 330–351. [CrossRef]
15. Bengochea, G. Algebraic approach to the Lane-Emden equation. *Appl. Math. Comp.* **2014**, *232*, 424–430. [CrossRef]
16. Bengochea, G.; Verde-Star, L. An operational approach to the Emden-Fowler equation. *Math. Meth. Appl. Sci.* **2015**, *38* 4630–4637. [CrossRef]
17. Arqub, O.A.; Osman, M.S.; Abdel-Aty, A.H.; Mohamed, A.B.A.; Momani, S. A numerical algorithm for the solutions of ABC singular Lane–Emden type models arising in astrophysics using reproducing kernel discretization method. *Mathematics* **2020**, *8*, 923. [CrossRef]
18. Singh, M.; Singh, K. An efficient technique based on higher order Haar wavelet method for Lane–Emden equations. *Math. Comp. Sim.* **2023**, *206*, 21–39.
19. Izadi, M. A discontinuous finite element approximation to singular Lane-Emden type equations. *Appl. Math. Comp.* **2021**, *401*, 126115. [CrossRef]
20. Wazwaz, A.M.; Rach, R.; Duan, J.S. Adomian decomposition method for solving the Volterra integral form of the Lane–Emden equations with initial values and boundary conditions. *Appl. Math. Comp.* **2013**, *219*, 5004–5019. [CrossRef]
21. Iacono, R.; De Felice, M. Constructing analytic approximate solutions to the Lane-Emden equations. *Phys. Lett. A* **2015**, *379*, 1802–1807. [CrossRef]
22. Sahu, P.K.; Ray, S.S. Numerical solutions for Volterra integro-differential forms of Lane-Emden equations of first and second kind using Legendre multi-wavelets. *Electron. J. Differ. Equ.* **2015**, *28*, 1–11.
23. Wong, J.S. On the generalized Emden–Fowler equation. *Siam Rev.* **1975**, *17*, 339–360. [CrossRef]
24. Habets, P.; Zanolin, F. Upper and lower solutions for a generalized Emden-Fowler equation. *J. Math. Anal. Appl.* **1994**, *181*, 684–700. [CrossRef]
25. Rufai, M.A.; Ramos, H. Solving third-order Lane–Emden–Fowler equations using a variable stepsize formulation of a pair of block methods. *J. Comp. Appl. Math.* **2023**, *420*, 114776. [CrossRef]
26. Zhang, Y. Positive solutions of singular sublinear Emden-Fowler boundary value problems. *J. Math. Anal. Appl.* **1994**, *185*, 215–222. [CrossRef]

 *mathematics*

Article

Charged Cavitation Multibubbles Dynamics Model: Growth Process

Ahmed K. Abu-Nab [1,2,*], Amerah M. Hakami [3] and Ali F. Abu-Bakr [1]

[1] Department of Mathematics and Computer Science, Faculty of Science, Menoufia University, Shebin El-Koom 32511, Egypt; alibakrm@yahoo.com

[2] Moscow Institute of Physics and Technology, Phystech School of Applied Mathematics and Informatics, Dolgoprudny 141700, Russia

[3] Department of Mathematics, Faculty of Science, Jazan University, Jazan 82723, Saudi Arabia; amhakami806@gmail.com

* Correspondence: ahmed.abunab@yahoo.com or ahmed.kamal87@science.menofia.edu.eg; Tel.: +20-1092568892

Abstract: The nonlinear dynamics of charged cavitation bubbles are investigated theoretically and analytically in this study through the Rayleigh–Plesset model in dielectric liquids. The physical and mathematical situations consist of two models: the first one is noninteracting charged cavitation bubbles (like single cavitation bubble) and the second one is interacting charged cavitation bubbles. The proposed models are formulated and solved analytically based on the Plesset–Zwick technique. The study examines the behaviour of charged cavitation bubble growth processes under the influence of the polytropic exponent, the number of bubbles N, and the distance between the bubbles. From our analysis, it is observed that the radius of charged cavitation bubbles increases with increases in the distance between the bubbles, dimensionless phase transition criteria, and thermal diffusivity, and is inversely proportional to the polytropic exponent and the number of bubbles N. Additionally, it is evident that the growth process of charged cavitation bubbles is enhanced significantly when the number of bubbles is reduced. The electric charges and polytropic exponent weakens the growth process of charged bubbles in dielectric liquids. The obtained results are compared with experimental and theoretical previous works to validate the given solutions of the presented models of noninteraction and interparticle interaction of charged cavitation bubbles.

Keywords: charged bubbles; interparticle interaction; growth process; analytical solution; Plesset–Zwick technique

MSC: 76M35; 35Q31; 35Q05; 76M20

Citation: Abu-Nab, A.K.; Hakami, A.M.; Abu-Bakr, A.F. Charged Cavitation Multibubbles Dynamics Model: Growth Process. *Mathematics* **2024**, *12*, 569. https://doi.org/10.3390/math12040569

Academic Editor: Arsen Palestini

Received: 4 January 2024
Revised: 19 January 2024
Accepted: 25 January 2024
Published: 14 February 2024

1. Introduction

Cavitation bubbles dynamics is a basic scientific subject with many fascinating and intricate dynamical properties that are of general interest [1]. More than a hundred years ago, many scientists and researchers began studying cavitation bubble dynamics and their potential uses in an attempt to reduce damage to ship propellers. Since then, bubbles have attracted enormous scientific and technological interest [2,3]. Many significant applications arise from cavitation bubble dynamics, which exhibit volumetric oscillations because of pressure imbalances. Different dynamic pressure imbalances give rise to bubbles of different cavitations, which exhibit numerous volumetric oscillations that have a wide range of use in many important applications. Certain acoustic and induced-laser cavitation bubbles [4–6], for instance, are used for medication and gene delivery [7,8], therapeutic biological systems [9–12], ultrasonic cleaning [13], sonoluminescence [14], inkjet printing [15], and bubble propulsion [16]. The efforts of researchers [1–15] help the researchers to understand and develop the bubble dynamics and its application, so these results enhance the scientific fields.

The cavitation bubbles are usually millimetre- or micrometre-sized oscillating bubbles. Air weapon bubbles and submerged blast bubbles, which can be metre-size-varying bubbles, are essential elements used in underwater implosion and geophysical studies [16,17]. Moreover, oscillating bubbles that range in size from millimetres to metres, known as hydraulic bubbles, trapped air bubbles, and heat-generated steam bubbles, can play a significant role in the operation of engines, reactors, and turbines [18,19]. Many research projects and applications are still being conducted on the use of bubble dynamics in discoveries and different applications for bubbles of different sizes.

Science started looking at bubble dynamics theoretically in the early 20th century. The Rayleigh–Plesset equation was derived, which is a classical equation that provides an accurate description of the oscillation of bubbles in incompressible fluids [20]. The Rayleigh–Plesset equation did not take into account energy lost due to acoustic frequencies, such as pressure waves resulting from the collapse of a bubble, as it relied on incompressible fluids. As a result, this equation becomes inappropriate when the collapse in the bubble radius or the energy lost is important and cannot be neglected. Weakly compressible bubble models were established, taking into account the weak compressibility of the fluid outside the bubble. The most widely used of them was the Keller–Mikis model [21], which was developed using the incompressible Bernoulli equation and the wave equation. Based on perturbation theory, Prosperetti and Lezzi [22,23] proposed a new model for describing behaviour dynamics that took the fluid's compressibility into account. Subsequently, many different models [24–26] were presented that made a significant contribution to theoretical studies of bubble dynamics in compressible fluids.

It is notable that, because bubbles have multiple oscillation cycles, boundaries, and scales, their dynamics are complex and present significant challenges for theoretical, numerical, and experimental research, regardless of whether the bubbles originate from natural or artificial sources. Understanding the physics of bubbles under various conditions and the basis for deciphering and comprehending a wide range of bubble dynamics and behaviour phenomena, as well as how they can be used in diverse industrial and biological applications, depend heavily on theoretical research. Recently, bubble dynamics [27] were investigated theoretically under consideration of the effect of magnetic field and liquid electrical conductivity where the authors [27] obtained the analytical results of the behaviour of single bubble dynamics in a generalized Newtonian fluid, especially how the impact of magnetic field weakens the gas bubble growth. Additionally, the development and application of analytical and numerical methods to study bubble dynamics in mathematical models has garnered increased attention in the last few years [28–33].

To the best of our knowledge, the mathematical models of bubbles used in all prior research on how frequencies affect the behaviour of multibubbles were considered, demonstrating that these bubbles are not charged. However, it has been shown that when exposed to acoustic forces, air and gas bubbles in liquids are electrostatically charged. A long-standing issue is the charging deposition on bubbles at bubble–liquid interfaces [34,35]. Experimental evidence has confirmed that the phenomena is related to the movement of ionic charge from the liquid onto the surface of the bubble. The dynamics of driven charged bubbles remain poorly understood, although charged bubbles have numerous potential uses in the creation of electro-aerosol sprays, which are made of highly charged particles, wastewater treatment [36], biological medicine [37], and the production of food [38].

Additionally, significant progress was made when the modified Rayleigh–Plesset equation for an acoustically single-frequency generated gas bubble was used, taking into account the existence of charge Q on the bubble's surface. When a charged bubble is present, its effective surface tension is lowered, which causes the bubble to enlarge in radius and then rapidly collapse to a minimal radius. Furthermore, it was observed that the charge raises the maximum achievable bubble radius and accelerates the occurrence of the period-doubling-bifurcations route to chaos [39].

The goal of this work is to present the theoretical and analytical study of nonlinear dynamics of charged bubbles. The study investigates the noninteracting and interacting charged cavitation bubbles in dielectric liquids where the proposed models are solved analytically based on the Plesset–Zwick method. The validation and verification of the proposed models are discussed in the text. A graphic representation of the results is estimated by Mathematica software (ver.13.1). The comparison between the current model with available published results are revealed in this study.

2. Model

This investigation highlights the significance of nonlinear Rayleigh–Plesset differential equations in comprehending complexity and intricate phenomena and treatment processes across different applied sciences. It is found that several mathematical and physical approaches are discussed to investigate nonlinear Rayleigh–Plesset differential equations, including numerical solutions, linearization methods, quadrature solutions, asymptotic analysis, and analytical solutions, which are investigated in our study. The analytical study of nonlinear dynamics of charged cavitation bubbles is introduced in dielectric liquids. For that, the physical problem is analysed in Figure 1, where the charged cavitation bubbles are in the dielectric liquid. This is supposing that the translational motion of charged bubbles and gravity force are neglected. The current physical situation has two models: the first model is to study the noninteracting, charged cavitation bubbles and the second one is in the case of interacting, charged cavitation bubbles. The proposed model is formulated, solved, and discussed in further sections.

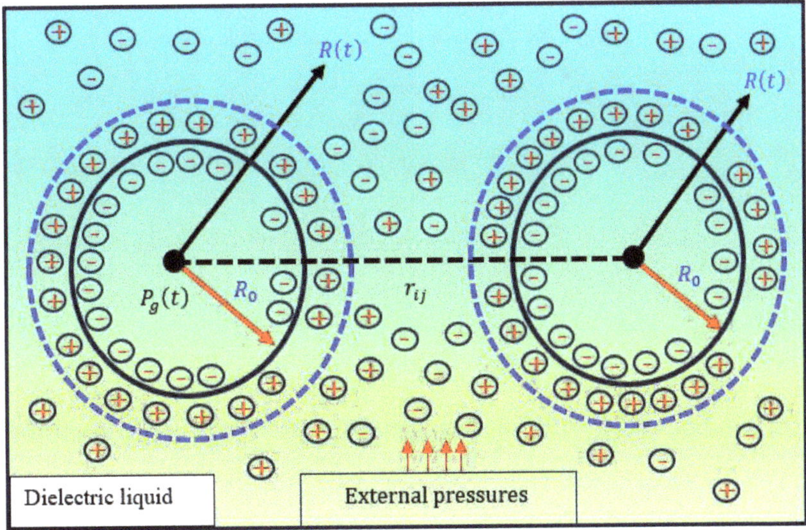

Figure 1. Sketch charged multibubbles dynamics; $(+)$ and $(-)$ are the positive and negative of electric charges. External pressures are defined in the text.

2.1. Noninteraction-Charged Cavitation Bubble

In our approach, the mechanism of charged cavitation microbubble dynamics occurs in a viscous mixture of vapour and superheated, incompressible Newtonian fluid between a two-phase flow (namely, an extended charged-Rayleigh–Plesset model) [39,40] can be expressed as:

$$\rho(R\ddot{R} + \frac{3}{2}\dot{R}^2) = (P_k + P_\eta + P_\sigma + P_Q + (P_v - P_0)). \tag{1}$$

Here, P_k is the pressure due to polytropic effects, which can be expressed in charged liquid as:

$$P_k = \left(P_v - P_0 + \frac{2\sigma}{R_0} - \frac{Q^2}{8\pi\varepsilon R_0^4} \right) \left(\frac{R_0}{R} \right)^{3\kappa} \text{ and } \kappa = \left\{ \begin{array}{l} 1 \\ \frac{4}{3} \text{ or } \frac{5}{3} \end{array} \right. \tag{2}$$

Moreover, P_σ and P_η refer to the acting pressures because of the forces of the surface tension and viscous effects, respectively, which can be read as:

$$P_\sigma = \frac{2}{R}\sigma. \tag{3}$$

and

$$P_\eta = 4\frac{\dot{R}}{R}\eta, \tag{4}$$

where σ is the surface tension. η is the viscosity dynamic.

In our study, P_Q is the charged pressure in the permittivity of the dielectric space-filling liquid ε in the system of dielectric liquid, which is defined as:

$$P_Q = \frac{Q^2}{8\pi\varepsilon R^4} \tag{5}$$

Here, Q is the electric charge. $\varepsilon = 85\,\varepsilon_0$; ε_0 refers to initial permittivity.

Combining Equations (1)–(5), the charged-Rayleigh–Plesset model in dielectric liquid for charged single cavitation bubble becomes:

$$\rho\left(R\ddot{R} + \frac{3}{2}\dot{R}^2\right) = \left(\left(P_v - P_0 + \frac{2\sigma}{R_0} - \frac{Q^2}{8\pi\varepsilon R_0^4} \right) \left(\frac{R_0}{R} \right)^{3\kappa} - \frac{2}{R}\sigma - 4\frac{\rho\dot{R}}{R}\eta + \frac{Q^2}{8\pi\varepsilon R^4} + (P_v - P_0) \right). \tag{6}$$

The pressure of the charged bubbles [8] $P_g(t)$ can be expressed as:

$$P_g(t) = \left(P_v - P_0 + \frac{2\sigma}{R_0} \right) \left(\frac{R_0}{R} \right)^{3\kappa}. \tag{7}$$

From Equations (6)–(8), Equation (6) becomes:

$$R\ddot{R} + \frac{3}{2}\dot{R}^2 = \frac{1}{\rho}\left(P_g(t) - P_0 \right) - \frac{Q^2}{8\pi\rho\varepsilon R_0^4}\left(\frac{R_0}{R} \right)^{3\kappa} - 4\frac{\dot{R}}{R}\eta - \frac{2}{\rho R}\sigma + \frac{Q^2}{8\pi\rho\varepsilon R^4} + \frac{1}{\rho}P_v. \tag{8}$$

The pressure difference [41] $(P_g(t) - P_0)$ can be stated as:

$$P_g(t) - P_0 = \mathbb{Z}_1(T_R(t) - T_s), \tag{9}$$

where $\mathbb{Z}_1$ defines a constant, which will be calculated below. T_b and T_s are the instantaneous temperature of the gas surrounding the charged bubble and the saturation temperature, respectively.

Combing Equations (8) and (9), Equation (8) becomes:

$$R\ddot{R} + \frac{3}{2}\dot{R}^2 = \frac{1}{\rho}\mathbb{Z}_1(T_b(t) - T_s) - \frac{Q^2}{8\pi\rho\varepsilon R_0^4}\left(\frac{R_0}{R} \right)^{3\kappa} - 4\frac{\dot{R}}{R}\eta - \frac{2}{\rho R}\sigma + \frac{Q^2}{8\pi\rho\varepsilon R^4} + \frac{1}{\rho}P_v. \tag{10}$$

The approach can be solved by taking the initial and boundary conditions into account, which can be expressed as:

$$R(t_0) = R_0,\ \dot{R}(t_0) = \dot{R}_0,\ \ddot{R}(t_0) = 0,\ T_R(t_0) = T_0, \tag{11}$$

$$R(t_m) = R_m,\ \dot{R}(t_m) = \dot{R}_m,\ \ddot{R}(t_m) = 0, \tag{12}$$

where 0 and m represent, respectively, the initial and maximum values. Applying the condition (9) into (10), the $\mathbb{Z}_1$ becomes:

$$\mathbb{Z}_1 = \frac{\mathbb{Z}_2}{T_0 - T_\infty};$$

(13)

$$\mathbb{Z}_2 = \frac{3}{2}\rho\dot{R}_0^2 + 4\frac{\rho\dot{R}_0}{R_0}\eta + \frac{2}{R_0}\sigma - P_v.$$

Combining Equations (10) and (12), Equation (10) takes this form:

$$R\ddot{R} + \frac{3}{2}\dot{R}^2 = \frac{1}{\rho}\left(\frac{\Delta T_B^*}{\Delta T_0} + 1\right)\mathbb{Z}_2 - \frac{Q^2}{8\pi\rho\varepsilon R_0^4}\left(\frac{R_0}{R}\right)^{3\kappa} - 4\frac{\dot{R}}{R}\eta - \frac{2}{\rho R}\sigma + \frac{Q^2}{8\pi\rho\varepsilon R^4} + \frac{1}{\rho}P_v.$$

(14)

Here $R\ddot{R} + \frac{3}{2}\dot{R}^2 = \frac{1}{2R^2\dot{R}}\frac{d}{dt}\left(R^3\dot{R}^2\right)$, $\Delta T_0 = T_0 - T_\infty$; is the initial value of over-temperature and ΔT_T^* is the solution of temperature equation (i.e., [42–44]), which stated as:

$$\Delta T_B^* = T_R - T_0 = -\left(\frac{a_l}{\pi}\right)^{\frac{1}{2}}\int_0^t\left(\left(\int_0^t R^4(x_2)dx_2\right)^{-1/2}\left(R^2(x_1)\left(\frac{\partial T}{\partial r}\right)_{r=R(x)}\right)\right)dx_1,$$

(15)

where a_l is the diffusion coefficient.

The temperature gradient $\frac{\partial T}{\partial r}$ can be evaluated via the equilibrium of gas diffusion at the microbubble wall [43] as follows:

$$\left(\frac{\partial T}{\partial r}\right)_{r=RS} = \frac{4}{3}\pi\frac{\frac{d}{dt}(\rho_g R^3)}{a_l A}; \quad A = 4\pi R^2.$$

(16)

Here A is the surface area of bubble. $\frac{\partial T}{\partial r}$ is the concentration gradient at the surface of bubble. T defines the temperature of the given medium. To complete the solution, Equation (16) is transformed to a dimensionless equation, via which aids these transformations as:

$$\Psi = \left(\frac{R}{R_0}\right)^3, v = \frac{\Omega}{R_0^4}\int_0^t R^4(x_2)dx_2, \Omega = \sqrt{\frac{2R}{\rho_L R_0^3}}, \frac{ds}{dt} = \frac{1}{3}\Omega R_0\Psi^{\frac{2}{3}}\Psi', \frac{d^2R}{dt^2} = \frac{1}{3}\Omega^2 R_0\Psi\left(\Psi\Psi'' + \frac{2}{3}\Psi'^2\right).$$

(17)

On the other hand, we can convert ΔT_B^* and $\left(\frac{\partial T}{\partial r}\right)_{r=S}$ in dimensionless forms.

$$\left.\begin{array}{c}\Delta T_B^* = -\frac{\rho_v R_0}{3a_l}\left(\frac{\Omega a_l}{\pi}\right)^{\frac{1}{2}}\int_0^v\left((v-\varsigma)^{-\frac{1}{2}}\Psi(\varsigma)\right)d\varsigma \\[2mm] \left(\frac{\partial T}{\partial r}\right)_{r=S} = \frac{S_0\rho_g}{3a_l}\Omega\Psi^{\frac{2}{3}}\Psi\end{array}\right\}.$$

(18)

With help via Equations (17) and (18), Equation (13) can be put in a dimensionless equation as:

$$\frac{1}{6\Psi'}\frac{d}{dv}\left(\Psi^{\frac{7}{3}}\Psi^2\right) = \frac{1}{\rho\Omega^2 R_0^2}\mathbb{Z}_2 - \mathbb{Z}_3\int_0^v\left((v-\varsigma)^{-\frac{1}{2}}\Psi'(\varsigma)\right)d\varsigma - \frac{Q^2}{8\pi\rho\varepsilon\Omega^2 R_0^2}\left(\frac{1}{\Psi^{\frac{1}{3}}}\right)^{3\kappa} - \frac{4}{3}\frac{4}{\Omega R_0^2}\Psi^{\frac{1}{3}}\Psi'\eta - \frac{2}{\rho\Omega^2 R_0^2}\frac{1}{\Psi^{\frac{1}{3}}}\sigma +$$

$$\frac{Q^2}{8\pi\rho\varepsilon\Omega^2 R_0^2}\frac{1}{\Psi^{\frac{1}{3}}} + \frac{1}{\rho\Omega^2 R_0^2}P_v$$

(19)

where $\mathbb{Z}_3 = \left(\frac{\Omega a_l}{9\pi}\right)^{\frac{1}{2}}\frac{\rho_v L\mathbb{Z}_2}{\rho\Omega^2\Delta T_0 R_0 k_l}$.

When the charged microbubble dynamics are a complete growth, the inertial forces are neglected and the boundary conditions in Equation (11) are verified. Mathematically, these mean $R(t_m) = R_m, \dot{R}(t_m) = \dot{R}_m, \ddot{R}(t_m) = 0$ and $\frac{1}{6\Psi'}\frac{d}{dv}\left(\Psi^{\frac{7}{3}}\Psi^2\right) \to 0$. Then, Equation (19) reduces to:

$$\int_0^v \left((v-\xi)^{-\frac{1}{2}}\Psi'(\xi)\right)d\xi = \frac{1}{\mathbb{Z}_3}\left[\frac{1}{\rho\Omega^2 R_0^2}\mathbb{Z}_2 - \frac{Q^2}{8\pi\rho\varepsilon\Omega^2 R_0^2}\left(\frac{1}{\Psi_m^{\frac{1}{3}}}\right)^{3\kappa} - \frac{4}{3\Omega R_0^2}\Psi_m^{\frac{1}{3}}\Psi'_m\eta - \frac{2}{\rho\Omega^2 R_0^2}\frac{1}{\Psi_m^{\frac{1}{3}}}\sigma + \frac{Q^2}{8\pi\rho\varepsilon\Omega^2 R_0^2}\frac{1}{\Psi_m^{\frac{1}{3}}} + \frac{1}{\rho\Omega^2 R_0^2}P_v\right] \quad (20)$$

To complete the solution of Equation (20), we use these assumptions: $\xi = \xi_1 v$, and $\beta(v) = \gamma v^{\frac{1}{2}}$; γ denotes a constant, we obtain:

$$\gamma = \frac{2}{\mathbb{Z}_3\pi}\left[\frac{1}{\rho\Omega^2 R_0^2}\mathbb{Z}_2 - \frac{Q^2}{8\pi\rho\varepsilon\Omega^2 R_0^2}\left(\frac{1}{\Psi_m^{\frac{1}{3}}}\right)^{3\kappa} - \frac{4}{3\Omega R_0^2}\Psi_m^{\frac{1}{3}}\Psi'_m\eta - \frac{2}{\rho\Omega^2 R_0^2}\frac{1}{\Psi_m^{\frac{1}{3}}}\sigma + \frac{Q^2}{8\pi\rho\varepsilon\Omega^2 R_0^2}\frac{1}{\Psi_m^{\frac{1}{3}}} + \frac{1}{\rho\Omega^2 R_0^2}P_v\right]. \quad (21)$$

Then $\beta(v)$ becomes:

$$\beta(v) = \frac{2}{\mathbb{Z}_3\pi}\left[\frac{1}{\rho\Omega^2 R_0^2}\mathbb{Z}_2 - \frac{Q^2}{8\pi\rho\varepsilon\Omega^2 R_0^2}\left(\frac{1}{\Psi_m^{\frac{1}{3}}}\right)^{3\kappa} - \frac{4}{3\Omega R_0^2}\Psi_m^{\frac{1}{3}}\Psi'_m\eta - \frac{2}{\rho\Omega^2 R_0^2}\frac{1}{\Psi_m^{\frac{1}{3}}}\sigma + \frac{Q^2}{8\pi\rho\varepsilon\Omega^2 R_0^2}\frac{1}{\Psi_m^{\frac{1}{3}}} + \frac{1}{\rho\Omega^2 R_0^2}P_v\right]v^{\frac{1}{2}} \quad (22)$$

Applying Equation (22) into $R = R_0\Psi^{\frac{1}{3}}$, the charged microbubble radius becomes:

$$R = R_0\left[\frac{2}{\mathbb{Z}_3\pi}\left[\frac{1}{\rho\Omega^2 R_0^2}\mathbb{Z}_2 - \frac{Q^2}{8\pi\rho\varepsilon\Omega^2 R_0^2}\left(\frac{1}{\Psi_m^{\frac{1}{3}}}\right)^{3\kappa} - \frac{4}{3\Omega R_0^2}\Psi_m^{\frac{1}{3}}\Psi'_m\eta - \frac{2}{\rho\Omega^2 R_0^2}\frac{1}{\Psi_m^{\frac{1}{3}}}\sigma + \frac{Q^2}{8\pi\rho\varepsilon\Omega^2 R_0^2}\frac{1}{\Psi_m^{\frac{1}{3}}} + \frac{1}{\rho\Omega^2 R_0^2}P_v\right]\right]^{1/3}v^{\frac{1}{6}} \quad (23)$$

To introduce v versus time t, Equation (23) is utilized into Equation (17), the result is defined as:

$$v^{\frac{1}{6}} = \left(\frac{\Omega}{3}t\right)^{\frac{1}{2}}\left[\frac{2}{\pi\mathcal{L}_2}\left[\frac{1}{\rho\Omega^2 R_0^2}\mathbb{Z}_2 - \frac{Q^2}{8\pi\rho\varepsilon\Omega^2 R_0^2}\left(\frac{1}{\Psi_m^{\frac{1}{3}}}\right)^{3\kappa} - \frac{4}{3\Omega R_0^2}\Psi_m^{\frac{1}{3}}\Psi'_m\eta - \frac{2}{\rho\Omega^2 R_0^2}\frac{1}{\Psi_m^{\frac{1}{3}}}\sigma + \frac{Q^2}{8\pi\rho\varepsilon\Omega^2 R_0^2}\frac{1}{\Psi_m^{\frac{1}{3}}} + \frac{1}{\rho\Omega^2 R_0^2}P_v\right]\right]^{2/3} \quad (24)$$

The charged noninteracting microbubble radius can be calculated as:

$$R = \left[\frac{2}{\mathbb{Z}_3\pi}\left[\frac{1}{\rho\Omega^2 R_0^2}\mathbb{Z}_2 - \frac{Q^2}{8\pi\rho\varepsilon\Omega^2 R_0^2}\left(\frac{1}{\Psi_m^{\frac{1}{3}}}\right)^{3\kappa} - \frac{4}{3\Omega R_0^2}\Psi_m^{\frac{1}{3}}\Psi'_m\eta - \frac{2}{\rho\Omega^2 R_0^2}\frac{1}{\Psi_m^{\frac{1}{3}}}\sigma + \frac{Q^2}{8\pi\rho\varepsilon\Omega^2 R_0^2}\frac{1}{\Psi_m^{\frac{1}{3}}} + \frac{1}{\rho\Omega^2 R_0^2}P_v\right]\right]^{1/3}\left(\frac{2}{\mathbb{Z}_3\pi}\right)^{\frac{2}{3}}\left(\frac{\Omega}{3}\right)^{\frac{1}{2}}t^{\frac{1}{2}} \quad (25)$$

From Equation (25), the charged noninteracting microbubble radius becomes:

$$R = \left[\frac{2}{\mathbb{Z}_3\pi}\left[\frac{1}{\rho\Omega^2 R_0^2}\mathbb{Z}_2 - \frac{Q^2}{8\pi\rho\varepsilon\Omega^2 R_0^2}(\phi_0)^\kappa - \frac{4}{3\Omega R_0^2}\phi_0^{\frac{-1}{3}}\Psi'_m\eta - \frac{2}{\rho\Omega^2 R_0^2}\phi_0^{\frac{1}{3}}\sigma + \frac{Q^2}{8\pi\rho\varepsilon\Omega^2 R_0^2}\phi_0^{\frac{1}{3}} + \frac{1}{\rho\Omega^2 R_0^2}P_v\right]\right]^{1/3}\frac{\Omega^2\rho R_0}{\mathbb{Z}_3}\left(\frac{12a_1}{3}\right)^{\frac{1}{2}}Ja\,t^{\frac{1}{2}} \quad (26)$$

Here, the Jacob number ($Ja = \frac{\rho C_p \Delta T_0}{\rho_v L}$), thermal diffusivity ($a_l = \frac{k_l}{\rho C_p}$), and the initial void fraction can be defined as the ratio between the initial of the charged bubbles and the maximum volume of charged bubbles, which takes this form: $\phi_0 = \left(\frac{R_0}{R_m}\right)^3$. It is noted that the charged cavitation bubbles are generated, and appear when this constraint ($0 < \phi_0 < 1$) is satisfied.

2.2. Charged Cavitation Multibubble

In this section, the pressure due to the interparticle interaction of the cavitation of multibubbles and the model of the charged cavitation of multibubble is derived, then the pressure utilized in the spherical charged bubbles, respective to the volume modification, can be used to find the incompressible dielectric fluid and continuity with the equations of Euler [45] as follows:

$$\frac{\partial v}{\partial t} + v\frac{\partial v}{\partial r} = -\frac{1}{\rho}\nabla P, \quad (27a)$$

$$\frac{\partial v}{\partial r} + \frac{2}{r}v = 0, \tag{27b}$$

where $v(r,t)$ is the fluid velocity, $P(r,t)$ is the pressure in the dielectric fluids, and r is the distance from the center of the charged bubble. ∇P is the gradient function of the pressure P.

Subsequently, Equation (27b) is integrated with respect to r, on the surface of charged bubble, where supposing $v(r,t) = \frac{dR}{dt}$ and $R(r \to \infty, t) = 0$, then:

$$v = \frac{1}{r^2}(R^2 \frac{dR}{dt}). \tag{28}$$

In the following, using Equation (28) into Equation (27a), and supposing $(r \to \infty, t = 0)$, hence, integrating the results, t, we obtain:

$$P = \frac{\rho}{r}\frac{d}{dt}\left(R^2\frac{dR}{dt}\right) + O(\frac{1}{r^4}) \cong \frac{\rho}{r}\frac{d}{dt}\left(R^2\frac{dS}{dt}\right). \tag{29}$$

Noting that, the term $O(\frac{1}{r^4})$ is omitted because of the high order of $(\frac{1}{r^4})$, and the pressure charged fluid in Equation (27a) is the pressure caused by each charged bubble. In this approach, the subscripts i and j are used for the individual effects of each charged bubble (i.e., the interaction between i- and j- charged bubbles). Thus, the interparticle pressure is obtained as follows:

$$P_{\text{int}} = \sum_{J=1, J \neq i}^{2} P_j = \rho_l \sum_{J=1, J \neq i}^{N} \frac{1}{r_j}\frac{d}{dt}\left(R_j^2\left(\frac{dR_j}{dt}\right)\right). \tag{30}$$

It is supposed that the charged bubbles' centres remain unconverted and unaltered. For completing the calculations, interparticle interactions can occur between two charged bubbles, i.e., identical charged bubbles with the same distance and conditions:

$$R_i = R \text{ and } H = \sum_{J=2,}^{N}\left(\frac{1}{r_{1,j}}\right)^{-1}, \text{ for } i,j = 1,2,\ldots,N \text{ and } i \neq j.$$

On the other hand, due to the charged bubbles having the same dynamics, H defines the distance between the centers of the charged bubbles: N is the number of charged bubbles. Consequently, we obtained:

$$P_{\text{int}} \to \frac{\rho}{H}(N-1)\frac{d}{dt}\left(R^2\frac{dR}{dt}\right), N = 1,2,3,\ldots. \tag{31}$$

Again, H and N are the distance between each pair of charged cavitation bubbles and the number of charged cavitation bubble, respectively.

Combining Equations (8) and (31), the charged-Rayleigh–Plesset model in dielectric liquid, considering interparticle interaction of the cavitation bubbles, becomes:

$$R\ddot{R} + \frac{3}{2}\dot{R}^2 = \frac{1}{\rho}\left(\left(P_v - P_0 + \frac{2\sigma}{R_0} - \frac{Q^2}{8\pi\varepsilon R_0^4}\right)\left(\frac{R_0}{R}\right)^{3\kappa} - \frac{2}{R}\sigma - 4\frac{\rho\dot{R}}{R}\eta + \frac{Q^2}{8\pi\varepsilon R^4} + (P_v - P_0) - \frac{\rho}{H}(N-1)\frac{d}{dt}\left(R^2\frac{dR}{dt}\right)\right) \tag{32}$$

Again, applying this relation $\frac{d}{dt}\left(R^2\frac{dR}{dt}\right) = R^2\ddot{R} + 2R\dot{R}^2$ and the pressure $P_g(t)$ into Equation (32), the charged multibubbles under the effect of interparticle interactions between bubbles becomes:

$$\frac{d}{dt}\left(R^2\frac{dR}{dt}\right) = \frac{1}{\rho}(P_g(t) - P_0) - \frac{Q^2}{8\pi\rho\varepsilon R_0^4}\left(\frac{R_0}{R}\right)^{3\kappa} - 4\frac{\dot{R}}{R}\eta - \frac{2}{\rho R}\sigma + \frac{Q^2}{8\pi\rho\varepsilon R^4} + \frac{1}{\rho}P_v - \frac{1}{H}(N-1)\left(R^2\ddot{R} + 2R\dot{R}^2\right) \tag{33}$$

Applying the conditions in Equation (11) into Equation (33), the nonlinear differential equation of charged multibubbles becomes:

$$\frac{1}{2R^2\dot{R}}\frac{d}{dt}\left(R^3\dot{R}^2\right) = \frac{1}{\rho}\left(\frac{\Delta T_B^*}{\Delta T_0}+1\right)\mathbb{ZZ}_2 - \frac{Q^2}{8\pi\rho\varepsilon R_0^4}\left(\frac{R_0}{R}\right)^{3\kappa} - 4\frac{\dot{R}}{R}\eta - \frac{2}{\rho R}\sigma + \frac{Q^2}{8\pi\rho\varepsilon R^4} + \frac{1}{\rho}P_v - \frac{1}{H}(N-1)\left(R^2\ddot{R}+2R\dot{R}^2\right) \tag{34}$$

Here, $\mathbb{ZZ}_1 = \frac{\mathbb{Z}_2}{T_0-T_\infty}$; $\mathbb{ZZ}_2 = \frac{3}{2}\rho\dot{R}_0^2 + 4\frac{\rho\dot{R}_0}{R_0}\eta + \frac{2}{R_0}\sigma - P_v + \frac{2\rho}{H}(N-1)R_0\dot{R}_0^2$, $\Delta T_0 = T_0 - T_\infty$, and ΔT_T^* were defined in a previous section in (15).

By applying the relation between Equations (17) and (18) into Equation (34), Equation (34) applied to charged multibubbles can be put in a dimensionless equation as:

$$\frac{1}{6\Psi'}\frac{d}{dv}\left(\Psi^{\frac{7}{3}}\dot{\Psi}^2\right) = \frac{1}{\rho\Omega^2 R_0^2}\mathbb{ZZ}_2 - \mathbb{ZZ}_3\int_0^v\left((v-\xi)^{-\frac{1}{2}}\Psi'(\xi)\right)d\xi - \frac{Q^2}{8\pi\rho\varepsilon\Omega^2 R_0^2}\left(\frac{1}{\Psi^{\frac{1}{3}}}\right)^{3\kappa} - \frac{4}{3\Omega R_0^2}\Psi^{\frac{1}{3}}\Psi'\eta - \frac{2}{\rho\Omega^2 R_0^2}\frac{1}{\Psi^{\frac{1}{3}}}\sigma + \frac{Q^2}{8\pi\rho\varepsilon\Omega^2 R_0^2}\frac{1}{\Psi^{\frac{4}{3}}} + \frac{1}{\rho\Omega^2 R_0^2}P_v - \frac{1}{H}(N-1)\left(\left(\frac{1}{3}\Psi^{\frac{8}{3}}\Psi'' + \frac{2}{9}\Psi^{\frac{5}{3}}\dot{\Psi}^2\right) + \frac{2}{9}R_0\Psi^{\frac{5}{3}}\dot{\Psi}^2\right) \tag{35}$$

where $\mathbb{ZZ}_3 = \left(\frac{\Omega a_l}{9\pi}\right)^{\frac{1}{2}}\frac{\rho_v L\mathbb{ZZ}_2}{\rho\Omega^2\Delta T_0 R_0 k_l}$.

In the case where charged microbubble dynamics undergo complete growth, the inertial forces are neglected and the boundary conditions in Equation (11) are satisfied, mathematically, then $R(t_m) = R_m$, $\dot{R}(t_m) = \dot{R}_m$, $\ddot{R}(t_m) = 0$, and $\frac{1}{6\Psi'}\frac{d}{dv}\left(\Psi^{\frac{7}{3}}\dot{\Psi}^2\right) \to 0$. Then, Equation (35) converts to:

$$\int_0^v\left((v-\xi)^{-\frac{1}{2}}\Psi'(\xi)\right)d\xi = \frac{1}{\mathbb{ZZ}_3}\left[\frac{1}{\rho\Omega^2 R_0^2}\mathbb{ZZ}_2 - \frac{Q^2}{8\pi\rho\varepsilon\Omega^2 R_0^2}\left(\frac{1}{\Psi_m^{\frac{1}{3}}}\right)^{3\kappa} - \frac{4}{3\Omega R_0^2}\Psi_m^{\frac{1}{3}}\Psi'_m\eta - \frac{2}{\rho\Omega^2 R_0^2}\frac{1}{\Psi_m^{\frac{1}{3}}}\sigma + \frac{Q^2}{8\pi\rho\varepsilon\Omega^2 R_0^2}\frac{1}{\Psi_m^{\frac{4}{3}}} + \frac{1}{\rho\Omega^2 R_0^2}P_v - \frac{1}{H}(N-1)\left(\left(\Psi_m^{\frac{8}{3}}\Psi''_m + \frac{2}{9}\Psi_m^{\frac{5}{3}}\dot{\Psi}_m^2\right) + \frac{2}{9}R_0\Psi_m^{\frac{5}{3}}\dot{\Psi}_m^2\right)\right] \tag{36}$$

In order to complete the solution (36), we use these assumptions: $\zeta = \xi_1 v$, and $\beta(v) = \gamma v^{\frac{1}{2}}$; γ denotes a constant, and the result is:

$$\gamma = \frac{2}{\mathbb{ZZ}_3\pi}\left[\frac{1}{\rho\Omega^2 R_0^2}\mathbb{ZZ}_2 - \frac{Q^2}{8\pi\rho\varepsilon\Omega^2 R_0^2}\left(\frac{1}{\Psi_m^{\frac{1}{3}}}\right)^{3\kappa} - \frac{4}{3\Omega R_0^2}\Psi_m^{\frac{1}{3}}\Psi'_m\eta - \frac{2}{\rho\Omega^2 R_0^2}\frac{1}{\Psi_m^{\frac{1}{3}}}\sigma + \frac{Q^2}{8\pi\rho\varepsilon\Omega^2 R_0^2}\frac{1}{\Psi_m^{\frac{1}{3}}} + \frac{1}{\rho\Omega^2 R_0^2}P_v - \frac{1}{H}(N-1)\left(\left(\Psi_m^{\frac{8}{3}}\Psi''_m + \frac{2}{9}\Psi_m^{\frac{5}{3}}\dot{\Psi}_m^2\right) + \frac{2}{9}R_0\Psi_m^{\frac{5}{3}}\dot{\Psi}_m^2\right)\right] \tag{37}$$

and $\beta(v)$ becomes:

$$\beta(v) = \frac{2}{\mathbb{ZZ}_3\pi}\left[\frac{1}{\rho\Omega^2 R_0^2}\mathbb{ZZ}_2 - \frac{Q^2}{8\pi\rho\varepsilon\Omega^2 R_0^2}\left(\frac{1}{\Psi_m^{\frac{1}{3}}}\right)^{3\kappa} - \frac{4}{3\Omega R_0^2}\Psi_m^{\frac{1}{3}}\Psi'_m\eta - \frac{2}{\rho\Omega^2 R_0^2}\frac{1}{\Psi_m^{\frac{1}{3}}}\sigma + \frac{Q^2}{8\pi\rho\varepsilon\Omega^2 R_0^2}\frac{1}{\Psi_m^{\frac{1}{3}}} + \frac{1}{\rho\Omega^2 R_0^2}P_v - \frac{1}{H}(N-1)\left(\left(\Psi_m^{\frac{8}{3}}\Psi''_m + \frac{2}{9}\Psi_m^{\frac{5}{3}}\dot{\Psi}_m^2\right) + \frac{2}{9}R_0\Psi_m^{\frac{5}{3}}\dot{\Psi}_m^2\right)\right]v^{\frac{1}{2}} \tag{38}$$

Applying Equation (38) into $R = R_0\Psi^{\frac{1}{3}}$, the charged multibubble radius becomes:

$$R = R_0\left[\frac{2}{\mathbb{ZZ}_3\pi}\left[\frac{1}{\rho\Omega^2 R_0^2}\mathbb{ZZ}_2 - \frac{Q^2}{8\pi\rho\varepsilon\Omega^2 R_0^2}\left(\frac{1}{\Psi_m^{\frac{1}{3}}}\right)^{3\kappa} - \frac{4}{3\Omega R_0^2}\Psi_m^{\frac{1}{3}}\Psi'_m\eta - \frac{2}{\rho\Omega^2 R_0^2}\frac{1}{\Psi_m^{\frac{1}{3}}}\sigma + \frac{Q^2}{8\pi\rho\varepsilon\Omega^2 R_0^2}\frac{1}{\Psi_m^{\frac{1}{3}}} + \frac{1}{\rho\Omega^2 R_0^2}P_v - \frac{1}{H}(N-1)\left(\left(\Psi_m^{\frac{8}{3}}\Psi''_m + \frac{2}{9}\Psi_m^{\frac{5}{3}}\dot{\Psi}_m^2\right) + \frac{2}{9}R_0\Psi_m^{\frac{5}{3}}\dot{\Psi}_m^2\right)\right]\right]^{1/3}v^{\frac{1}{6}} \tag{39}$$

To introduce v versus time t, applying Equation (39) into Equation (17), we obtain:

$$v^{\frac{1}{6}} = \left(\frac{\Omega}{3}t\right)^{\frac{1}{2}}\left[\frac{2}{\pi \mathbb{Z}\mathbb{Z}_3}\left[\frac{1}{\rho\Omega^2 R_0^2}\mathbb{Z}\mathbb{Z}_2 - \frac{Q^2}{8\pi\rho\varepsilon\Omega^2 R_0^2}\left(\frac{1}{\Psi_m^{\frac{1}{3}}}\right)^{3\kappa} - \frac{4}{3\Omega R_0^2}\Psi_m^{\frac{1}{3}}\Psi_m'\eta - \frac{2}{\rho\Omega^2 R_0^2}\frac{1}{\Psi_m^{\frac{1}{3}}}\sigma + \frac{Q^2}{8\pi\rho\varepsilon\Omega^2 R_0^2}\frac{1}{\Psi_m^{\frac{1}{3}}} + \frac{1}{\rho\Omega^2 R_0^2}P_v - \right.\right.$$
$$\left.\left.\frac{1}{H}(N-1)\left(\left(\Psi_m^{\frac{8}{3}}\Psi_m'' + \frac{2}{9}\Psi_m^{\frac{5}{3}}\dot{\Psi}_m^2\right) + \frac{2}{9}R_0\Psi_m^{\frac{5}{3}}\dot{\Psi}_m^2\right)\right]\right]^{2/3} \tag{40}$$

After making some simple calculations based on the Jacob number, initial void fraction, and thermal diffusivity, the charged interacting-bubble radius becomes:

$$R = \left[\frac{2}{\mathbb{Z}\mathbb{Z}_3\pi}\left[\frac{1}{\rho\Omega^2 R_0^2}\mathbb{Z}\mathbb{Z}_2 - \frac{Q^2}{8\pi\rho\varepsilon\Omega^2 R_0^2}(\phi_0)^\kappa - \frac{4}{3\Omega R_0^2}\phi_0^{\frac{-1}{3}}\Psi_m'\eta - \frac{2}{\rho\Omega^2 R_0^2}\phi_0^{\frac{1}{3}}\sigma + \frac{Q^2}{8\pi\rho\varepsilon\Omega^2 R_0^2}\phi_0^{\frac{1}{3}} + \frac{1}{\rho\Omega^2 R_0^2}P_v \right.\right.$$
$$\left.\left. - \frac{1}{H}(N-1)\left(\left(\phi_0^{\frac{-8}{3}}\Psi_m'' + \frac{2}{9}\phi_0^{\frac{-5}{3}}\dot{\Psi}_m^2\right) + \frac{2}{9}R_0\phi_0^{\frac{-5}{3}}\dot{\Psi}_m^2\right)\right]\right]^{1/3}\frac{\Omega^2\rho R_0}{\mathbb{Z}_3}\left(\frac{12a_1}{3}\right)^{\frac{1}{2}}J_a t^{\frac{1}{2}} \tag{41}$$

3. Validation and Verification Model

To find evidence for the current mathematical approaches of the charged cavitation bubbles, we begin with Equation (32) for charged cavitation multibubbles in dielectric fluids, considering the impact of the interparticle interaction of charged bubbles, where we use Equation (6) for a single charged cavitation bubble as the distance between the charged bubbles H (or r_{ij}) approaches infinity (means mathematically $H \to \infty$ or $r_{ij} \to \infty$) and is verified by:

$$\lim_{H\to\infty}\frac{(N-1)}{H}\frac{d}{dt}\left(R^2\frac{dR}{dt}\right) \to 0,$$

for $N > 1$, and N is the number of charged bubbles.

Additionally, Equation (6) reduces to the results of the dynamics of a single charged bubble during the growth process in [41], from the method based on Plesset–Zwick transformation [43].

On the other hand, the current results of the noninteracting- and interacting charged cavitation bubbles are introduced in a dielectric liquid with the previous available studies in different fluids, such as experimental data [30], Forster and Zuber model [31], Mohammadein et al. models [32,44], and the Plesset–Zwick model [43], as shown in Table 1. Table 2 shows the models and solutions which were utilized in the present study. Moreover, the obtained results hold greater significance in comprehending the intricate behaviour of charged bubbles in the different industrial and technological domains.

Table 1. Characterization of the current models of charged cavitation bubbles and previous studies [31,32,43,44] during the growth process.

Model	Mathematical Formula	Solution	Description
Current Model (6)	$R\ddot{R} + \frac{3}{2}\dot{R}^2 =$ $\frac{1}{\rho}\left((P_v - P_0 + \frac{2\sigma}{R_0} - \frac{Q^2}{8\pi\varepsilon R_0^4})(\frac{R_0}{R})^{3\kappa}\right.$ $\left.- \frac{2}{R}\sigma - 4\frac{\dot{\rho}R}{R}\eta + \frac{Q^2}{8\pi\varepsilon R^4} + (P_v - P_0)\right)$	$R = \left[\frac{2}{\mathbb{Z}_3\pi}\left[\frac{1}{\rho\Omega^2 R_0^2}\mathbb{Z}_2 - \frac{Q^2}{8\pi\rho\varepsilon\Omega^2 R_0^2}(\phi_0)^\kappa\right.\right.$ $- \frac{4}{3\Omega R_0^2}\phi_0^{\frac{-1}{3}}\Psi_m'\eta - \frac{2}{\rho\Omega^2 R_0^2}\phi_0^{\frac{1}{3}}\sigma$ $\left.\left.+ \frac{Q^2}{8\pi\rho\varepsilon\Omega^2 R_0^2}\phi_0^{\frac{1}{3}} + \frac{1}{\rho\Omega^2 R_0^2}P_v\right]\right]^{1/3}\frac{\Omega^2\rho R_0}{\mathbb{Z}_3}\left(\frac{12a_1}{3}\right)^{\frac{1}{2}}J_a t^{\frac{1}{2}}$	No n-interaction of charged cavitation bubbles in dielectric liquids
Current Model (31)	$R\ddot{R} + \frac{3}{2}\dot{R}^2 =$ $\frac{1}{\rho}\left((P_v - P_0 + \frac{2\sigma}{R_0} - \frac{Q^2}{8\pi\varepsilon R_0^4})(\frac{R_0}{R})^{3\kappa}\right.$ $- \frac{2}{R}\sigma - 4\frac{\dot{\rho}R}{R}\eta + \frac{Q^2}{8\pi\varepsilon R^4} + (P_v - P_0)$ $\left.- \frac{\rho}{H}(N-1)\frac{d}{dt}(R^2\frac{dR}{dt})\right)$	$R(t) = \left[\frac{2}{\mathbb{Z}\mathbb{Z}_3\pi}\left[\frac{1}{\rho\Omega^2 R_0^2}\mathbb{Z}\mathbb{Z}_2 - \frac{Q^2}{8\pi\rho\varepsilon\Omega^2 R_0^2}(\phi_0)^\kappa\right.\right.$ $- \frac{4}{3\Omega R_0^2}\phi_0^{\frac{-1}{3}}\Psi_m'\eta - \frac{2}{\rho\Omega^2 R_0^2}\phi_0^{\frac{1}{3}}\sigma$ $+ \frac{Q^2}{8\pi\rho\varepsilon\Omega^2 R_0^2}\phi_0^{\frac{1}{3}} + \frac{1}{\rho\Omega^2 R_0^2}P_v - \frac{1}{H}(N-1)$ $\left.\left.\left((\phi_0^{\frac{-8}{3}}\Psi_m + \frac{2}{9}\phi_0^{\frac{-5}{3}}\Psi_m^2) + \frac{2}{9}R_0\phi_0^{\frac{-5}{3}}\Psi_m^2\right)\right]\right]^{1/3}$ $\frac{\Omega^2\rho R_0}{\mathbb{Z}_3}\left(\frac{12a_1}{3}\right)^{\frac{1}{2}}J_a t^{\frac{1}{2}}$	Cavitation multibubble in dielectric liquids

Table 1. *Cont.*

Model	Mathematical Formula	Solution	Description
Forster and Zuber model [31]	$R\ddot{R} + \frac{3}{2}\dot{R}^2 = \frac{1}{\rho}\left((P_v - P_0) - \frac{2}{R}\sigma - 4\frac{\rho\dot{R}}{R}\eta\right)$	$R(t) = J_a(P\,a_l t)^{\frac{1}{2}}$	Single cavitation bubble in Newtonian fluid
Mohammadein et al. model [44]	$R\ddot{R} + \frac{3}{2}\dot{R}^2 = \Delta P - \frac{2\sigma(t)}{\rho R} - 4\frac{\dot{R}}{R}\eta$	$R(t) = \frac{3\rho R_0 R_0^2 + 8\epsilon\eta\rho R_0^2 \dot{R}_0 + 4\sigma(1-\phi_0^{\frac{1}{3}})}{3\rho R_0 R_0^2 - 2bR_0\Delta P_0 + 8\epsilon\eta R_0 + 4\sigma} J_a\left(\frac{12a_l}{\pi}t\right)^{\frac{1}{2}}$	Single cavitation bubble in Newtonian fluid
Plesset and Zwick model [43]	$R\ddot{R} + \frac{3}{2}\dot{R}^2 = \frac{P(R) - P_0}{\rho}$	$R(t) = J_a\left(\frac{12a_l}{\pi}t\right)^{\frac{1}{2}}$	Single cavitation bubble in Newtonian fluid
Mohammadein et al. model [32]	$R\ddot{R} + \frac{3}{2}\dot{R}^2 = \Delta P - \frac{2\sigma(t)}{\rho R}$	$R(t) = \frac{3\rho R_0^2 + 4B_2\rho_g R_0(1-\phi_0^{\frac{1}{3}})}{3\rho R_0^2 - 2b_2\Delta P_0 + 4B_2\rho_g R_0}\left(\frac{12a_l}{\pi}t\right)^{\frac{1}{2}}$	Single cavitation bubble in Newtonian fluid

4. Results and Analysis

In this study, the mathematical approaches are formulated and described based on the Rayleigh–Plesset model of charged bubble dynamics in dielectric fluid. The solution of the charged bubble model gives us the analytical solutions and behaviour of noninteracting and interacting charged bubbles. The obtained solutions reveal the main role of physical configuration on the behaviour dynamics of charged cavitation bubbles under the effect of an electric field. To calculate this, the different values of physical configurations (e.g., in refs. [27,42]) are found by: $\rho_l = 1000$ kg.m^{-1}, $\rho_g = 1.308$ kg.m^{-1}, $R_0 = 0.001$ m, $R_m = 0.005$ m, $\dot{R}_0 = 0.1$ m.s^{-1}, $\eta = 0.077$ Pas, $\sigma = 0.05$ N.m^{-1}, $C_{Pl} = 4179$ J(kg.K)$^{-1}$, $L = 533{,}000$ J.kg^{-1}, and $k_l = 0.6786$ W.m^{-1}.K^{-1}, $\Delta T_0 = 1.5$ K. The results of the present study on the nonlinear dynamics of charged cavitation bubbles under the effect of an electric field are shown in Figures 2–9, in dielectric liquids where the obtained figures illustrate the influence of the physical parameters as electric charges and polytropic exponents on the growth process of noninteracting and interacting charged cavitation bubbles in dielectric liquids. All graphical representations of the given results are important, not only in explaining the physical configuration of the present model but also in verifying the given solutions. Obtaining this motivation, the given solution in the model's approaches is displayed graphically. All graphical representations of the results are estimated by the symbolic software program (Mathematica software version @13.1), which will be utilized to plot the graphs.

4.1. Effect of Electric Charges and Polytropic Exponent on Charged Cavitation Multibubble Growth

Figure 2 reveals the impact of electric charge Q on growing cavitation bubbles in the dielectric field where the activity of charged cavitation bubbles is increasing with the decrease in electric charge. From that, we obtain the influence of electric charge weakens the growth process of charged cavitation bubbles. On the other hand, Figure 2 shows the comparison between the behaviour of noninteracting and interparticle interaction between charged cavitation bubbles where the growth of noninteracting charged bubbles $(N = 1)$ is higher than in the case of interacting charged bubbles $(N > 1)$. The role of polytropic exponent k on the growth process is shown in Figure 3, where the growth process decreases with the increase in polytropic exponents in dielectric liquids.

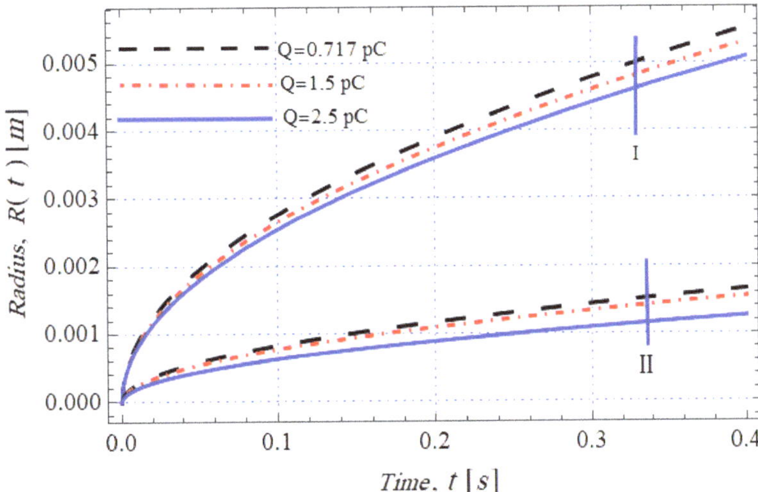

Figure 2. The growth process of charged bubbles dynamics versus time for different values of charged field; I-model of noninteracting bubbles and II-model of interacting bubbles, $H = 0.02$ m, $N = 3$, and $k = 1$.

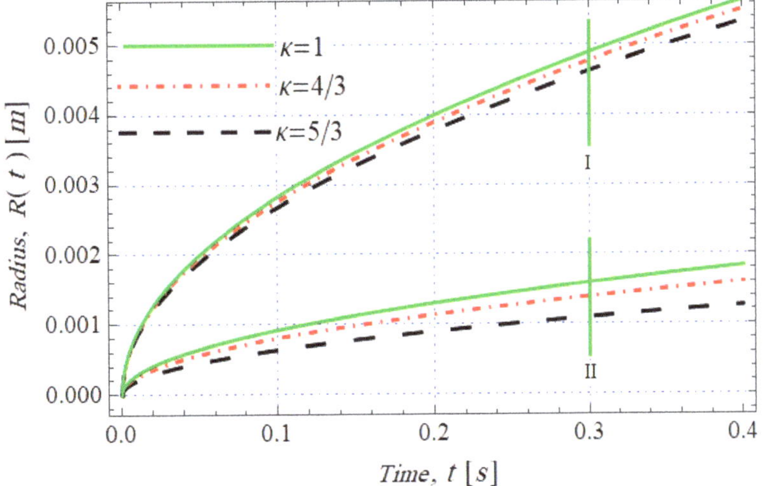

Figure 3. Growth process of charged bubbles dynamics versus time for different values of polytropic exponent; I-model of noninteracting bubbles, and II-model of interacting bubbles, $H = 0.02$ m, $N = 3$.

4.2. Effect of the Number of Charged Bubbles and Charged Bubble–Bubble on Charged Cavitation Multibubble Growth in Dielectric Liquids

Figures 4 and 5 depict the main role of the parameter of the number of cavitation bubbles "N" and the distance between the charged bubbles "H" in our approach, where the increase in the number of bubbles N on the nonlinear cavitation dynamics reduces the behaviour of the growth process. However, the increase in the distance between the charged bubbles on the behaviour of cavitation dynamics significantly enhances the growth process. Figure 6, illustrate the relation between the cavitation radius R and the parameters of the charged field and number of bubbles, respectively, during the growth process at one instant ($t = 1.0$ s), where it is found that the radii of charged bubbles are inversely proportional to the charged field and the number of bubbles.

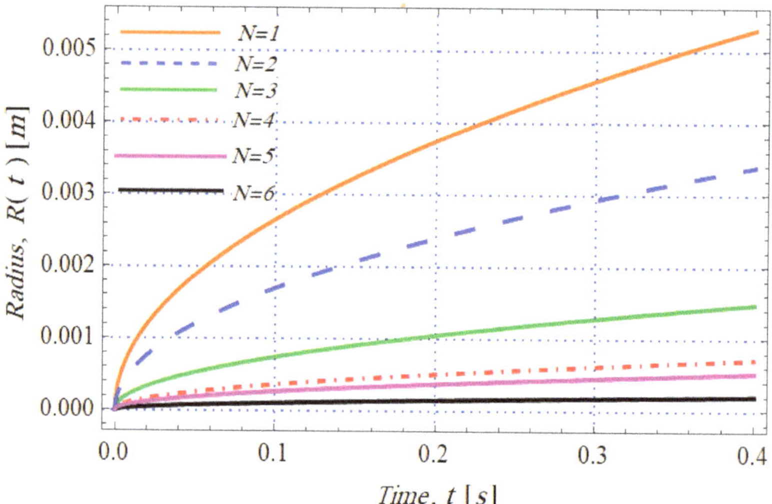

Figure 4. Growth process of charged cavitation multibubble dynamics versus time at the different values of the number of bubbles N. $H = 0.02$ m, $k = 1$.

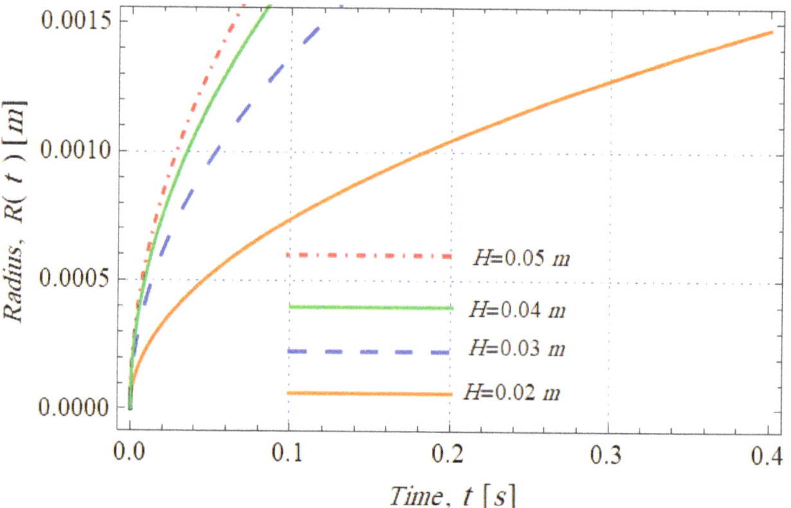

Figure 5. Growth process of charged cavitation multibubble dynamics versus time at the different values of distance between the bubbles, $N = 3$ and $k = 1$.

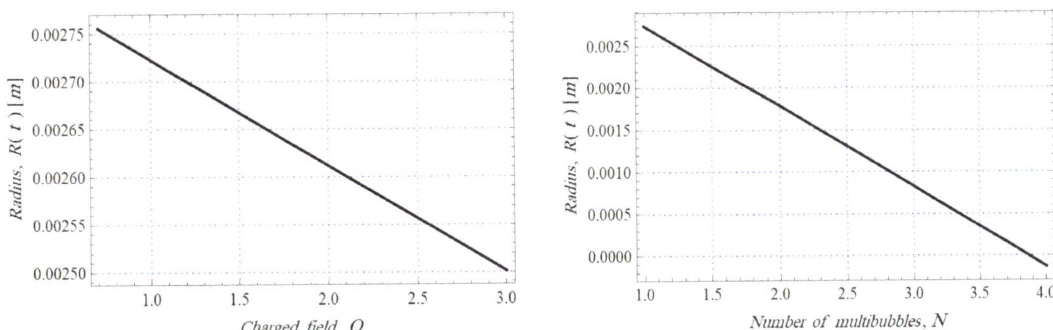

Figure 6. The relation between the cavitation radius R and the parameters charged field and number of multibubbles, respectively, on the growth process at one instant ($t = 1.0$ s).

Figure 7 reveals the results of the single and interparticle interaction of charged cavitation bubbles in a dielectric liquid with the previous available studies in different fluids (as Newtonian liquids (nondielectric liquids), nanofluids) such as experimental data [30], the Forster and Zuber model [31], Mohammadein et al. models [32,44], and the Plesset–Zwick model [43]. These results are the comparison between them. It is found that, firstly, the obtained results agree with the published works in [30–32,43,44]; secondly, the activity of the charged bubbles in the dielectric liquids is significantly lower than in the other published works [30–32,43,44] due to the effects of electric charges.

Ultimately, we recommend using these results when formulating the physicality and modelling of charged bubbles and their applications. It is found that the results obtained give good agreement when compared with experimental and theoretical previous works, and will help the academic community understand the intricate behaviour of charged bubbles in their different industrial and technological applications.

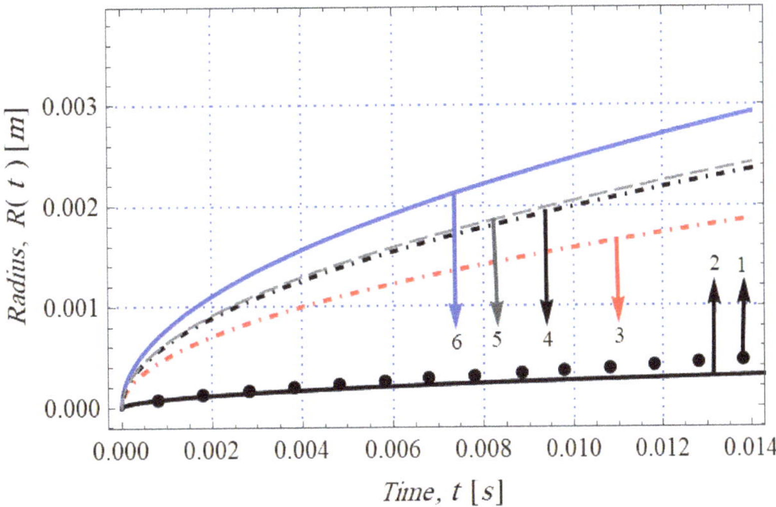

Figure 7. The comparison between the proposed model of the growth process for charged bubble dynamics versus time at $N = 3$, $H = 0.02$ m, black solid line 1: proposed model, line 2: experimental data [30], line 3: Forster and Zuber model [31], line 4: Mohammadein et al. model [44], line 5: Plesset and Zwick model [43], line 6: Mohammadein et al. model [32].

4.3. Effect of the Dimensionless Phase Transition Criteria and Thermal Conductivity on Charged Cavitation Multibubble Growth in Dielectric Liquids

It is notable that dimensionless phase transition criteria (namely, Jacob number $Ja = \frac{\rho C_p \Delta T_0}{\rho_v L}$) is very important in the study the charged bubbles in dielectric liquids. Moreover, the dimensionless phase transition criteria are depended on the value of superheating liquid ΔT_0. So, Ja can be calculated in Table 3 It is noted that the dimensionless phase transition criteria are increasing when the superheating liquid ΔT_0 increase. As following Figure 8, it is noted that the growth process of charged bubbles as a function of time and void fraction is proportional to the dimensionless phase transition criteria Ja. From the results of Table 3 and Figure 8, we obtain the dimensionless phase transition criteria is a dominant of the growth layers of charged bubbles under effect of interparticle interaction of charged bubbles in dielectric liquids. Figure 9 shows the growth process of charged bubbles' dynamics versus time and initial void fraction with different values of thermal diffusivity. We find that the layers of growth of a charged cavitation bubble is proportional to the thermal conductivity k_l. Consequently, an increase in the dimensionless phase transition criterion and thermal conductivity enhances the growth process of charged multiple cavitation bubbles in dielectric liquids.

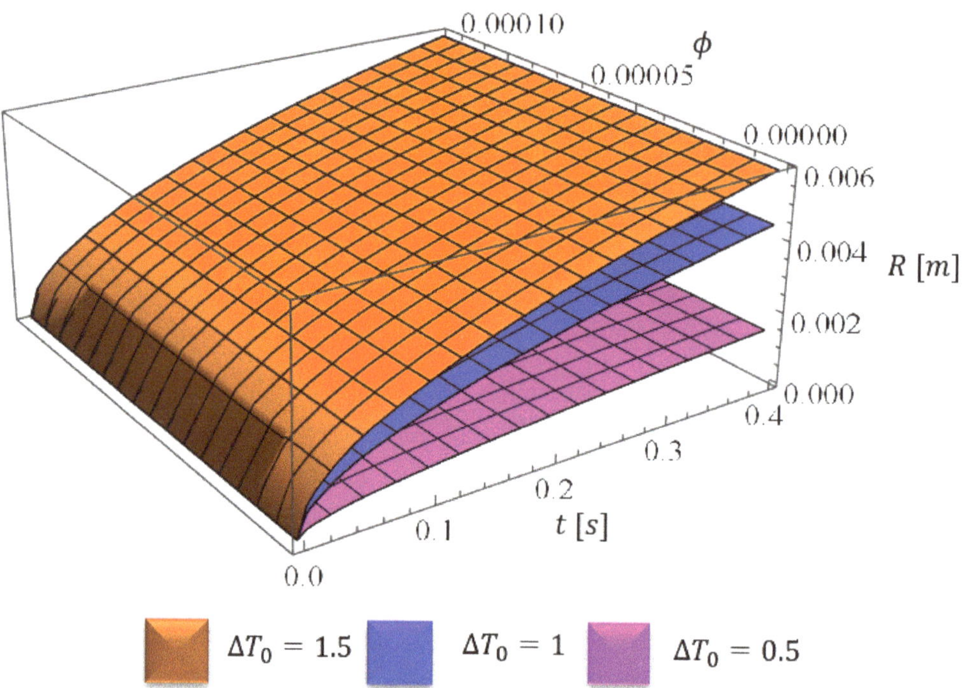

Figure 8. The growth process of charged bubbles' dynamics versus time and initial void fraction at different values of superheating liquid ΔT_0.

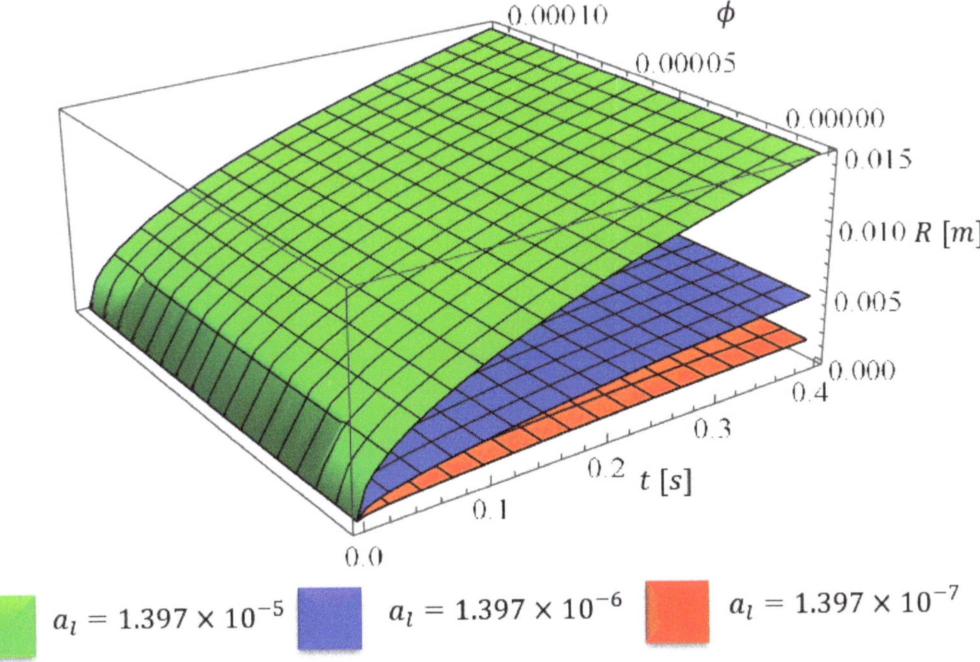

Figure 9. The growth process of charged bubble dynamics versus time and the initial void fraction at different values of thermal diffusivity a_l.

4.4. Estimation the Proposed Different Pressures during the Growth Behaviour of Charged Cavitation Multibubbles in Dielectric Liquids

In this subsection, the proposed different pressures are estimated during the growth behaviour of charged cavitation multibubbles in dielectric liquids. Table 3 illustrates the effect of the growth process on the different pressures such as pressure due to polytropic effects P_k, pressure due to the surface tension P_σ, pressure due to viscous forces P_η, and charged pressure P_Q by permeability, which were stated in Equations (2)–(5), respectively.

Table 2. Numerical calculations of various pressures for nonlinear bubble dynamics in dielectric fields.

	P_k		P_σ		P_Q	
t	Single Charged Bubble $N = 1$	Charged Multibubbles $N = 2$	Single Charged Bubble $N = 1$	Charged Multibubbles $N = 2$	Single Charged Bubble $N = 1$	Charged Multibubbles $N = 2$
0.1	-3.51×10^{15}	-1.61×10^{16}	30.91	110.78	1.08×10^{18}	1.792×10^{20}
0.2	-1.24×10^{15}	-5.72×10^{16}	21.85	78.33	2.71×10^{17}	4.48×10^{19}
0.3	-6.77×10^{14}	-3.11×10^{16}	17.84	63.95	1.21×10^{17}	1.99×10^{19}
0.4	-4.39×10^{14}	-2.02×10^{16}	15.45	55.39	6.79×10^{16}	1.12×10^{19}
0.5	-3.14×10^{14}	-1.44×10^{16}	13.82	49.54	4.35×10^{16}	7.16×10^{18}
0.6	-2.39×10^{14}	-1.11×10^{16}	12.62	45.23	3.02×10^{16}	4.97×10^{18}
0.7	-1.89×10^{14}	-8.73×10^{15}	11.68	41.87	2.21×10^{16}	3.65×10^{18}
0.8	-1.55×10^{14}	-7.15×10^{15}	10.93	39.16	1.69×10^{16}	2.81×10^{18}

Table 3. a: Calculations of dimensionless phase transition criteria, J_a based on superheating liquids ΔT_0. b: calculations of thermal diffusivity, a_l based on thermal conductivity k_l.

a			
ΔT_0 [K]	1.0	1.5	2.0
Dimensionless phase transition criteria, J_a	12.47	18.71	24.95
b			
$k_l [J/(s\,m\,K)$	0.613	0.713	0.813
Thermal diffusivity, a_l $[m^2/s]$	1.397×10^{-7}	1.624×10^{-7}	1.852×10^{-7}

5. Conclusions

The nonlinear dynamics models of charged cavitation bubbles and their results for the growth process in dielectric liquids are formulated and solved analytically based on the Plesset–Zwick method. We conclude that:

- The impact of electric charge on growing charged cavitation bubbles reduces the growth process.
- The behaviour of the noninteracting charged cavitation bubbles is higher than in the case of interacting charged cavitation bubbles in dielectric liquids.
- The polytropic exponent weakens the growth process of charged bubbles in dielectric liquids.
- An increase in the dimensionless phase transition criterion and thermal diffusivity enhances the growth process of charged multiple cavitation bubbles in dielectric liquids during the growth process.
- The obtained results of noninteracting and interacting charged cavitation bubbles models in dielectric liquids agree with the published works [30–32,43,44] for different types of the fluids.

The obtained findings would be significant in understanding the complex behaviour of charged cavitation bubbles in practical applications, especially when considering the charged surface tension. Moreover, the current results should be taken into consideration at organization of interacting charged cavitation bubbles and their applications.

Author Contributions: A.K.A.-N.: writing—original draft preparation, methodology, review and editing, software, supervision, validation, conceptualization, formal analysis, and data curation; A.M.H.: writing—original draft preparation, methodology, review and editing, software, validation, conceptualization, formal analysis, and data curation; A.F.A.-B.: writing—original draft preparation, methodology, review and editing, software, supervision, validation, conceptualization, formal analysis, and data curation. All authors have read and agreed to the published version of the manuscript.

Funding: This paper is based upon work supported by Science, Technology & Innovation Funding Authority (STDF) under grant number 48262.

Data Availability Statement: Data are contained within the article.

Conflicts of Interest: The authors declare no conflict of interest.

Nomenclature

Nomenclature

Parameter	Description	Unit
P	Pressure	N.m^{-2}
Q	Charge	pC
σ	Surface tension of liquid surrounding the bubble	N.m^{-1}
η	Viscosity tension of liquid surrounding the bubble	Pa.s
T	Temperature	K
ε	Permittivity	–

κ	Polytropic coefficient	–
$\Delta T_0 = T_0 - T_\infty$	Initial temperature difference	K
$\Delta T_B^* = T_b\text{-}T_0$	The temperature difference defined by Equation (15)	K
a_l	Thermal diffusivity of the liquid	$m^2.s^{-1}$
k	Thermal conductivity	$W.m^{-1}.K^{-1}$
ρ	Density	$Kg.m^{-3}$
ρ_l	Density of the liquid surrounding the bubble	$Kg.m^{-2}$
Ψ	Dimensionless volume variable defined by Equation (17)	–
$\mathbb{Z}_1, \mathbb{Z}_2, \mathbb{Z}_3$	Constants are defined in Equations (12) and (19)	–
$\mathbb{ZZ}_1, \mathbb{ZZ}_2, \mathbb{ZZ}_3$	Constants are defined in Equations (34) and (35)	–
R	Charged bubble radius	m
$\dot{R}$	Instantaneous bubble wall velocity	$m.s^{-1}$
$\ddot{R}$	Instantaneous bubble wall acceleration	$m.s^{-2}$
N	Number of bubbles	–
H	Distance between the bubbles	–
ϕ_0	Initial void fraction defined by Equation (26)	–
Ja	Jacob number given by Equation (26)	–
∇	Del operator	
Subscripts		
b	Boundary	
s	Saturation	
l	Liquid	
g	Gas	
0	Initial	
m	maximum	

References

1. Zhang, A.; Li, S.; Cui, P.; Li, S.; Lium, Y. A unified theory for bubble dynamics. *Phys. Fluids* **2023**, *35*, 033323. [CrossRef]
2. Rayleigh, L. On the pressure developed in a liquid during the collapse of a spherical cavity. *Philos. Mag.* **1917**, *34*, 94–98. [CrossRef]
3. Lauterborn, W.; Kurz, T. Physics of bubble oscillations. *Rep. Progr. Phys.* **2010**, *73*, 106501. [CrossRef]
4. Abu-Nab, A.K.; Omran, M.H.; Abu-Bakr, A.F. Theoretical analysis of pressure relaxation time in N-dimensional thermally-limited bubble dynamics in Fe$_3$O$_4$/water nanofluids. *J. Nanofluids* **2022**, *11*, 410–417. [CrossRef]
5. Bai, L.; Xu, W.; Deng, J.; Li, C.; Xu, D.; Gao, Y. Generation and control of acoustic cavitation structure. *Ultrason. Sonochem.* **2014**, *21*, 1696–1706. [CrossRef] [PubMed]
6. Abu-Bakr, A.F.; Abu-Nab, A.K. Towards a laser-induced microbubble during lithotripsy process in soft tissue. *Bull. Russ. Acad. Sci. Phys.* **2022**, *86* (Suppl. S1), S1–S7. [CrossRef]
7. Stride, E.; Coussios, C. Nucleation, mapping and control of cavitation for drug delivery. *Nat. Rev. Phys.* **2019**, *1*, 495–509. [CrossRef]
8. Dollet, B.; Marmottant, P.; Garbin, V. Bubble dynamics in soft and biological matter. *Annu. Rev. Fluid Mech.* **2019**, *51*, 331–355. [CrossRef]
9. Pahk, K.; Gelat, P.; Kim, H.; Saffari, N. Bubble dynamics in boiling histotripsy. *Ultrasound Med. Biol.* **2018**, *44*, 2673–2696. [CrossRef]
10. Abu-Nab, A.K.; Mohamed, K.G.; Abu-Bakr, A.F. Microcavitation dynamics in viscoelastic tissue during histotripsy process. *J. Phys. Condens. Matter.* **2022**, *34*, 304005. [CrossRef]
11. Abu-Nab, A.K.; Mohamed, K.G.; Abu-Bakr, A.F. An analytical approach for microbubble dynamics in histotripsy based on a neo-Hookean model. *Arch. Appl. Mech.* **2023**, *93*, 1565–1577. [CrossRef]
12. Abu-Bakr, A.F.; Mohamed, K.G.; Abu-Nab, A.K. Physico-mathematical models for interacting microbubble clouds during histotripsy. *Eur. Phys. J. Spec. Top.* **2023**, *232*, 1225–1245. [CrossRef]
13. Landel, J.R.; Wilson, D.I. The fluid mechanics of cleaning and decontamination of surfaces. *Annu. Rev. Fluid Mech.* **2021**, *53*, 147–171. [CrossRef]
14. Gaitan, D.; Crum, L.; Church, C.; Roy, R. Sonoluminescence and bubble dynamics for a single, stable, cavitation bubble. *J. Acoust. Soc. Am.* **1992**, *91*, 3166–3183. [CrossRef]
15. Lohse, D. Fundamental fluid dynamics challenges in inkjet printing. *Annu. Rev. Fluid Mech.* **2022**, *54*, 349–382. [CrossRef]
16. Wu, S.; Zuo, Z.; Stone, H.A.; Liu, S. Motion of a free-settling spherical particle driven by a laser-induced bubble. *Phys. Rev. Lett.* **2017**, *119*, 084501. [CrossRef] [PubMed]
17. De Graaf, K.L.; Brandner, P.A.; Penesis, I. Bubble dynamics of a seismic airgun. *Exp. Therm. Fluid Sci.* **2014**, *55*, 228–238. [CrossRef]

18. Goh, B.; Gong, S.; Ohl, S.-W.; Khoo, B.C. Spark-generated bubble near an elastic sphere. *Int. J. Multiph. Flow* **2017**, *90*, 156–166. [CrossRef]

19. Kluesner, J.; Brothers, D.; Hart, P.; Miller, N.; Hatcher, G. Practical approaches to maximizing the resolution of sparker seismic reflection data. *Mar. Geophys. Res.* **2019**, *40*, 279–301. [CrossRef]

20. Plesset, M. The dynamics of cavitation bubbles. *J. Appl. Mech.* **1949**, *16*, 277–282. [CrossRef]

21. Keller, J.; Miksis, K. Bubble oscillations of large amplitude. *J. Acoust. Soc. Am.* **1980**, *68*, 628. [CrossRef]

22. Prosperetti, A.; Lezzi, A. Bubble dynamics in a compressible liquid—Part 1: First-order theory. *J. Fluid Mech.* **1986**, *168*, 457–478. [CrossRef]

23. Lezzi, A.; Prosperetti, A. Bubble dynamics in a compressible liquid—Part 2: Second-order theory. *J. Fluid Mech.* **1987**, *185*, 289–321. [CrossRef]

24. Herring, C. *Theory of the Pulsations of the Gas Bubble Produced by an Underwater Explosion*; Columbia University, Division of National Defense Research: New York, NY, USA, 1941.

25. Trilling, L. The collapse and rebound of a gas bubble. *J. Appl. Phys.* **1952**, *23*, 14–17. [CrossRef]

26. Keller, J.; Kolodner, I.I. Damping of underwater explosion bubble oscillations. *J. Appl. Phys.* **1956**, *27*, 1152. [CrossRef]

27. Abu-Nab, A.K.; Elgammal, M.I.; Abu-Bakr, A.F. Bubble growth in generalized-Newtonian fluid at low-Mach number under influence of magnetic field. *J. Thermophys. Heat Trans.* **2022**, *36*, 485–491. [CrossRef]

28. Sun, S.; Chen, F.; Zhao, M. Numerical simulation and analysis of the underwater implosion of spherical hollow ceramic pressure hulls in 11,000 m depth. *J. Ocean Eng. Sci.* **2022**, *8*, 181–195. [CrossRef]

29. Mohammadein, S.A. The derivation of thermal relaxation time between two-phase bubbly flow. *Heat Mass Transf.* **2006**, *42*, 364–369. [CrossRef]

30. Dergarabedian, P. The rate of growth of vapor bubbles superheated water. *J. Appl. Mech.* **1953**, *20*, 537–545. [CrossRef]

31. Forster, H.K.; Zuber, N. Growth of a vapor bubble in a superheated liquid. *J. Appl. Phys.* **1954**, *25*, 474–478. [CrossRef]

32. Mohammadein, S.A.; Mohammed, K.G. Growth of a gas bubble in a supersaturated liquid under the effect of variant cases of surface tension. *Int. J. Mod. Phys.* **2011**, *25*, 3053–3070. [CrossRef]

33. Olek, S.; Zvirin, Y.; Elias, E. Bubble growth predictions by the hyperbolic and parabolic heat conduction equations. *Warme-Stoffabertragung* **1990**, *25*, 17–26. [CrossRef]

34. Atkinson, A.J.; Apul, O.G.; Schneider, O.; Garcia-Segura, S.; Westerhoff, P. Nanobubble technologies offer opportunities to improve water treatment. *Acc. Chem. Res.* **2019**, *52*, 1196–1205. [CrossRef] [PubMed]

35. McTaggart, H.A. The electrification at liquid-gas surfaces. *Philos. Mag.* **1914**, *27*, 297–314. [CrossRef]

36. Alty, T. The origin of the electrical charge on small particles in water. *Proc. R. Soc. Lond A* **1926**, *112*, 235–251.

37. Dastgheyb, S.S.; Eisenbrey, J.R. Microbubble applications in biomedicine, Handbook of Polymer Applications in Medicine and Medical Devices. In *Plastics Design Library*; William Andrew Publishing: Oxford, UK, 2014; Volume 11, pp. 253–277.

38. Thi Phan, K.K.; Truong, T.; Wang, Y.; Bhandari, B. Nanobubbles: Fundamental characteristics and applications in food processing. *Trends Food Sci. Technol.* **2020**, *95*, 118–130. [CrossRef]

39. Hongray, T.; Ashok, A.; Balakrishnan, J. Effect of charge on the dynamics of an acoustically forced bubble. *Nonlinearity* **2014**, *27*, 1157–1179. [CrossRef]

40. Grigor'ev, A.I.; Zharov, A.N. Stability of the equilibrium states of a charged bubble in a dielectric liquid. *Tech. Phys.* **2000**, *45*, 389–395. [CrossRef]

41. Mohammadein, S.A.; El-Rab, R.A.G. The growth of vapour bubbles in superheated water between two finite boundaries. *Can. J. Phys.* **2001**, *79*, 1021–1029. [CrossRef]

42. Mohammadein, S.A.; Shalaby, G.A.; Abu-Bakr, A.F.; Abu-Nab, A.K. Analytical solution of gas bubble dynamics between two-phase flow. *Res. Phys.* **2017**, *7*, 2396–2403. [CrossRef]

43. Plesset, M.; Zwick, S. The growth of vapor bubbles in superheated liquids. *J. Appl. Phys.* **1954**, *25*, 493–500. [CrossRef]

44. Mohammadein, S.A.; Mohamed, K.G. Growth of a vapour bubble in a viscous, superheated liquid in two phase flow. *Can. J. Phys.* **2015**, *93*, 769–775. [CrossRef]

45. Khojasteh-Manesh, M.M. Numerical investigation of the effect of bubble-bubble interaction on the power of propagated pressure waves. *J. Appl. Comput. Mech.* **2019**, *5*, 181–191.

MDPI
St. Alban-Anlage 66
4052 Basel
Switzerland
www.mdpi.com

Mathematics Editorial Office
E-mail: mathematics@mdpi.com
www.mdpi.com/journal/mathematics

9 783725 807390